JUDICIAL REVIEW IN AN OBJECTIV _ _.rı

How should courts interpret the law? While all agree that courts must be objective, legal scholars differ sharply over what this demands in practice: fidelity to the text? To the will of the people? To certain moral ideals?

In *Judicial Review in an Objective Legal System*, Tara Smith breaks through the false dichotomies inherent in dominant theories – various forms of Originalism, Living Constitutionalism, and Minimalism – to present a new approach to judicial review. She contends that we cannot assess judicial review in isolation from the larger enterprise of which it is a part. By providing careful clarification of both the function of the legal system as well as of objectivity itself, she produces a compelling, firmly grounded account of genuinely objective judicial review. Smith's innovative approach marks a welcome advance for anyone interested in legal objectivity and individual rights.

Tara Smith is a professor of philosophy at the University of Texas at Austin. She is the author of *Moral Rights and Political Freedom*; *Viable Values: A Study of Life as the Root and Reward of Morality*; and *Ayn Rand's Normative Ethics: The Virtuous Egoist*. Her writings have been translated into several languages including Chinese, Japanese, and Hebrew.

Judicial Review in an Objective Legal System

TARA SMITH

University of Texas at Austin

CAMBRIDGE
UNIVERSITY PRESS

32 Avenue of the Americas, New York NY 10013-2473, USA

Cambridge University Press is part of the University of Cambridge.

It furthers the University's mission by disseminating knowledge in the pursuit of
education, learning and research at the highest international levels of excellence.

www.cambridge.org
Information on this title: www.cambridge.org/9781107534957

First published 2015
First paperback edition 2015

A catalogue record for this publication is available from the British Library

Library of Congress Cataloguing in Publication data
Smith, Tara, 1961– author.
Judicial review in an objective legal system / Tara Smith, University of Texas at
Austin.
    pages. cm.
Includes bibliographical references and index
ISBN 978-1-107-11449-4 Hardback
ISBN 978-1-107-53495-7 Paperback
1. Law – Interpretation and construction. 2. Objectivity.   3. Judicial review.
4. Rule of law.   I. Title.
K290.S63 2015
347'.012–dc23   2015011612

ISBN 978-1-107-11449-4 Hardback
ISBN 978-1-107-53495-7 Paperback

Contents

Contents

Acknowledgments

My thinking about the issues discussed in this book has benefited enormously from discussions with many people over the past several years. In settings ranging from the classroom to conferences and workshops to discussion groups, students, colleagues, and others have posed sharp questions and probing criticisms and provided patient guidance for my initial forays into legal philosophy. Space does not permit me to name all of those whose contributions have made a difference. I am particularly thankful, however, to Onkar Ghate, Tom Bowden, Robert Mayhew, Greg Salmieri, Steve Simpson, Larry Salzman, Dana Berliner, Adam Mossoff, and Amy Peikoff. In Austin, Al Martinich, Matt Miller, and Arif Panju have supplied a steady stream of congenial intellectual agitation about legal practices and legal principles (joined, for different periods of our ongoing discussion group, by Wesley Hottot, Andrew Ingram, Sam Krauss, Adam Phillips, Steve Davey, and Michael Sevel).

Funding from the BB&T Chair for the Study of Objectivism and the Anthem Foundation has allowed me to organize related workshops and conferences and to hire research assistants. I am very grateful to these institutions, as well as to those assistants for their labors: Kate Ritchie, Malcolm Keating, Jerry Green, Sam Krauss, Simone Gubler, and Megan Hyska, who prepared the Index. I am also grateful to the University of Texas for granting me leave time to devote to the book, and to the *Washington University Jurisprudence Review* for allowing me to use material originally included in my article "Neutrality Isn't Neutral: On the Value-Neutrality of the Rule of Law," which appeared in its volume 4, issue 1, in 2011.

At Cambridge, John Berger and his staff have been a pleasure to work with. Their support – in spirit as well as in meticulous material detail – is much appreciated.

The large number of people listed here should in no way be read to diminish the substantial benefits I have reaped from each of them. Nor, my appreciation.

Introduction

The proper conduct of judicial review has been intensely contested over the last few decades. While the issue has a longer history, the *Roe* decision in the 1970s and the Robert Bork nomination battle in the 1980s brought the stakes into sharper focus and invigorated the debate in ways that continue to pulse today. The basic question in dispute is: When courts are asked to clarify what a regime's laws mean and, correspondingly, the kinds of actions that its laws permit and forbid, what are the primary considerations that should guide courts' reasoning? What is the proper method for judges to employ in order to understand the law correctly?

While several answers have been offered over the years, all of them suffer from fatal defects. This book seeks to learn from their missteps – as well as from their kernels of truth – in order to elaborate a portrait of objective judicial review. Its scope is somewhat broader, however. For my exploration of the question has led me to conclude that we cannot understand the proper manner of conducting judicial review without understanding the objectivity of a legal system itself. That is, the essential requirements of objectivity in judicial decision making derive from the fundamental character of objective law. For it is only within a larger legal system that the courts play their vital role. Indeed, the failure to appreciate this is one of the principal ways in which the prevalent accounts of judicial review go wrong. While few would detach their accounts of proper review entirely from the larger legal system, theorists typically give insufficient attention to what objective law truly is and work with seriously misguided conceptions of it that distort their prescriptions for objective review. Accordingly, my purpose in the book is not to chart a how-to manual that can be neatly slotted into the existing debate, perfectly symmetrical with all the sorts of prescriptions offered by the advocates of Original Understanding or Strict Construction or Popular Constitutionalism, for instance. While my theory does offer prescriptions for judicial review, it hopes to make a deeper contribution by showing the essential requirements of objective law and, on that basis, the guidelines that are essential for objective judicial review.

Before we proceed, I should note a few qualifications about the range of the book's ambitions. First, I am speaking of U.S. law. While some of my claims about proper review will apply in other legal systems, my primary object is to understand how judicial review should be conducted in the United States and I am taking for granted a basic familiarity with this legal system's structural and philosophical rudiments. (I will directly discuss some of its philosophical underpinnings in Chapter 4, however, and will refer to them in places throughout.) Second, I am speaking primarily of constitutional law, although some of my claims will extend to questions of meaning that arise for statutory, regulatory, contract, and other law. I will not take up the question of exactly which those are, nor the possible differences in proper review in these realms. My main aim is to illuminate an objective understanding of the Constitution, since that is the foundation of the U.S. legal system and, as such, it is what governs the legal status of particular statutes, regulations, and the rest.

Finally, a couple of terminological points. I will frequently speak of "the court," which might naturally lead a reader to think that I am speaking of the U.S. Supreme Court. While that will often be the case, because I believe that the basics that characterize proper judicial review are the same for all tiers of the judiciary, I will speak interchangeably of "the court," "courts," and "the judiciary." Since the tiers stand in a hierarchy of authority, legitimate questions arise about what differences might be appropriate for judicial review at the different levels. Because I see that issue as derivative from the core issue that I tackle, however, I will not address those questions in this book. Thus, nothing more should be read into my variable use of the plural or the singular. (When I say "the court" rather than "courts," for instance, one should not suppose that I am staking a claim about proper review that is necessarily unique to the Supreme Court or that differs at lower levels of the judiciary.) I will also occasionally use "adjudication" to refer to judicial review, although "adjudication" is obviously a broader term. I do this simply for economy of phrasing. As long as these parameters are borne in mind, I do not expect that any of what follows will be unclear.

1. WHO CARES?

The significance of our subject is plain. To do things by law is to do them by force. The government of a given society enjoys the exclusive authority to compel people to behave in certain ways by physical means – by guns, shackles, prisons. It may coerce compliance with its edicts. A nation's laws, in turn, establish how that unique authority may be exercised. Courts, when asked to clarify the meaning of these laws, determine whether we actually live in a law-governed society and enjoy the attendant benefits. Because of what the law is, however, courts' power should be appreciated at a deeper level. Insofar as judges articulate what the laws mean, they control how government power is used. In practice, the way in which courts interpret the law translates into how individuals are treated by the legal system.

Because the law is a potent instrument, in other words, judicial review is a potent instrument. When judges do not apply the law as they should – when their reasoning is guided by inappropriate considerations, whether deliberately or inadvertently – legal power is misused and individual rights suffer. Those are the stakes.

Not surprisingly for such a vital issue, judicial methodology hardly wants for attention. While popular interest spikes when a high court vacancy looms or a presidential election seems likely to affect the federal bench's composition, legal scholars have spilled rivers of ink in efforts to identify the appropriate contours of judicial methodology, elaborating an array of theories that include Originalism of various forms (such as Original Intent, Textualism, and Original Public Understanding), Perfectionism, Minimalism, Pragmatism, Progressive Constitutionalism, Popular Constitutionalism, Common Law Constitutionalism, Justice-Seeking Constitutionalism, and Judicial Engagement. Broadly, the alternatives typically fall into one of three camps:

- some form of Originalism, which abhors the "judicial activism" that treats the law as malleable and calls, instead, for fidelity to the original meaning of the law
- some form of Living Constitutionalism, which resists the stifling "dead hand of the past" that would freeze words' meanings to those of a particular historical period and urges, instead, that law's meaning be alive to contemporary circumstances
- Minimalism, a prescription that urges courts to rule as modestly and narrowly as possible, in ways that will leave the lightest imprint on law's practice beyond what is absolutely necessary to resolve the immediate dispute

A rare strand of agreement emerges in the growing cries of frustration with the alternatives on offer – which tends to spur the proliferation of still further entrants that often turn out to be, at root, merely more of the same.[1]

---

[1] Truly, it is difficult to keep track. In addition to the continuous spawning of new variations (such as "Original Methods Originalism," lately championed by Michael Rappaport and Michael

None of the existing theories succeeds. My account is not a variation of Originalism or Living Constitutionalism or any of the others. I do believe that several of the leading accounts offer important individual points. Yet the overall debate is a minefield of loaded terms, false dichotomies, half-truths, and straw men (evidenced in the prevalent charges of "activism," "legislating from the bench," and "making law," as well as in calls for "deference to the democratic branches," "flexibility," "evolving meaning," and "balancing"). To be clear: some of these ideas do have valid applications. Courts sometimes do engage in inappropriate activism, for instance, and balancing *by an objectively proper standard* is sometimes called for. Yet all too frequently, these tropes are hurled in ways that cloak invalid assumptions and thus obscure rather than illuminate. The climate of debate is thick with suspicion of ulterior ideological agendas, as many participants seem spring-loaded to read opponents' words in their least tenable light.

The reason is not that all the parties are either fools or knaves. Objective adjudication is difficult, thanks to the abstractness of the ideal and the complexity of many of the cases to which it must be applied. Moreover, the stakes are large and emotionally charged, which can easily distract people from exercising their most careful judgment. Yet the deeper explanation for the sterility of debate lies in theorists' failure to consider judicial review in sufficiently fundamental terms. The proper manner of conducting judicial review depends on the function of judicial review; that, in turn, depends on the function of the legal system itself. Further, precisely because they do not confront the basic function and the basic authority of a legal system, many theories harbor misguided assumptions concerning the legitimate place of value considerations in judicial review. And while nearly everyone in the debate agrees that courts' primary responsibility is to objectively maintain the law of the land, their accounts of how to do that are distorted by misconceptions of what objectivity *is*.

In order to explain the foundations that are necessary to understand proper judicial review, therefore, this book examines the essential nature of objectivity and the specific ways that objectivity should guide a legal system. My account pays particular attention to the authority of law. For without a firm grip on a legal system's authority, we cannot understand what legitimately qualifies as the law that judges (and other interpreters) are to be faithful *to*. It

McGinness, *Originalism and the Good Constitution*, Cambridge, MA: Harvard University Press, 2013), several of these schools go by various names and portions of some overlap with portions of others. All of this makes an accurate, up-to-date catalog elusive. For a few helpful, if inevitably incomplete, taxonomies, see Sotirios Barber and James Fleming, *Constitutional Interpretation: The Basic Questions*, New York: Oxford University Press, 2007, p. 64; and Philip Bobbitt, *Constitutional Fate*, New York: Oxford University Press, 1982, pp. 3–7.

is only when informed by a sound understanding of all of these, we will see, that we can appreciate what objectivity in judicial review demands.[2]

2. DISTINCTIVE PERSPECTIVE

My approach makes several distinctive claims. Foremost, I argue that an understanding of objective judicial review requires a thorough understanding of objectivity itself as well as of objectivity's particular demands of a legal system. Judicial review is but one significant activity within a larger legal system whose parts are designed to work in tandem to perform a specific task. As a single component of a coordinated enterprise, the proper exercise of judicial review is determined by its role in serving that mission. Prescriptions for judicial review, accordingly, can only be evaluated in that context – by reference to the fundamental principles of a proper, larger system.

Objectivity, I will argue, is not (contrary to its usual portrait) passive assent to ready-made truths. Elaborating on the insights of Ayn Rand in this sphere, I explain how objectivity consists of a specific manner of using one's mind in order to "get one's conclusions right." It is only by achieving a particular relationship between subject and object that a person can accurately understand the aspects of reality relevant to his inquiry and can claim objective validity for his conclusions.

Further, I show how the authority of a legal system is critical both to the objectivity of that system and to objectivity in judicial review. The purpose of judicial review is to ensure governance by the law; courts police the lawfulness of a government's use of its power. Without a firm grip on what constitutes valid law, however, this would be impossible. And we cannot understand what counts as valid law (law that *should* be upheld by courts) without understanding the authority of the law. We must understand what legitimates the legal system's unique power to compel obedience to its strictures in order to know exactly how far that power extends and what constitutes its objective use.[3]

---

[2] While the term "objectivity" is not always featured in debates about competing methods of judicial review, the concept is virtually always implicit in claims concerning fidelity to law. Judges must follow *this* method, most theorists will argue, or this other method, in order to maintain objective law. Part of my larger thrust, in fact, is that objectivity's position in the shadows is one of the barriers that obstructs a correct understanding of judicial review. We need to confront the nature of objectivity head-on in order to appreciate its requirements for jurists. The failure to understand correctly objectivity's fundamental character and correlative requirements is largely responsible for the missteps that have marred efforts on this subject.

[3] In claiming that the authority of a legal system is critical to the objectivity of that system, I mean that unless the system's exercise of power is grounded in valid authority, the legal system is not objective. At the same time, a legal system would forfeit its authority if it strayed

Legal philosophy is derivative from political philosophy, I believe, and the basic framework of a proper legal system is determined by more fundamental issues addressed in that field – most pivotally, by conclusions concerning the purpose of government. I explain the moral authority of a legal system in these terms, therefore, arguing that law's moral authority is grounded in individual rights. The only legitimate use of the kind of power that a government wields – and the only valid reason for any institution's having such power in the first place – is its necessity to protect individual rights.

When it comes to the question of judicial review, we will see how misguided images of objectivity and misconceptions of law's authority distort the debate. Originalists, for instance, tend to project artificial expectations of what objective law is and of what courts must do to interpret it faithfully. By underappreciating the role of judgment in an objective process, they adopt an overly rigid image of what fidelity to law actually is. Living Constitutionalists, on the other hand, tend to give too great a role to personal judgment and thereby release review from the constraints imposed by the enduring law.

3. OVERVIEW

The book falls into two parts. The first examines the fundamental character of objectivity in a legal system. It begins, in Chapter 1, by examining objectivity itself. Drawing from arenas in which its basic character is most readily recognized, I puncture the mystique of objectivity by breaking down the simple essentials of what objectivity consists of, why we should seek it, and what we must do in order to be objective. In doing so, I distinguish objectivity not only from its obvious alternative, subjectivism, but also from "intrinsicism," the belief that that which is objective is simply given and capable of being known in a relatively passive, effortless way.[4] In truth, I argue, objectivity consists in a volitional, deliberate

from the demands of objectivity. So in this respect, the inverse is also true: the objectivity of a legal system – in its actual operation – is critical to the authority of that system. In different ways, objectivity and authority each support the other. Authority questions will be explored in depth in Chapters 4 and 5.

4   This threefold distinction between objectivity, subjectivism, and intrinsicism is taken from Ayn Rand. Realists, such as Plato, who regard the referents of concepts as universals inherent in things, would exemplify the intrinsicist position, in her view, while nominalists who regard concepts' referents as wholly products of man's consciousness would be subjectivists. The "view from nowhere" model of objectivity associated with Thomas Nagel, among others, would be a contemporary instance of intrinsicism. Nagel, *The View from Nowhere*, New York: Oxford University Press, 1989. Rand explains the three alternatives more fully in *Introduction to Objectivist Epistemology*, ed. Harry Binswanger, New York: Penguin, 1990, 2nd edition, pp. 52–54 and 79; and, in its particular application to questions of value, in "What Is Capitalism?" in *Capitalism: The Unknown Ideal*, New York: Signet-Penguin, 1967,

method of using one's mind so as to apprehend accurately the object(s) of one's concern. It demands scrupulous adherence to relevant evidence and strictly logical inference therefrom. While this chapter delves into the characteristically difficult terrain of epistemology, it is crucial to position ourselves to understand objectivity in the law.

Chapter 2 tackles the core conditions necessary for objectivity in a legal system, arguing that three features are crucial: law's content, law's administration, and law's justification. In more colloquial terms, a legal system's propriety turns on what the system does, how it does it, and why it does it (*why*, in the sense of the authority beneath all that it does). Deviations in any one of these areas, we will see, undermine the integrity of the system and compromise its objectivity.

Chapter 3 highlights a particular implication of a legal system's objectivity that is rarely appreciated, but which is especially significant for judicial review. Nearly everyone agrees that the touchstone of judicial fidelity is the Rule of Law. That is the ideal that judges are obligated to uphold. Contrary to its prevalent portrayal, however, this ideal is not value neutral. I argue that the Rule of Law is, in fact, a moral ideal. Indeed, the reason why the law *should* be objectively upheld is that doing so serves a morally valuable end. And that end must factor into the reasoning of courts that are charged to interpret the law. Far from impeding the objectivity of judicial decision making, a clear understanding of values' role in proper law is what makes possible its objective interpretation. In practice, the insistence that judicial review should be sterilized of all traces of value only invites the influence of inappropriate values by default, since the leverage of *some* values in a legal system is inescapable.

In order to understand the justification beneath an objective legal system, Chapters 4 and 5 explore the law's authority. Chapter 4 addresses the moral authority of a legal system, explaining the basic moral premises that underwrite the legitimacy of its very enterprise. This chapter is thus somewhat different in kind from the others, addressing the questions of political philosophy that lay the foundation for the conception of proper law that my account relies upon. Specifically, this chapter grounds a legal system's warrant to coerce in the purpose of government and identifies that purpose as the protection of individual rights. It explains how the initiation of force is inimical to human life and, correspondingly, why it must be removed from human interactions. If men are to flourish while living together in society, they must be free from

---

pp. 21–23. Also see elaboration in Leonard Peikoff, *Objectivism: The Philosophy of Ayn Rand*, New York: Dutton, 1991, pp. 142–150, 245–247.

the arbitrary imposition of force. This is what authorizes the protective rule of a government.

Chapter 5 examines a system's internal legal authority, that which is properly bedrock *as law*. What should serve as the ultimate arbiter of how legal power may be used? I answer by examining the two leading candidates, common law and constitutional systems. Notwithstanding the considerable contributions that common law has offered to sound legal practices, by identifying a number of its severe shortcomings (including its overvaluing stability and confusion of wisdom with authority), I show how the sovereignty of a constitution is a superior means of fulfilling the legal system's function. Such an explicit, definitive repository of a system's ultimate authority allows that legal system to integrate its fundamental principles better, to discipline its practices more strictly to conform to those principles, to guide better everyone living under it, and, by all these means, simply to govern better – that is, to govern more consistently and more effectively in accordance with the proper principles.

Having established the defining elements of an objective legal system, the second part of the book traces the implications for judicial review. Chapter 6 critiques the leading schools of thought on proper judicial methodology. It examines Textualism, Public Understanding Originalism, Popular Constitutionalism, Perfectionism or Living Constitutionalism, and Minimalism, focusing the critique, in each case, on the ways in which these theories misconstrue either the basic nature of objectivity or the requirements of objectivity in a legal system (or both). In highly abbreviated terms: Textualism misunderstands the objective meaning of language; Public Understanding Originalism confuses objective meaning with original-ness of intended meaning; Popular Constitutionalism misconstrues the authority of the law and the role of the Constitution; Perfectionism misconstrues the relationship between the philosophy that animates the law and the law itself; and Minimalism steers courts away from the proper object of judicial review.

In Chapter 7, I present an account of objective judicial review. Drawing on the explanations of objectivity and objective law given in Part One, this chapter identifies the most basic guideposts that must steer a court, if it is to honor objective law. Using the function of judicial review as an abiding compass, I emphasize two factors as vital for proper review: unswerving focus on the law (as opposed to attention to a number of extraneous considerations that are commonly invoked); and scrupulously logical respect for the full context of the law – including its animating principles – in order to glean the meaning of any of its individual elements. I also discuss those features of personal character, intellectual and moral, that best suit a person to adhere to the regimen of objective review.

My account of proper review in Chapter 7 is premised on a wider legal system whose several parts are all basically functioning as they should. Because the proper functioning of the courts cannot be understood apart from the actions of the other branches, however, Chapter 8 considers how justices should proceed when those branches are not living up to that ideal – in other words, the situation that courts face today. Without attempting comprehensive details prescribing how judges should proceed within a flawed system, I chart the most significant measures that courts should employ if they are to begin to restore greater objectivity to our law. Principally, I argue, courts should reject the doctrine of three-tiered scrutiny that has reigned for roughly a century and revive strict scrutiny (rationally strict), across the board.[5] Doing so would go a great distance toward restoring valid presumptions to legal determinations of government authority. Further, judges must exert the courage that is often required to resist various ancillary pressures and to acquit the full responsibilities of their obligation to the law.

Consistent adherence to my counsel for judicial review would carry far-reaching repercussions for certain entrenched social arrangements and is thus likely to trigger concerns about unfairness in disrupting people's associated expectations. In addressing these concerns, I stress the difference between finding the law and identifying the legal remedy that is most just, in such circumstances. The practical changes necessitated by objective methodology, I argue, need not be imposed at a stroke, without warning. At the same time, it is important to appreciate that the longstanding familiarity of unjustified legal practices does not justify the maintenance of such practices.

⤺

The reason to care about the proper exercise of judicial review is the same reason to care about objectivity in a legal system: to enable that system to fulfill its function. The power of a legal system is immense. To do things by law, as we observed, is to do them by force. Thus it is equally imperative that a legal system not exceed its mandate, that it not stray beyond the specific reason for its having the power that it does. A clear understanding of what the mission and authority of a legal system are, therefore, along with an understanding of the objective exercise of its power, are prerequisites for understanding the distinct requirements of judicial review. That is what I hope to provide.

Most theories of proper review profess that their methodologies are faithful to the law. Because they have not adequately grappled with what objective law

---

5   *US v. Carolene Products Company* 304 US at 152 (1938) is widely seen as the font of tiered scrutiny.

is, however, they are not. Only the kind of account that I offer here, I think, by virtue of its grounding in a sound understanding of objectivity – both objectivity in principle, as it applies in any sphere, and objectivity in its particular application to a legal system – truly honors the law. Consequently, this account offers a prescription for judicial review uniquely capable of delivering the value that is properly sought by a legal system, namely, the protection of individual rights.

PART I

AN OBJECTIVE LEGAL SYSTEM

1

Objectivity – Getting Reality Right

1. INTRODUCTION

The law largely consists of a set of abstractions: rules designed to govern myriad individual cases. It is because the proper application of these abstractions in particular cases is not self-evident that disputes arise and the judiciary is called upon to resolve these disputes objectively. Thus, it behooves us to understand what its doing so – what *objective* review – consists of.

In order to understand objectivity in judicial review, however, we must first understand objectivity's demands in a legal system more broadly. That, in turn, depends on a firm understanding of objectivity itself. Clarifying objectivity is the task of this chapter. While we do not require the depth or detail of an epistemologist, we do need a solid grasp of the essential nature of objectivity in order to be able to assess the objectivity of law and of different methods of judicial reasoning that attempt to uphold the law.

Familiar as the concept is and ready as people are to complain about others' perceived failures to be objective, prevailing notions of objectivity are mottled with confusions. The term is bandied about to mean different things, hiding disparate assumptions concerning what an objective process does and does not provide. These tend to surface when we disagree over whether a particular person *is* objective and discover that our differences arise, at least in part, from conflicting conceptions of exactly what objectivity demands. It is precisely because many legal thinkers do not accurately understand the nature of objectivity that they favor modes of judicial review that ultimately pull jurists away from fidelity to the law. Taken-for-granted misconceptions can drastically distort our standards of objective law. The exact manner in which they do so should become clearer as I develop these ideas over the course of the book. For now, our aim is to distill the essence of objectivity and solidify our grasp of its basic nature in any sphere, so that we will be well equipped to deploy it in the legal domain. The account of objectivity that I present is based on that of Ayn Rand.[1]

Examining objectivity, I should caution, brings us into some highly abstract territory. While I will guide us along a relatively simple path and use accessible examples, there is no way around the fact that objectivity is an abstract subject. The kind of discussion necessary to clarify objectivity and that occupies much of this chapter is not representative of the rest of the book. Only by laying this groundwork carefully, however, can we have a secure foundation for our subsequent investigation of objectivity in a legal system and objectivity in judicial review.

2. WHY SEEK OBJECTIVITY?

To begin, let us attend to the kind of thing that objectivity is. What is its genus? Objectivity is a method of using one's mind. On a given question, given a variety of observations, information, and purported information vying to attain the status of knowledge in a person's mind, "objectivity" designates a particular manner of considering such factors, in reaching conclusions. Whether one is deciding which job applicant to hire, which school to attend, how much to spend on a car, or whether to believe in a god, global warming, or that the latest iPhone is better than the latest Android, objectivity is a particular manner of arriving at answers.[2]

It is important to recognize that, contrary to the way in which people frequently speak, strictly, *reality* is not objective. Facts – existing phenomena – are neither objective nor nonobjective; they simply are. If a particular rose is red, that rose is red; if the speed of the car caused the severity of the damage, then the speed was responsible for the severity of the damage. It is human beings who can be either objective or nonobjective in the ways that we think about phenomena. Objectivity is a particular discipline for directing our thinking.[3]

---

[1]   In subsequently referring, at times, to "my account," it should be understood both that Rand is the originator of the basic picture of objectivity that I am elaborating and that my understanding of her view may be mistaken in places. While I do not believe that it is, that possibility is inescapable.

[2]   The concept of "objectivity" can refer either to the process of reaching a conclusion or to the conclusions themselves, as illustrated in our routinely making such remarks as "the investigative committee is not doing its work objectively" or "the decision to deny his appeal was not objective." Also, I will frequently refer to just one of the specific types of thinking processes that can be objective (such as reaching a conclusion, answering a question, making a decision, forming a belief, accepting a belief, etc.) to represent the full gamut of relevant thinking processes.

[3]   Strictly, the term "objective" can be used in either a metaphysical or an epistemological sense. In its metaphysical usage, objectivity refers to a thing's existence independent of consciousness. Epistemological objectivity, by contrast, pertains to a person's manner of using his mind

Why should we seek objectivity? What is to be gained from being objective? Why does it make sense to subject our mind's activity to *any* particular discipline, for that matter?

Essentially, because we want to be right. We want our beliefs to be true and our conclusions to be valid. Recognizing (at least implicitly) that effective action in any domain requires a sound understanding of relevant phenomena, we employ the method of objectivity to help us build reliable foundations for our beliefs, appraisals, and the actions that we take on their basis. When hiring, for example, we would like to accurately gauge candidates' strengths, weaknesses, capabilities, and suitability for the position. When treating an illness or planning a vacation, we would like to accord an array of facts their appropriate place so as to achieve our principal aim. Again, we discipline our thinking by the rigors of objectivity, most basically, because we want to be sure of things. We want knowledge.

This much concerns what we seek. We also realize, however, that in order to gain knowledge, we must respect certain facts. Perhaps most obvious is the fact that evidence does not speak for itself. Facts do not disclose themselves to us or announce their significance in relation to other facts and to a particular person's questions or decisions. Since *we* speak for the observations that we make, we need to make sure that we speak in a way that is faithful to them – that correctly represents what we observe and what it signifies.

Human beings are notoriously fallible. We are not automatically correct in the beliefs that we adopt. (I thought my balance was $2,567 when it was actually $2,657. I thought Bill would be a good branch manager, but the responsibilities overwhelmed him. We thought the bridge was safe to walk across, but it turned out to be otherwise.) For this reason, we need a means of sifting true beliefs from untrue and valid inferences from invalid.

The desire for accurate understanding does not suffice, due to another basic fact that creates the need for objectivity: the Primacy of Existence. This is the label that Rand bestowed on what is essentially a form of realism: the thesis that a thing's existence and identity (its specific nature) are independent of human beings' observations, attitudes, and beliefs about that thing's

to think about that which exists. My analysis concentrates on this epistemological sense. I discuss this distinction in "The Importance of the Subject in Objective Morality: Distinguishing Objective from Intrinsic Value," *Social Philosophy and Policy* volume 25, no. 1 (2008), pp. 139–143, and in "'Social' Objectivity and the Objectivity of Value," in *Science, Values, and Objectivity*, eds. Peter Machamer and Gereon Walters, Pittsburgh: University of Pittsburgh Press, 2004, pp. 150–156. Also see Rand, "Who Is the Final Authority in Ethics?"in *The Voice of Reason*, ed. Leonard Peikoff, New York: Penguin, 1988, pp. 18; and Peikoff, *Objective Communication*, ed. Barry Wood, New York: Penguin, 2013, pp. 84–86.

existence and identity. If I have a lung tumor, I have that tumor whether I or anyone else knows it or would like to believe it. If a certain configuration of substances, temperature, atmospheric pressure, and other conditions causes a particular chemical reaction, my ignorance of that or my misunderstanding of the relationships involved does not alter this fact. Existents and their identities are independent of our thoughts about their existence and identities. (By "existent," I refer to anything that exists, regardless of its metaphysical category. Thus physical objects, properties, events, actions, emotions, plans, and relationships are among the many things that qualify. For they all exist.)[4]

Reality is resolute, we might say (although this is obviously metaphorical). The implication for us is that if we are to gain knowledge of reality, we must deliberately direct our minds according to means that honor this fact, firmly resisting any inclination to confuse internal thoughts with thought-independent facts. And among the realities that we must respect is the nature of the human mind itself.

Human thought is volitional. Our minds do not automatically operate in an exclusively fact-finding, logical way. (Contrast certain physiological processes such as the circulatory or digestive systems, which automatically perform their functions [at least, normally they do].) Individuals control how they use their minds, and process affects product: How a person uses his mind affects the validity of the beliefs that he arrives at. This, too, then, helps us to explain why we need to adopt a deliberate method of thinking. The way that a person goes about exercising his mental faculty (identifying, distinguishing, inferring, etc.) is up to him. He faces alternative paths in selecting which questions to pose, which leads to pursue, which thoughts to dismiss, which ideas to credit, when to draw a halt to the process of thinking and when to seek further information or to consider implications from a different angle, and so on. Some such paths are much better than others, however – better for the purpose of *getting it right* – of accurately understanding the nature of the object in question.

For all these reasons, then – the Primacy of Existence, human beings' fallibility, and human thought's volitional character – human beings require the discipline of objectivity.

---

4 For further explanation of the Primacy of Existence, see Rand, *Introduction to Objectivist Epistemology*, expanded second edition, ed. Harry Binswanger, New York: Penguin, 1990, pp. 53–54, 245–252, 109–110; Peikoff, *Objectivism: The Philosophy of Ayn Rand*, pp. 17–23, 118; Allan Gotthelf, "Ayn Rand's Theory of Concepts: Rethinking Abstraction and Essence," in *Concepts and Their Role in Knowledge: Reflections on Objectivist Epistemology*, eds. Allan Gotthelf and James G. Lennox, Pittsburgh: University of Pittsburgh Press, 2013, pp. 6, 10; and Gregory Salmieri, "Conceptualization and Justification," in *Concepts and Their Role in Knowledge*, pp. 43–44.

At the same time, it is important to appreciate that no method can offer a fail-safe guarantee of correct conclusions. Nothing will convert us into infallible beings. While we should earnestly seek reliable conclusions and genuine knowledge, the standards for assessing our means of seeking them must be realistic to our actual capacities.[5] Consequently, the fact that an objective conclusion is not *necessarily* accurate should not be regarded as refutation of a particular conclusion's objectivity or of objectivity's usefulness. (Because many people find this counterintuitive, I will explain the point more fully later in the chapter. I raise it here, however, to set expectations on an appropriate track at the outset.) There is no means by which human beings could attain such fanciful epistemological power; a realistic account of objectivity will not pretend to. The method of objectivity, however, when properly understood, is *the* means by which human beings can best position themselves to know whereof they speak. By identifying the most fundamental features that distinguish reality-tracking thinking, objectivity charts the path for doing everything that we can to reach accurate conclusions. And that, again, is our reason for seeking objectivity: to furnish the firmest ground possible for our conclusions to hug the facts.

3. THE CORE OF OBJECTIVITY

So what is objectivity?[6]

While the average person might struggle to provide a precise formulation, it is a thoroughly familiar concept, routinely used, of which most people carry a working understanding. Starting with a few commonplace ways of thinking about objectivity will help us to zero in on its essential character.

---

[5] They must themselves be objective, in other words. We will understand this claim more fully, as I explain the core of objectivity in the balance of the chapter. I also discuss the fallibility of objective reasoning in "'Social' Objectivity and the Objectivity of Value," 2004, pp. 153–154, and "The Importance of the Subject in Objective Morality," pp. 135–136.

[6] While my portrait of objectivity is drawn from Rand's account, I do not think of Objectivism as having a monopoly on the concept and I do not mean to equate objectivity with the Objectivist view of it. The phenomenon of objectivity long preceded Rand's discussion. Plenty of people over the centuries have been objective in their approaches to numerous issues, large and small. Moreover, people gradually developed the *concept* of objectivity as a self-conscious, deliberate method of using one's mind, weighing evidence, teasing out inferences, and so forth. (It is difficult to imagine the sciences' progress without it.) Just as various theorists have advanced our understanding of objectivity's signature characteristics, I would expect future epistemologists further to extend and refine our understanding of objectivity. Because Rand offers the most sound and illuminating account of objectivity's fundamental character to date, in my judgment, I exploit her account to shed light on objectivity in a legal system and in judicial review.

Let us begin with a very broad way of distinguishing the objective: A belief is objective when it is held for reasons, as opposed to being held arbitrarily or baselessly. In seeking objectivity, one seeks to overcome reliance on hearsay, faith, or sheer unsubstantiated opinion.[7] Slightly more carefully: A belief is objective when it is held for good reasons. Even more precisely: when it is held for the right reasons, those that are most indicative of the truth of the specific claim at issue. While many things might be true of a particular subject and while I might have very good reason to believe those things, not all of them give me good reason to embrace every possible conclusion about that subject. Knowing that Tim is tall, for example, does not mean that I should hire him for the position at the bank. Knowing that Tim is from Alabama does not mean that I should fire him from his position at the bank. That Tim is a Democrat with thirty years of government service does not mean that I should vote for him or marry him.[8]

The ideal of objectivity reflects recognition that some considerations are more telling than others, in demonstrating a specific claim's validity. Objectivity is a screen, first, for the relevance of various considerations and then, more critically, for determining their place (if any) in logical support for a claim.

A. Going Public?

Many people equate the objectivity of a process with its publicness – the process's being overt, transparent, available for all to observe. Organizations sometimes boast that their procedures for reaching decisions are "out in the open." *Anyone can see how we do things* and, the implication is often projected, our methods are, by virtue of that, perfectly objective. On this view, objectivity is a function of openness.[9]

While public accessibility *is* often a feature of objective methods, this does not capture the core of objectivity. By probing the value of publicness, we can see why not.

---

[7]   Several specific logical fallacies reflect this rejection of the baseless, which is often what lurks beneath appeals to authority, to popularity, to tradition, or emotion (whether those appeals are explicit or implicit).

[8]   Obviously, I am leaving aside the extremely unusual circumstances in which some of these facts could be relevant to the decision in question. Ordinarily, the facts cited give no reason to act in the ways noted.

[9]   Not everyone who boasts of transparency claims such objectivity, but many do, as do many people who treat transparency as providing objectivity.

When the grounds for a conclusion are openly given, the conclusion can be externally checked. Others can follow the same procedures and apply the same criteria to see if the results correspond. The implication – which is both valid and important – is that objective conclusions are not a mysterious insight that results from privileged information or special methods exclusively known to a select few. Rather, claims are justified on the basis of their procedural pedigree. Openness, in other words, suggests that it is not authority that governs (which would be arbitrary), but thinker-independent facts.

Moreover, the accessibility of conclusions' foundations to public scrutiny (the methods employed as well as substantive premises relied upon) allows for constructive critique of those foundations. The more that outsiders can know about the factors that governed, the better our prospects for discovering any errors in methods or in the specific conclusions that were reached by using them. It also allows us to hold accountable the people who employ those methods. In this way, openness testifies to good faith and confidence that one's reasoning is sound. "Opening up the books" conveys that one does not fear scrutiny and shows a commitment to getting things right, given that it does invite the possibility of others' finding errors in one's processes.

Useful as all of these features are, however, they speak more to the appearance and periphery of objectivity than to its essence. Publicness, per se, wholly concerns the display of one's method. While transparency can be an excellent aid for identifying faults and needed corrections of methods used in reaching conclusions, it does not identify what those methods are or what distinguishes them as objective. A person can be objective in reasoning about an issue in private, after all, without anyone else knowing how he is proceeding. Moreover, when publicly available conclusions and their foundations are corroborated by others, that does not tell us that those results are correct. Those who affirm a conclusion may all be mistaken.

Willingness to publicize one's methods is a good sign, to be sure. It is a sign that one is not hiding a conscious arbitrariness and believes that his methods will withstand outside scrutiny. Yet it is only that. *Will* they withstand such scrutiny? And, more important, *should* they? Will they accomplish the work that we ask of objective methods, namely, helping us to get our conclusions right?

B. The Scientific Method

To answer these more fundamental questions, we do better by considering what is probably the most commonly cited model of objectivity, the scientific method. What are its hallmarks?

In using the scientific method, one begins by making observations. Research is rooted in *looking* – in sensory, perceptual experience. (I use "looking" as a shorthand for whichever of the five senses is most germane for the phenomena being inspected.) It is only after this that a person seeks to understand his observations by describing, and then by forming a hypothesis about what is actually so (i.e., about the nature of the phenomena in question).

Next, he tests his hypothesis. In this phase, the critical elements that distinguish a procedure as scientific include such things as:

- studying a large and diverse sample of specimens under varying conditions
- careful and thorough observation, followed by meticulous precision in reporting those observations
- repetition of trials, so as to exclude distortions potentially introduced by accidental factors in a given test
- holding different variables constant in different trials, so as to isolate the role of each of the possibly salient factors
- blind or double-blind testing, eliminating subjects' and researchers' knowledge of one another's identity, so as to exclude the potential influence of such knowledge

Some of the particulars will vary, depending on the kind of phenomena and specific hypotheses being investigated, and we could inventory these elements in somewhat differing ways or at differing levels of detail. For our purposes, though, the lesson is clear. The scientific method is a discipline employed in a systematic effort to eliminate possible distortions from a person's thinking about a given phenomenon. This effort is driven by the aim of understanding the actual reality in question. The goal is not simply agreement among those who are considering a question. The scientific method seeks accuracy. It seeks to identify the facts. It seeks, as I put it earlier, to *get reality right*. Those who use it do so to gain *knowledge*.

Consider testing a pharmaceutical for its efficacy in treating mid-stage colon cancer. To assess that efficacy, researchers need to hone in on salient aspects of the drug's effects on those taking it. They need to gain knowledge of the actual phenomena that indicate the nature of the drug in that respect. Many other features of the drug, such as its taste or expense or side effects, are irrelevant.[10] What is important for us is that it is not enough to conduct testing that, whenever repeated, yields the same results or gains the consensus of a wide variety of researchers. In order to be sure that researchers are not being

---

[10] Certain of its side effects will obviously be relevant to the question of the overall advisability of a person's taking the drug, but that is a distinct question from the efficacy of the drug.

systematically misled about the efficacy of the drug, tests designed to adhere to the scientific method seek to reveal the drug's actual nature. Accuracy is the gold standard.[11]

Objectivity is a discipline that properly governs the full gamut of subjects that people think about, not only those issues that are typically classified as "scientific" or that are most readily testable by physical means. Yet the scientific method's signature features illuminate the essence of objectivity in all spheres. For the scientific method is actually an application of objectivity and it allows us to appreciate that objectivity is, at its core, a reality-anchored and logic-guided method of reaching conclusions. To be objective is to be guided, fundamentally, by reality – by the *nature of the thing* in question. More exactly, it is to be guided in one's thinking by the nature of those phenomena that bear on the answer to the specific questions being asked or the specific hypothesis being evaluated.

The objective inquirer proceeds on the basis of what each factor *is*, as best as he can discern, rather than what he might like to believe it is, what certain others think it is or traditionally have thought it was, or what he has some other incentive to say that it is (such as a financial, political, or social incentive). When it comes to drawing inferences from what he observes, he adheres to the correlative discipline: His reasoning is guided scrupulously by logic. A person might make a mistake, of course; trying to be logical does not assure success in actual conformity with all of its rigors. (A person might simply fail to grasp the logical implications of a certain fact, for instance, through no avoidable fault, in that instance.) But a person is objective to the extent that he does his honest best to accept only those conclusions that comply with rules of logical inference. He strives to proceed solely by the relevant evidence and logical inferences therefrom.

C. *The Role of Purpose*

How can a person determine what the relevant facts are, however? The answer will depend on his purpose.

In any particular use of objectivity, we cannot know the concrete elements that objectivity demands without knowing what the person is after. If I wish to evaluate job candidates, the qualities to heed and the weight to

---

[11] More exactly, it is conduciveness to accurate conclusions that is the standard, rather than actual accuracy. As I noted earlier, conscientious objectivity cannot guarantee success in reaching accurate results. Again, I will say more on this when discussing fallibility in the next section.

assign them depend on what the job is: sales manager, wedding planner, rugby coach? Does the sales position involve managing a division of 14 people or 400? Appropriate criteria derive from these types of considerations as well as from my vision of how those roles can best be fulfilled. Which qualities do I regard as most critical to a worker's success in delivering the result that I seek? Along similar lines, in order to grade student papers objectively, the purpose of the assignment (what it intends to assess and to teach) must inform the criteria employed. Note that more generally, researchers who employ the scientific method do so in order to answer a specific question, and what that question is determines which observations and associated considerations are salient for objective conclusions. (Factors irrelevant to a cough syrup's safety, such as its taste, for instance, might be relevant to determining its appeal to children.)

Important as a person's purpose is to determining the precise factors that will distinguish an objective verdict in a given case, it remains, more basically, *reality* that determines what he must do in order to achieve that purpose. A person's purpose does not single-handedly dictate the objective course of action, in other words. Reality – external facts that obtain independently of a person's purpose – and his purpose are both essential to determine the particulars of objectivity in any specific application. But it is crucial to respect the proper division of labor. The overarching purpose of objectivity is always to get reality right: to accurately understand facts. Whatever the more specific end (such as hiring a manager, testing for hepatitis, evaluating a new boyfriend, or assembling a rugby team), the ongoing, governing meta-concern is to accurately understand reality. Within that framework, then, a person's more circumscribed purpose is needed to determine which particular facts to heed and in what exact ways.

D. Misconceptions

Given this portrait of objectivity's basic character, we should be able to appreciate the failings of several popular conceptions of objectivity. While each reflects grains of truth, they are, by themselves, extremely misleading.

Neutrality
One frequently hears that to be objective is to be neutral or impartial. An objective conclusion is not tainted by the values of the inquirers. (While neutrality and impartiality are not the same thing, people frequently treat them as if they are. Since the difference is not important for my larger point, however, I will not pursue it.)

While it is true that an inquirer's particular values or ends should not distort his procedures or conclusions (as was clearly reflected in the rigors imposed by the scientific method), objectivity's relationship to values is not as simple as sheer exclusion. While certain values should not play certain roles in an objective process of reasoning about an issue, objectivity does not banish values, as such. Indeed, the pivotal role played by purpose in determining what an objective procedure will consist of, in any specific case, entails that objectivity cannot be completely value indifferent. In its application to a given case, in fact, objectivity imposes some of the specific requirements that it does because of a value that is sought – the value placed on answering a certain question (about a drug's potency, a job applicant's capabilities, etc.). That purpose injects value judgments into the process. Consequently, a person's being "objective" and being "value driven" are not mutually exclusive (although we must be careful about the type of influence that values exert in drawing conclusions).

What it is important to recognize is this: What constitutes the *answer* to a specific question is not determined simply by the values of the inquirer (e.g., by the fact that I *want* the drug to be approved because of all the money I have invested in it). The objective manner of arriving at the answer to any question, however, does depend, in part, on what the question is. And that – the question that is raised – bespeaks the valuing of certain knowledge. Thus, it is a mistake to demand that an objective inquiry be utterly devoid of value. Without a val-ued purpose, we would have no reason to pursue a question and no basis by which to understand objectivity's specific demands in addressing it.

Evenhandedness

Another frequent characterization of objectivity holds that it consists of even-handedness or treating like cases alike. In grading papers, the idea is, one should maintain consistent standards (assuming that we are speaking of stu-dents in the same class). In evaluating bids on a city contract or mediating between two sides in a dispute, one should accord an equal hearing and apply the same standards in assessing each party's case.

While objectivity *is* typically reflected in such a policy, this characteriza-tion is superficial. Evenhandedness does not reach to the core of objectivity. The reason to treat like cases alike is more telling. For more important than likeness of treatment is the propriety of treatment. If I grade all students by the same standard but it is an inappropriate standard, I am not grading objectively. Repeating an error does not eliminate the error. Equal treatment can be a sign that one is treating cases objectively (or at least that one is attempting to); to deliberately eschew disparate criteria avoids one type of arbitrariness. Yet it does not disavow all types of arbitrariness and it does not deliver objective results.

Consider: What if I am grading only one student? How should I grade *him*?[12] Moreover, in order to treat like cases alike, one must determine which are "like cases." If that is not itself done objectively, then any subsequent regularity in treating individual cases cannot render the process as a whole objective.

What these questions reveal is that a comparison of treatments is not enough. Understanding *appropriate* similarities or differences in treatment is derivative from the underlying nature of objectivity. Whatever sameness of treatment is sometimes required is so only because of objectivity's more fundamental requirements. To think that objectivity is a matter of being evenhanded represents, at best, a slice of its surface.

Interchangeability

Finally, another widespread misconception equates objectivity with interchangeability. The way to be objective, we frequently hear, is to "put yourself in the other guy's shoes." Any single person's vantage point should make no difference to the conclusion reached. Correspondingly, this model considers a conclusion objective when it is the conclusion that anyone would arrive at, once he imagines himself in another's position. The conclusions of objective inquirers will converge.[13]

This conception mistakes a frequent effect of objectivity for the deeper phenomenon that is (at least often) responsible for it. The agreement of people who occupy differing vantage points might be a promising sign that certain sorts of inappropriate factors are not distorting their thinking methods, but it is only that. Agreement, per se, does not identify why we should arrive at the conclusion they have reached, does not tell us how to find the correct result, and does not tell us what the correct result consists of.

The failings of this conception of objectivity are in certain respects similar to those that proved fatal to the "evenhanded, like treatment" conception. Notice that it measures objectivity in entirely social terms: The relationship

---

[12] Assume that I have never taught the course before and that there is no ready comparison class that I might use as guidance.

[13] On reflection, the instruction given by this model becomes murky. Exactly *what* should be altered when adopting another person's perspective, and which elements should not be altered? Am I to imagine what he feels? What he thinks? What he should feel or think? What is actually true of his situation, regardless of his thoughts or feelings? *Which* facts that mark his situation? Further, with whom should one swap perspectives – everyone affected? Those most affected? Unaffected third parties? Obviously, some theorists have addressed such questions and articulated more careful theories, but the most popular and most influential versions of this notion tend to be coarse and ill thought through.

between what one person thinks and what others think is treated as decisive. As long as different people swapping places could agree on a result, that suffices for objectivity. The problem, however, is that nothing disciplines these people; in this account, nothing binds their reasoning to the actual facts (that is, to reality). Pure interchangeability, by itself, is a completely subjectivist standard.[14]

In truth, objectivity is not a function of who believes something or of how many endorse a belief, but of the basis on which a belief is held. Does this conclusion reflect logical inference about the observed relevant phenomena (given the other available information), or not? Rather than recognizing that *who* professes a belief is immaterial to its validity, however, the interchangeability model simply expands membership of the group whose opinion is considered decisive. When enough people agree about *x*, it holds, that is the objective truth about *x*. Obstinately, reality does not play along. Any number of people's consensus that *x* is so does not make it so, thus this conception of objectivity leaves it unable to do objectivity's job: to facilitate people's acquisition of knowledge.[15]

The grain of truth that lends credence to the interchangeability notion is that under certain conditions, rational inquirers equipped with the same information, possessing the same level of intelligence, and employing the objective method *will* reach the same conclusion. That does not entail that that convergence of opinion is what constitutes objectivity, however. What we are after, by adhering to the method of objectivity, is knowledge, awareness of what is actually so. Given the Primacy of Existence, consensus is not an adequate substitute.

This interchangeability model is closely related to another refrain frequently heard when someone asserts the objectivity of a claim: the rejoinder *Who's to say?* This is typically intended as a decisive, unanswerable veto of the allegedly objective assertion. The interchangeability model of objectivity is sometimes tacitly treated as the premise beneath this refrain inasmuch as it

[14] "Subjectivism," in essence, is the belief that a thing's nature is dependent on the consciousness of the person(s) considering it.
[15] Because of specialized training, education, experience, and the like, some individuals' opinions on certain matters do warrant greater attention than others'. People *become* genuine experts or authorities in certain areas due to their acquiring knowledge of the relevant body of material, however. Their opinions warrant attention, accordingly, not simply because they are theirs, but because these people have made themselves more knowledgeable about the subject in question. Their claim on our attention, we might say, comes not from who they are, but from the work and knowledge in virtue of which they have become who they now are. I discuss the failings of a social conception of objectivity further in "'Social' Objectivity and the Objectivity of Values," especially pp. 144–160.

posits that when everyone "says" – that is, when people agree about the truth of a claim – *that* "who" provides an adequate basis to underwrite the objectivity of a claim. As long as we fall short of such consensus, however, no view can be regarded as objectively justified. In other words, no one can "say."

The "who's to say" objection to assertions of objectivity, however, is guilty of the same type of error as the interchangeability conception in that it attributes unwarranted significance to people's verdicts on an idea. Just as the number of people accepting a belief is irrelevant to the validity of that belief, so the identity of the person(s) accepting a belief is irrelevant to the validity of that belief. Objectivity is not, fundamentally, a question of "who."

Alongside the interchangeability premise, the other idea that animates the "who's to say" protest is the conviction that no one is naturally privileged, specially endowed with an inside track on truth, reserved exclusively for him. And this is certainly true. No person's claim should be accepted as objective simply because it is he who claims it. The conclusion too often drawn from this observation, however – namely, that no one can claim the truth of a claim unless everyone would agree about that truth – does not logically follow. If, concerning a particular thesis, some people have relevant experience while others do not and some people have relevant training while others do not and some people have relevant skill and facility with the type of reasoning and subject involved while others do not and – what is most important – if some people adhere to the strictures of objectivity while others do not, then, indeed, those people are in a position to declare a conclusion objectively valid. And we have abundantly more reason to attend to their conclusions than to alternatives not reached on similar grounds. The reason we should do so is not these people's membership in an anointed, mysteriously privileged caste that issues arbitrary professions of objectivity, but their knowledge of the relevant material and the validity of the arguments they provide for the conclusions that they affirm.

These people are by no means rendered infallible by having acquired a body of knowledge or having adhered to the rigors of objective thinking. It would not be rational for others to treat their word as gospel. But they are distinguished by their presentation of strong arguments – arguments which remain open to refutation by anyone who can make better use of the objective method to offer a still stronger argument for a different conclusion. The point is, personal identity in itself does not make one person's claim more credible than anyone else's claim.

In essence, the answer to the query "Who's to say?" is: anyone who can prove his case. Expert or amateur, the test is in reality, not personality.[16]

---

[16]   For related discussion, see Rand, "Who is the Final Authority in Ethics?"

While a proper account of objectivity should not be confused with any of these commonplace shorthands, then, their appeal is understandable. A conclusion should not be what it is *just because* it happens to be a particular individual who conducted the experiments or did the hiring. A particular type of interchangeability is appropriate, as is a particular type of evenhandedness and a particular type of neutrality. Each of these accounts opposes a form of subjectivism that is rightly booted from objective processes. Spotlighting particular ways of deviating from objectivity, however, does not provide an account of what objectivity itself consists of.

In seeking to grasp the essence of objectivity, I think, it is most helpful to remember that objectivity has a job to do: We seek to be objective in order to gain an accurate understanding of reality – of actual, mind-independent existents. And the way for human beings to do that, in the most fundamental terms, is to ground their thinking in observation of reality and to remain faithful to what they observe through the conscientious use of logic. Thus, the characterization that I presented earlier: In its essence, an objective procedure is reality-anchored and logic guided. We employ the discipline of objectivity in order to get reality right, in our minds. Reality itself is the throughline, the fundamental standard, that unites and distinguishes all objective processes.[17]

Before proceeding, I should address a possible misgiving. One might wonder how this portrait of objectivity will hold in regard to law, which is man-made rather than simply given or found. How can a conception of legal objectivity draw from respect for the Primacy of Existence, given that the existence of law is due to human beings' actions rather than to any prior, man-independent natural phenomena? Moreover, law's character as normative rather than descriptive – as action guiding rather than purely fact reporting – may also seem to cloud the prospects for this model of objectivity in the legal sphere. If objectivity revolves around *getting reality right*, how can that apply to rules that are created and changed by us?

On modest reflection, these questions pose no great difficulty. While the law *is* a set of man-made rules rather than a report of facts in nature, once made, law has a definite identity, and that is the reality to which jurists must

---

[17] Whenever I speak of the need for objectivity in order to understand "mind-independent" or "thought-independent" reality, I refer to the *present* thought(s) of those now considering the issue *about* that issue. I am not claiming that no thought may have ever been involved in creating or shaping what the object in question is. Beliefs, emotions, plans, designs, and numerous other thought-involving phenomena could themselves be the object of an inquiry (e.g., Why was my anger at him so intense? Is Johnson's assessment of the coach fair?). The point is simply that once an object has been brought into existence (be it a mental object such as an emotion or evaluation or any other type), it has an identifiable nature, and that nature does not depend on the beliefs or attitudes of the people now thinking about that object.

be faithful. Recall that "reality" does not need to be physical to be genuine. To be objective, I have argued, is to be guided "by the nature of the thing in question ... it is to be guided in one's thinking by the nature of those phenomena that bear on the answer to the specific questions being asked or the specific hypothesis being evaluated." This is necessary for legal objectivity as it is for any other type.

The normative character of laws does create space for variation in specific legal findings *within* the parameters of the adopted laws. It permits bounded variation, in other words. But this, likewise, represents no threat to objectivity insofar as action-guiding instruction must respect the fact that often there may be more than one way to do something. If I tell you to "go to the grocery store" or to "exercise regularly," you might abide by these instructions by adopting a variety of routes to the store or regimens of physical activity. The same goes for laws.

That "Congress shall have power to ... provide and maintain a navy"[18] does not dictate a precise set of one-and-only actions by which Congress might fulfill this responsibility. Similarly, when a state defines battery as "the intentional use of force or violence upon the person of another,"[19] it leaves to others the determination of whether a particular person's actions in a purported battery constitute such a use of force or violence. It does so on the recognition that "battery" designates a certain *kind* of action and that whether a particular action is of that kind requires thoughtful scrutiny. It does not reflect any withdrawal of commitment to objectivity or dilution of the basic requirements of objectivity. While laws differ in their specificity of instruction and the corresponding scope of discretion left to individuals in selecting the precise means by which they will respect the law, objectivity requires respect for the law, however broad or particular its specific demands.

4. THE OBJECTIVITY OF HIGHER ABSTRACTIONS

If this much conveys the core of objectivity, we should also address objectivity's demands when its subject matter is more abstract. For objectivity is more difficult, and is certainly more contested, when more abstract assertions are at issue. The instruction to "go by reality" or "stay anchored in the object" may seem reasonable enough when the object in question is directly perceivable by our senses. It is easy to agree to the objectivity of the claim that "this boy is blonde," for instance, when we are all now looking at a blonde boy. It

---

[18]   U.S. Constitution Article I, Section 8.

[19]   This is a part of the Louisiana penal code's definition of battery (section 33).

is harder to verify the objectivity of the claim that that boy is irresponsible, or tenacious, or fair-minded. Similarly, that Jones regularly gives each of his children the same allowance is more readily verifiable than that Jones is a just father. How can we be objective about such more abstract claims? And in judicial review, obviously, courts are not primarily concerned with disputes of the sort that lend themselves to clear-cut resolution through purely physical scrutiny. While police officers, bomb squads, and medical examiners must be objective in handling physical evidence (ballistics, blood stains, carpet fibers, etc.), the appellate judiciary "gets the theoretical questions." Its work is more abstract.[20]

Notice that in form, the basic question that judicial review poses for courts is: "Is this a case of that?", where the "this" is a (usually) complex set of actual circumstances that are legally disputed in a specific case, and the "that" is an abstract category, such as a "tax," "search," "speech," "public use," "regulation of commerce" or "establishment of religion." For example: Does this police use of a GPS device constitute a search? A search of the sort that requires a warrant? Does this courthouse's posting of the Ten Commandments constitute an establishment of religion? Does the right to free speech protect publication of cartoons that mock a religious creed? Is a government mandate to purchase health insurance a tax?

It is at these levels that agreement grows more elusive and many people believe that objectivity is impossible. Because we cannot put a "search" or an "establishment of religion" under a microscope to resolve our differences by physical inspection, some conclude that claims to objectivity must be surrendered.

That conclusion does not follow, however. In one respect, it is an understandable mistake. For the greater the number of steps that a reasoning process takes from simple reports on things that are directly perceivable (such as that a boy is blonde), the greater the occasions for potential missteps and for such errors to infect subsequent inferences. The possibility of going astray, however,

---

[20] This is a very loose characterization, as the division of labor is hardly all-or-nothing. The results of judges' reasoning are directly practical, and judges may not disregard what they learn about physical evidence in a case, just as those agents of a legal system who most directly handle physical specimens must employ certain theoretical understanding. The very concept of "evidence" presupposes judgments about the relationship of information to broader hypotheses, such as a person's involvement in a crime. Correlatively, a police investigator must recognize not simply that "this is gunpowder residue" or "these are fingerprints," but the potential significance of such facts to ascertaining the guilt or innocence of various parties and the ways that he should, as a result, handle these prints or residue. An objective thinking process is, by its nature, abstract. Even the recognition that "these are fingerprints" is a conceptual identification.

is only that: a possibility. It is precisely to guard against its becoming actuality that we must insist on adherence to the standard of objectivity.

Before I proceed, it is important to acknowledge that the discipline of objectivity *is* more intellectually demanding at higher tiers of abstraction. Two factors are primarily responsible for this.

First, by "tiers" of abstraction, I refer to a claim's proximity to perceptual awareness. The more abstract the claim, the greater its distance from a person's direct, immediate perception in terms of the number of steps of reasoning required to reach that conclusion. "Pet" is a more abstract concept than "dog," for example. I can see that an animal is a dog more readily than I can know that it is a pet; the latter classification rests on further knowledge about that animal. "Garment" is a more abstract concept than "shirt." A "right" is a more abstract concept than "demand," just as "demand" is more abstract than "statement" (which itself is more abstract than "noise"). A person needs to understand a greater number of relationships and to make a greater number of distinctions in order to correctly deploy the more abstract concepts ("pet," "garment," "right," etc.) than he does to correctly deploy the less abstract ("dog," "shirt," "demand," etc.).

In the law, the individual concepts whose meaning and application are most often contested each rest on a number of layers of observation and inference. The concept of a "search" incorporates beliefs and conclusions concerning the nature of an activity and the purpose of an activity, among other things. The concept of "property" builds on conclusions about the relationship between a physical object and a particular person in their relationships to other persons – typically, on the basis of such considerations as how the object in question came to exist and the means by which a person acquired physical possession of it.[21] A firm grasp of legally salient concepts typically involves mastering a network of complex relationships to other phenomena and concepts. And the correct application of these concepts to a specific case (*was* this use of the GPS an unconstitutional search? *Is* that downtown development a "public use?" Did the eviction of residents respect the owners' property rights?) requires still further skills of deft conceptual navigation. Thus, the sheer degree and complexity of the abstractness typical of legal concepts makes the proper exercise of judicial review demanding.

The second factor responsible for the challenge of maintaining objectivity in judicial review is the fact that many of the salient legal concepts are normative, by which I mean that the concepts themselves rest on certain judgments about what should be the case (as opposed to what is the case). Just as, outside

---

[21] I am leaving aside intellectual property for simplicity.

the law, familiar concepts such as "delicious" or "stingy" or "useless" or "edifying" incorporate certain evaluations of the objects to which these are ascribed, so, in a legal system, the concepts of "due process," "equal protection," "private property," "probable cause," "impartial jury," and many others reflect evaluative conclusions. These concepts are formed on the basis not only of pure descriptions, but on conclusions concerning ideals – judgments about what is good or desirable. And the standards by which such judgments are made must themselves be validated. It is here that many people balk, denying the possibility of objective validation.

While the relationship between factual and evaluative assertions is too large a topic for us to undertake here,[22] in its essence, the objective validation of evaluative conclusions is no different in kind from the validation of any other abstractions. The justification for claiming that certain ends are worthwhile or that certain goods belong to a person by right are obviously much more complex than claims that a boy is blonde or a soup is salty, but they are no more suspect, in principle, than are other crucial normative concepts that people employ on a regular basis, regarding such things as how to grow wheat or how to care for a newborn baby or a flea-infested dog. Consider, more generally, claims that particular substances are nutritious or toxic, or that certain activities are physically therapeutic or psychologically healthy. We can make such determinations on grounds that are either objective or nonobjective, depending on the basis supporting the underlying relationships that they implicitly affirm (e.g., the relationship between a certain amount of water and the production of wheat). Claims about those relationships are assertions of fact, subject to the usual sorts of verification that are appropriate for other assertions of fact. The ends pursued can themselves be questioned, of course (why care about wheat production? What is the good of nutrition?), but these, too, as I have argued elsewhere, can be justified by identifying their grounds in still deeper layers of fact, such as the requirements of organisms' survival.[23]

---

[22] I discuss this in depth in *Viable Values*, chapters 4 and 5, and more briefly in *Ayn Rand's Normative Ethics*, chapter 2; and "The Importance of the Subject in Objective Morality," pp. 131–135. Also see Rand, "The Objectivist Ethics," in *The Virtue of Selfishness*, New York: New American Library, 1964; "Causality vs. Duty"; Peikoff, *Objectivism*, chapter 7, especially pp. 241–248.

[23] I do not maintain that value judgments, at any level, can be deduced from judgments of fact, but that value judgments can be (and routinely are, without provoking controversy) induced from relevant observations of fact, logical reasoning, and the adoption of certain ends. The propriety of these ends is justified, in part, by their inescapability for the "propriety" and possibility of pursuing any ends and of employing any normative standards – crucially, including the standards and requirements of logic or reason itself. Indeed, the intelligibility of the categories of "valid" or "appropriate" ends or means rests on tacit assumptions of ends that would be served by adhering to such standards. Objectivity itself is a normative concept.

Again, while this is a more involved issue than I can do justice to here, note that consistent skepticism about the possibility of objectively valid normative conclusions would undermine the very concern with *proper* judicial review. There would be no point in pursuing it if one firmly believed that no objective grounds can be had for distinguishing between proper and improper ways of conducting review.[24]

To return, then, to our main track: While objectivity is a more demanding achievement in regions of higher and more value-inflected abstractions, it is equally possible and all the more crucial, inasmuch as more will logically follow from claims about the meaning of wider abstractions. More hinges on higher abstractions. Notice that the overall goal of objectivity remains the same, namely, to get our conclusions right. Thus, the central question posed for higher or more contested levels of abstractions is the same as at lower levels: What must we do in order to reach valid conclusions? And the answer, in its essence, remains the same: logically adhere to the relevant facts of reality. However simple, sophisticated, or consequential the questions involved, this is what objectivity demands. Insofar as the aim of being objective is unchanged and the reality that we are attempting to understand is unchanged (it is still governed by the Primacy of Existence), so is the instruction of objectivity for our thinking. At higher and more consequential regions of abstraction as at the lowest, its standard and basic discipline remain: volitional fidelity to reality.

A full explanation of how to achieve this would require explanation of the fundamental nature of concepts. Because concept formation is the most basic level at which we can get things right or wrong by proceeding objectively or not, it is the building block that sets the pattern for objective thinking in the acquisition of all knowledge. Even a sketch of concept formation, however, would be much more intricate than is appropriate here. For neither a judge nor the ordinary citizen needs an explicit, detailed epistemological analysis of objectivity in order to know and abide by its basic character and requirements.[25]

For more careful elaboration of this, see Smith, *Viable Values*, pp. 101–111, *Ayn Rand's Normative Ethics*, pp. 21–33, and "The Importance of the Subject in Objective Morality," pp. 132–134. Also see Rand, "Causality vs. Duty," pp. 118–119; and Peikoff, *Objectivism*, pp. 244–245.

[24] It may also be worth noting a different kind of factor that makes some people particularly skeptical of the possibility of objectivity in judicial review: the stakes. Since a legal system's rules are imposed by force and individual rights stand to be either respected or violated by the use of legal power, some fear that heightened concern with the outcomes of legal decisions is so strong as to overwhelm people's ability to maintain objective standards.

[25] For an excellent explanation of concept-formation that serves as the basis for my analysis of objectivity, see Rand, *Introduction to Objectivist Epistemology*; and Peikoff, *Objectivism*, chapter 3. Further debate about the account, including its application to certain animated

What is most important to understand about higher-level objectivity, for our purposes, is the basic way in which "fidelity to reality" is maintained in these regions. Objective thinking at more abstract altitudes is largely a matter of correct classification. That is, it consists of accurately recognizing which discrete existents are of the same kind and which should be classified in different categories. (Is it a tax? Is it a penalty? Is it something else?) Most critical for the judiciary is what we commonly refer to as "thinking in principle." This is the ability to discern the essences of various phenomena and to interrelate them accordingly. When faced with numerous distinct situations, thinking in principle is the ability to isolate the fundamental common denominator that runs through some of them but not others. (What is it, for instance, that unifies certain animals of differing shapes and sizes and capacities as dogs? What is it that unites certain practices as religious?) To do so objectively is to do so on the basis of features that do, indeed, distinguish one set of items from others.

No two existents are identical. However alike even two same-issue postage stamps may be in many respects, each is a discrete existent, inescapably incorporating unique variations. When we classify distinct things as nonetheless the same, in their essence (e.g., as "toxic" or "tenacious" or as a "search" or a "trespass" or an "exercise of religion"), we are recognizing a fundamental similarity among those things that withstands their other differences. To do so objectively is to do so on appropriate grounds – that is, on the basis of their actual similarity.

At the same time, similarity is relative. Sameness is not a freestanding characteristic that any one thing can either possess or fail to possess. Two or more items (two toxins, two searches, two trespasses, etc.) can be the same only *in* certain respects and *when contrasted* with other things that differ from them in those respects. That contrast class is crucial. While no two existents are exactly alike in the sense of being identical, many things are sufficiently alike in certain respects so as to make it useful and valid to mark them off mentally as forming a distinct category (and correspondingly, to treat them differently in action). Doing so is standard practice in a legal system, whose rules obviously designate the legal status of specified categories of actions (*all* exercises of religion, *all* conducting of searches, and so on).

The point is, an objective thinker is able to sift those features that are essential to a thing's identity as a member of a certain class from those that are peripheral, and thus to understand what does and does not belong in a given

issues in contemporary epistemology, can be found in the essays in Gotthelf, ed., *Concepts and Their Role in Knowledge.*

category. He is a good screener. However abstract or complex the categories being considered, he can see past things' superficial similarities and differences[26] and penetrate to essentials, appreciating which variations in features are possible within a given category while still respecting the integrity of that kind's distinctiveness. He understands which differences *make* a difference to a thing's fundamental identity as the kind of thing that it is.[27]

Hierarchy and Context

Objectivity, I have said, is reasoning that is fundamentally object anchored and logic guided. In a certain respect, the second is redundant. For on a proper conception of logic, reality is what adherence to its discipline provides: Logic's strictures are designed to keep a course of thinking grounded in facts; that is, in the actual nature of the specific object or phenomena in question. As a person's thinking rises beyond claims concerning that which is directly observed through perception, logic is the chord by which he maintain his conclusions' warrant from reality.

In order to adhere to logic and to reach objective conclusions, it is especially helpful to recognize two features of knowledge: Knowledge is hierarchical and context relative. Deliberate attention to these features serves as a check to help maintain a person's thinking's grounding in reality. Here again, while I cannot offer a full explanation of these, it will be helpful to elaborate briefly on each, given that objectivity depends on respect for both of them.[28]

The Hierarchical Structure of Knowledge
Knowledge of some things builds and depends on knowledge of others. One cannot understand what a pet is without understanding what an animal is. One cannot understand theft without understanding property. One cannot

---

[26] "Superficial" relative to the purpose of distinguishing the categories being distinguished or of understanding the differences between them.

[27] A properly formed conceptual categorization is a tool, we might say, somewhat like a pair of spectacles that enables you to see the world more sharply. Valid concepts and objective abstract thinking allow you to observe the world *in a particular way*, namely, in terms of those features that are most essential to understanding your principal object. It is important to recognize that *what* you are seeing (the object) remains what it is, independently of your use of tools – just as when I look through the lenses of different strengths of eyeglasses the *world* does not change.

[28] Rand especially emphasized the significance of these features. See Rand, *Introduction to Objectivist Epistemology*, pp. 42–47, 102–103, 231–235, 239, 22–25, 204–215; and Peikoff, *Objectivism*, pp. 121–141. For much fuller discussion, also see material cited in Note 25; and Peikoff, *Understanding Objectivism*, pp. 195–198.

understand the concept of a divorce without first understanding the concept of marriage. Countless everyday ideas – *student, vehicle, carbohydrate, anger, autobiography, software* – reflect this. Certain ideas are necessary in order to make possible others. And the same holds in regard to all sorts of far more sophisticated knowledge, whether we are speaking of single concepts or complex propositions. (One cannot understand fractions without first understanding whole numbers; one cannot understand algebra without first understanding arithmetic; one cannot understand emotions without first understanding consciousness.)

The application of this for objectivity is direct: In order to assess the validity of any particular claim, a person must assess the validity of all the underlying conclusions on which it stands. No claim can be objective if any of its presuppositions is itself unwarranted. Consequently, an objective thinker must identify all the lower rungs of a claim's logical ladder and make sure that each is sturdily grounded in reality.

The more complicated the claim whose objectivity is being assessed and the more extensive its logical scaffolding, naturally, the more demanding this test of objectivity will be. A larger number of elements and a more diverse range of relationships will have to be scrutinized, with the possibility of error correspondingly magnified. Yet the essential point is straightforward: Adherence to objectivity requires conscientious respect for the hierarchical structure of knowledge. Departures from that structure break the bond by which ideas are tied to reality. The person who asserts conclusions while neglecting their cognitive underpinnings is selectively choosing which facts to heed (assuming that he does heed some), while omitting others that are a crucial part of the explanation of why an abstract claim is true and the basis on which he can know it. Consider, for instance, making the claim that U.S. foreign policy should be one of isolationism or one of humanitarian interventionism or one of national security, without having addressed questions concerning the proper purpose of a nation's foreign policy, the proper purpose of government, the exact meaning of national security, interventionism, and isolationism, or the principles that should guide all uses of government power. Such indifference to cognitive hierarchy effectively declares that the person making the claim knows his conclusions independently of knowing their explanatory, logical roots. Rather than deliberately adhering to all of the relevant aspects of reality in order to validate his conclusions (which is what the objective method demands), this person introduces an alternative touchstone of truth, namely, whatever he chooses to believe. He may well offer *some* considerations in defense of his viewpoint, but if he does not systematically work through the logic of all of its underlying foundations, he is essentially treating his preferences as a rival to reality which trumps respect for it. This is not objective thinking.

The Contextual Character of Knowledge

The second aspect of knowledge that carries significant repercussions for objectivity is the fact that knowledge is contextual. It is always conditioned by the information that is available to a person at a given time. Knowledge is not acquired in a vacuum and is not acquired by an epistemic Superman. The requirements of objectivity must be understood accordingly: Objectivity is relative to a given context.[29]

Knowledge is always held by a specific individual; it is the knowledge *of someone*. This carries two major implications concerning the relevance of context. First, human beings are not omniscient. Even on a delimited subject, no one, however expert, can know everything that might be known in the fullness of time. Our standards of objective knowledge, accordingly, cannot require that they do. A person can only reason about the material available to him. He can be more or less conscientious in seeking out that material and in reasoning logically about the material that he finds. But he cannot be faulted for failing to be omniscient, infallible, or for failing to know now what he might later come to know in future months or years. The demands of objectivity must be relative to his other knowledge and cognitive position at a given time.[30]

Second, a person always has a reason for seeking to reach a conclusion about a subject; his interest in the issue is motivated. What the objective manner of proceeding consists of is derivative from this. Objectivity is relative to a

---

[29] Notice how natural it is to heed context in setting our expectations for the objectivity of a linguistic translation. What it is that one is translating – a recipe, poem, legal contract, letter, drug prescription, and so forth – makes a great deal of difference to the standards that are appropriate to demand, to ensure objectivity. For interesting related discussion, see David Bellos, *Is That a Fish in Your Ear? Translation and the Meaning of Everything*, New York: Faber & Faber, 2011, especially pp. 33, 319–322.

[30] As a simple illustration, consider the deliberations of a jury. It is perfectly possible for each of its members to proceed with scrupulous objectivity at every turn in assessing the evidence and arguments brought before it, yet to discover, years after rendering its verdict, that it had erroneously acquitted a man who was actually guilty. That its verdict proved to be factually incorrect (it did not "get reality right") does not show that its method was defective or not what it should have been. Relative to the information available as well as (let's stipulate) the further information they had reason to believe existed and would bear on the accuracy of their conclusion, their methods might have been impeccably fact grounded and logic guided. For more on the compatibility of objectivity with fallibility, non-omniscience, and actual error, see my discussions in "The Importance of the Subject in Objective Morality," pp. 135–136, and " 'Social' Objectivity and the Objectivity of Values," pp. 153–154.

person's specific purposes. Which pieces of information it is rational to consider and what weight to assign them in drawing inferences depends (in part) on the purpose of the inquiry.

To see this, bear in mind that knowledge is not the same thing as facts. Facts obtain independently of a person's awareness of them. "Knowledge" refers to mental content (*what* a person knows) or to the state of a particular person's mind in relation to specific mental content; it designates the cognitive status that the content occupies in his thinking. "Do I know it?" we sometimes ask ourselves, "or do I merely believe it, or suspect it, or imagine it, or fear it, or hope it?"[31] As we noted earlier, evidence does not speak for itself. It neither interprets itself nor applies itself. (Strictly, no information even is evidence apart from its being understood as standing in a supportive logical relationship to a particular claim.) *How* evidence speaks – what it says – depends largely on what the thinker does with it. Yet a person's mind is always, necessarily, at a particular stage of knowledge: on a given date, he will have learned certain things and not others (about financial planning, pharmacy, surveillance technology or the death penalty). That existing body of knowledge is the network with which any new information must be assimilated and within which any additional knowledge must logically sit. What it is rational and objective to infer about a given notion x, accordingly, depends on what else the person knows about x and about a range of other things that have bearing on x. In other words, his particular context is crucial.

A person cannot understand how to classify or evaluate an item, apart from other knowledge. He can observe that there's a *something* here, but to correctly identify what it is and what he can and should infer from it he must draw on other pertinent facts, many of which will reflect his own particular knowledge and aims. To be clear: That thing is what it is (and is *all* that it is) regardless of anyone's attention or ignorance or interest. Yet whenever a person is considering a subject, he is doing so from a particular cognitive context – a position of particular knowledge and ignorance and purposes. These inform which of its aspects are most salient. Is he evaluating job applicants for the position of police lieutenant or sous chef? Is he debating whether to buy a particular property as a vacation home or an investment vehicle? While many propositions will be true of any given existent, only some of these will matter to the purpose for which he is considering it.

---

[31] Believing, suspecting, imagining, etc. are the types of cognitive status in question. Much finer-grained distinctions could be carved in this territory, but they are not necessary in order to appreciate the essential difference between the factual content that a statement stands for and the status of that claim in a specific person's mind (his believing it, doubting it, regarding it as probable, as impossible, etc.).

What all of this demonstrates is the fact that objectivity is context relative. What it is logical for a particular person to believe today depends (in part) on other material that he brings to the inquiry. The inferences that logically follow from one set of starting points and purposes will be different from those that follow from a different set. This does not mean that objectivity is entirely a function of individuals' cognitive perspectives. The object that a person is trying to understand exists "out there," independent of us; the realist Primacy of Existence still holds. It remains possible for a person to think and draw conclusions either objectively or nonobjectively. The crucial thing to recognize, however, is that what constitutes an objective understanding of material is a function of the identity of the thinker as well as of the thing thought about.

Objective conclusions are not free-floating phenomena. They are formed and held by individual minds. For that reason, our standard of objectivity must take certain features of those minds into account (the basic character of the human mind as well as particular features of the specific mind in question).

Recognition of the role of context does not relax the rigor of objectivity. It does not convert it into subjectivism. Within any particular context, there remain proper and improper ways of proceeding (ways that would be objective and ways that would be nonobjective). Appreciating the relevance of context, however, respects the fact that thinking and conclusions are always an individual's thinking and conclusions and that what it is logical for one person to think about object x at a particular time depends on a host of preexisting beliefs that will not be shared by everyone else who might think about x.

The relational, contextual nature of objectivity also indicates how objective knowledge can be revised over time. As a person's experience expands and his knowledge extends, he could discover that his earlier knowledge was incomplete in important respects.[32] He might have identified gold as a metal, for instance, long before realizing that it is also an element. Subsequently learning the latter does not refute the objectivity of the conclusion that he had previously held in a different context. Similarly, he may have misunderstood and misclassified certain plants or animals, excluding items that should be included in a certain category or including items that should be excluded. (Whales are not fish, it turns out, but marine mammals, and tomatoes are a fruit.)[33]

---

[32] The expansion of a person's experience does not necessarily or inevitably extend his knowledge; contrary to popular wisdom, a person "learns from experience" only if he exerts a deliberate and objective effort to do so.

[33] For a good discussion of objectivity in relation to "conceptual change" (scare quoted because exactly what changes is part of the issue to be clarified), see James B. Lennox, "Concepts, Context, and the Advance of Science," in *Concepts and Their Role in Knowledge: Reflections on Objectivist Epistemology*, pp. 112–133.

As a person learns more about all sorts of things and considers their accurate identification *and* as a person's understanding of the exact dimensions of similarity that distinguish members of one class from others becomes more precise (such as with whales, fish, and mammals), he will command a wider, stronger, and more reality-rooted basis for making these judgments correctly. (I can better classify individual dogs as collies or as Labradors, for instance, the more fine-grained my knowledge of what makes a collie and of what makes a Labrador.)

To call a claim objective is not to canonize the present state of knowledge about the object in question as irrefutable for all time, regardless of future evidence and reasoning. Such a posture would clearly defy objectivity, by elevating the subject's belief over the reality of the object's nature. Recognition of the contextual character of objectivity, rather, is an implication of the fact that knowledge is not acquired in one gulp. A person does not abruptly transform from ignorance of a subject to complete, "final" knowledge of that subject overnight. Experience unfolds in stages and knowledge is built cumulatively, by drawing lessons from numerous episodes. Because our experience is never exhaustive, we continually encounter new factors to consider. (*What is this thing? What kind of thing is it? Is it of a more distinct type, within that kind? What is its relationship to things of this other kind, and of that kind – e.g., to sharks or cod or horses, or to property or privacy or political freedom?*) Doing so will sometimes alter our previous conclusions, however objectively formed those conclusions were at the time they were first made. The point is, because knowledge of a subject is never "finished," "over," a safely "been there, done that" proposition, objectivity does not presume possession of knowledge that can never be improved upon. What an assertion of objectivity does assert is that, *in the state of knowledge at the relevant time,* the (objective) conclusion most fully and most accurately reflects the nature of the existents in question and the relationships among them.

(Notice that the advance of knowledge and of new means of doing things are responsible for many of the thorny questions that are posed for judicial review. What had been an objective understanding of "speech" or a "search" in 1787 requires updating, in later years, due to subsequently developed technologies for engaging in speech or a search. My point is not that definitions of concepts require revision and reformulation with each new discovery or invention that carries ramifications for the pursuit of those activities. It is, rather, that previously nonexistent questions and relationships need to be sorted out in order for us to understand concepts' objective meanings. *Is* the publication of photographs a form of speech? *Is* that use of a thermal imaging device a form of a search? Because such questions would not have even arisen before certain capacities were devised, objective claims about the meaning and scope of the relevant concepts must be updated in the sense that they must take into account all present knowledge.)[34]

Both the contextual and hierarchical character of knowledge, then, are crucial to a proper, realistic understanding of objectivity. (In other words, to an objective understanding of objectivity.) When an idea is snatched from its context or isolated from its position in a hierarchical ladder of knowledge, it can easily appear to have a different logical status than it actually does. To guard against this, active checks on the contextual and hierarchical integrity of one's thinking serve as intellectual ground plugs that maintain the connection between one's thoughts and the reality that they seek to *get right*.

5. FURTHER MISCONCEPTIONS – OBJECTIVITY'S CUSTOMARY BAGGAGE

The assertion that a claim is objective is often met with skeptical derision. What is responsible for this hostility, I think, is a grab-bag of assumptions that a claim to objectivity is the claim of a belief's fixed, rigid certainty, insisted upon by people who are some combination of dogmatic, closed-minded, authoritarian, and sanctimonious. None of these assumptions is warranted, however. In order to disentangle a proper conception of objectivity from look-alikes that give it a bad name, let me address a few frequent confusions.

First, bear in mind that on the account that I have given, assertions of claims' objectivity are *conclusions* based on observation and inference, rather than arbitrary stipulations. As such, they are testable – and revisable. When further observation or more careful inference points to a conclusion that is different from the claim initially regarded as objective, that claim is (properly) changed. This is not a refutation of its objectivity, however, as I explained earlier. At the time that it was thought to be the objective truth, that belief may well have been perfectly objective *relative to* all other knowledge available at that time and to the most rigorous, reality-respecting, logic-guided efforts exerted by the inquirers in question. An assertion of a claim's objectivity is not

---

[34] Also note an important implication of the portrait of objectivity that I have painted. The objective thinker must be thorough: Every conclusion that he draws must stand the tests of direct observation, of the logic of the inferences that he builds on his observations, as well as of consistency with his other knowledge. Because every item that a person files as knowledge is potential material to be used in his subsequent thinking about other issues (used as a premise, for instance, or as an example, or as a general principle under which to subsume certain other new thoughts and observations, etc.), objective conclusions about any issue depend on painstaking respect for reality at every turn.

a profession of infallibility about that claim. Remember that objectivity is context relative and much of the relevant context is a person's other knowledge at a given time.

Another fatal confusion: In seeking to avoid subjectivism, people frequently lapse into what they assume is the only alternative, "intrinsicism," a term that Rand coined to refer to the belief that objectivity is inherent in certain facts. On the intrinsicist model, reality *contains* objective truths, in effect; these are simply given and a person is objective when he recognizes and faithfully reports such truths. Being objective amounts to being a sort of stenographer, taking dictation. When we think about what objectivity is designed to do, however, we should realize that this poses a false alternative and that intrinsicism is not the model of objectivity that I have defended.[35]

Remember that objectivity concerns *how* human beings reach conclusions, the basis on which we can know things. The point of adhering to its discipline is to ground our beliefs in reality, to make them accurately reflect the way things are. The conclusions that we accept are, ultimately, claims about what is so. The question of whether or not a person is being objective, accordingly, concerns whether he is using his mind in the manner that is best suited to succeed in that quest – to *get reality right*, to gain genuine knowledge. In this way, objectivity pertains to a specific relationship: that between what a person does with his mind and the independent existents that he is attempting to understand through the use of his mind.

Contrary to prevailing assumptions of the available options, therefore, objectivity is not determined exclusively by the object (something "given," a finished product which reveals itself to human beings, like an image in a mirror), nor is it determined exclusively by the subject (by a person's beliefs or attitudes about a given object, "the eye of the beholder"). Rather, objectivity is relational: it depends on achieving and maintaining a certain relationship between what is "in here" (the beliefs and activities of a person's mind) and what is "out there" (that which exists independently of his mind). Neither object nor subject – by itself – delivers objectivity or knowledge.

---

[35] Realists such as Plato and Aristotle exemplify the intrinsicist viewpoint insofar as they regard concepts or universals as a special type of existent that lies inherent in certain things, independently of man's consciousness. For in-depth explanations of intrinsicism, see Rand, *Introduction to Objectivist Epistemology*, pp. 52–54, 78–82; Peikoff, *Objectivism*, pp. 142–151, and Peikoff, *Understanding Objectivism*, pp. 171–208; Smith, "'Social' Objectivity and the Objectivity of Values," pp. 155–160, and Smith, "The Importance of the Subject in Objective Morality," pp. 128–131; and on intrinsicism in regard to values, Rand, "What Is Capitalism?" pp. 21–23. Also see my brief discussion in the Introduction.

Far from the intrinsicist's image of the objective person as a passive recipient of fixed points of knowledge, then, on my account objectivity requires and results from an active process. (It is the antithesis of a no-brainer.[36]) The objective person must deliberately monitor his thinking on an ongoing basis, checking to ensure that his reasoning about an issue is evidence based and logically integrates with everything else that he knows. Objectivity does not reflect "the view from nowhere," as some contend, since nowhere is fictional and useless, for steering us to reality-grounded conclusions.[37] It is actual individuals, each of whom stands *some*where and *is* someone, who need guidance. Objectivity is not an ideal for ghosts or fairies or fanciful projections of "better" beings who are omni-perspectival or a-perspectival. Objectivity is a discipline of thinking intended to guide human beings to reach sound conclusions.[38]

Given my emphasis on objectivity as relational, it is important to warn against another frequent confusion. On my conception, the relevant relationship is between thinker and object; it is not between different people's thoughts. That is, people frequently suppose that if any view can be legitimately considered objective, it must be that view that wins the assent of the greatest number of people, the view that carries the day in the eyes of most others.

In fact, this notion of objectivity simply represents another species of subjectivism. It regards objectivity as a relationship between thoughts or thinkers and omits altogether the very aim of being objective, namely: our coming to understand external, thought-independent reality. It makes objectivity a popularity contest, more a poll taker than a reality tracker. While winning others' assent is often a consequence of objectively demonstrating a valid conclusion and while, for those people who are equipped with the same information and who are proceeding objectively in reasoning about that information, consensus will be the result, such a convergence of opinions is not what objectivity consists of. Consensus as such does not help anyone to know reality.

Finally, my acknowledgment of the fallible, revisable character of objective knowledge may seem surprising, given widespread assumptions about the implications of objectivity. It is important to grasp that those assumptions are mistaken.

---

[36] Objectivity does not require a so-called big brain, but it demands the active, disciplined, methodical use of the brain that one has.

[37] Thomas Nagel, *The View from Nowhere*, New York: Oxford University Press, 1989.

[38] The contextual nature of objectivity reflects the fact that any cognitive process takes place "somewhere" and that where that is matters to how it is rational for a specific person's thinking to proceed.

When one claims that a person or process or claim is objective, while that does carry a casual, conversational implication about the external fact of the matter (namely, that the stated belief is correct and offers an accurate depiction of the object in question), it does not alter the subject matter of objectivity. In the epistemological sense that I have been analyzing, objectivity pertains to the method by which a conclusion is reached. We must not "metaphysical-ize" objectivity by applying those standards or attributing those characteristics that are appropriate to mind-independent existents to mind-dependent conclusions. Knowledge remains *knowledge*, even when we deem a particular claim of knowledge "objective." That is, "knowledge" refers to the character of certain mental content; it does not refer (directly) to the object of such knowledge, to that which it purports to be knowledge about. The designation "objective," similarly, does not attach to external, mind-independent reality. A belief that is objective is still a belief, an item in a person's mind. Correspondingly, in order to understand what an objective belief is (or what a belief must be, in order to qualify as objective), we must attend to certain features of the person whose belief it is (including his context of other knowledge) and specifically, to the steps by which he reached the belief. Simply studying the object in question and discovering that it is not exactly as the purportedly objective person had held is not adequate grounds for concluding that he was not objective.

When it comes to the possibility of correcting claims to objective knowledge, therefore, any air of paradox should evaporate. Objectivity is not the assertion of a belief's actual, after-the-fact "match" with belief-independent reality. Indeed, no such omniscient, context-transcending hindsight is possible, since any retrospective can itself be reevaluated still later. (Monday morning quarterbacking is a lifelong occupation.) To claim that one's belief is objective *is* to assert that, based on the best of current reasoning and knowledge, it is the belief about the nature of the relevant reality that it is rational to hold. But it is not the assertion of eternal irrefutability.

In sum, unfounded expectations of objectivity, such as the supposition that "if a claim is objective, it can't be wrong," make it natural to conclude that no one can be objective. My account, however, exposes the errors of these expectations.

6. CONCLUSION

What does all of this amount to? The most important thing to understand, in trying to secure a solid grasp of objectivity, is the fact that it has a job to do. In any realm of activity, we seek objectivity in order to gain the strongest possible assurance that our conclusions are correct. To warrant such confidence, I have argued that the single, fundamental requisite is logical allegiance to reality. This is the touchstone of all objective thought.

As a somewhat rough approximation, we might say that a claim is objective when it is based on the way things really are *as best as you can tell*. A little more exactly: as best as a particular human being, using his distinctive means of acquiring knowledge, can ascertain at a given time. An account of objectivity itself, then, is an attempt to identify what that "best" consists of: the types of actions that it requires and the standards that we should demand of ourselves in order to make our thinking reality-faithful. If a person is adhering to the objective method, that *is* the best that he can do and that any normative standard can ask.[39]

It follows, on this account, that objectivity concerns an activity. Objectivity is not a sort of beatified status naturally endowed in select claims or individuals. Objectivity is practiced – the condition is achieved and the label is earned – by deliberate, disciplined work. And for this reason, the familiar refrain "Who's to say?", often invoked to dismiss assertions of objectivity, completely misses the point. As an argument against the possibility of objectivity, it misunderstands the kind of thing that objectivity is. A claim's objectivity is not a function of who asserts it, but of the basis on which one does so.

While assertions of objectivity at higher levels of abstraction tend to be more contested than those at lower rungs (e.g., "he is within his rights" as opposed to "he is blonde"), I have sought to show that these can be every bit as objective as the most basic. A higher-level abstraction is as objective as are each of the premises and conclusions on which it stands. If those rungs that are required to support a claim themselves withstand the test of evidence and logic, then that claim is objective. What is crucial to appreciate is that the standard at all levels is the same: fidelity to reality. And this fidelity is achieved through our only means of ascertaining reality: direct perceptual observation and logical inference. However brief and straightforward or extensive and complex the chain of reasoning needed to validate a particular conclusion, objectivity, in its essence, is the discipline of governing one's thinking exclusively by strict adherence to facts and logic.

Objectivity, again, is a means to an end. We seek to be objective in order to *get reality right*. Having explained the basic way to do that, we will turn next to consider the implications for a legal system.

---

[39] One might think of objectivity as a mental protection device, adopted to guard against inappropriate factors distorting a thinking process by distracting it from those considerations that it needs to pursue in order to understand the nature of the object it seeks to understand.

2

Objectivity in a Legal System – Three Cornerstones

1. INTRODUCTION

What does objectivity require in law? If, essentially, objectivity consists in methodically maintaining a logical, reality-anchored relationship between a person's conclusions about an object and the actual nature of that object, how is that method realized in the operation of a legal system? How will its central elements be manifested?

A thorough answer to this question would require a book of its own, addressing numerous implications of objectivity in regard to the legislative process, rules of evidence, punishment, election to office, and so on. While we do not need to consider an objective legal system in that detail in order to establish the foundations for objective judicial review, because judicial review is one particular task within a larger whole, we do need to understand how the basic conditions of objectivity shape that whole. That is our task in this chapter.

Building on the account of objectivity given in Chapter 1, I will begin by indicating the rudiments needed for a legal system to be objective. In particular, I will argue that a legal system's objectivity turns on three dimensions. The bulk of the chapter elaborates, explaining how each of these is crucial to ensure objectivity. It is also critical, however, to appreciate that the three work in concert. Because the law is a tightly integrated *system*, failings in any one of the three dimensions disrupts the ability of the others to do their part in delivering objective law.[1]

---

[1] I am borrowing some of my characterization of objective law from my essays "Objective Law," in *A Companion to Ayn Rand*, eds. Allan Gotthelf and Greg Salmieri, Malden, MA: Wiley Blackwell, 2015, and "Humanity's Darkest Evil: The Lethal Destructiveness of Non-Objective Law," in *Essays on Ayn Rand's*, Atlas Shrugged, ed. Robert Mayhew, New York: Lexington Books, 2009, pp. 335–361.

2. LEGAL OBJECTIVITY – A PRELIMINARY SKETCH

A legal system is the formal institution through which a government serves its function. It consists of the rules that will coercively govern social relationships (since government action is, by its nature, coercive), along with all of the practical apparatus necessary to establish and implement those rules – encompassing everything from policies determining how laws will be adopted, altered, and enforced, procedures for investigating, prosecuting, and punishing violations of laws, through the selection of personnel and management of government buildings and equipment.

While institutions can be quite complex, for an institution to be objective, according to the parameters explained in Chapter 1, it must have a valid mission and be organized in a way that is rationally conducive to its serving that mission. The institution is "what it should be" both in that we have compelling reason to have that institution (it serves a rational purpose) and good reason for it to be structured, and for its power to be distributed, in the ways that they are. It is designed and operates so as to optimally serve its central purpose. In an objective legal system, all decisions are made – all policies and procedures are adopted and carried out – for the right reasons, and it is the purpose of government that establishes what those "right reasons" are.

In order to understand the objectivity of a legal system, a few features are especially salient. First, a legal system is empowered with a particular, unusual instrument by which to accomplish its purpose: physical force. It governs by coercion. Laws are attended with coercive sanctions and citizens are compelled to comply with the law on pain of penalties that are imposed against their will (fines, imprisonment, wages seized, restricted physical movement in the form of house arrest or orders not to leave the state, and so on).[2] And the authority to exercise this power is unique. Normally, no one may force

---

[2] Alexander Hamilton observed that "Government implies the power of making laws. It is essential to the idea of a law, that it be attended with a sanction: or, in other words, a penalty or punishment for disobedience.... This penalty ... can only be inflicted in two ways: ... by the coercion of the magistracy or by the coercion of arms.... Sentences can only be carried into execution by the sword." *Federalist Papers* 15, in *The Federalist: The Gideon Edition*, eds. George W. Carey and James McClellan, Indianapolis: Liberty Fund, 2001, p. 72.

  In the same vein, John Locke characterized political power as the "right of making laws with penalties of death," *Second Treatise on Government*, chapter 1, section 3, ed. C.B. MacPherson, Indianapolis: Hackett, 1980, p. 8, and described the magistrate's unique prerogative "to give laws, receive obedience, and compel with the sword." *A Letter on Toleration*, Indianapolis: Hackett, 1983, p. 27. I am employing the standard modern understanding of what a state is, often associated with Max Weber, who characterized a state as "a human community that (successfully) claims the monopoly of the legitimate use of physical force within a given territory." "Politics as a Vocation," 1919, p. 1, lecture retrieved from:

another person to act against his will. The government, however, may. (I am assuming a legitimate government.) In a proper society, the government holds a monopoly on the legitimate initiation of physical force. Given this unique authority, it is important to recognize that the stakes of legal objectivity are high: a person's ability to act free from the unjustified imposition of force.[3]

Second, a legal system is a *system*: a network whose constituent elements are designed to work together to achieve the government's primary, overarching mission. Correspondingly, the exact way in which a single component of that system serves the primary goal will not always be direct or transparent, and its propriety cannot be assessed in isolation from the larger network.

Third, insofar as a legal system establishes the social rules to which citizens will be held accountable, it is important to recognize the relationship between rules and action. For our purposes (to understand the objectivity of a system of legal rules), two features stand out. First, rules' scope is deliberately broad; their prescriptions are intended to govern a variety of individual cases on multiple distinct occasions. To bring any field of activity under the dominion of rules is to regularize how decisions on those occasions will be made. If I am on a diet whose one rule is "no carbohydrates," for instance, then all incarnations of carbohydrates on all occasions are to be resisted.

Moreover, rules distill prior reflection concerning what those individual decisions should be. Rather than proceeding on a case-by-case, start-from-scratch basis, a regimen of rules draws on conclusions reached by prior deliberation about what the best means of proceeding are. Good rules reflect principled, rational conclusions concerning the most salient similarities and differences between discrete cases that dictate the ways in which different cases should be treated as similar to one another and the ways in which they should be treated as different. In this way, a legal system's rules are a vital means of maintaining its objectivity, ensuring that the legal system's actions are justified by their service to its principal mission.[4]

A legal system, again, is the institutional mechanism by which a government exercises its unique power. All of its elements must be rationally coordinated so as to achieve its primary purpose. Its power is bestowed for a specific purpose; its power is legitimately exercised insofar as it adheres to that purpose.

---

http://www.sscnet.ucla.edu/polisci/ethos/Weber-vocation.pdf. Jeremy Waldron discusses this idea of the state in "Toleration and the Rationality of Persecution," in *Justifying Toleration*, ed. Susan Mendes, New York: Cambridge University Press, 1988.

3   I say "unjustified" to allow for the fact that certain preemptive and defensive uses of force are justified.

4   I will say more about rules in the discussion of the Rule of Law in Chapter 3.

3. LEGAL OBJECTIVITY IN GREATER DETAIL

This account of objective law is, thus far, merely a sketch. We need to gain a sharper image of objectivity's distinct demands in this sphere. For a legal system to be objective, what are the more specific requirements that must be met?

One natural way to think of law's objectivity would be to posit that a legal system is objective when it says what it means and means what it says. It openly states how its power will be wielded – the rules with which it will demand compliance – and it faithfully adheres to the announced rules. Objective law communicates clearly and follows through accordingly, applying its rules in an evenhanded manner. Under such a regime, people can know what to expect and have a fair chance to comply. The law of the land is clear and constant.[5]

While these are vital ingredients for an objective legal system, this account is incomplete. For what if *what* the law "says" is inappropriate? What if the activity restricted by a particular law is not the type that the government should be restricting? A legal system's transparency and consistency in enforcement do not ensure that the system is exercising its powers for the right reasons – that it is, in that respect, *getting it right* (which is always the aim of striving for objectivity). Given that the exact demands of objectivity in any sphere are dependent on the purpose of the enterprise, we cannot assess the objectivity of a legal system without also attending to the content of its laws. Is the enforcement of *these* laws serving the system's larger function?

In short, objectivity in a legal system must be concerned with what that system does as well as with how forthrightly and how consistently it does it. Legal objectivity is a function of the kinds of conduct that the government requires, prohibits, and otherwise restricts as well as of its manner of administration.[6]

Even this is incomplete, however. In order to determine what constitutes proper content, we must understand the authority of the system as a whole: what the law is to be used to accomplish and the license by which it may exercise its unique coercive power to serve that end. The way to determine whether specific legal prescriptions are valid, in other words, is by reference to their underlying rationale in relation to the system's authorizing mission. By what warrant should the legal system govern these things and not those? Why should it protect a person's freedom to travel but not to trespass?

---

[5] Recall from Chapter 1 that public visibility is often regarded as central to objectivity.

[6] For convenience, I will frequently use "government" interchangeably with "legal system," although, obviously, the two are not identical. For purposes here, however, this should create no confusion. If the difference between them is ever significant in our discussion, my usage will make that clear.

Why should it protect the practice of religion but not of rape? Or should it? We cannot know what the legal rules should be unless we know *why* they should be – that is, what authorizes a legal system's having any such restrictive powers at all.

What all of this indicates is that objectivity in a legal system turns on three essential factors. In broad terms, it is a function of what the legal system does, how it does it, and the authority by which it does what it does. While the bulk of the chapter will elaborate on each of these, let me briefly explain the basic reasoning before providing the fuller argument.

From what we have said already, the need for proper content of law should be fairly plain. A government's laws tell people how its power will be used. Even more basic than this expressive role, however, laws *are* the ways in which that power is used (assuming that the government in question faithfully adheres to its laws). That is, a nation's laws constitute its policy concerning the exercise of its power. Consequently, for a government to govern as it should, the content of its laws is crucial. A nation's laws must restrict exactly those things – and only those things – that are necessary in order for the legal system to fulfill its function. When the content of laws is misguided (whether knowingly or not), the enforcement of those laws does not amount to the government doing its job. It is doing more or less than that, but it is not exercising its distinct power in the manner authorized by its mission.

By the same sort of reasoning, because the best-made rules in terms of content can be prevented from having their desired effect by certain types of misguided application, the *how* of a legal system – its basic manner of administration – is also crucial for objective law. If laws whose prescriptions are objectively impeccable are interpreted subjectively or applied erratically, the value of that valid content is undermined. It does the individual to whom the law is applied no good. While the substantive *do's* and *don'ts* that a legal system imposes may naturally seem to determine that system's objectivity, because that content is not the sole determinant of how legal power is used and of whether the legal system actually accomplishes its mission, it is not the sole measure of the system's objectivity. If a legal system is to fulfill its charter, the administration of its extensive array of interconnected parts and powers must scrupulously adhere to the standards set by its mission.

Finally, however thoughtfully designed the mechanical procedures by which a legal system adopts and enforces its rules, we cannot know which rules should be so carefully implemented without understanding the authority beneath those rules. This third dimension is necessary in order to judge the first – to evaluate the content of the laws and to determine whether it is legitimate (i.e., whether the actions that the law restricts are properly restricted).

How to administer a legal system obviously depends on what it is that you are administering. Yet truly, at an even more fundamental level, both the *what* and the *how* – the content and the administration of a legal system – stem from the system's *what for*, its reason for being. We cannot know the standards by which to evaluate either the content of laws or the manner of implementing laws apart from understanding the authorizing mission of the system. Only on that basis could we objectively assess what content of laws is legitimate and which modes of administration are legitimate.

In essence, again, a legal system's objectivity depends on its *what, how*, and *why*. In substance, what do its laws do? What kinds of actions of private individuals do they restrict and what kinds of disciplines do they impose on the government itself? In manner, how does it govern? Do its policies and practices in administering the law rationally adhere to its mission? And by what authority does it exercise its power? Are the foundations on which it makes each of its countless decisions justified by that distinct warrant?[7]

Objectivity does not require flawlessness. No system could assure that and, as we explained in Chapter 1, objectivity does not imply infallibility. A legal system committed to being objective, however, must strive to honor each of these facets of its operation. Let me now explain them in more depth.

A. What: *Objectivity in Laws' Content*

The first condition for objectivity in a legal system concerns laws' content. The substantive requirements imposed by a nation's laws must be completely consonant with the fulfillment of its overarching mission. A legal system has a job to do. Certain facts which are independent of our choosing dictate the most effective means of doing it. While human beings may enjoy a certain range of choice in determining precisely how to get the job done, the success of our methods requires that we respect the relevant, framing facts. A government devoted to the protection of individual rights, for example, will require certain kinds of laws (e.g., prohibiting theft and murder) and exclude others. A government devoted to a different purpose – such as the glory of Allah, the wealth of the monarch, or economic egalitarianism – would need to adopt a different set of laws.

---

7   The logical chain between animating mission and policy particulars will often be lengthy and may include forks that present equally legitimate alternatives. The number of layers and the options at certain junctures do not alter the basic fact, however, that at every turn, laws' administration must be consonant with its foundational authority.

This is not to imply that each conceivable purpose of government dictates, in detail, a single way of achieving that purpose. Circumstances usually permit a range of variation in the exact rules. Facts do not dictate and objectivity does not compel *the* one and only correct age for citizens' voting eligibility, correct length of a manslaughter sentence, or proper congressional term of office. While the permissible ranges for certain rules have definite boundaries, within those boundaries, differences in particulars can be equally rational. The larger point, however, is important: The content of a legal system's rules must further the purpose for having the system and establishing the government's power in the first place. Laws that defied their reason for being would entail that the government is not exercising its power *for the right reasons*. As such, these laws would not be objectively justified.

Notice that this component of legal objectivity is perfectly in tune with popular assumptions about the criteria for evaluating a legal system's propriety. People routinely debate what our laws should and should not do: Should gay marriage be legally recognized? Should assisted suicide be permitted? How long should a copyright's protections extend? Should I be compelled to buy medical insurance? Common complaints similarly reflect the belief that the legal system must *get the content right*. "Those regulations are excessive," people lament, "we've gone too far." Or, they contend, the government is failing to do what it is charged to do: "They ought to do more to protect our privacy," "to stop online bullying," "to make mortgages affordable." Whatever the merits of any of these complaints, they testify to the widespread understanding that an objective legal system should govern certain things and not others. The substance of its laws is crucial to its overall legitimacy.

One of the obvious lessons of this dimension of objectivity is the importance of law*making*. Those charged with writing the law must identify the kinds of activities that should be restricted, the kinds of restrictions needed for the government to perform its role, and then formulate the particular rules by which it will do this. However innocent in motivation, laws that are non-objective in their content misuse the government's power; they unleash the unjustified use of force. Further, when mistakes that infect enacted laws are permitted to stand without correction, the longer-term effect is to obscure people's understanding of what the proper guiding principles are. Laws of unjustified content are a misleading, corrosive model of what the objective exercise of legal power is.[8]

---

[8] Laws that fail this first condition of objectivity will typically be either misguided in conception or misguided in execution, through clumsy or insufficiently thoughtful formulation. A further kind of case also bears notice, however. A law that might have been valid in both its original

Given the logical dependence of laws' proper content on laws' authorizing mission, this explanation of the *what* facet of objective law will be more
complete when I address authority more directly, a little later in the chapter.
Further, in Chapter 4, I will argue that the proper function of government
is the protection of individual rights. Correspondingly, in an objective legal
system, all laws must be based on individual rights and aimed at their protection. Even apart from that particular view of a legal system's mission, however, my more basic claim about valid content should be unobjectionable. An
objective legal system reflects a government's proper ends and imposes rules
that are necessary to achieve those ends. Laws are not objective when, in the
substance of their requirements, they deviate from the legal system's mission
by prohibiting action that it has no authority to prohibit or by allowing action
that it has no authority to allow. That, again, is the yardstick: Laws should do
everything necessary – and only what is necessary – in order to accomplish the
mission for which the legal system is created.[9]

B. How: *Objectivity in the Administration of Law*

The second condition of objectivity in a legal system concerns *how* it operates: its structure and manner of administration. This encompasses the legal
system's basic division of authority among different branches and organs
(federal, state, local; military and civilian; cabinet departments, administrative agencies, etc.), its procedures for selection of all government personnel,
and policies governing how laws are made and how laws are enforced. All

conception and its original statement might, over time, come to be dominantly interpreted and
applied in ways that are not objectively justified. Many would argue that the government's interpretation of "public use" in exercising its eminent domain powers under the Takings Clause
of the Fifth Amendment is just such a case. Another example, some would contend, is Honest
Services Law. Its requirement that "officeholders and employees owe a duty to act only in the
best interests of their constituents and employers" may seem unobjectionable (law quoted by
Adam Liptak, "Elusive Line Between 'Obnoxious' Dishonesty and the Criminal Kind," *New York
Times*, October 13, 2009). Yet many complain that it is increasingly being construed to encompass actions to which it does not properly apply. A Wisconsin honest services law, for example,
was used in 2006 to convict a civil servant who had awarded a contract to the best bidder according to the stated criteria but had failed to penalize the company for its slapdash presentation.
The civil servant was sentenced to eighteen months in prison for depriving the public of honest
services. Reported in "Too Many Laws, Too Many Prisoners," *The Economist*, July 24, 2010, p. 28.
   My immediate point is not to argue the merits of these laws or of these specific interpretations of them, but simply to indicate another avenue by which nonobjectivity can creep into a
legal system's exercise of its power.
[9] A similar portrait is suggested in Bernard H. Siegan, *Drafting a Constitution for a Nation or
Republic Emerging into Freedom*, Fairfax, VA: George Mason University Press, 1994, pp. 40–41.

the mechanics of its day-to-day work, in other words, from its procedures for criminal investigations and resolution of civil disputes to national defense and the issuing of passports and patents, must conform to standards of objectivity. However valid the content of a nation's laws, if they are not administered objectively, their value is erased.

As we have seen already, the basic requirements of objectivity in any sphere of activity depend on the purpose of that activity. All of the administrative components of a legal system, correspondingly, must be tested against that measure: the government's overarching mission. And any particular element of its operation must be evaluated in that context: in light of its larger mission and the ways in which different parts of that legal system are designed to work in tandem to serve that mission. (This will have direct implications for the proper conduct of judicial review, as we will see in Chapters 6–8.)

Here again, many popular criticisms of our legal system reflect the conviction that failings in its administration sabotage objective law. Consider complaints about clogged courts and judicial backlogs that lead to the uneven application of law (such as when innocent people are induced to plead guilty, simply to achieve resolution of their cases).[10] Or complaints that money and special interests influence lawmakers in ways that make their decisions subjective, rather than objective.[11] People also lament the complexity of many laws whose language is opaque, whose length is overwhelming, and whose technical requirements seem inscrutable.[12]

Several of the features that distinguish the objective administration of a legal system are straightforward and relatively uncontroversial. The laws must

---

[10]   According to John R. Emshwiller and Gary Fields, "Federal and state court statistics show over 90% of all convictions come through plea bargains." "Decisions Open Door to Appeals of Pleasure Bargains," *Wall Street Journal*, November 24–25, 2012.

[11]   The objection is not necessarily stated in those terms, but that is its gist: that lawmakers are not fulfilling their responsibilities by making decisions on the right basis.

[12]   The Affordable Care Act is 20,202 pages. Franklin Foer, "New Frontiers of Failure," *The New Republic*, December 9, 2013, p. 4. On the increasing average length of legislation, see "Outrageous Bills," *The Economist*, November 23, 2013, p. 32. Moreover, according to *The Economist*, laws concerning "corporate governance or the environment are often impossible to understand." "Too Many Laws, Too Many Prisoners," *Economist*, July 24, 2010, p. 28. The *Economist* laments the "opacity" of business regulations and the fact that frequently "it is unclear what exactly is illegal." "The Criminalisation of American Business," August 30, 2014, p. 9. For further elaboration, also see "Criminalizing the American Company – A Mammoth Guilt Trip," *Economist*, August 30, 2014, pp. 21–24 and, specifically on the effects of legislation's length and complexity, "Over-Regulated America," *Economist*, February 18, 2012, p. 9.

      Without pursuing the overly technical statement of many legal requirements that compound people's confusion, suffice it to say that when legislators feel the need to propose anti-gobbledygook laws, it is a bad sign. See Matthew Yglesias, "Government by Gobbledygook," *Slate*, January 20, 2012.

be public: openly available for all to know. If a legal system's rules are effectively to guide people's behavior, people must know what the rules are. Open statement of the rules also allows people to observe whether the announced standards are those that are actually being used and to hold legal officials accountable.[13]

Similarly, the individual provisions of an objective legal system must be mutually consistent. Laws or policies that conflicted with one another could not all be respected, since adherence to one would mean violation of another, and to that extent, something other than the stated law would be called upon to determine how a person is actually treated by the legal system.

Yet another fairly obvious demand of objectivity is law's consistent enforcement. This is essential if the legal system is to serve its function. Properly, a legal system adopts a particular set of laws and policies on the premise that their governance provides the most effective means of its accomplishing its work. If, however, it abides by those rules inconsistently, it is injecting alternative standards that serve alternative ends. Whether intentionally or not, it is only intermittently practicing its professed standards and is, in fact, exercising its coercive power to serve unauthorized aims. When a legal system's rules are not consistently enforced, in short, it is not those rules that actually govern.[14]

The Crucial Import of Laws' Statement

What is not as well appreciated, yet absolutely vital to a system's objectivity, is the statement of its laws. While a legal system betrays its mission when it enacts laws or exercises its power in ways that serve ends other than those for which it holds power, it also does so when, even while intending to respect the bounds of its authority, it formulates its laws in vague or equivocal terms.

As we noted earlier, a proper understanding of a legal system's mission does not dictate a single, uniquely acceptable set of rules by which a legal system can serve that mission. The rational performance of its work permits a certain range of acceptable alternatives. Within that range, officials enjoy discretion in adopting the exact rules by which the system will operate. An important consequence, however, is a legal system's responsibility to make clear the precise rules by which it will exercise its power and to which it will hold people accountable.

---

[13] I will say more on this and on some of the other features of law's objective administration in Chapter 3's discussion of the Rule of Law.

[14] People's awareness of such inconsistency also exacts a toll on their respect for the system, which, in turn, can weaken their willingness to comply with the law, particularly on those occasions when they have doubts about the wisdom of a particular law.

Correspondingly, objectivity demands that a nation's laws eschew vagueness and ambiguity. Laws should be written so as to eliminate all possible ground for variable interpretation. If laws are stated so loosely that significantly different meanings could be reasonably assigned to them, then the *same* law will not govern all cases. Unclear law precludes consistent application.

By their nature, laws are abstract; they are intended to govern numerous, distinct cases. Human judgment is always needed to determine the rational application of an abstraction, such as a law, to a particular set of circumstances. Thus, abstractness itself is not the problem. The difficulty arises when laws do not clearly articulate what the relevant abstraction is. In order to be objective, laws must make plain the essential nature of the phenomena they refer to – the actions called for and the restrictions imposed.

Precision in the formulation of a law obviously cannot avert all logical questions about that law's proper application. Only careful discrimination can determine whether the Constitutional prohibition of unreasonable searches prohibits the police's use of a GPS device on a particular occasion or whether freedom of speech encompasses a deceitful representation of one's military accomplishments. Precision does close off most, however; it minimizes what is open to reasonable question. And in this way, the clear and exact statement of law facilitates the consistent application of laws. It is a lynchpin of legal objectivity.[15]

While the logic of this may seem elementary, U.S. law frequently falls foul of this condition of objectivity. Consider laws that prohibit "unfair methods of competition" and "anti-competitive practices,"[16] or prohibitions on "predatory" pricing and lending.[17] Does a company's bundling some of its more and less popular products together constitute a form of such predation? Does its offering rebates, which obviously affect the ultimate price that a consumer pays? Do the reasons for a firm's pricing matter, such as a competitor's prices or market share? Indeed, does the success of a firm's competitors determine whether that first firm is complying with the law? (Company A might charge the same prices in 2019 that it charged in 2018, but the strength or weakness of its competitors will make those prices look more or less "predatory.")

---

[15] The basic idea has long been recognized in the judicial practice of striking down statutes as "void for vagueness." The legal rationale is usually that such laws either fail to satisfy the Sixth Amendment requirement that a person "be informed of the nature and cause of the accusation" or that their vagueness precludes due process.

[16] Federal Trade Commission Act of 1914, quoted in *The Abolition of Antitrust*, ed. Gary Hull (New Brunswick, NJ: Transaction, 2005), p. 164.

[17] See, for instance, the Robinson-Patman Act of 1936 (also known as the Anti-Price Discrimination Act, 15 U.S.C. Sec. 13).

The Federal Communications Commission's rules governing net neutrality prohibit "unreasonable discrimination" in allowing some packets of electronic data to travel faster than others, but it does not make clear the kinds of discrimination that are "unreasonable." Because its rules also advise that allowing "pay for priority" (i.e., for speedier service) would "raise significant cause for concern," the signals sent are murkier still: While the government is not explicitly banning such discrimination, it is simultaneously announcing that it is not inclined to allow it.[18]

Since the landmark *Bakke* decision in 1978, affirmative action law has turned heavily on the concept of "diversity," since the Court ruled that use of racial preferences in higher education is permissible if pursued for the sake of diversity.[19] Even many advocates of affirmative action, however, recognize that this ideal's nebulous character makes it impossible to know whether or not one's actions are lawful. Because the types of diversity, the degrees of diversity, and the appropriate measures of diversity that justify discrimination are dim and fluid, the laws' requirements are a moving target.[20]

The lesson from all of this is obvious. When the law is not expressed in forthright and exact terms, it is impossible for the governed to know the rules; a person cannot be sure whether his action is permissible. As Jeremy Waldron has observed, if a legal system is to be objective, it is not enough that it vaguely indicate that *something* is expected of a person; it "must let a person know what is expected of him."[21]

To be objective, therefore, laws should be stated in terms that name the kinds of existential actions that they refer to. They should refrain from using terms that are evaluative or that are typically applied in subjective ways, such as "predatory," "unfair," or "indecent." Laws should not incorporate terms

---

[18] "A Tangled Web," *Economist*, January 1, 2011.

[19] *Regents of the University of California v. Bakke*, 438 US 265 (1978).

[20] This explains the ongoing stream of litigation over diversity ever since, including such notable cases as *Grutter v. Bollinger* 539 US 306 (2003), *Gratz v. Bollinger* 539 US 244 (2003), and *Fisher v. University of Texas* 570 US (2013). For discussion of the difficulty of compliance that results from the law's uncertain meaning, see Adam Liptak, "College Diversity Nears its Last Stand," *New York Times*, October 16, 2011. The fact that somewhat different measures of diversity are used to define "compelling state interests" in the economic and employment arenas than in the educational realm also fosters confusion.

[21] Jeremy Waldron, "Vagueness and the Guidance of Action," *Philosophical Foundations of Language in the Law*, eds. Andrei Marmor and Scott Soames, Oxford: Oxford University Press, 2011, p. 70. I also discuss this in "Objective Law" and in "Humanity's Darkest Evil." For related discussion of the perils of nonobjective law, see Ayn Rand, "America's Persecuted Minority: Big Business," *Why Businessmen Need Philosophy*, eds. Debi Ghate and Richard E. Ralston, New York: New American Library, 2011, pp. 77–95.

whose application may legitimately vary, depending on the beliefs, tastes, or preferences of the person applying them.[22]

It is worth explaining this point in some detail. Consider the concept "delicious." While this concept has an objective, readily intelligible meaning, its application to a particular meal depends on the taste of the diner (the subject). The same applies to "handsome," "risqué," "offensive," and countless other concepts. Correspondingly, a law stipulating that all meals served to the armed forces must be delicious or a prohibition on government personnel wearing risqué attire to work would be impossible to apply in a uniform manner. More accurately, applying such laws objectively would require serving an endless variety of meals and forbidding a vast array of clothing, in order to satisfy the infinitely varying tastes of human beings.

It is important to appreciate the lesson here. The point is not that wherever people disagree about a concept's meaning or proper application, objectivity is impossible and a legal system may not venture. The point, rather, is that where the *objective* application of a concept depends on factors that legitimately vary from subject to subject (such as taste in food or attire), then that law – at least as formulated – is nonobjective. What determines what can "legitimately" vary? The overarching purpose of the legal system – that which a proper legal system is to guard people against. That is, because individuals' varying tastes have no direct or necessary bearing on whether or not they are doing something that should occasion government censure, that variability per se is legitimate *from the standpoint* of the legal system's concerns (however unacceptable it might be from certain other standpoints, such as those of a particular moral code or of Emily Post's standards of good taste).

To put the point more simply, the reason for having a legal system determines how its coercive power may be used. And that reason affords no grounds for its treating individuals differently on the basis of anyone's subjectively varying tastes.

A full explanation of why this is and of the objective administration of law depends on the authority of the law, which I have not yet addressed, so I cannot fully vindicate this claim here. I can indicate, however, a little more of the basic reasoning.

If (as I believe and as I will discuss in Chapter 4) the mission of the legal system is to protect individuals' rights from others' initiation of force and if

---

[22] In the next several paragraphs, I will use "beliefs," "tastes," "preferences," "opinions," "judgment," and "attitudes" interchangeably, using any one of these terms as a shorthand that could refer to any and all of them, as appropriate in a given case. This coarse batching is purely for ease of expression and should not make any material difference to my claims about the propriety of such terms in objective law.

(as I also believe) the actual initiation of force in any given case is a matter of fact that is independent of individuals' varying opinions about whether such an initiation has taken place, then the laws of an objective legal system will be indifferent to such variations in individual opinion. The legal system will have no reason to care about what tastes good *to you* or what offends *my* prudish sensibilities, for example, nor to care about your particular political or moral or religious convictions. It will have no reason to inject such personally tailored considerations because deference to such subjective considerations would be at odds with its mission and legitimate purview.

The lesson here is admittedly intricate, as it turns on some fine distinctions. Certain subjective preferences *can* sometimes properly affect the objective application of law. Jones's use of Lopez's property is not theft, for example, if Lopez freely gave that property to Jones; Ben's sexual intercourse with Helen is not rape if Helen freely consented. The pivotal decisions here were clearly matters of individuals' preference. What these spotlight, however, is the difference between the meaning of a law and its correct application on a specific occasion. They do not refute my basic claim: that objective laws must be stated by naming existential actions rather than variably applied evaluations of actions.

It is fine for individually variable preferences to play a role (a specific, limited role) in determining whether a concrete action is *of* a certain kind (whether Jones committed theft, for instance, or whether Ben committed rape, both of which depend largely on the expressed preferences of Lopez and Helen). When pivotal terms in a law's very statement are reasonably taken to refer to different things by different individuals, however – indeed, when those terms can only instruct action after such subjective "finish" is applied – that renders the *kind* of thing that is governed by the relevant law itself uncertain. And this is what objective law cannot abide: the use of subjective language in the statement of law that makes the kind of actions governed by that law contingent for their identity on individual legal officials' opinions. (Better for a law to ban "public nudity," for instance, than "unseemly attire in the streets," or to ban "stepping on an American flag" than "disrespectful behavior toward national symbols.")[23]

Again: Individual opinion may play a role in determining whether a person's action on a particular occasion constitutes a violation of the law because

---

[23] I am referring to certain statements as "better" here only in regard to this aspect of such laws' propriety: the verbal formulation of a law, rather than its overall propriety. The point is that, for the purpose of governing *any* particular kind of action, statements of the law that is to do so can be better or worse – clearer and less ambiguous or dimmer and more uncertain.

it is of the kind governed by that law (*was* this a case of rape?), but it may not determine the very kinds of things that the law concerns. This requirement of objective law is rooted in the legal system's foundational mission. The terms in which laws are stated should not introduce evaluations of any type other than the type that is necessary for the legal system to fulfill its authorized function.

We can summarize all of this discussion of subjective language in the statement of law in terms of three critical failings. First, to state laws in subjective terms is to make the laws and the actions that they refer to nebulous. It strips them of a firm identity and a stable, objectively knowable meaning. Second, in its practical effect, this places law*making* power in the hands of those whose responsibility is to apply the law, rather than to create it. Since the meaning of such laws is effectively incomplete until filled in by the interpreter, it extends rule-creating power to that interpreter. And third, the reliance on subjective language in laws' very formulation cedes unjustified power to individuals' attitudes toward irrelevant features of their actions. Such laws stray into aspects of actions' desirability that fall beyond those that are salient to the legal system's ability to fulfill its function. In doing so, the legal system expropriates power that it does not legitimately possess.

My larger contention, again, is that objective law must record and communicate its provisions directly, by clearly identifying the existential actions that it pertains to. Ill-formulated law deprives citizens of a fair chance to comply with the law, precludes the consistent, principled application of law, and functions, in practice, like retroactive law: a person only learns after having taken an action whether that action was legally permissible.[24]

---

[24] As further examples of how the U.S. legal system sometimes fails to satisfy this condition, consider The Gas Price Spike Act (H.R. 3784) introduced by Ohio Representative Dennis Kucinich in early 2012, which called for the creation of a Reasonable Profits Board and decreed that "the term 'reasonable profit' means the amount that is determined by the Reasonable Profits Board to be a reasonable profit." (*Investors Business Daily*, January 24, 2012). Or consider the Federal Communications Commission's rules prohibiting indecency on broadcast television networks under which, as Justice Ruth Bader Ginsburg observed during the oral arguments of *FCC v. Fox Television, et. al.*, in 2012, "one cannot tell what's indecent and what isn't." (Theodore J. Boutros, "Broadcast 'Indecency' on Trial," *Wall Street Journal*, January 17, 2012. For a good critique of such restrictions, see Don Watkins, "Fleeting Freedom: The Indecent Assault on Broadcasters," *American River Messenger*, November 2008, retrieved from http://www.americanrivermessenger.com/pdf_files/vol_3_pdfs/Vol3Iss21.pdf).

Or again, consider obscenity law's reliance on the "LAPS" test, adopted by the Supreme Court in *Miller v. California* and *Paris Adult Theater I v. Slaton* (1973), which holds that the yardstick of obscenity is:

(a) whether "the average person, applying contemporary community standards" would find that the work, taken as a whole, appeals to the prurient interest ... (b) whether the work depicts or describes, in a patently offensive way, sexual conduct specifically defined by the applicable state law, and (c) whether the work, taken as a whole, lacks

A still more fundamental problem lurks: When legal language is vague or equivocal, the effect is to dissolve the limits of the government's power. If a law can be reasonably understood to mean any of several distinct things, then legal power is an amorphous, continually shifting grab bag whose boundaries are chimerical and whose tentacles are endless. The meaning of the law and, correlatively, the respective domains of individuals' freedom and government authority, are created on the spot, merely ad hoc fixes of specific disputes. When a law's meaning is not clearly knowable in advance but instead acquires a meaning from decisions of those applying the law in a particular case, the government is not truly *applying* a preexisting rule at all. Since the "law" in question does not have a singular, identifiable meaning, the people are governed, rather, by whatever exercise of power is adopted on that occasion by whoever happens to hold the relevant decision-making power. The practical result is the constriction of individuals' freedom. When an ill-formulated law might mean *a or b or c or d*, the safest way for a person to avoid legal liability is to avoid engaging in any of those activities: *a* and *b* and *c* and *d* – despite the fact that some of them fall perfectly within his rightful freedom.[25]

> serious literary, artistic, political, or scientific value." (these last terms explain the acronym LAPS)
>
> Consider, further, the Food and Drug Administration's requirement that certain of pharmaceutical manufacturers' promotional materials contain a "fair balance between effectiveness and risk information." See the FDA's "Guidance for Industry – Presenting Risk Information in Prescription Drug and Medical Device Promotion," at http://www.fda.gov/downloads/Drugs/ GuidanceComplianceRegulatoryInformation/Guidances/UCM155480.pdf; and Stella Daily's discussion in "How the FDA Violates Rights and Hinders Health," *The Objective Standard* 3:3, Fall 2008, p. 106.
>
> Finally, consider sexual harassment law. The U.S. Education Department's Office of Civil Rights has published a series of "clarifications" of this law's requirements over the years. In May 2013, its mandatory guidelines for the adjudication of harassment complaints at colleges and universities defined sexual harassment as "any unwelcome conduct of a sexual nature," including "verbal conduct." Moreover, it decreed, the allegedly harassing behavior need not be offensive to an "objectively reasonable person of the same gender in the same situation." (Quoted in Carlin Romano, "Civility and Sex Speech," *Chronicle of Higher Education*, July 3, 2013.) While the OCR does offer some further guidance, what remains pivotal is whether or not the proscribed action is "unwelcome." For discussion of "the capaciousness of the concept" of sexual harassment, see Katie Roiphe, "In Favor of Dirty Jokes and Risque Remarks," *New York Times*, November 13, 2011. One can read the OCR's clarifications themselves at the Equal Employment Opportunity Commission's website: http://www.eeoc.gov/.
>
> We might also note that many laws' appeal trades on the positive connotations of their labels, such as the Dream Act or the Patriot Act. The allure of such labels typically distracts attention from careful inspection of whether the law's provisions are sufficiently exact and whether they are objectively justified.
>
> [25] I am assuming that the vague law in question aims to restrict something that properly should be restricted, but simply casts its net too broadly. One of its likely interpretations, in other

It is also important to appreciate that when the laws that government offi-cials are charged to apply are ambiguous, even officials who are well-intended will offend. Where the law does not provide a clear standard for cases' objec-tive resolution, the wisdom and integrity of a given official are fruitless. For a law that can be rationally interpreted to refer to significantly different things can only be applied by the arbitrary selection of one of those. The fact that the person selecting might mean well and earnestly try to discern an objective meaning does not restore objectivity to the law itself or enable its objective application. A law that is badly made (in terms of nonobjective content or nonobjective formulation) cannot be objectively applied. And a person who is subject to it cannot be objectively governed.[26]

Plainspoken precision in formulation, in short, is necessary in order to ratio-nally evaluate the validity of a law, to provide principled limitations to govern-ment's power, and for citizens to understand the rules to which they will be held coercively accountable.

C. Why: *Objectivity of Law's Authority*

The most crucial component of objectivity in a legal system – because it stands at the base of all the rest – is the authority by which that system rules. The system must be morally justified in wielding its power. Without this at the legal system's foundation, neither the content of its rules nor the manner in which it administers them could be objective.

Bear in mind the unique nature of a legal system's power: it rules by force. As we noted earlier, a government enjoys the ability – and the moral license – to force people to act in certain ways regardless of those individuals' desire to act in those ways.[27] A person must comply with the law on pain of fine,

---

words, does name a kind of action that should be restricted by law. For a chilling discussion of government officials eager to exploit such equivocal statements of law, see Roger Lowenstein, "The Greed Police," *New York Times Magazine*, September 22, 2011. (The piece has a different title in the online edition.) Lowenstein characterizes the law on insider trading as "ambigu-ous enough to allow for a range of interpretations" (p. 37), and he focuses on the deliberately aggressive policy pursued by the Securities and Exchange Commission to use relevant rules' ambiguity as means to punish and discourage activities that are not clearly illegal. He quotes a former SEC enforcement director, Linda Thomsen, as approvingly remarking that "the genius of insider trading law ... is its flexibility" (p. 38).

[26] For more on this, see my "Humanity's Darkest Evil" and "Objective Law," and Rand, "The Pull Peddlers," in *Capitalism: The Unknown Ideal*, New American Library, New York: 1967, p. 188.

[27] I use "license" here to refer strictly to morally valid authority and not in the increasingly popu-lar sense of license as unconstrained permission or as exemption from or indifference to all normative bounds.

imprisonment, and so forth. Normally, no one (morally) may impose his will on another person by force. In order for the government's exercise of this power to be justified, therefore, it must have moral warrant. That warrant derives from its reason for being.

I will explain this in much greater depth in Chapter 4, which is devoted to law's moral authority, but the immediate point is that the authority of a legal system stems from and depends on its fidelity to its founding mission. (I am assuming here that that mission is itself legitimate.) The use of force is permissible only for a specific purpose: to guard or defend against others' initiation of force. The scope of a legal system's authority is, correspondingly, bounded by that purpose. Every aspect of a legal system must be designed and deployed in ways that are reasonably expected to achieve its mission. Because that commissioning purpose is specific and limited, however, so is its authority to act. An objectively valid legal system exercises its power by strict adherence to its distinguishing function.

As with the other dimensions of an objective legal system, the demand that it possess authority for its actions is implicit in familiar complaints that the government is overstepping its sphere of responsibility. Consider objections to the legally mandated purchase of medical insurance or participation in Social Security, for instance, or to restrictions on the consumption of marijuana or "super-sized" soft drinks, or to invasions of privacy incurred by airport security measures or the government's surveillance of people's smart phone data. Regardless of whether one agrees with any of these objections and whatever the ultimate merit of these legal policies, the point is simply that people expect a legal system to respect definite boundaries on its authority.

The authority of a legal system is, as I indicated, foundational to the propriety of its other features. A mistaken conception of what a legal system's authority is will engender the adoption of laws whose substantive requirements are not objectively valid and means of administering the law that are not objectively valid. People will believe that laws of unwarranted content *are* valid and, correspondingly, sanction the unwarranted exercise of legal power. While the content of a given law could make sense relative to a very particular aim and while its manner of enforcement might also be valid relative to that aim, if the government lacks authority for pursuing that aim itself, then that law is not a legitimate exercise of government power.

Most proposed laws are (understandably) framed in terms of some seemingly desirable end that they will serve, such as helping hurricane victims, stopping bullying, or reducing credit card interest rates. However desirable a given end may in fact be (by certain measures, at least), objectivity in a legal system requires that we assess it in the full context: is anyone entitled to force people to act to achieve that end? Is doing so within the legitimate scope of a government's coercive mandate?

The point is straightforward. When a legal system strays from its mandate, any apparent objectivity in regard to other facets of its operations is merely that – apparent. For that law lacks its requisite foundation. Without a good answer to the *why* question – the authority by which it exists – *no* content could be validated.

It is not only content that hinges on a correct understanding of the authority of law. Misconceived authority will also corrupt the administration of law. When certain laws are not authorized components of a legal system, their apparently proper application will require actions that thwart other features of an objective system. Consider, for example, a law that bars the immigration of individuals who pose no threat to the rights of citizens. (I am thus leaving aside criminals, violent enemies of the state, people who pose health risks, and the like.) Assume, for our purposes here, that the substance of this law exceeds the legal system's rightful authority.[28] As such, it should not be enforced. Insofar as it is a duly enacted law which has satisfied the relevant formal hurdles, however, it should be enforced.[29]

Laws such as this, whose substantive demands are not objectively justified, place legal officials in an untenable position. It is a commonplace that legal officials' responsibility is to enforce the law of the land regardless of their personal opinions of those laws; the occasional gap between the two is not a problem uniquely created by misconceptions of legal authority. What is at issue here is not simply a law that is controversial, however. Our concern is with law that is not justified by a proper understanding of the authority of government power. In this situation, a legal official has *good reason* to resist enforcing that law. Yet at the same time, from a more circumscribed perspective, he should enforce it. That is the nub of the problem.

In practice, these conflicting imperatives are resolved by the subjective selection of one or the other by whoever is in charge on a given occasion. The danger is not that a typical legal official will cavalierly disregard the instruction of the law and administer it however he chooses. The point is that, because the instruction provided by the legal system is itself schizophrenic, that official has no alternative but to employ considerations that, *from the standpoint of*

---

[28] In fact, I believe that such a law does exceed that authority and is not justified, but that requires a separate argument that is not necessary for the immediate point.

[29] Anti-immigration measures enacted in various states of the United States in the past several years have brought this dilemma into sharp relief. Many Americans believe that, however pristine their procedural pedigree, these measures violate the principles that lend our legal system its legitimate authority and correlative claim on our allegiance.

objective law, are arbitrary. He must choose between the two mutually incompatible instructions of the legal system by some criterion other than those supplied by the legal system. While it is endemic in his role that a legal official must exercise his best judgment about a law's proper application on any specific occasion, the insoluble problem generated by laws of bogus authority is that *no* application can be proper. Not in the full context, that is; not in light of all of the salient facts.

An incorrect understanding of the authority of law, in other words, injects inconsistencies into a legal system that place the official responsible for carrying out the law under impossible demands. He is expected to conform to two contradictory contexts: one in which the law in question is presumed, like all laws, to represent a valid use of government power, and one in which it does not. Because the very standards of objectivity have been warped by the inclusion of laws that lack genuine authority and that are incompatible with the valid laws, the legal official *cannot* do his job objectively.[30]

I shall say more about the interplay of objective law's three dimensions in the next section. What I wish to emphasize here, however, is the fundamentality of authority. Errors in understanding the proper scope of a legal system's authority naturally lead to the adoption of laws whose substance is not objectively valid. These, in turn, lead to failures of objectivity in the administration of law. And when laws cannot be enforced according to purely objective standards, those responsible for enforcing them are invited – indeed, required – to employ subjective criteria. Over time, the effect of this is to normalize the reign of inappropriate bases for determining the application of laws, which only further distorts people's understanding of what proper laws and proper administration are.

---

[30] Complaints about over-criminalization sometimes reflect this. See, for instance, Alex Kozinski and Misha Tseytlin, "You're (Probably) a Federal Criminal," in *In the Name of Justice*, ed. Timothy Lynch, Washington, DC: Cato Institute, 2009; Harvey Silverglate, *Three Felonies a Day*, New York: Encounter Books, 2011; "Too Many Laws, Too Many Prisoners," *The Economist*, July 24, 2010, p. 28; and "As Federal Crime List Grows, Threshold of Guilt Declines," *Wall Street Journal*, September 27, 2011. The concern is that when enforcement resources are extended to enforce rules that should not exist, a legal system's ability to perform its job effectively is compromised. The excess of rules to be upheld overtaxes that system and necessitates inappropriately selective enforcement – the nonobjective administration of law. Resources are always limited, of course, and enforcement officials inevitably must decide which cases are most worth pursuing. The particular problem created by laws of misconceived authority, however, is that when over-criminalization literally does occur (i.e., laws criminalize actions that objectively should not be), officials are compelled to resort to inappropriate factors to make those decisions. Rather than simply deciding how best to deploy limited resources to uphold appropriate laws, under these circumstances, officials must choose *between* laws. Among its other problems, this also has the effect of giving these officials lawmaking power.

4. THE IMPERATIVE FOR LEGAL INTEGRITY

From examining the three cornerstones of an objective legal system, it should by now be clear how this portrait of objective law reflects my account of objectivity itself. As always, the reason that we seek the discipline of objectivity is ultimately practical: there's a job to be done and we seek to *get it right*. We have seen that an objective legal system, correspondingly, is designed and operates precisely in those ways that are necessary for a government to fulfill its distinctive function. Objectivity enables the government to accomplish its mission and constrains it from doing anything other than that.

It is especially important to recognize the integrated character of an objective legal system – the need for each of its three facets to be strictly objective and to work in tandem, so that law's unique power is used exclusively in the role for which it exists. Any deviation from objectivity in regard to what the law commands, its manner of administration, or the basis on which it acts would betray the mission of government. However innocuous or isolated they may seem, such departures drive a wedge into the legal system by pitting some parts against others. A nonobjective interpretation of the free exercise of religion clause that results in some people's exemptions from restrictions to which others are properly subjected, for example, creates a conflict between that which is required to enforce that erroneous conception of religious freedom and that which is required to enforce the correct conception of religious freedom.[31] Zoning restrictions that are premised on an improper understanding of a legal system's authority or of religious freedom's protections similarly create tensions with property rights.[32]

Obviously, one might challenge these particular examples; argument is needed to demonstrate exactly what action constitutes a departure from objectivity. The point, however, is plain: the need for consistency throughout a legal system. More exactly, the need for its consistent objectivity. Because

---

[31] Through a different prism, we can also see a conflict with the requirements of equal protection, which would not abide such favored treatment of the religious. In Chapter 8, I will discuss the contretemps over this issue that grew out of the Affordable Care Act's requirements of religious institutions' provision of employee health insurance. *Hosanna Tabor*, a less discussed 2012 case in which the Supreme Court upheld a "ministerial exemption" under the rubric of religious freedom, also pitted EEOC rules about compliance with equal protection laws against particular interpretations of religious freedom.

[32] On the conflict between cities asserting their authority to impose zoning restrictions and religious groups protesting by appeal to federal laws recognizing such groups' right to use their property as their faith commands, see Jess Bravin, "Church Turns to Higher Authority in Zoning Battle," *Wall Street Journal*, November 16, 2011.

the system's *what*, *how*, and *why* naturally affect one another, errors cannot be contained. A mistake in regard to any one of them creates an apparent basis for further deviations. And, most fundamentally, it allows the misuse of the legal system's power. Those who are meant to be protected by that system are, instead, injured by it, as their rights are constricted. When a legal system is nonobjective, force is used without warrant and individual rights are not protected.[33]

5. CONCLUSION

While all three of the dimensions that I have highlighted are critical to the provision of objective law, authority is the anchor. We cannot know what a legal system should rule or how it should rule, in order to rule objectively, unless we securely understand *that* it should rule and why – the grounds on which it may rightfully wield its tremendous power. Because the legal system's distinctive instrument is physical force and because the use of force by one person against another requires moral justification, a legal system's authority for its activities is vital to its objective propriety. (Without a good answer to the *why* question, in other words, no manner of doing its work could be objectively valid.)

We have seen, in this chapter, the basic condition needed for legal authority to be objective: the legal system must adhere to its mission. But what is its mission? I have referred to it without yet fully explaining it. While a complete defense would be a subject for a separate, far different book in political philosophy, because objectivity in any enterprise stems from the purpose of that enterprise, it will be helpful to probe certain major aspects of law's purpose and authority a little further. Doing so will give sharper resolution to the shape and substance of objective law. Thus, I examine these over the next three chapters.

---

[33] Aggravating the damage is the fact that people are led to believe, by the sheer existence of a seemingly proper government, that they *are* being protected, which discourages them from seeking more reliable protection. I discuss this effect briefly in "Humanity's Darkest Evil."

3

The Moral Imperative of the Rule of Law

1. INTRODUCTION

In order for judges to uphold the law, they must have a clear understanding of how much "the law" encompasses. On my view, an understanding of valid law rests on an understanding of the moral authority of the law. I will explain what that moral authority is in Chapter 4 and its implications for proper judicial review in Chapter 7. Here, though, it is important to correct a prevalent misconception that undercuts the ability of a legal system to perform its work.

"Objective law" is not the idiom in which people most commonly think of the propriety of legal systems. They speak more readily of the Rule of Law, a rough stand-in which they regard as a universally desirable ideal and the essential prerequisite of a legal system's legitimacy. Indeed, around the world, emerging nations and reforming regimes are enthusiastically encouraged by a host of governments, international bodies, nongovernment organizations and private institutions to seed and nurture the Rule of Law.[1] An array of Indexes measure specific indicators of the Rule of Law that are then used to make decisions about foreign aid, investment, alliances, and other forms of international cooperation.[2] The Rule of Law has become the gold standard of respectability, "a universal secular religion."[3] While those in charge of a given legal system

---

[1] The World Bank and International Monetary Foundation are prominent among these. Western donors have poured billions of dollars into Rule of Law projects over the past few decades. See "Order in the Jungle," *The Economist*, March 15, 2008, p. 84.

[2] The World Justice Project's influential Rule of Law Index lists nine general conditions, further subdivided into 52: http://worldjusticeproject.org/rule-of-law-index. Economists have been particularly attentive to the concept since Hernando de Soto, *The Mystery of Capital*, Basic Books, 2000 explored the legal conditions that are most conducive to nations' economic growth.

[3] Tom Bingham, *The Rule of Law*, Allen Lane, 2010, quoted in *The Economist*, February 13, 2010, p. 84. Niall Ferguson identifies the Rule of Law as one of Western civilization's 6 "killer apps,"

may not always live up to their professed devotion to the Rule of Law, few would deny the ideal's propriety.[4]

Domestically, as well, people frequently criticize specific acts of the U.S. government as imperiling the Rule of Law. Over the past few decades, a parade of deeds have been denounced in some quarters on exactly these grounds, including: specific surveillance and detention practices adopted by both the Bush and Obama administrations in the "war on terror," the powers assumed by central bankers at the Federal Reserve and Treasury Departments during the 2008 financial crisis, the use of Presidential Signing Statements, recess appointments, the suspension of various provisions of the Affordable Care Act in 2013 and 2014, Congressional "reconciliation" processes for enacting legislation, and the Supreme Court's ruling in *Bush v. Gore*.[5]

While the Rule of Law *is* integral to an objective legal system, I believe that the dominant conception of what it consists of is seriously flawed. For the Rule of Law is widely assumed to be value neutral and ideologically agnostic. On this conception, it does not commit a government to any particular substantive ends or moral convictions. Communists and capitalists, individualists and collectivists, egalitarians and libertarians, believers and atheists can all, allegedly, benefit from its purely formal scaffolding. Insofar as people view the Rule of Law as desirable, they do believe that it has some value, of course; it is not value vacant. But that value arises entirely from its instrumental efficacy. Joseph Raz has likened the Rule of Law to a sharp knife, equally serviceable for noble or for ignoble purposes.[6] Indeed, this versatility is widely seen as its

---

responsible for the West's dominance over the past 500 years. Niall Ferguson, *Civilization: The West and the Rest*, New York: Penguin, 2011.

4   Joseph Raz observes as much in "Formalism and the Rule of Law," *Natural Law Theory: Contemporary Essays*, ed. Robert George, Oxford: Clarendon Press, 1992, p. 309. Cynics occasionally surface, such as Critical Legal Studies theorists who see the concept as a mask of oppression. Larry Solum discusses this at *Legal Theory*, Legal Theory Lexicon 017: The Rule of Law: http://lsolum.typepad.com/legal_theory_lexicon/2004/01/legal_theory _le_3.html.

5   In his dissent in *Bush v. Gore*, Justice Stevens wrote that "the identity of the loser is perfectly clear. It is the Nation's confidence in the judge as an impartial guardian of the Rule of Law," 531 US 98, at 129 (2000).

6   Joseph Raz, "The Rule of Law and Its Virtue," *The Authority of Law: Essays on Law and Morality*, New York: Oxford University Press, 1979, p. 225. Also see Matthew H. Kramer, "On the Moral Status of the Rule of Law," *Cambridge Law Journal* 63, March 2004, p. 65, and Kramer, *Objectivity and the Rule of Law*, New York: Cambridge University Press, 2007, pp. 102, 103, 143. For further elaboration of Raz's rather complex view, also see Raz "About Morality and the Nature of Law," 48 *American Journal of Jurisprudence* 1, 2003, pp. 1–15, and "Formalism and the Rule of Law," cited in Note 4 in this chapter. I discuss this view at greater length in "Neutrality Isn't Neutral: On the Value-Neutrality of the Rule of Law," *Washington University Jurisprudence Review*, volume 4, no. 1, 2011, pp. 49–95.

strength, the very feature that allows the ideal to transcend people's deeper moral, political, and religious differences.[7] What makes the Rule of Law desirable, on this model, is thought to be entirely procedural, exclusively a function of the administrative features that it requires. The substantive direction of its governance and its likely practical effects, however, are considered separate questions to be addressed by other aspects of a society's values. In the words of Antonin Scalia, such "formalism ... is what makes a government a government of laws and not of men."[8]

In fact, I think, this is a mistake. And the error carries significant implications for our understanding of proper standards of objectivity in a legal system and, correspondingly, for the proper exercise of judicial review.[9] As we saw in Chapter 2, the objective validity of a legal system depends on what it does, how it does it, and why – on the authority by which it acts. Indeed, the proper administration of law depends on what the legal system is trying to accomplish, just as the objectivity of methods employed in any enterprise necessarily depends, in part, on the purpose of that enterprise. If we renounce concern with specific purposes, we surrender the very basis for distinguishing some procedures as objective and others as nonobjective. We cannot determine what law's proper form *is*, in other words, apart from considering a legal system's authorizing mission and the corresponding content of its laws. The champions of the value neutral conception of the Rule of Law, however, elevate form into all-important prominence, shedding concern with the other components, all three of which must actually work together to make a system legitimate. However admirable a particular legal system might be in certain respects, without moral justification for its exercise of power, it lacks the authority requisite for its objective validity. What I hope to make clear in this chapter is that that authority cannot be attained independently of the ends that the legal system is designed to advance. Given the distinct power of a legal

---

7   See Brian Z. Tamanaha, *On the Rule of Law: History, Politics, Theory*, New York: Cambridge University Press, pp. 94–95; and Raz, "Formalism and the Rule of Law," p. 309.
8   Antonin Scalia, *A Matter of Interpretation*, ed. Amy Gutmann, Princeton: Princeton University Press, 1997, p. 25. Also see John V. Orth, noting an understanding of the Rule of Law as "'having no defined, nor readily definable, content,'" *Due Process of Law*, Lawrence, KS: University Press of Kansas, 2003, p. 31, note 34. (Orth is quoting David M. Walker, *The Oxford Companion to Law*, New York: Oxford University Press, 1980, p. 1093.)
9   Bear in mind that the court's precise role is to uphold the Rule of Law. While all employees of a legal system are obligated to respect the bounds of their authority, the judiciary is uniquely responsible for resolving disputes about whether legal officials are doing so. By determining, in concrete cases, what constitutes fidelity to the law, courts' work hinges on an understanding of what this ideal encompasses. An accurate grasp of the proper place of values within that ideal is thus critical, if the judiciary is to perform its job properly.

system, legal authority can be justified only by the substantive ends that that power is used to serve.[10]

The value neutral conception of the Rule of Law is not universal; others have challenged it, defending "thicker" conceptions.[11] And while the Rule of Law *is* vital to an objective legal system, my contention is that the value neutral conception drains the ideal of its lifeblood and thus of its claim on us. Because this misconception is so prevalent and because it threatens proper standards of objective law, therefore, before explaining what the moral authority of a proper legal system is (the task of Chapter 4), in this chapter, I will explain why the Rule of Law is a moral good. This should deepen our understanding of how a legal system's moral authority is indispensable to its objective propriety.[12]

(To cast the issue in the terms of Chapter 2, the value neutral model exalts the administration of a legal system at the expense of its substance and purpose – revering its *how* in isolation from its *what* and *why*. Yet even if we examine the value neutral notion on its own terms and completely leave aside my three-part analysis of a legal system's objectivity, we should be able to see why a value neutral conception cannot stand up as a genuine ideal.)

I will begin by presenting the basic conditions most widely accepted as distinguishing a society that enjoys the Rule of Law. Next, I will briefly canvas the core of its appeal. Then, in the heart of the chapter, I will explain the twofold basis of my view, elaborating on how both the purpose of a legal system and the distinctive instrument of a legal system mandate the moral justification of a legal regime's governance.[13]

2. THE BASIC ELEMENTS OF THE RULE OF LAW

The Rule of Law is typically thought to consist of respect for a number of formal conditions, all of which concern the administration of a legal system.

---

[10] Indeed, any attempt to prevent values from exerting a role in the operation of a legal system will, in practice, only permit the subterranean influence of potentially inappropriate values, by default. Why this is so should become clearer as we proceed.

[11] See "Order in the Jungle," pp. 84–85, and my "Neutrality Isn't Neutral," pp. 51–52. Jeremy Waldron injects a third dimension to the form–substance analysis which he calls "natural Justice" or "procedural due process." Waldron, "The Rule of Law and the Importance of Procedure," in *Getting to the Rule of Law*, ed. James E. Fleming, New York: New York University Press, 2011, pp. 3–31.

[12] Throughout this chapter, I am using "value neutral" to refer to neutrality specifically in regard to moral value, rather than to all possible forms of value.

[13] Much of what follows is a compressed presentation of arguments made in greater depth in my "Neutrality Isn't Neutral," Note 6 in this chapter.

While different theorists specify the conditions in more or less detail and under slightly differing labels and descriptions, their lists share considerable common ground.[14] The basic kinds of formalities required to protect society from the alternative Rule of Men are relatively uncontroversial. It is widely agreed, for instance, that the Rule of Law requires that legal rules be written and that they be clearly formulated. They must be broad in scope, since they will be used to govern a wide variety of individual situations. Laws should be made publicly known in advance of their application and may not impose retroactive obligations (no ex post facto law).

Further, under the reigning conception of the Rule of Law, legal rules must be settled and stable. This requires not that they be immutable, but demands that laws not change frequently, erratically, without reasonable notice, or in defiance of previously approved procedures for their alteration. Moreover, a nation's laws must be mutually consistent, they may not impose conflicting demands. The application of the rules must also be consistent, such that laws are enforced impartially and like cases are treated alike. When two individuals violate the same law to which specific penalties are attached (as with many traffic violations, for instance), each of them should be given the relevant penalty.[15] This entails that government officials be as accountable to the law as are private citizens.[16] Further, the Rule of Law demands that laws' authority is supreme – not only in name, but in the actual operation of the legal system. No one may be "lawfully made to suffer in body or goods except for a distinct breach of law,"[17] and by the same token, nothing other than the law may determine how legal power is exercised.[18]

---

[14] Waldron has tallied several theorists' conditions. By his count, Albert Venn Dicey named three principal conditions, "John Rawls four, Cass Sunstein came up with seven, Lon Fuller had eight, Joseph Raz eight, John Finnis eight, Lord Bingham eight ... Robert Summers ... eighteen." Waldron, "Thoughtfulness and the Rule of Law," *British Academy Review* 18, Summer 2011, p. 2. Waldron's own account is included in that essay. Richard Epstein offers a list of eight in *Design for Liberty: Private Property, Public Administration, and the Rule of Law*, Cambridge, MA: Harvard University Press, 2011, pp. 19–20. John Finnis elaborates eight in *Natural Law and Natural Rights*, Oxford: Clarendon Press, 1980, pp. 270–273.

[15] Barring the types of extenuating circumstances that would occasionally tell against this.

[16] According to Thomas Carothers, the Rule of Law "can be *defined* as a system in which the laws are public knowledge, are clear in meaning, and apply equally to everyone." Carothers, "The Rule of Law Revival," *Foreign Affairs*, 1998, emphasis his, quoted in Waldron, "Thoughtfulness and the Rule of Law," p. 2.

[17] Dicey, quoted in Epstein, *Design for Liberty*, p. 17.

[18] Another influential voice in discussions of the Rule of Law, Friedrich Hayek, declared that "stripped of all technicalities, [the Rule of Law] means that government in all its actions is bound by rules fixed and announced beforehand." Quoted in Epstein, p. 17. Note that the oft-invoked constitutional concept "due process of law" itself reflects respect for the Rule of

This list is not meant to be a definitive, comprehensive statement, but simply to indicate the types of conditions widely thought to constitute the Rule of Law. While most of the differences in scholars' precise articulations of these conditions are comparatively inconsequential, others are potentially more significant. (Is citizens' access to courts vital to the Rule of Law, for instance? Is trial by jury? Does the legal system need to assure judicial independence?) For our purposes, fortunately, it is not necessary to resolve these questions or to settle on a single, correct statement of the requisite conditions. For the aspect of the Rule of Law that I wish to challenge logically precedes this level of difference and is shared by many theorists who themselves favor slightly different accounts of those conditions:[19] My target is the prevalent belief that satisfaction of the Rule of Law's requirements amounts to a purely formal achievement, devoid of moral value. In fact, I think, a sound understanding of objective law and of its implications for judicial review demands appreciating that the Rule of Law ideal cannot be value neutral. So let me make the case for its value.

3. THE BASIC APPEAL OF THE RULE OF LAW

The basic appeal of the Rule of Law can be distilled into a handful of elements. Three features, I think, capture the core of why people widely regard it as a worthy and important ideal.

A. Rules

Part of the attraction rests in the fact that the Rule of Law offers all the advantages provided by any system of rules. In whatever domain they govern, rules

Law. For its implication is that we must "go by the rules," that we must deliberately and painstakingly abide by the law.

More complete discussions of the basic conditions of the Rule of Law include Albert Venn Dicey, whose 1885 *An Introduction to the Study of the Law of the Constitution* expounded the fundamental precepts of the unwritten British constitution; Lon L. Fuller, *The Morality of Law*, New Haven: Yale University Press, 1964; Brian Z. Tamanaha, *On the Rule of Law*; Matthew Kramer, *Objectivity and the Rule of Law*, chapter 2; Tom Bingham, *The Rule of Law*; Andrei Marmor, "The Rule of Law and its Limits," *Law and Philosophy* 23, pp. 1–43, 2004; Richard Fallon, " 'The Rule of Law' as a Concept in Constitutional Discourse," *Columbia Law Review* volume 97, no. 1, January 1997, pp. 1–56; Francis Fukuyama, *The Origins of Political Order: From Pre-Human Times to the French Revolution*, New York: Farrar, Straus, & Giroux, 2011; Larry Solum, "The Rule of Law," Legal Theory Lexicon 017, cited in Note 4 in this chapter. Much simpler but useful discussion turns up periodically in *The Economist*, as in "Order in the Jungle," March 15, 2008, p. 84, and "The Paper Chase," June 25, 2011, pp. 40–42.

[19] To put the thought differently, we cannot identify what the necessary conditions of the Rule of Law are, let alone the precise optimal statement of them, until we have a firm grasp of the value that such conditions are to serve.

simplify decision-making processes, provide a definitive standard for the resolution of disputes, and allow effective coordination of people's activities. In
social contexts, adherence to established rules facilitates the predictability that
enables fruitful cooperation.[20]

Moreover, when something is respected as a rule, people typically follow it
without revisiting the merit of its content. Since rules' guidance is intended to
govern multiple cases on an ongoing basis, people do not continually consider
afresh whether a given rule's prescription is advisable in the case at hand. To be
governed by rules is to accept rules' authority as decisive and to leave behind
debates about what each rule should command. In this way, a regime of rules
provides the significant value of closure, *settling* things.[21] All of these benefits
attach to a system of legal rules, as to any other. (To be clear: This does not
mean that respect for rules demands thoughtless compliance or the refusal to
ever contemplate rules' need for revision. Rules can be a tremendous aide to
thought, but they are not a substitute for it. To respect a rule system, however,
is to affirm the basic propriety of the rules' content and to make deference to
the rules' instruction the default. It does not require that one regard the rules
as unerring.)[22]

Insofar as the Rule of Law is rule *by* law, it involves regulation of the future
by the past.[23] Decisions made by earlier lawmakers govern indefinitely, unless
they are altered through specified procedures. Governance by law is thus a
discipline. To adopt laws is to commit to acting only within their constraints;
to subsequently abide by those laws is to honor that commitment.[24] The premise of this discipline is that those who made the rules did so wisely, after due
deliberation about all relevant considerations.

---

[20] For good discussion of these and other features of rule systems, see Larry Alexander and
Emily Sherwin, *Demystifying Legal Reasoning*, New York: Cambridge University Press, 2008,
pp. 11–15; and Raz, *The Morality of Freedom*, Oxford: Clarendon Press, 1986, pp. 57–62. Todd
Zywicki also discusses the benefits of adherence to rules in "The Rule of Law, Freedom, and
Prosperity," foreword to *Supreme Court Economic Review*, volume 10, University of Chicago,
2003, pp. 11–14.

[21] Indeed, this is why people often "make it a rule" to standardize certain of their quotidian practices, such as where they keep their car keys or where they park their car in a particular lot: to
reduce the need for later thought.

[22] For discussion of the role of thought in the proper employment of rules, see Waldron,
"Thoughtfulness and the Rule of Law."

[23] Jed Rubenfeld, *Revolution by Judiciary*, Cambridge, MA: Harvard University Press, 2005,
pp. 141, 112.

[24] By "abide" here, I mean deliberately to obey the law because it is the law, as opposed to taking
actions that merely happen to conform with the requirements of the law but that are not taken
for that reason.

B. Objectivity

Another facet of the Rule of Law's appeal rests in its objectivity. In this context, a few aspects of objectivity are especially salient.

First, under the Rule of Law, the rules are knowable – overt, publicly available for all to be aware of. As we saw in Chapter 1, this aspect of objectivity provides several significant benefits. It enables the rules to genuinely guide both those who govern and those who are governed. Only when a person knows the legal status of different actions can he conduct his affairs accordingly. (To the extent that the laws themselves are properly made, such greater compliance with laws means that people will be acting in ways most conducive to the legal system's larger aims.) Further, the visibility of the laws exposes them to criticism, which can lead to their improvement. And still further, it provides a clear standard to which government officials can be held accountable. Since respect for the limits of government power is crucial to the proper exercise of that power, this aspect of objectivity alone is invaluable.[25]

A second salient aspect of the Rule of Law's objectivity is its requirement that laws be applied consistently, rather than by the subjective preferences of the particular individuals who happen to hold power at a given time. The Rule of Law insists on like treatment of like cases and the relevant likeness is *by the law* – that is, as determined by the criteria set forth in the law's relevant provisions. This aspect of law's objectivity allows a person to know both the content of the legal rules and that those rules are, indeed, the standard to which he will be answerable. It thereby fosters respect for law – respect both in the form of actual compliance and in sustaining people's belief in the legal system's integrity (which can also motivate future compliance).

The third facet of objectivity that is pronounced in people's devotion to the Rule of Law reflects the desire for fairness. The knowability of the rules that a person will be held responsible to obey and consistency in their application are necessary in order to provide people with a fair chance to comply with the law and avoid the government's penalties. "It is only right," we normally think, "that all are held answerable to the same set

---

[25] Francis Fukuyama depicts accountability as, historically, one of the three conditions most essential for a healthy political order. The public character of objective law also indirectly tends to foster stability, inasmuch as laws that were altered frequently or without warning would not be knowable. Sotirios Barber and James Fleming are among the many who emphasize the Rule of Law's providing a sense of predictability, security, and control over one's life, *Constitutional Interpretation: The Basic Questions*, New York: Oxford University Press, 2007, p. 183. Also see *The Federalist* # 1 on this, ed. Jacob E. Cooke, Middletown, CT: Wesleyan University Press, 1961, pp. 3–7.

of known-in-advance rules that are applied in the same known-in-advance ways." Insofar as the subjects of a given legal system are similar to one another in the relevant respects and insofar as 2 cases or 2,000 cases are similar in whether or not they violate a particular law, the legal system's treatment of these cases should be the same. Because the Rule of Law insists on this public access to the rules and consistency of their application, it further contributes to legal objectivity.

C. Reason (as Opposed to the Arbitrary)

The heart of the appeal of the Rule of Law, however, is best revealed by contrast with its fundamental alternative, the Rule of Men. Strictly, of course, it is inescapably men who make and enforce the laws of a given society. The Rule of Law does not offer a source of law that is utterly different in kind – bolts from the heavens, revelations of legal propriety that are supplied by god or nature or any other nonhuman device. A little more precisely, therefore, we can say that the Rule of Law concerns *how* men adopt and treat the laws of their society. (This will carry important implications for a proper understanding of judicial review.)

The Rule of Law represents men acting by principles, adhering to pre-considered conclusions about proper uses of government power. The Rule of Men, by contrast, spurns such principles; those in power refuse to be bound by prior reflection or by any disciplines that issue from it. Whatever the laws officially on the books may be, living under the Rule of Men is, in its effects, no better than living under no law, since the men in command treat the laws as tissue, empty words that impose no genuine constraints on their power. They assert their ability to have their way as all the "authority" they require. While, under the Rule of Law, the application of legal sanctions depends on individuals' conformity to preestablished rules, under the Rule of Men, it is ad hoc opinions rendered after the fact that command our lives.[26]

---

[26] See Kent Greenawalt, *Law and Objectivity*, New York: Oxford University Press, 1992, p. 142. In the words of the Roman emperor Justinian, law is simply that which "has pleased the prince," whereas the prince himself "is not bound by the laws." Quoted in Tamanaha, *On the Rule of Law*, p. 13. What Justinian embraced, James Madison feared. He opposed the Alien Enemies Act on the ground that it would fuse an individual ruler's will with the law, "[leaving] everything to the President;" under that Act, Madison warned, "His will is the law." Quoted in Richard Boyd, "The Madisonian Paradox of Freedom of Association," *Social Philosophy and Policy* 25, Summer 2008, p. 252.

Notice, further, that when the Rule of Law is replaced by the Rule of Men, the distinction between legal questions and political questions dissolves. Because the rulers employ whatever reasoning they like to serve whatever ends they like, no division between questions of conformity with the relevant rules – legality – and questions of substantive policy in determining what the governing rules should be is respected.[27] While officials might maintain lip service to law, decisions about how to "apply" laws in a given case are actually no different in kind from decisions about what the laws should be – or, more exactly, about which outcome the persons in power would prefer, in that instance. *All* questions are treated as political, in other words, insofar as they are answered by individual governors' case-by-case choices of how to wield their power; concern for adherence to rules and boundaries is cast aside.[28]

Although the idea of the Rule of Law was merely in an embryonic stage in the ancient world, Aristotle recognized the essence of the alternative. In his view, "He who bids the law rule may be deemed to bid God and Reason alone rule, but he who bids man rule adds an element of the beast.... The law is reason unaffected by desire."[29] The Rule of Law, in other words, is the rule of men who have exercised reason to adopt a principled set of legal rules and who subsequently adhere to them, logically applying those conclusions across a multitude of actual cases. The Rule of Men, by contrast, forsakes reason and thereby delivers us to the untamed urges of the physically powerful – sheerly

---

[27] I am using "political" here to designate just that: the proper substance of the laws (which is among the basic questions of political philosophy), leaving aside other meanings often associated with the term "political" today, such as those involving popularity, electoral power, and the like.

[28] This is why many people reject the Legal Realist doctrine that the law is what judges say it is as a sham. By rendering the law unknowable and invisible (if still existent at all), such Realism is, in the words of Ayn Rand, a "formula for tyranny." It is the antithesis of objective law. Rand, WKCR interview on "Objective Law," quoted in *Objectively Speaking: Ayn Rand Interviewed*, editors Marlene Podritske and Peter Schwartz, New York: Rowman & Littlefield, 2009, p. 60. For elaboration of the Realist doctrine, see Brian Leiter, "American Legal Realism," in *The Blackwell Guide to the Philosophy of Law and Legal Theory*, Malden, MA: Blackwell, 2005, pp. 50–66.

[29] Aristotle, *Politics*, Book III, 1286, cited in Tamanaha, *On the Rule of Law*, p. 9. Also see Book III, 1287 a 28-b 6, and, concerning the Rule of Law more broadly, 1282 b 1–12. Plato also offered useful discussion. In *The Laws*, for example, the Athenian stranger insists that the authorities be *"ministers* of the law" because "the preservation or ruin of a society depends on this more than on anything else." Plato, *Laws*, 715d, translation A.E. Taylor, in *Plato: Collected Dialogues*, eds. Edith Hamilton and Hamilton Cairns, Princeton: Princeton University Press, 1961. Earlier, the Athenian statesman Solon had exerted considerable influence on the adoption of policies that were later recognized as seeds of the Rule of Law ideal. For discussion, see John David Lewis, *Early Greek Lawgivers*, London: Duckworth, 2007, especially pp. 71–73; and Tamanaha's discussion more generally of the classical origins of the Rule of Law, pp. 7–14.

because they *are* powerful. The Rule of Men leaves control of the government's arsenal to the unreasoned "element of the beast."[30]

Centuries later, those thinkers who propelled the ideal of the Rule of Law into wider consciousness and practical influence clearly understood the fundamental vice to be conquered by the Rule of Law as arbitrariness in the exercise of government power. Edward Coke, William Blackstone, Hugo Grotius, Samuel Pufendorf, and John Locke, for example, all explained the value of the Rule of Law as resting largely in its replacement of arbitrary exertions of power (as by capricious monarchs) with the reasoned.[31] A.V. Dicey, whose 1885 *An Introduction to the Study of the Law of the Constitution* is widely recognized as a landmark in establishing the modern concept of the Rule of Law as an explicit desideratum, emphasizes the rejection of arbitrary power as a critical distinguishing feature.[32]

---

[30] Justice Robert Jackson, in his opening statement at the Nuremberg trials (where he served as chief prosecuting counsel for the United States), struck an Aristotelian theme in asserting that to refrain from vengeance and instead submit a nation's "captive enemies to the judgment of the law is one of the most significant tributes that Power has ever paid to Reason." Quoted in Michael Walzer, "Trying Political Leaders," *The New Republic*, June 10, 2010, p. 35.

　As one scholar has characterized Aristotle's position, "in one sense, humans do not rule – law does.... But more precisely, law and men must rule together." Robert Mayhew, "Rulers and Ruled," in *Blackwell Companion to Aristotle*, ed. Georgios Anagnostopoulos, Malden, MA: Wiley Blackwell, 2009, pp. 531. Waldron contends that Aristotle is highlighting the *activity* of reasoning in the Rule of Law, as opposed to the "eternal verities of reason" associated with Natural Law doctrine. Waldron writes that "[w]hen we celebrate being ruled by law what we are celebrating in large part is that sort of influence of reasoning ... in the way we are governed."

[31] See, for instance, John Locke, *Second Treatise of Government*, Indianapolis: Hackett, 1980, Sections 136–137, 142, 151–153. J.M. Kelly, A *Short History of Western Legal Theory*, Oxford: Clarendon Press, 1992, offers a helpful review of the ideal's evolving meaning over centuries. I discuss this historical conception a little further in "Neutrality Isn't Neutral."

　Another way of characterizing this demand for reason to replace the arbitrary might be to say that historically, the adoption of the conditions exemplified by the Rule of Law marked an attempt to replace the absolutism of a monarch with the absolutism of law.

[32] Dicey, pp. 120–121. As noted earlier, Dicey treated the unwritten English constitution as the model of the Rule of Law and he believed that it was marked by absence of arbitrary power. For discussion of how the tradition of British common law, despite being largely unwritten, provided the Rule of Law, see Arthur R. Hogue, *Origins of the Common Law*, Indianapolis: Liberty Fund, 1966, especially pp. 53–54, 251–252.

　Note that the related ideal of constitutionalism, which is arguably a necessary component in establishing the Rule of Law, is also a means of combating arbitrariness and taming the exercise of power. Ulrich Preuss emphasizes that under constitutionalism, a law must be "immune from the arbitrariness and vacillations of the power holder. The law is the embodiment of reason which checks the passions of the ruler." Moreover, "The form of the law domesticates the will power of the sovereign ruler and thus forces it to exercise its power in a reasonable manner. Essentially, the law is not will, but reason." Ulrich K. Preuss, "The Political Meaning of Constitutionalism: British, French, and American Perspectives," in *Readings in*

The larger point is that both historically and today, when concerns about limiting the discretionary powers of government officials remain at the core of debates over respect for the Rule of Law, the rejection of arbitrary rule is central to the Rule of Law's appeal.

4. WHY THE RULE OF LAW IS A MORAL IDEAL

With this understanding of the basic character and appeal of the Rule of Law, we can now consider my contention that the Rule of Law is a valid ideal that should command our allegiance only because of its moral propriety. The support for this is grounded in two central facts: both the purpose of the law and the means by which law is enforced require moral justification. While I will treat each of these in turn, truly, they are not fully separable.

A. *The Purpose of the Law Is Moral*

The function of government is a moral one. As I discussed in Chapter 2 and as I will explain much more fully in Chapter 4, a proper government is created to protect individuals against the initiation of force (which is an evil) and to place the retaliatory use of force under objective control. As such, it is a good. A legal system's reason for being is to serve this moral objective. What people frequently fail to appreciate, however, is that this informs the proper form of its laws as well as their substance.

In law, as in many areas, form follows function. As John Adams observed, we cannot sensibly consider the best form of government without clearly understanding the end of government.[33] While this does not mean that a legal

the *Philosophy of Law*, eds. John Arthur & William H. Shaw, 4th edition, 2006, Upper Saddle River, NJ: Pearson Prentice-Hall, p. 533.

Separately a word on my use of "arbitrary" in the text: A conclusion or decision is arbitrary when it is reached on no particular basis and for no particular reason in a context in which reasons *are* called for, to justify the conclusion in question. While lawfulness (either natural or manmade) implies constancy governed by abiding, underlying truths (such as with the laws of gravity), that which is arbitrary is random, irregular, erratic. When it comes to human action, because an arbitrary action's root source is non-general and non-principled, its explanatory significance and predictive powers are nil. A decision that is arbitrary provides no basis for expecting similar circumstances to be handled in a similar fashion in the future.

The arbitrary is not to be confused with the irrational, which might attempt to follow reason but simply fail. The arbitrary is scornful of reason; the irrational (at least in many cases) is more like a failed suitor – making an unsuccessful yet good faith attempt to track the relevant reality and proceed on the appropriate basis. (Note that "irrational" can be used to refer either to a person's deliberate indifference to reason or to a person's flawed execution of reasoning.)

[33] Adams, "Thoughts on Government," in *The Revolutionary Writings of John Adams*, ed. C. Bradley Thompson, Indianapolis: Liberty Fund, 2000, p. 287.

system's purpose will dictate every detail of its correct implementation (on some decisions, the government can choose from equally legitimate alternatives), it does entail that certain features in its formal administration must be rejected because they would impede the legal system's ability to successfully serve its mission. In order for a legal system to function not only as an *effective* rule system (as that set of rules that actually governs), in other words, but to serve its more particular substantive purpose, certain forms of administration will be required.[34]

The simplest way to see this is by imagining that a very different account of the formal conditions necessary for the Rule of Law had been proposed. Forget the familiar conditions that require laws' clarity or consistency or equal application, for instance, and try to imagine some alternate set of Rule of Law requirements. How would we assess its adequacy? We could not, without relying on assumptions concerning the ultimate ends of the legal system. Such ends will inform any criteria of assessment.

While you or I might regard retroactive law as flagrantly offensive to the Rule of Law, notice that it would not be inimical to *any* conceivable ends that a legal system might embrace. Under certain forms of egalitarianism, for instance, retroactive application of property laws or tax laws might be expedient means of attaining the wealth distribution that is sought. If a government held that certain economic outcomes are of paramount importance, why should it accept formal constraints that would impede that? In a similar vein, the requirement of the equal application of laws – however vital that mainstay may seem to many of us – could interfere with the achievement of other ends that are prized more highly. Theocrats of a particular faith, for instance, might reject the premise of men's equal rights that undergirds that formal requirement. Some men, in the theocrats' view, are more entitled than others and a proper legal system should reflect this. To do otherwise would defy the will of their god. My point is simply that when the overarching substantive aims of a legal system diverge in significant ways, the reason to insist on the most familiar set of formal Rule of Law conditions disintegrates.[35]

Consider the issue from a different direction. If a nation's rulers were scornful of individual rights, why should they seek to maintain the Rule of Law (at least, as its contents are normally conceived)? What would be gained by

---

[34] Dicey defends the Rule of Law largely on the grounds of its substantive benefits, treating a legal system's formal and substantive features as intimately entwined. See Dicey, especially pp. 116–118, 121, and 219. Also see Hogue, pp. 251–252. Epstein similarly views the Rule of Law's formal conditions as constraining the substance of what a legal system so bound will be able to do.

[35] Hogue comments on this relationship in regard to divine-right monarchs, p. 243.

adhering to that template of legal etiquette? While a few answers suggest themselves, it is easy to see that none supplies the kind of reason needed to underwrite a firm obligation to the Rule of Law.

One possible answer is that a particular ruler simply likes order and predictability; he is more comfortable knowing what to expect.[36] A legal system administered according to the familiar conditions concerning laws' generality, internal coherence, advance notice, and so on seems most likely to give him that. Another possible reason for respecting the Rule of Law's conditions is the dictator's belief that such regularity will produce greater compliance from his subjects. If he has very definite desires about how he would like people to behave, then it could be prudent to make his wishes clear to them, to punish all violators equally harshly, and so forth, so as to make their obedience most likely. This regularity might also be efficient by demanding fewer police resources to keep people in line.

The Rule of Law might also seem to offer a different benefit, namely, the appearance of justice. Because of its superficial similarities with certain characteristics of a just regime, this look-alike lends the dictator's system moral credibility. Keeping up the facade by maintenance of conventional Rule of Law conditions could help to disguise the substantive injustice underneath, leading people to suppose that his is a proper system that is worthy of their submission.

No doubt, we could imagine still further conceivable bases for a rights-hostile ruler's adoption of familiar formal conditions. What is significant for my claim, however, is that none of these supplies reason to conclude that the Rule of Law is objectively good – that it is, in fact, a worthwhile ideal which all should honor. These "reasons" for a dictator's adherence to Rule of Law formalities are utterly accidental, all contingent upon his peculiar beliefs and desires, which themselves could be completely unfounded. While they indicate that respect for the Rule of Law might sometimes be a shrewd tactic, they do not show that it holds any more abiding moral authority.

The point, again, is that the formal requirements of the Rule of Law do not constitute a proper ideal independently of what they serve. When they are in fact ideal, they are so only because of the value of the ends which they advance. If they were truly value neutral *or* if the end that they served were not a worthy one, they would forfeit their claim on us.[37]

---

[36] For simplicity, I will speak of a single dictator, although it could obviously be a group that holds power.

[37] Again, I defend this view in much greater depth in "Neutrality Isn't Neutral," where I pursue further rounds of objection and reply to the basic line of reasoning presented here. I also

Properly, a legal system's formal conditions are what they are because of that system's substantive mission. Form cannot be severed from function. The propriety of a set of formal conditions proceeds from their overarching purpose.

B. *The Law's Morally Salient Means*

Suppose one agrees that the formal conditions required by a legal system reflect beliefs about the substantive purpose of that system. Nonetheless, one might wonder, must a legal system's purpose be a moral one? Could it not be amoral? Why suppose that the Rule of Law's formal requirements must reflect moral ends?

The answer lies in the context – more specifically, in what a legal system uniquely does. While the distinction between substantive ends and the subset comprised of morally substantive ends is certainly a valid one, in this particular context – when discussing the conditions required by a legal system – it is irrelevant. For it ignores the critical facts of what a legal system is for and the means by which it exercises its authority. While I have thus far focused on the purpose of the Rule of Law to spotlight its moral value, what is even more basic to its moral character is the means by which legal rules are enforced.

People commonly suppose that an honorable legal system must give people a fair chance to comply with its restrictions. The reason that we insist on such formalities as advance notice of legal rules, rules' clear and straightforward expression, internal consistency, and so forth, is the presumption that failing to respect such conditions would be unjust. This is obviously a moral judgment, however. And what is important for us to appreciate is the *reason* that it would be unjust, namely, the means employed to apply a nation's laws: physical force. It is a general precept of morality that no one may subject another person to force without moral justification. Because force is the means by

address the contention that certain bare conditions are required simply to supply a genuine *rule* system – truly capable of guiding people's choices – even while that system's moral character may be dependent on the addition of further ends. This suggestion, I argue, falls prey to the same basic failing: the alleged propriety of doing something *in a particular way* (however sparsely we specify the content of that way) depends on the end that will be thereby served. Unless we have compelling grounds for adopting that end, the alleged propriety of that manner of doing things will have no traction. See "Neutrality," pp. 78–80.

Note that the debate over the legitimacy of the concept of substantive due process is often a reflection of the same issue of whether legal procedures can be proper (*due* process) without at least tacitly relying on substantive ideals. For good defense of the concept of substantive due process, see Timothy Sandefur, "In Defense of Substantive Due Process, or the Promise of Lawful Rule," *Harvard Journal of Law and Public Policy*, volume 35, no. 1, Winter 2012, pp. 283–350.

which legal rules are imposed, however, this means that the exercise of legal power requires morality's authorization.[38]

As we have discussed in earlier chapters, to do things by law is to do them by force (either its direct application or threat thereof). The law does not merely suggest or encourage certain behavior; it compels it. The law commands people to do certain things regardless of their wishes, on pain of penalties that are coercively imposed: We'll garnish your wages; we'll restrain you from seeing her; we'll put you in prison. This is perfectly legitimate, for certain purposes – but only for those purposes. Indeed, it is because the initiation of force against the innocent is not morally permissible that we establish government to protect us against it. If the government is to fulfill that role properly, however, its legal system must establish rules and practices that do not themselves violate the rights that they are intended to protect. Because force is not generally permissible and may only be used against a person on very specific grounds, the operation of a legal system requires moral license. The government's use of force, in other words, like all uses of force, must stand on a moral foundation.[39]

It may be helpful to consider the point from a slightly different angle. To make legal rules is to rely on suppositions about what we are entitled to force people to do. Insofar as these legal rules are designed to prohibit certain types of actions and insofar as prohibiting actions via force is itself a moral issue, to make laws is to take a stand on that moral question. This is in the fabric of legal work. In order for a government to be morally justified, therefore, its uses of force must be morally justified. Accordingly, both the content of its laws and the administration of its laws (including their formal requirements) must strictly adhere to its mission. Since all aspects of laws are ultimately imposed by the government's monopoly on the use of force, all of them are in need of moral sanction.[40] In order for the Rule of Law to be an ideal that societies

---

[38] That precept is not without dissenters, but it is clearly widely accepted. I explain why the precept should be accepted at length in *Moral Rights and Political Freedom*, Lanham, MD: Rowman & Littlefield, 1995, and I will address it in Chapter 4. Also see my "Objective Law;" and Leonard Peikoff, *Objectivism: The Philosophy of Ayn Rand*, pp. 310–324.

[39] Not all laws are direct commands requiring anyone to engage or refrain from a particular type of action, of course; some, instead, prescribe the manner in which an action must be taken in order to gain legal protection. Laws stipulating procedures for adopting a child or marrying, for instance, or laws governing how to bestow power of attorney on another person or how to incorporate as a business would be examples of this type. No one is required *to* marry or to incorporate. Even in these cases, however, legal protection of those transactions demands a person's conformity with government strictures. For further discussion of this, see "Neutrality Isn't Neutral," pp. 84–86.

[40] This does not mean that each requires its own separate justification, but simply that all features of the law must maintain its requisite moral character.

truly should respect, therefore, it cannot consist simply of formal routines that look respectable. Rather, it must be morally superior to the Rule of Men. The stakes – individuals' title to be free from the initiation of force – demand that. When what is in question is the use of the government's coercive power, in other words, to be amoral would be immoral.

Notice that when people debate the substance of laws – Should stem cell research be limited? Should health insurance be mandatory? Should gun use be regulated? Should gay marriage be legal? – they can easily envision the repercussions of alternative positions. The abstractions involved in the Rule of Law's conditions, by contrast – formalities concerning clarity or promulgation or internal consistency – often seem arid technicalities, remote from actual experience: *Where's the juice? What does that have to do with me?* It is crucial to recognize, however, that deviations from those formal conditions do real damage. They prevent a government from fulfilling its mission of protecting individual rights. And worse, they convert a legal system into a positive threat to those rights. When a proper formal condition of the Rule of Law is breached, the harm that is done is far from "value neutral."

To see this more vividly, recall some of our discussion in Chapter 2. There, I explained how ambiguity in the statement of law (a violation of the formal condition of clarity) serves to shrink a person's rightful freedom. Because, under a law that could be reasonably understood to mean several different things (mandating "diversity" or prohibiting "indecency," for instance), a person must confine his actions to those that would not violate *any* of those meanings, his scope of freedom is unjustly restricted. He is legally compelled to refrain from acting in ways that are properly prohibited *as well as* from acting in ways that are not. (Strictly, to "shrink" a person's rightful freedom of action is to destroy it. By limiting the range of action that is, properly, his to control, one deprives him of that control – that is, of the freedom to act as *he* chooses.)[41]

Breaches of other appropriate formal conditions (concerning laws' internal consistency or promulgation or retroactive enforcement, for instance) inflict similar damage. I cannot obey two laws that impose conflicting requirements. To be held accountable to such laws is to be placed in an untenable position – in the morally indefensible position of being liable to legal punishment *regardless of what I do.* The same applies to retroactive law. The same applies

---

[41] Law that is ambiguous thus satisfies the promulgation condition in name only. It does not serve the purpose for which the law should be promulgated, namely, to provide people with knowledge of what conduct is actually demanded of them. Such empty formalism does no good for those who are subjected to it.

to laws that are not promulgated. All of these transgressions of law's proper formal conditions violate individuals' *moral* rights.

The larger lesson is that the Rule of Law cannot be value neutral. To make rules is to make choices about the kinds of actions that will be permitted and punished by the sanctions of that rule system. In the case of law, because of the mechanism of enforcement, these rules reflect judgments about which types of actions should be respected as rightfully a man's own to rule and which may be controlled by others (controlled by force). It is thus impossible to install legal rules that do not reflect a view of the proper relationship between the government and the individual. What is important for my purposes is that the inescapably moral character of these decisions pertains to law's formal features as much as to law's content. Certain methods of constructing and administering a legal system (allowing ambiguity or inconsistency, for instance) would be antithetical to the purpose of government and, correspondingly, would undermine that government's legitimacy.

As form follows function, so does authority. When a government exercises its power in ways that deviate from its function, whether this is manifested in the substance of its laws or in their formal administration, it forfeits its authority.[42]

C. How a Misconception of Objectivity Distorts Images of the Rule of Law

Having demonstrated the moral character of the Rule of Law, it may still be helpful to address one of the principal rationales that animates the erroneous but widespread presumption that the Rule of Law is value neutral. For its thinking stems directly from a confusion concerning the nature of objectivity.[43]

Many people assume that if the Rule of Law is a mark of an objective legal system, then it must be value neutral, since objectivity itself is value neutral. Indeed, common complaints about judges who employ political preferences as bases for their rulings testify to the fact that the Rule of Law is understood to be apolitical (and correlatively, in many minds, amoral). To "moralize" the Rule of Law as I do, critics would charge, abandons its distinctive character

---

[42] The point is not to indict any legal system that ever errs as wholly invalid. There is a fundamental difference between a legal system that is essentially proper, although imperfect, and a legal system that is corrupt in its very core – whose characteristic way of using its power is not morally justified. Notice that when a legal system is essentially sound, we can reasonably expect its improvement when failings are discovered. When a system is essentially corrupt, by contrast, we have no grounds for comparable hope. Such a regime is indifferent to the propriety of its use of power.

[43] Bear in mind that I continue to use "value neutral" to refer to the idea of moral neutrality and not, for instance, to an amoral instrumental utility.

and destroys the very legal-political barrier whose significance I emphasized in Part 3.

Despite the initial plausibility of this reasoning, my analysis of objectivity in Chapter 1 should make it easy to see its error. For this argument relies on a hollow conception of objectivity. Since value neutrality is the immediate focus, let us pursue it by examining the nature of neutrality.

Like objectivity, neutrality is never an end in itself. Proper decision making in any realm is determined, in large measure, by what one is seeking to accomplish. When neutrality *is* appropriate, it is so in order to serve an end that is regarded as valuable. As a familiar form of neutrality, consider impartiality in a selection process. If a college admissions policy, for example, seeks to be impartial by being nondiscriminatory, it tacitly relies on an understanding of what such neutrality consists of. Toward which characteristics should decision makers turn a blind eye? Toward an applicant's race? Sex? Sexual orientation? Toward his grades or religion or physical disability? Cognitive disability? For any set of answers, we can reasonably ask why the school should ignore these aspects of the applicants' profiles and not others. The answer to that question will reflect the particular goal that is sought through the use of these standards. A policy of neutrality has a purpose, in other words, and it is the value placed on that purpose that determines the exact contours of the neutrality that is adopted.

This dependence of appropriate neutrality on valued ends applies to a legal system as much as to any other enterprise. Neutrality is a means, rather than a good in its own right; it is a method of reaching decisions that deliberately excludes certain factors in order to ground the decisions on others deemed more appropriate because of their bearing on the goal. It is thus a confusion to treat this means (neutrality) as if it carried independent authority. Insistence on the value neutrality of the Rule of Law ideal, however, does exactly that. Only by ignoring the value that is sought *through* certain forms of neutrality can neutrality itself seem desirable. When neutrality is in fact appropriate, it is so in order to serve a particular, chosen purpose. As such, it is decidedly not value neutral.[44]

The assumption that law should be apolitical or amoral is seductive, I think, because it rests on a partial truth (from which many draw an invalid conclusion). The use of values to play certain roles *is* inappropriate in the objective

---

[44] We should be alert to the fact that the terms "value neutral" and "apolitical" are themselves sometimes ambiguous in regard to the exact kinds of values and roles for values that they mean to exclude. For further discussion, see my "Neutrality Isn't Neutral," pp. 67–69.

operation of a legal system. Police officers should enforce the laws on the books concerning the rights of protestors or of abortion providers or of handgun owners, for instance, rather than the laws that they wish had been enacted. To recognize the moral character of the Rule of Law, as I have urged, would not license government officials' rogue injection of their personal preferences to determine the exercise of legal power. The fact that values should not play that role does not show that values should play no role, however. The appropriate neutrality of certain elements within a legal system does not demonstrate the value neutrality of the system itself.

Judges must recognize the values that are implicit in the law in order to understand the law accurately and to apply it objectively. When a judge is called on to apply a particular immigration law, for example, if he does not appreciate the purpose of the law and the guiding principles of the larger system of which this is a part, he will not understand its proper application in complicated cases. The meaning of any law depends on its context, and principles and purposes (which reflect values) are essential elements of that context.[45]

In short, while we need to be careful to specify the exact way in which values properly influence the Rule of Law, it is too sweeping to claim that the Rule of Law must be shorn of all values. The belief that it should be retains the misguided model of objectivity as value free that I have refuted.

5. CONCLUSION

People widely insist that courts should uphold *the law*, whatever that law might be and regardless of judges' own wishes that certain laws were different. This demand is perfectly appropriate. In guarding against judges' indulgence of their personal preferences, however, we must not become blind to another danger that lurks within the law itself, namely, the possibility that what it commands is not justified – that it exercises power beyond its authorized purpose. We must recognize that a rule's passage through certain procedural hoops or satisfying other purely formal criteria does not ensure that rule's legitimacy. The thin, value neutral model of the Rule of Law, unfortunately, diverts our attention from the *what* and the *why* of a legal system, blinding us to the

[45] This does not claim that meaning is determined entirely by context, but simply that context constrains meaning, such that text alone is insufficient. Justice John Roberts offered several simple examples of this phenomenon in his majority opinion in *AT&T v Federal Communications Commission*, no. 09-1279 (2011) citing the meanings of "golden opportunities," "golden boy," "craft," and "crafty," among others, as clearly context dependent. See Adam Liptak, "Justices' Opinion is Wrapped in an English Lesson," *New York Times*, March 2, 2011. Naturally, I will say much more to support this view of meaning in my discussion of judicial review in later chapters.

possibility that a given law, regardless of its procedural pedigree and formal characteristics, may be nonetheless invalid according to the full meaning and robust standards of objective law.

The Rule of Law is not simply a utilitarian device of no particular moral character. While a smoothly functioning legal system definitely has its merits and is preferable, *other things being equal*, to a less efficient system, efficacy as such is not a good. In the service of vice, it is no virtue.[46] The formal conditions that compose the Rule of Law offer a genuine ideal that people *should* actively seek only if the government demanding those conditions enjoys valid authority and exercises that authority to serve its proper function. The Rule of Law warrants respect insofar as the government is doing what it is charged to do. The "ideal-ness" of the Rule of Law, in other words, cannot be maintained apart from the fact that by respecting its conditions, we advance a *good*.

Contrary to the Rule of Law's aura of hollow formality, then, by honoring its conditions, we help to ensure the proper exercise of government power. When a legal system's form is made to follow its function, respecting its formal conditions advances that function.

Distilled to its essence, the alternative between the Rule of Law and the Rule of Men is the alternative between the rule of reason and the rule of force. In this context, the rule of reason takes the form of a moral doctrine: the rule of rights. The Rule of Law offers rule by the conclusions of reason about proper uses of government coercion. The Rule of Men, by contrast, is rule by might – by brute physical power, applied as subjectively and randomly as the urges of those wielding it. The violation of any of the Rule of Law's proper formal conditions means that the government's power to force people to act in particular ways is unleashed from the discipline of rational restraint. For when, in defiance of the Rule of Law's conditions, we are subjected to vague laws or to conflicting laws or to retroactive laws or to laws that are applied to some members of a society but not others on no valid basis, this means that some men are using the power of law to control other men in defiance of the reason for which and the right by which they hold that power. Might is making right.

This is not merely a breach of empty niceties of form. The Rule of Men is wrong. It deprives individuals of something that is theirs: their rightful freedom. The Rule of Law, conversely, in its maintenance of proper conditions, is right. It is morally good.

---

[46] Which is why rights-respecting nations condemn sinister regimes' (such as North Korea's) bolstering of their arsenals or acquisition of nuclear weapons, despite its strengthening those governments' ability to govern effectively.

4

The Moral Authority Beneath the Law

1. INTRODUCTION

By laying bare the inadequacy of a "Rule of Law" devoid of moral warrant, Chapter 3 underscored the need to understand a legal system's moral authority. Given its unique title to coerce compliance with its rules, the source of this authority is critical to distinguish a proper legal system from the order imposed by a band of well-armed thugs.

As I explained it earlier, objectivity in any domain demands that a conclusion be anchored in reality. How does that apply here? What is the anchor for a legal system's authority to forcibly compel people to obey its edicts and, correspondingly, what makes it proper (as opposed to simply expedient) for the people governed by a particular legal system to comply with it?

The answer rests in remembering that a legal system is the practical mechanism through which a government carries out its mission. Its moral authority must be understood in that framework: It arises from those facts that create the need for such an institution in the first place. A legal system's moral authority is not self-bestowed; no regime may arrogate to itself the license to act as it does, acquiring authority by self-declared decree. Because we are inquiring into the basis of legal authority, the explanation must rest in facts external to the legal system itself.[1] And for this reason, an account of law's moral authority cannot stand apart from more foundational conclusions in political philosophy (which, in turn, rely on conclusions of moral philosophy). Because those are themselves large and contested questions, I can hardly provide a complete demonstration of law's moral authority here. I will, however, present the basic logical structure of the case along with some explanation of why it is a strong

---

[1] We will analyze legal authority, the ultimate arbiter of legitimacy *within* a legal system, in Chapter 5. In this chapter, therefore, I will sometimes use "authority" as a shorthand for moral authority.

case. (It is worth recognizing that any account of the moral authority of the law must at least tacitly take stands on such deeper questions. Insofar as one regards a legal system as a legal system that is entitled to certain respect, one implies its possession of moral legitimacy. Indeed, even the denial of a legal system's moral authority or the denial that it requires moral authority would stand on assumptions about moral propriety. Thus, the reliance on presuppositions concerning morality is not unique to my theory.)

Essentially, I will contend that the requisite anchor for the moral authority of a legal system rests in that system's serving the proper function of government, which is to safeguard individuals' freedom by banning the initiation of physical force. The bulk of the chapter is devoted to explaining why this *is* the function of government, which I will do by elaborating five more basic facts about man's nature and needs that create the need for an institution to play this specific role. Some of these facts offer descriptive observations concerning the conditions of human existence, while others incorporate evaluations of what is good for human beings. It is the union of the two that creates the need for a government to protect individuals' freedom of action.

The implications of this issue for our eventual concern with judicial review should not be difficult to appreciate. The legitimate authority of the law (of a particular legal system as a whole) naturally constrains the conceivable identity of the law and, correspondingly, what any particular provision of its written expression could genuinely mean. A legal system's moral authority sets the context for understanding what its constituent laws are. The legal system could not be interpreted as sanctioning activities that the government lacks the basic authority to engage in (at least, not rationally interpreted). Since law's authority is limited, so must law's meaning be. A better understanding of a legal system's rightful scope of command, therefore, will help us understand any particular provision's objective meaning.[2]

---

[2]   If a legal system's authority can extend no farther than its moral authority, one might suspect that this entails the embrace of Natural Law or endorsement of the thesis that an unjust law is not truly a law. It does not. Essentially, that supposition would confuse the conditions necessary to enjoy the Rule of Law, which is an ideal, with the question of whether a legal system exists in a given area, which is a simpler, non-normative matter of fact. Bear in mind that my concern throughout the book is to understand a legal system that *should* be respected, that is objectively proper. Thus, my contention that a proper legal system requires moral authority does not stake a claim in the distinct dispute between Positivists and Natural Lawyers over what *constitutes* law. I should note, though, that my account of an objective legal system does disavow some important features found in many versions of Natural Law, particularly metaphysical moral realism and claims to the self-evidence of certain prescriptive legal truths.

   It is also important to recognize that many contemporary advocates of Natural Law (such as John Finnis, Robert George, Mark Murphy) reject the stringent "unjust law is no law" thesis and adopt more qualified variants. For good discussion of some of these views, as well as

2. AUTHORITY FLOWS FROM FUNCTION

To orient our inquiry into a legal system's moral authority, we should begin by reminding ourselves of what authority itself is. Consider its occurrence in a range of areas: authority in the military, in the workplace, in the classroom; between parent and child, coach and players, director and actors, warden and prisoner. Authority is a relationship in which one party holds title to restrict another party's actions in certain respects.[3] As a philosophy professor, for example, I may determine the writing assignments required for students to pass a course that I teach; I may not impose restrictions on students' diet or dating or off-campus attire.

In colloquial terms, the person with authority gets to boss another around. When the person truly holds the relevant authority, it is rightful bossing; his imposition of restrictions is legitimate. Broadly, one party enjoys the authority to restrict another in a certain domain when his doing so is justified by the relevant standards. What those standards are will depend heavily on the purpose

of the Positivism-Natural Law debate more broadly, see Mark C. Murphy, *Natural Law in Jurisprudence and Politics*, New York: Cambridge University Press, 2006, pp. 29–59; Murphy, *Philosophy of Law*, Malden, MA: Blackwell Publishing, 2007, pp. 35–36; John Finnis, *Natural Law and Natural Rights*, pp. 9–18 and 290; Murphy, "Natural Law Theory," *Blackwell Guide to the Philosophy of Law and Legal Theory*, eds. Martin P. Golding and William A. Edmundson, Malden, MA: Blackwell, 2005, pp. 15–28; and Brian H. Bix, "Legal Positivism," *Blackwell Guide to the Philosophy of Law and Legal Theory*, pp. 29–49. The strong version of Natural Law is most associated with Aquinas, who wrote that "every human law has just so much of the nature of law as it is derived from the law of nature. But if in any point it deflects from the law of nature, it is no longer a law but a perversion of law," *Summa Theologica*, Question 95, Second Article, and that laws "contrary to human good" are "acts of violence rather than laws, because, as Augustine says, 'A law that is not just seems to be no law at all,'" *Summa*, Question 96, Fourth Article, in *The Political Ideas of St. Thomas Aquinas* ed. D. Bogongiari, New York: Haffner, 1969, pp. 58 and 71–72. More recently, Michael Moore wrote that "for something to be a law at all it must necessarily not be unjust," Moore, "Law as a Functional Kind," in *Natural Law Theory*, ed. Robert George, Oxford: Clarendon, p. 189. For further elaboration of my view in relation to the Positivism-Natural Law debate, see "Neutrality Isn't Neutral," pp. 88–90, and, particularly on the false alternative that the two schools pose, "Objective Law," *A Companion to Ayn Rand*.

A further worry might also arise, namely, that affording such a role to law's moral authority will allow too great a power to judges' beliefs about moral authority. While I do believe that judicial review demands a certain kind of philosophical reasoning from judges, I discuss the crucial limitations of judges' use of philosophy in Chapter 6, explaining how judges are not to impose their personal philosophies over the law, and in Chapter 7, when I address the concern that my account of proper judicial methodology may seem overly philosophical. The issue also surfaces in Chapter 8, where I treat the proper exercise of judicial review in today's context. I explain the limited nature of the philosophy that judges should employ more directly in "Why Originalism Won't Die," pp. 178–179 and 211–213.

3   The "party" could be a single person or several or an organization, company, or other institution such as a university, a club, or a league. For simplicity, I will speak of parties as if they designate single persons. Note that some dictionary definitions of "authority" treat authority as a power, while others identify it as a rightful power or "title." Since we are seeking to distinguish authority from sheer power, our focus is on the latter, "title" sense of authority.

of the enterprise. Is the overall goal a student's education, for instance? Is the goal a military mission's success?[4]

Our question is: What licenses a legal system to command people in ways that no one else may? To coercively compel individuals to comply with the rules that it lays down? The answer, in the most fundamental terms, is: the fact that its doing so makes possible all the benefits of living in society.

Human beings stand to gain incalculably from ongoing interaction with one another. The advantages of living in organized society are almost too manifest to cite and certainly too abundant to capture here. Consider the knowledge that a person can gain from the experience and insights of others. Consider the intellectual advances available from exchanging information and conjectures, from sharing lessons, undertaking joint investigations, building on the hypotheses and criticisms, the refinements, innovations, and discoveries that other individuals offer in every area of human activity, from mechanics, mining, and medicine through communication and travel to clothing, cuisine, and the arts.

Consider, also, the trade that society makes possible – trade in the material goods and services that people produce, from the mundane necessities of bread, shoes, plumbing, or heating through pharmaceuticals and pacemakers to the luxuries of an automobile, a symphony, a contest of fantasy football, or a Reese's peanut butter cup.[5]

---

4   Note that we can challenge someone's exercise of his authority without challenging his possession of it. Also, to assert a person's authority is to affirm the propriety of the restrictive, superior-subordinate relationship in which the two parties stand. Because moral authority is one species of wider moral propriety, that authority relationship acquires its propriety from the same foundations, and must ultimately be judged by the same standard, that governs all moral values. I have argued elsewhere that values are rooted in the necessary conditions of life. It is the fact that living organisms must act to satisfy the conditions of their existence that furnishes the objective foundation for distinguishing things as good or bad, as valuable or not valuable, and correspondingly, for all derivative concepts such as "right," "wrong," "virtuous," "vicious," and "morally proper." The validation of these concepts lies in the fact that some modes of action are essentially conducive to an organism's existence and others are deleterious to it. While the defense of that standard is beyond our purposes here, what may be helpful for understanding a legal system's moral authority is that the ultimate justification of that authority will be grounded in that legal system's service to human beings' objective well-being.

For explanation of values' roots in the conditions of existence, see my *Viable Values: A Study of Life as the Root and Reward of Morality*, Rowman & Littlefield, 2000; *Ayn Rand's Normative Ethics – The Virtuous Egoist*, Cambridge University Press, 2006, chapter 2; Harry Binswanger, *The Biological Basis of Teleological Concepts*, Marina del Rey, CA: ARI Press, 1990. My account is an elaboration of the theory that Rand originated. See Rand, "The Objectivist Ethics," in *The Virtue of Selfishness*, New York: Penguin, 1964; "Causality vs. Duty," in *Philosophy: Who Needs It*, New York: Bobbs Merrill, 1982; and Leonard Peikoff, *Objectivism: The Philosophy of Ayn Rand*, chapter 7.

5   The enjoyment of luxuries offers its own type of contribution to a person's existence and serves a particular type of need. As I discuss in *Viable Values*, the distinction between needs and wants is not nearly as sharp as people commonly suppose. See *Viable Values*, pp. 130–143.

Consider, still further, the spiritual values that other people bring to one's life – the emotional and psychological rewards that uniquely result from sharing our experiences.[6] Through relationships ranging from the most remote and impersonal to the most intimate, other people routinely enlighten, amuse, or inspire; they provide understanding, comfort, and camaraderie. Not everyone does this, by any means, nor does anyone do it unfailingly, but this is a kind of value uniquely available from other human beings.

These are simply the broadest categories of social benefits. The point is, living in society is an objective value to human life. Myriad forms of interaction with others make a person's existence exponentially easier and richer than it would otherwise be – more secure, more comfortable, more rewarding, more fun. The benefits of society are attainable, however, only under certain conditions. It is rational, therefore, for people to organize themselves on terms that will preserve those conditions that make society's advantages possible. It is these basic ground rules that a legal system properly identifies and enforces.

All of that, as I indicated, is the most fundamental explanation of a legal system's moral authority. We can understand this more fully, however, by narrowing our focus to a legal system's more distinctive mission.

The only reason for granting an institution a monopoly on the initiation of force is the protection of individual rights. Properly, government is established and endowed with the power that it has because that power is needed to safeguard the freedom that is necessary for human well-being. (I will say much more on this connection in the next part of the chapter.) Consequently, the substance and administration of a legal system (the *what* and the *how*, in the terms of Chapter 2) must be designed to do these things. Essentially, a legal system possesses moral authority insofar as it exerts its coercive power exclusively in the ways that are necessary to accomplish its mission. If a specific legal system is dedicated to that mission (as evidenced in its manner of exercising its power), then people *should* obey it as a means of serving their rational interest. The propriety of a legal system's governance and of people's obedience is entirely determined by the government's activities being in service to that end.

A legal system's moral authority, in other words, is an organic outgrowth of its reason for being. Just as form follows function, so authority follows function.

---

[6] By "spiritual," I do not mean religious or mystical, but simply those aspects of human consciousness that are often described as our psychological or emotional experience. "Spiritual" characterizes phenomena of consciousness, while "physical" characterizes phenomena of material bodies.

A legal system holds moral authority on the condition that it exercises its power responsibly, consonant with its reason for having that power.[7]

It follows, then, that not every legal system can legitimately claim moral authority. A given regime might enjoy widespread obedience without possessing moral title to rule as it does. A legal system that brazenly violated individual rights would be antithetical to the purpose of having a government and, as such, could not possess moral authority. It might be powerful insofar as it effectively intimidated multitudes into submission, but that is a different issue. A legal system maintains its authority by using its power to do its job (just as the authority of a coach or a teacher is contingent on his using his power in ways that serve the larger purpose for which he has it).[8] The authorizing commission of a legal system, however justified in its inception, does not grant to that system *carte blanche*, the indefinite and unqualified title to use its power in whatever ways and for whatever ends it likes. A government's license to practice law, so to speak – that is, to exercise force – is conditioned on its fidelity to the purpose for which it holds that power.

Before proceeding, it may be helpful to underscore the objective character of this account of the law's moral authority. At base, I am arguing, a legal system's authority is a matter of fact, rather than opinion. It is not a product of people's beliefs or preferences. On the account that I have begun to provide, certain immutable conditions of human existence underwrite the law's authority. In light of the widespread presumption that it is some form of popular consent that supplies the law's authority, this is significant.

Many people suppose that a government is legitimate when and because a great number of people agree that it is. (Social contract theory is an obvious form of this.) This view is subjectivist. It treats authority as created and shaped by the beliefs of subjects rather than by prior, belief-independent phenomena. On my account, in contrast, the law's authority flows from the recognition of

---

[7] The appropriate standard here is not infallibility (for the reasons discussed when I explained the demands of objectivity in Chapter 1). Roughly, a legal system is legitimate insofar as (a) it seeks to act only in ways that are necessary to fulfill its function, (b) it adopts a rational plan for doing so, and (c) its actual execution of that plan (its practical governance) essentially does so.

The broader belief that power should be commensurate with purpose is hardly original. See, for instance, Alexander Hamilton, who considered it "a maxim in ethics and politics" that "every power ought to be commensurate with its object" (*Federalist* 31), and James Madison, who contended that "a good government" implies both "fidelity to the object of government" and "a knowledge of the means by which that object can be best attained" (*Federalist* 62). *The Federalist*, edited by George W. Carey and James McClellan, Indianapolis: Liberty Fund, 2001, pp. 150 and 322.

[8] I am not claiming that there will always be a singular precise manner of achieving those ends (one *and only one* way), but that the legal system's actions must fall within the permissible range. More on this, later in the chapter.

man's need for freedom. Authority is not hostage to any group's consensus for the simple reason that man's needs are not a fancy of any group's consensus. The fundamental conditions of human life are not dependent on anyone's say-so. The law's authority is grounded on human beings' nature – specifically, on our need for the freedom from force that only a proper government can provide.[9]

While this highlights the objective character of my account of authority, it obviously anticipates some of the argument of the next section. So let me turn to that explanation of the specific grounds beneath these claims to objectivity. Although a proper legal system's dependence on deeper principles of political and moral philosophy cannot be fully demonstrated here, it is important for understanding law's moral authority to know the major planks that underwrite it.[10]

3. THE MORAL AND POLITICAL FOUNDATIONS BENEATH LAW'S MORAL AUTHORITY

Given that the authority of a legal system depends on that system's serving its proper function, the way to understand its authority more fully is to understand the system's reason for being. Five premises, I think, are most critical to this:

A. Each man is an end in himself
B. Reason is man's means of survival – his most basic means of serving his objective well-being
C. Reason requires freedom from others' initiation of force

---

[9] The denial that popular agreement is the source of a legal system's moral authority is compatible with the propriety of certain other political decisions' being left to the people's agreement (such as the selection of specific legislative representatives). The determination of exactly which decisions those are is peripheral to our purposes here. What is important, however, is that the answer must be guided by the overarching mission of the legal system. Within a proper system, popular agreement could legitimately resolve questions on which all of the alternatives would themselves respect individual rights. If democratic will were obeyed at the cost of individual rights, however, it would defeat the purpose for which the legal system holds its power. We will discuss this further in Chapter 6.

[10] I have elaborated in much more depth on different aspects of the claims that follow in *Moral Rights and Political Freedom*, especially chapters 1–2 and 6–9; *Viable Values*, chapters 4 and 5; and *Ayn Rand's Normative Ethics*, chapter 2. Further explanations of these claims are in Rand, "The Nature of Government," and "Man's Rights," in *Capitalism: The Unknown Ideal*; Peikoff, *Objectivism: The Philosophy of Ayn Rand*, pp. 310–324 and 350–369; and Adam Mossoff and Fred Miller, "Political Theory – A Radical for Capitalism," in *A Companion to Ayn Rand*, 2015.

D. Each man is entitled to freedom of action – that is, each man has the right to his own life, which is the right to lead his life free of others' forceful interference

E. Man requires government in order to protect his right to freedom

Notice that these premises are of two types. The second and third concern the requirements of human existence. The first and fourth are evaluative judgments that imply prescriptions; they entail the propriety of certain kinds of actions. The fifth represents the conclusion from the others. The overall thrust is that certain facts of nature, coupled with the recognition of individuals' well-being as their proper end, provide the foundations for the moral authority of a legal system. Man needs to have a government because his happiness is properly his highest end and because man can only achieve that happiness under certain conditions. The security of those conditions is the mandate of a legal system.[11] Let me elaborate on the logic of each.

A. *Each Man Is an End in Himself*

The most basic feature of morality that informs a legal system's moral authority is the fact that each man is an end in himself. It is right for him to treat his life as such, pursuing his well-being as his highest end. And it is right for others to respect a man's doing so. A society's political arrangements, accordingly, must recognize this fact. It is because an individual's happiness is his proper end that an institution sanctioned to use force against individuals must do so in ways that are consonant with this. The only reason for having such an institution is its necessity, in order to combat those who would interfere with that.

This first premise is so basic and so widely accepted that I will not directly argue for it here.[12] This is not to say that in the grander scheme, if one were offering the complete demonstration of the role of government, it would not require argument; it does, and I offer a much fuller defense of egoism in *Viable Values*, where I explain the entire phenomenon of values as rooted in and

---

[11] I am presupposing the propriety of Rand's theory of rational egoism, defended elsewhere. See Smith, *Viable Values; Ayn Rand's Normative Ethics*, chapter 2; Rand, "The Objectivist Ethics," "Causality vs. Duty"; and Peikoff, chapter 7, especially pp. 229–241. Also, in what follows, I will use the terms "life," "existence," "happiness," "well-being," and "flourishing" interchangeably. I explain the justification for doing so in depth in *Viable Values*, chapter 5. As I demonstrate there, the standards for assessing human happiness and well-being are ultimately objectively grounded in the same kind of facts of human nature as those that ground standards for measuring human life or existence.

[12] Widely accepted in the political sphere, that is. Many people are inconsistent in their respect for this idea in action and evade the conflict between its implicit egoism and their professed moral beliefs in the propriety of self-sacrificial service to others.

relative to the demands of human life.[13] I will not engage that here, however, primarily because I expect few of my readers would deny the idea that we should treat individuals as ends in themselves or would embrace the attendant implication that some individuals are, by birth, more morally entitled than others; that some men are properly, by nature, fodder to be subordinated to the ends of others. Indeed, the very concern with legal *authority* – the attempt to justify morally a government's forcing individuals' compliance with its rules – seems to presuppose it. Why would such a justification be sought, if individuals were not ends in themselves? Two points are worth brief comment, however.

First, perhaps the most commonly cited justification of government power is self-defense. Nearly everyone would agree that government is needed as a means of people's defending themselves against both external and internal aggressors. Observe the implication that self-interest is permissible – that a person may treat his life as an end in itself and resist those who would obstruct his doing that. Yet self-defense can be legitimate only if self-promotion is legitimate – "promotion," here, meaning the considered pursuit of one's rational interest by means that respect the similar interests and rights of others. The reason that self-defense is permissible, in other words, is the propriety of a specific kind of egoism. Men are justified in pursuing their security only because they are justified in pursuing their happiness.

Contentious though this claim is, it is important to recognize, I think, because it informs the proper function of government. A government's function could not be at odds with more basic requirements of morality – at least, not if that government aspired to *moral* legitimacy.

The second observation hearkens back to a view that we commented on in Section 2, the widespread belief that popular consent provides the basis of law's authority. While I reject that view, it is not difficult to understand its appeal. It draws on the assumption that it would be wrong to treat people in certain ways unless those people had agreed to that treatment. And I concur; it would be wrong. To believe that, however, is to imply that a man is an end in himself. That is, the reason that an individual's consent is required to justify certain ways of treating him is that his life is his, to lead as he chooses (subject to the requirement that he respect others' same status).[14] What is often lost when drawing the erroneous conclusion that people's agreement is the basis of law's authority, however, is the fact that individuals' autonomy does not

---

[13] *Viable Values*, chapters 4 and 5.
[14] Throughout, it is important that all my assertions of individuals' rights or title to freedom be understood as subject to this condition. A person would forfeit his rights by violating the rights of others.

encompass its *every* possible exercise. Nor would every conceivable restriction that others might impose on him be an infringement of his proper freedom or at odds with respecting him as an end in himself. There are certain things that one man (morally) may do to another without his consent, such as restrain him from violating another man's rights (restrain him from physically assaulting an innocent person, for instance). The thief who has been apprehended need not agree to society's punishment for such punishment to be morally permissible. Thus, my argument against consent as the source of law's authority stands. The pertinent point here is to see how embedded this first premise of legal authority (the belief that each man is an end in himself) is, to routine thinking about proper social relations.

B. Reason is Man's Means of Survival

The second plank beneath law's moral authority is a fact about the fundamental nature of human existence: reason is man's most basic means of survival. A human being's existence is neither an immutable given that will naturally continue in perpetuity, nor a condition that is wholly determined by factors beyond his control. Neither the course of his life nor the sheer continuation of his life is at the mercy of celestial spirits or DNA. A person's existence is possible only under certain conditions and his own actions are critical to the fulfillment of those conditions.[15]

Unlike other species, human beings are not genetically coded to meet all of our needs automatically, without conscious, chosen effort. "Schools of fish, flocks of birds, and herds of deer respond similarly, collectively, and almost instantly to predators. They don't stand (or fly or swim) around debating the matter."[16] Human beings, however, do – because we must. We are not conveniently "wired" in ways sufficient to maintain our lives. Man must figure out what he needs and how he can get it – what he needs to have as well as what he needs to do. Indeed, he must first recognize that he *has* needs. And he must take the actions that he then determines will satisfy those needs.

Human action is volitional. A person acts by choosing among alternatives.[17] In order to act in ways that will, in fact, meet his needs, *how* must he choose? On what basis should he evaluate his options?

---

[15] I am speaking of normal adults. Small children and those severely impaired in certain ways, obviously, must rely on others to meet their needs. The underlying fact, however, is that human life is sustained exclusively by specific types of human action.

[16] John Lewis Gaddis, *The Landscape of History*, New York: Oxford University Press, 2002, p. 111.

[17] Even when a person drifts relatively thoughtlessly into an action, he chooses to not focus his mind on exactly what each of his alternatives offers. To do something passively or carelessly is

In the most fundamental terms: by the guidance of reason. That is, by a dedicated commitment to gaining knowledge – to understanding the facts of reality that are relevant to his general situation and to the more specific alternatives that he faces. As a method for utilizing one's mental capacity, reason is the deliberate, disciplined effort to recognize factual evidence and to trace and respect the logical implications of that evidence in drawing conclusions and in taking actions. For the only way to satisfy the conditions of reality is by heeding reality. Any attempt to skirt this (by denial, by distorting evidence or comforting rationalizations, for instance) cannot help him to meet its demands and, at worst, will pose a definite hindrance to his doing so.[18]

The particular steps that rationality will demand in a given case depend on the situation – on the specific ends that a person is seeking, their relationship to the larger network of his other ends, and his relevant knowledge and resources (time, money, personnel, etc.). Whether the question is complex or simple and whether it carries momentous or relatively trivial repercussions, however, the throughline that distinguishes all rationality is the deliberate, systematic effort to identify, understand, and respect the way things are – the actual nature of all relevant phenomena independently of anyone's beliefs, appraisals, or wishes concerning those phenomena. As a man's mode of addressing questions and making decisions, reason reflects a basic and unwavering reverence for reality.[19]

The alternatives that men have tried simply do not work. Reliance on an authority figure or on a tradition, for instance, or deference to an idea's popularity or its emotional appeal or the flat rejection of all conceivable *grounds* of validation and adoption of a "conclusion" under the banner of "intuition" or "faith" have proven themselves incapable of fixing a faucet, eradicating an infection, flying a plane, or making a hammer that can drive a nail. Irrational techniques do not help people to learn the facts they need to know on any

---

   still a manner of *doing* it – "doing" in the sense that the person could have done otherwise, by
   acting more attentively, but chose not to.
[18] A person's ends themselves might be rational or irrational, depending on his basis for adopting
   them and their relationship to other of his ends and needs. Typically, a person simultaneously pursues an extensive array of ends of widely divergent kinds, breadth, and significance
   (e.g., save for retirement, get a dentist appointment, complete this course, enliven my social
   life, help Democrats be elected, fix the dishwasher). The ultimate rationality of any of them
   depends on that end's place within a rational life plan. And facts that are not of one's choosing
   (the most basic requirements of human existence) set the terms on which all other ends may
   be embraced.
[19] Obviously, this depicts rationality as very similar to objectivity. The two are nearly identical,
   I think, though I would characterize rationality as the broader phenomenon and objectivity
   as a more targeted tool of rationality, which consists of the deliberate, self-monitored effort to
   root one's reality tracking in the object rather than the subject.

given issue and do not help people to take the actions they need to take to satisfy the conditions of their existence.

This is not to say that deviations from reason visit immediate catastrophe. Most people survive some of their own irrationalities on a daily basis. Surviving them does not mean that one is untouched by them, however. Destructive consequences need not be severe or conspicuous to be genuine. A person weakens his chances of achieving his well-being when he acts in ways that defy the reality that sets its conditions. He weakens *himself* simultaneously, sabotaging his own development as the kind of person who can most effectively achieve his well-being. I court heart disease through certain dietary habits, for instance; I court bankruptcy by certain spending habits; I risk flunking out of college by certain study habits. And I weaken my willpower or integrity or honesty or productiveness by the evasions and lies and various other forms of faking that I indulge, to grease this slide away from reason.

The important point here is that irrationality is not sustainable. Only the kind of thought and action that respects reality can satisfy the conditions of a person's existence *in* reality. It is facts of nature that determine what man's needs are and the means that can satisfy them. Consequently, it is only by respect for those facts (that is, by reason) that man can acquire knowledge and hope to meet them.

In principle, it is reason that sustains humans' existence. The use of reason is not a guarantee of success, since other factors could defeat a man's rational efforts (disease or accidental injury, for instance). And the conscientious effort to be rational does not ensure that one's conclusions will always be accurate; rationality is not omniscience or infallibility. Lack of information and flawed inferences resulting from honest error could result in mistaken judgments. Nonetheless, within the range of things that a person controls, the basic manner in which way he uses his mind is the most critical determinant of his long-term success. It is the fundamental driver of human existence. And this is what is important for shedding light on legal authority.

Each man is an end in himself. If a man is to treat his life as an end and if he is to achieve the happiness that that makes possible, he must respect his need for rational action. If he is to take advantage of the benefits of living in society, however, his success depends on more than this. So let us proceed to the further conditions that are relevant here.

C. *Reason Requires Freedom from Force*

The next point that is important for understanding the moral authority of a legal system is the fact that reason requires freedom from other people's initiation of physical force. This is perhaps the most complex of these premises, since it presupposes a view of what rationality itself is. Here, once more, I will simply lay out the basics behind this claim in order to illuminate the critical relationship between reason and freedom.[20]

My claim is that a person's ability to employ reason successfully depends on his freedom from others' use of force against him. By "force," I mean physical contact or physical manipulation. Pressing, poking, or puncturing an object are obvious ways of applying force. Beating, stabbing, shooting, or shackling are just a few of the ways in which force can be exerted against a person. When others attempt to dictate a person's action by physical rather than intellectual means (by brandishing a gun rather than offering an argument, for instance), they are thwarting his capacity to use his mind in a rational way.[21]

To understand how force blunts thought, begin with the simple fact that thought and force are different in kind. Thinking is not essentially physical; it does not consist of the motions of matter. Physical force cannot make a person *think* something because thinking is not a physical process. While thought obviously relies on physical materials (brains, blood, neurons, etc.), thinking is a form of conscious experience and conscious experience is not reducible to non-conscious matter. Correspondingly, force cannot supply its victim with *reason* to affirm any particular conclusion. That is simply not the kind of thing that physical manipulation is capable of.

Let me break this down a little further with the aid of an example. The process of thinking about an issue essentially consists of making decisions about an array of choices. Whatever the principal question that one is considering – whether this mushroom is edible, whether copper conducts electricity, whether to join the Marines or marry Melissa, how to fix a flat tire or manage a company – to think is to confront a cascade of decisions about which particular thoughts and observations to pay attention to, which to credit, which to discard, how much to weigh each, how to relate them, as well as decisions

[20] I have gone into this in greater depth in *Moral Rights and Political Freedom*, chapters 6 and 7; and "Objective Law," *A Companion to Ayn Rand*, 2015. Also see penetrating discussion in Peikoff, *Objectivism: The Philosophy of Ayn Rand*, pp. 358–363; and Darryl Wright, "Reason and Freedom in Ayn Rand's Politics," in *The Philosophy of Capitalism: Objectivism and Alternative Approaches: Ayn Rand Society Philosophical Studies*, volume 3, eds. Greg Salmieri and Robert Mayhew, Pittsburgh: University of Pittsburgh Press, forthcoming 2016.

[21] Throughout, when I refer to uses of force, I am speaking of its unprovoked initiation unless the context clearly indicates otherwise (as when an innocent person uses force in response to another's initiation of force). Notice that we do not object to the dentist's drilling or to the surgeon's cutting precisely because these are not ordinarily unprovoked initiations, but, rather, are voluntarily submitted to. Also, I will speak of the use of force as encompassing either its direct application or the threat of its application. The reason for doing so should become clearer over the next few pages. (I also explain this in *Moral Rights and Political Freedom*, pp. 150–155.)

about which additional questions to pose and what inferences to draw. To think *rationally* is to address these choices in a particular manner, namely, by striving to grasp the actual nature of the phenomena in question. And to do that, at a more granular level, is to answer all these questions on the basis of factual evidence and logic. A person's procedure is rational insofar as he answers these questions in a rigorously evidence-tracking, logic-using, reality-pursuing manner.

Consider the issue of whom to support in a gubernatorial election. (For simplicity, assume that my aim is to support the candidate who I deem best qualified for the office.) As I consider which candidate to support, of the array of things that I hear about the various contenders, which should I accept as true? Of those that I do regard as true, which should I give weight, in my deliberations, and which should I dismiss as insignificant? What (if anything) should I do to seek out further information? And what particular types of information should I seek – more detail on the same issues about which I already know something (such as the candidates' positions on immigration or gun control), or information on other issues that I have not previously learned about? Which issues within each category? What about the candidates' broader "vision"?

Further, on the basis of knowledge that I have already acquired about the candidates, what inferences should I draw about their positions on other issues? Or about their abilities in regard to different aspects of the governor's responsibilities? Which aspects? What inferences should I draw about their character? About which aspects of their character? To what extent should any of those matter? More broadly, by what yardstick should I evaluate the relative merits of one candidate vis-à-vis others, given that none of them is my ideal?

The exact conclusion that rationality commends for a given individual will depend to some extent on that person's preexisting beliefs about the role of government, the responsibilities of governors, and certain other framing premises which may themselves be rational or not. A conclusion might be rational relative to particular premises but irrational from the wider perspective that recognizes the irrationality of those premises. The basic point for our purposes, however, should be clear: Whether a thinking process is rational or not depends on the way in which a person manages his mind in confronting the decision making that thinking, at bottom, consists of. However simple or complex the issue, the essence of a rational process is the same: drawing conclusions on the basis of relevant evidence and logical inference.

Another person's imposition of force, however, short-circuits this process. An ultimatum backed by force says: "Don't think, just do. Forget about *your* thoughts and your convictions; simply do as I command."

The lesson for our purposes is that a demand for obedience issued by the threat to use physical force – *vote for Pearson, or else* – is different in kind from the sorts of considerations that could make Smith's voting for Pearson a rational verdict on Pearson's suitability for office. The command, "Obey me" calls for a very different course of action than does the policy, "Be rational" (which instructs a person to seek out evidence, investigate the case for various alternatives, draw conclusions by logic, and take actions accordingly).

Now one might object here that in many circumstances, it *will* be rational to obey a credible threat of serious harm. Yet this misses the point. For the rationality of that decision – whether to obey or not – is distinct from the rationality of one's assessment of the candidates. The injection of force, in other words, changes the subject; it introduces a different question for the agent to answer. And whatever the rationality of a person's answer to that question ("should I obey the coercer or not?"), it is distinct from the rationality of his answer to the question he had been considering prior to the imposition of force (namely, who is the best candidate for governor).

To put the point slightly differently: The fact that if I fail to vote for Pearson my kneecaps will be shattered is not logical reason to conclude that Pearson is the most qualified candidate. Smith's taking action x *because Thug ordered him to under threat of force* is different from Smith's taking action x because Smith deems that action, by his own best judgment and independently of Thug's wishes or weapons, the course that is best supported by evidence and logic. To affirm a conclusion out of obedience is not to affirm it on the merits.

John Locke made the same basic case in his defense of religious toleration: "And such is the nature of the Understanding, that it cannot be compell'd to the belief of anything by outward Force. Confiscation of Estate, Imprisonment, Torments, nothing of that Nature can have any such Efficacy as to make Men change the inward Judgment that they have framed of things."

For, he continued,

> It is one thing to persuade, another to command: One thing to press with Arguments, another with Penalties.... But Penalties are no ways capable to produce such Belief. It is only *Light and Evidence* that can work a change in Men's Opinions. And that Light can in no manner proceed from corporal Sufferings, or any other outward Penalties.[22]

The larger point, again, is that force blunts its victim's use of reason. Force and threats of force might induce particular *behavior* in the victim, but it is

---

[22]   John Locke, A *Letter Concerning Toleration*, ed. J.H. Tully, Indianapolis: Hackett, p. 27.

incapable of producing his rational conclusions.[23] Reasoning is a strictly do-it-yourself activity; no one else can make your conclusions rational. Insofar as they are yours, their rationality depends on your manner of reaching them. The motions of a robot or the noises of a parrot are not indications of their reasoning or understanding.[24]

It will be instructive to consider another objection. The claim that reason requires freedom may seem vulnerable to obvious counterexamples, such as political dissidents who produce impressive work while censored or imprisoned. (Consider Solzhenitsyn and Dostoyevsky, for instance.) Further, many would argue, dictators employ repression and propaganda precisely because they are effective. Millions of North Koreans believe the lies they are fed. Like it or not, some would insist, propaganda works. And this tells against the claim that reason requires freedom. For it suggests that a rationally ordered society (whatever its moral status) can be achieved by means of force rather than freedom.[25]

While this line of argument carries an initial aura of realism, brief reflection reveals it to be based on a superficial understanding of reason. On the contention that propaganda works, it is important to ask: works how? To accomplish what, exactly? Undoubtedly, censors can control the material that people are

---

[23] As Leon Wieseltier has observed, "You cannot coerce somebody to believe; you can coerce them only to act as if they believe." Leon Wieseltier, "Freedom Games," *The New Republic*, October 25, 2012.

[24] Obviously, people can help one another in the acquisition of knowledge; we frequently gain a great deal from engaging with others' thinking, as I noted in discussing the benefits of living in society in section 2. The point, however, is that insofar as a belief is Bill's belief, its rationality depends on *his* manner of reaching it. Rationality is not a free-floating quality that attaches to certain beliefs and not others purely on the basis of the content of those beliefs. The same idea (e.g., that Pearson is the most qualified candidate, that wood is flammable) could be a rational belief for Bill to hold and irrational for Mary. To profess others' beliefs (even beliefs that are rational for those others) without understanding the basic case for them is not to be rational.

The full truth here demands more intricate explanation, but as Locke observed, "We may as rationally hope to see with other men's eyes as to know by other men's understandings.... The floating of other men's opinions in our brains, makes us not one jot the more knowing, [even if] they happen to be true." Locke, *An Essay Concerning Human Understanding*, Book I, ch III, "Other Considerations Concerning Innate Principles, Both Speculative and Practical," Section 24. Reasoning, as distinguished from various facsimiles, is ultimately a first-person, self-driven enterprise.

For much more on the necessarily self-directed character of reasoning, see Smith, *Ayn Rand's Normative Ethics*, pp. 113–117; *Moral Rights and Political Freedom*, pp. 40–42 and 147–155; and Yaron Brook and Don Watkins, *Free Market Revolution*, New York: Palgrave MacMillan, 2012, pp. 129–132.

[25] Thanks to an anonymous reader for the press for prompting me to address this sort of case. And for a version of this objection in the context of religious freedom, see Brian Leiter, *Why Tolerate Religion?* Princeton: Princeton University Press, 2013, pp. 10–12.

exposed to; they can manipulate the information that enters their intellectual environment and the ideas that people are permitted to consider. Further, by punishing anyone who would try to break out of the imposed boundaries, dictators can induce a person to *act as if* he believed certain things. I would also agree that dictators can manipulate people into actually believing certain things, albeit under false pretenses, on account of their having been misled. Because their minds have been denied access to relevant information, many people may sincerely believe that the North Korean dictator is the smartest man on earth.

What dictators cannot do, however, is control what a person does with his mind. And this is what is critical. Force cannot induce a person to think rational thoughts, reach rational conclusions, or gain genuine knowledge – understanding of a subject that is based on logical examination of relevant evidence. If a person is denied access to the full nature of existents because certain lanes of inquiry are forbidden, he cannot reach rational conclusions about the associated subjects. His conclusions – concerning genetics or geophysics, the solar system or an economic system, his beliefs about how an illness is contracted or how a generator is built – will be distorted by the constricted vision that he is permitted. Exactly *how* distorted, and whether certain authors' fiction (as opposed to nonfiction) might still offer value, will depend on the degree of repression. But the basic truth remains: Reason is a reality-seeking device. That is its mission – to help man gain knowledge of reality. When dictators forcibly forbid the investigation of certain portions of reality, however, reason cannot play that role. Reason's capacity to help a man to know reality depends on the unimpeded freedom to explore reality.[26]

When I say that reason requires freedom, I do not mean to imply that no one living without freedom in a dictatorship can be rational – at least, not in one ordinary sense of that ascription. It is important to distinguish assessments of a *person* as rational or not (based on the way that he uses his mind) from claims about the faculty of reason and the preconditions of its ability to serve its purpose. As I indicated earlier, a person's exercise of reason need not be flawless in order for that person to be credited as rational. He may be using his rational capacity to the best of his ability and cannot be faulted for factors beyond his control, such as others' depriving him of salient information. Yet in our desire to be fair in our assessment of the person, it is important not to lose sight of the reason for using reason, namely, the acquisition of knowledge.

Reason is man's means of understanding that which exists. Reasoning is valuable only insofar as it is our means of knowing reality. When that object is

---

[26] Thus Rand's observation that man "cannot function successfully under coercion," "Man's Rights," in *Capitalism: The Unknown Ideal*, 1967 edition, p. 322.

denied people due to restrictions of their freedom, it loses that value. People may be permitted to go through the motions of reasoning, but the results are rigged. They are kept from achieving the good – knowledge – that reason uniquely makes possible.

Again, all of this raises intricate questions concerning the essential nature of rationality that lie beyond our scope here. What is most important to reason's dependence on freedom is the fact that you cannot physically compel a mind to think rational thoughts or to take rational actions. The instruments that can be employed by force (hammers, handcuffs, blades, bludgeons) and the instruments employed by reason (observation, evidence, experiment, chains of deduction and induction) are fundamentally different in kind, and no type of physical mechanism or physical contortion can substitute for evidence or argument or logical inference. If, as I argued in the previous section, man's existence depends on his use of reason, then it further depends on his freedom. For reason requires freedom from others' imposition of physical force. Powerful as force is for moving matter, force is impotent when it comes to moving minds.

D. Each Man Is Entitled to Freedom of Action

The union of the premises asserted thus far – the belief that each man is an end in himself in combination with these facts observing human life's dependence on reason and on freedom – yields the fourth cornerstone of a legal system's moral authority: Each man is entitled to freedom of action. Each man holds the right to life, by which I mean that he is morally entitled to lead his life *by* his judgment, *for* his chosen ends, free *from* others' forceful interference.[27]

Because of widespread confusions that infect the concept of rights, a few clarifications are in order. First, the possession of rights exclusively concerns a person's *freedom* of action rather than the final, all-things-considered moral propriety of his action. The morality of a particular exercise of freedom (an action's virtue or rightness or conformity with a particular code of moral values) is a separate judgment. For certain purposes, it will be a more important judgment, but the immediate point is simply to recognize the significant difference between the two. It is perfectly possible for a person to use his rights in ways that are themselves immoral, yet which do not infringe on others' rights. Suppose that he engages in certain sexual activities or recreational activities that are, in fact, immoral. As long as his engagement does not infringe on the

---

[27] As noted earlier, this right obtains only as long as a man respects others' rights.

freedom of others, however, he *has* the right to act as he does. Similarly, suppose that a coward who betrays his own principles lacks moral integrity. If his betrayal does not affect others' freedom, his immorality is within his rights.[28]

The concept of rights addresses a jurisdictional issue: Who should control an individual's actions – that person himself, or someone else? The person who is wiser? Stronger? Holier? The group? Given that people frequently disagree about how a person should lead his life (in regard to specific decisions concerning his work or marriage or religious practices, for instance) and that people sometimes attempt to impose their views on others, the concept of rights is specifically designed to demarcate individuals' respective spheres of authority. And the object that rights protect, again, is a person's moral title to act by his own judgment, free from others' use of force. (Notice that it is not necessary that all members of a rights-respecting society subscribe to the exact same moral code. My neighbor's worship of a god that I find ludicrous, his expression of opinions I find noxious, or his engagement in sexual activities I find perverse leaves me no less free to conduct my life as I like. What is essential is simply that we deal with each other by voluntary choice rather than force. For that is the condition necessary for the exercise of reason.)

It is also important to recognize that the obligation to respect others' rights is in no way a diminution of a person's interest; it is not a sacrifice to be endured or an imposition required by some freestanding duty of reciprocity. Rather, because rational action is the wellspring of all the objective values that human beings create and from which we each stand to gain and because rational action is only possible to a person who is free, it is in each of our interest to respect other people's freedom. Doing so is a means of nurturing the conditions most conducive to our enjoying a relationship that can be truly beneficial – to me as well as to you.

And this feeds into the main idea, which is straightforward. As we saw earlier, a man stands to gain enormous values from living in society with others. He can realize those values, however, only by respecting the conditions that make them possible. The most fundamental of these is individuals' freedom of action. A person must be free in order to exercise his reason and he *needs* to exercise reason, in order to create genuine values that advance his life. This is why we should recognize each man's right to be free from others' initiation

---

[28] On the question of what kinds of actions *are* moral, see my *Ayn Rand's Normative Ethics*, which explains those major moral virtues that are the necessary means and manifestations of rational egoism. For further explanation of the distinct (although partially overlapping) domains of the questions of rights and of what *is* right, see *Moral Rights and Political Freedom*, pp. 18–23, and "Rights Conflicts: The Undoing of Rights," *Journal of Social Philosophy* 26, 2 (Fall 1995), pp. 141–158.

of force. It would make no sense to enter society without respecting that condition. Freedom is the sine qua non of a rational society – a society that it is rational for men to enter into because it allows them to flourish. Freedom does not guarantee that any particular individual will flourish or even that a given person will use his freedom wisely, in the attempt. It is a prerequisite, however. Correspondingly, a rational society is designed to ensure that men deal with one another through persuasion rather than coercion, through voluntary agreement rather than physical compulsion.

But I get ahead of myself. The point here is that if each man *is* an end in himself (Premise A), then each man is entitled to lead his life as he sees fit. He is entitled to be free.[29]

E. *Man Requires Government in Order to Protect His Right to Freedom*

For all of the reasons just presented, men need government. If reason *is* man's fundamental means of survival and if a prerequisite of the use of reason is freedom, and if each individual is an end in himself who is entitled to freedom of action, and if, as I discussed in section 2, people stand to gain incalculable riches from living in society with others, then it makes sense to establish an institution whose role is to protect the freedom that makes those values possible. While a person's exercise of reason always requires the absence of force (regardless of whether he is in a formal society), when people do wish to gain the advantages of society, a government dedicated to preserving their freedom

---

[29] I do not subscribe to the conception of rights as "side constraints" that is embraced by many libertarian thinkers. While it is true that any rightholder is morally obligated to respect the rights of others and is in that respect constrained (from trying to force others to do as he wishes), this is not what rights are *about*. To define rights in terms of constraints or even to feature that derivative aspect of rights is to miss their more fundamental nature and significance.

Consider: Why do human beings need rights? Why does the principle arise? Why should we refrain from forcing our will onto others in the way that rights declare? Answer: To protect individuals' freedom of action – which is necessary for individuals to be able to exercise their reason – which itself is necessary in order for individuals to be able to act in those ways that will advance their lives and well-being. This is the crucial, positive *good* that respect for rights delivers.

The notion that rights are essentially side constraints carries the undeniable taint of privation, loss, a price one must pay, with the tacit implication that a person would truly be better off if he were not under such inhibiting obligations. This is false, in my view. It fails to recognize the value of freedom in its enabling the benefits of rational action and the selfish value to me that results from others' being free, as well as from my own freedom. The side-constraints model mistakenly focuses on the indicated relationship *between* individuals ("hands off") without recognizing the good that is protected by men's honoring that relationship (their freedom of action) and all that that makes possible. My thinking about this notion has benefited from discussion with Onkar Ghate and Robert Mayhew.

is crucial. For beyond a very small scale, rights-respecting intercourse requires clear ground rules. Beneficial social existence depends on people's shared understanding of its requisite conditions, on their commitment to respect those conditions, and on an institution empowered to establish and enforce the exact rules by which they can do that.

A piecemeal, "each man for himself" mode of defense of rights might suffice in a tiny, homogeneous group in which disagreements were few and readily, rightfully resolved. The larger a group, the more diverse its members, and the more sophisticated their relationships (in forms of trade, for instance), however, the more natural it will be for conflicting expectations to arise. No sinister intentions are necessary for individuals sometimes to have honest disagreements about the exact lines of their respective authority and obligations. In these circumstances, it is necessary to have a single, recognized body authorized to make and enforce those rules of social conduct that will enable the society's members to maintain the freedom that makes their valuable interaction possible.

It is also important to appreciate that the government's role is not simply to punish those who have violated its rules, important though that is. The prevention of rights violations is at least equally critical. People are far better off when their freedom is steadily respected, without disruption, than when it is intermittent. While the capture and punishment of lawbreakers is certainly preferable to the alternative, better yet is the situation in which incursions on one's freedom themselves are rare. And for this reason, an important contribution of a proper legal system lies not simply in its after-the-fact response to lawbreaking, but in its advance issuing of valid rules spelling out the kinds of actions required to respect individuals' freedom. That is, a major part of a legal system's task is to identify exactly what individuals' spheres of rightful authority truly are and then to translate that into more specific rules by which those people could be effectively and rightfully governed. The greater the extent to which a legal system's rules are proper as well as efficiently enforced, the greater the actual freedom enjoyed by the people living under that legal system.

This does not entail that the correct identification of individuals' freedom will dictate a single acceptable set of laws. A variety of particular rule schemes may all be compatible with respect for individual freedom; in selecting between them, a legal system's responsibility is to adopt that set of laws which it rationally concludes will most effectively fulfill its function. (If one kind of law would be much easier to communicate or to enforce, for instance, without any loss to the freedom that laws are designed to protect, then it should choose that one.) In adopting its rules, a legal system must look both backward and forward: backward to ensure fidelity to the broad principle of rights that it is charged to safeguard; forward to the narrower question of specific means (laws and other mechanisms) that will enable it to do that most effectively. In those cases where alternatives equally satisfy both responsibilities, the alternatives are equally acceptable.

Not a Strict Transfer of Preexisting Authority

This observation points to a related feature of the authority of a legal system. What I am proposing is not a strict transfer of the very same authority that is held by private individuals, prior to a government's establishment, to that government. Rather, a proper government acquires special, new authority that did not predate it. Practical efficacy demands this. A legal system could not perform its work unless it held certain unique authority that is greater than the sum of the individuals' authority that it replaces. Lest this seem an unjustified extension of government power, let me explain.

As a private individual and outside the context of government, I am morally entitled to defend myself against others' violations of my rights. I may not go further than that, however, such as by coercively enforcing self-declared rules demanding others' compliance with my particular preferences about precisely *how* they respect my rights. As long as others respect my freedom of action, I may forcibly demand no more from them. A government, by contrast, may. Government is responsible for protecting the rights of many people, and this wider scope of responsibility also expands its authority in certain ways.[30]

Government's distinct function is to secure individuals' freedom. The protection of individuals' freedom is more than mere respect for their freedom, however; it requires more than noninterference. It is a positive undertaking. As such, it requires that the government anticipate likely kinds of incursions and take actions to forestall them. In order to safeguard all individuals' rights in an evenhanded way (since it has no basis for favoring some over others), a legal system will need to standardize its manner of handling discrete cases by adopting rules that demand a level of particularity in people's actions that no private individual would have the authority to impose. These rules might require that evidence or appeals in court be introduced in a particular format or on a specific schedule, for instance. They might require that a contract or child adoption conform to uniform criteria in order to be legally binding. In the absence of a legal system, it may be perfectly possible for one person to fully respect another's rights without having obtained two witnesses to a

---

[30] In certain ways, but by no means boundlessly. As ever, government legitimately enjoys only as much authority as is needed for it to fulfill its mission.

contract or having provided three photocopies of an affidavit. Nonetheless, once we seek the protection of a legal system, we must recognize that its effective governance requires more regularity in the particular means required to respect rights than would otherwise be permissible. In order to function as a single body whose rules must govern a tremendous number of people in a great variety of circumstances and whose rules must do so in a consistent, principled, objective manner, a legal system is licensed to demand greater particularity of conduct. Such tighter restrictions are the necessary means of its holding everyone to the same, proper standard.

The basic point, again, is that a legal system, because of its unique function and the means that are required to fulfill that function, acquires the moral authority to compel people in ways that private individuals, in personally defending their own rights, may not. Individuals' prelegal authority to defend their rights and a proper legal system's authority to *protect* individual rights are not perfectly symmetrical.[31]

And let me reiterate the broader claim of this fifth premise. For men to coexist profitably, they must coexist peaceably. More precisely, they must live force free – free of the initiation of force. In order for men to reap the values that life in society makes possible, they thus require an institution devoted to protecting their freedom from the initiation of force. They need a government possessing the authority to adopt appropriate laws and to forcibly compel compliance with those laws.

4. CONCLUSION

Because a legal system governs by force, it must enjoy the sanction of morality. While a given regime's power to compel obedience may be evident, the authority to do so requires a distinct, moral foundation. I have explained this authority as an outgrowth of the law's function.

---

[31] Despite this difference, it remains true that under an objective legal system, obedience to the law is in each person's interest. Just as my respect for others' rights is not a loss to be suffered, so my compliance with laws that are properly made and objectively administered is a net benefit for me. And the interest involved is far deeper than "stay out of jail" expediency. On the premise that freedom is a prerequisite for our ability to reason and to create objective values, anything other than an environment of freedom would impede individuals' optimal achievement of their well-being. When a legal system is objective in the three dimensions that I have emphasized (in its laws' substance, in laws' authority, and in its manner of administration), it is providing a profound value, enabling people to reap all the advantages that society makes possible. It would be personally counterproductive for any member of that society to act in ways that defy it.

The law's function, in turn, can be objectively ascertained. It is grounded in facts of human nature. It is not determined by polls of public opinion or decreed by a divine being; it is not a self-evident "read" from the cosmos or common sense. Rather, it is certain natural, inescapable facts about the conditions of human existence (specifically, man's need to reason and to be free of force, in order to be able to reason) that demonstrate the need for a government to perform a specific service: to protect individual rights to freedom of action. These facts provide the objective foundation for a legal system's authority.

To hold that authority, a legal system must confine its activities to those that are essential to its fulfilling its mission. It may only legitimately enact laws and adopt policies that fall within that mandate. Because it is created to perform a specific role, the function of the legal system is both the basis and the standard of its moral authority.

This clearer understanding of the moral authority behind the law should fortify our grasp of what an objective legal system is. Further, and more salient to judicial review, it should focus the context for understanding the meaning of law. For a law's valid meaning can extend no farther than the legal system's actual authority; no purported meaning that exceeded the system's authority could be properly enforceable.

Before delving into judicial review, however, we must complete the explanation of authority. While a legal system's moral foundation is crucial, a legal system does not operate as a direct order handed down from morality. A legal system comprises a complex network of practical mechanisms that actually exercise government power (numerous types of lawmakers, enforcement agencies, and arbitrators, for example, along with different divisions of police work, military and diplomatic work, etc.). These create another type of question about authority. Within a legal system, what is bedrock? What properly organizes and disciplines that system's components' exercises of their power? What determines whether a given police search yields evidence that is admissible in court, for instance, or whether a particular Environmental Protection Agency edict legitimately warrants enforcement? We must also understand distinctively legal authority, in other words. We turn to that in Chapter 5.

5

A Written Constitution – Bedrock Legal Authority

1. INTRODUCTION

Having identified the moral authority of law, we must next consider its legal authority. If we are serious about confining a legal system to exercise its power solely in the ways that are required for it to perform its proper work, it is important to identify exactly what constitutes the law that possesses the authority to govern. For an erroneous understanding of what *is* law and of the ultimate repository of a nation's law would permit unjustified uses of force – the direct breach of a legal system's moral authority. Observe, also, that disagreements over the meaning of law (the sort of dispute addressed by judicial review) often depend, in part, on differing assumptions concerning the authority of law. Or, to put it slightly differently, over the identity of the law that holds genuine authority. What *is* the actual law to be understood and applied? In short, the Rule of Law depends on clear knowledge of what the law is. Our aim in this chapter is thus to identify the ultimate arbiter of lawfulness. What is it, within a legal system, that should command final say? What should be bedrock in determining how, in fact, legal power may be used?

The question arises due to the naturally complex character of a legal system. A legal system is an intricate network consisting of numerous components responsible for different aspects of the government's overall mission. Different government offices make rules concerning such diverse realms as property, battery, immigration, child custody, religious freedom, international relationships, and military deployments. Each must decide how its rules will be made, how its officials will be selected, how its budget will be spent. It must adopt methods of communicating rules and of enforcing them and determine whether and how appeals of its actions will be considered. Which office governs a particular issue? What are the respective domains of the various offices and the relevant layers of decision-making authority?

On even such a quick survey, it is plain that within a legal system, disagreements will be inevitable. When such disagreements arise, what should be sovereign? Of the numerous agencies that have some claim to speak for the law, what are the boundaries of their respective authority and what should be respected as the law's last word, beyond further appeal? The clearer we can be in enunciating this, the fewer disputes will arise and the more efficiently the system can serve its function.

Obviously, the identification of legal supremacy will not eliminate hard cases or differences of opinion. Governance requires action, however, and proper governance requires the principled resolution of such questions. A legal system could not perform its work without an unequivocal arbiter. And because the legal system may act only within the bounds of its moral authority, an objective legal system must rest final legal authority in the manner that will best do that. Thus, our question: Where, within an objective legal system, should ultimate legal authority reside? What is the final law that the governed and governing alike are bound to respect?

The answer is: a written constitution. For this best serves the function of government. When properly made, a written constitution translates the mission and moral commitments of a government into legal practice by using those commitments to establish the government's specific powers and the boundaries around those powers.[1]

Today, amidst recent decades' flurry of constitution-making and constitution-revising around the world,[2] the merits of constitutional authority may not seem especially in need of defense. Does anyone really challenge it? Although few would directly deny the value of a written constitution, however, the propriety of its authority *is* threatened in an indirect yet potent way. Many people endorse a constitution *as well as* supplements which, in their actual use, can compromise a constitution's authority. A particular threat of this form, I think – and a threat to law's underlying moral authority – comes from the common law.

It may be jarring to think of common law as a threat. Historically, the common law has contributed numerous sound, useful features that are found in today's best legal systems. Many sensible, entrenched conventions

---

[1] The content of any particular constitution is obviously critical to whether or not it actually serves its moral purpose, but our aim here is simply to identify the form of legal authority that best accomplishes that purpose.

[2] Consider the establishment of post-Soviet republics, new states in the Balkans, fallout from upheaval in the Middle East, and new regimes in Africa, for instance. Latin American nations reportedly have a particular penchant for tinkering with their constitutions. "All Shall Have Rights," *The Economist*, March 15, 2014, pp. 15–16.

(concerning torts, contracts, free speech, and self-defense, for example) are the progeny of common law.[3] Precisely because of its constructive contributions, however, enthusiasts are sometimes seduced into assigning common law a greater title than it warrants. Therein lies the danger. Thus, I will frame our analysis of legal authority in terms of the relative merits of constitutional and common law.

In doing so, it is important to make a few things clear at the outset. As they actually developed, common law and constitutional law arose largely as means of dealing with different domains, private law and public law, thus they do not pose perfectly symmetrical alternatives.[4] And the two are rarely pitted as rivals, only one of which might be adopted to govern. The U.S. legal system, in fact, seems to benefit from both. (Indeed, the term "constitutional law," in this country, is often taken to encompass common law staples of legal doctrine and precedent as well as a constitution's text.) Yet common law is frequently invoked as carrying equal, if not greater, weight than the Constitution. We see this in a familiar kind of criticism of judicial decisions, namely, that they are insufficiently deferential to previous court rulings. Indignant complaints that the *Citizens United* ruling on campaign finance, for example, swept aside decades of precedent clearly imply that precedent should prevail. One routinely hears a host of court rulings, concerning everything from affirmative action and guns to gay marriage and voting rights, subjected to the same standard of evaluation, which presumes that precedent should sometimes trump the Constitution. Even the poster boy for strict adherence to the Constitution's text, Antonin Scalia, has referred to himself as an Originalist, but "not a nut," bowing to the presumed supremacy of precedent.[5] According to David Strauss, the U.S. legal system is most accurately characterized as a common law system in which precedent and past practices are as important as the Constitution itself.[6] Strauss also contends that the most impressive

---

[3] Certain practices in the administration of the law are also based on common law traditions, such as access to the courts and trial by jury.

[4] "Private" law refers, roughly, to that part of the law that governs relations between private citizens or groups rather than between citizens and the state. The law of torts and contracts exemplifies private law. For brief discussions of this distinction, see Raymond Wacks, *Law – A Very Short Introduction*, New York: Oxford University Press, 2008, pp. 36–37; Douglas E. Edlin, *Judges and Unjust Laws: Common Law Constitutionalism and the Foundations of Judicial Review*, Ann Arbor: University of Michigan Press, 2008, p. 77; and Brian Z. Tamanaha, *On the Rule of Law: History, Politics, Theory*, p. 56.

[5] Antonin Scalia, "On Interpreting the Constitution," The Wriston Lecture, given at the Manhattan Institute, November 17, 1997. His exact words: "I am an originalist. I am a textualist. I am not a nut." Retrieved from http://www.manhattan-institute.org/html/wl1997.htm.

[6] David Strauss, *The Living Constitution*, New York: Oxford University Press, 2010, p. 3.

achievements of U.S. constitutional law are the product of the "living" constitution that is the common law.[7]

For these reasons, then, I will explain the legal authority of a written constitution primarily by comparison with common law. In doing so, I certainly recognize the common law's considerable contributions. It is largely because of those contributions, in fact, that lining up the two can sharpen our appreciation of the distinct advantages gained by embracing a written constitution as the proper repository of final law.

The plan: I will begin, in Section 2, by explaining the basic nature of common law and sketching those considerations that most seem to counsel our allegiance. Section 3 will expose the common law's frailties – frailties particularly for its occupying the role of sovereign authority. Then in Section 4, I will elaborate on the significant values uniquely made possible by a written constitution. These should make plain its superiority and its necessity. Finally, I will consider the natural suggestion of hybrid legal authority, the thought that we should build on the best of constitutional and common law in combination to deliver objective law. Such a proposal, I will argue, falls prey to the same subordination of individual rights that is fatal to common law itself.

2. COMMON LAW AUTHORITY

A. *What Common Law Is*

The term "common law" is widely used to refer to a variety of closely related but distinct phenomena. For our purposes, it is most helpful to distinguish three principal senses of the term. "Common law" most often refers to either a historical system of governance that has been used in specific times and places; a method of reasoning used to resolve legal controversies; or the substantive legal doctrine that results from the use of that method.[8]

In the first, historical sense, "common law" designates a system of governance that is built not on a foundational, canonical text such as the U.S. Constitution, but on multiple traditions and precedents that acquire the character of law gradually and cumulatively, over an extended time.[9] The paradigm instance is Great Britain from roughly the twelfth century to the

---

[7] Strauss, *The Living Constitution*, p. 46.
[8] Edlin, pp. 22ff. Edlin offers a very helpful discussion, including additional, more finely grained distinctions between meanings of the term. "Common law" is also sometimes meant to encompass two or more of its possible senses, referring, for instance, both to a body of authoritative legal materials as well as the process of adhering to those materials in deciding cases.
[9] Strauss, *The Living Constitution*, p. 3.

present day (although the purity of its common law has been attenuated over
the last century). While the British never adopted a single, comprehensive
statement identifying legal bodies or powers that would serve as the final locus
of its law, the rulings issued in earlier controversies, along with a handful of
specific charters and acts, have been treated as the bases from which jurists
should extract principles of guidance for the resolution of present disputes.
(Those other materials include the Magna Carta of 1215, the Petition of Right
of 1628, the Bill of Rights of 1689, the Act of Settlement of 1701, and the Habeas
Corpus Act of 1679.)[10] Judicial opinions in previous cases are regarded as a
source of the law to be followed in the present.[11]

Integral to this system of governance is a particular method of reasoning
that is used to determine the meaning and proper application of law. This is
the second sense in which "common law" is often used – to name this mode
of reasoning.[12] When a legal system anticipates certain kinds of disputes and
adopts general rules to prevent them or to resolve them (in the form of
a legislative statute or agency regulation, for instance), courts are given a
straightforward procedure for deciding cases, namely: Follow the relevant
rule. The court must determine whether any legal rules apply to the case
before it, of course, and whether exceptional circumstances might alter a
rule's usual requirements, but if a rule does apply, the court's remaining task
is simply to determine exactly what is required for that rule to be obeyed
in that particular case. If a statute decrees that no alcohol may be sold on
Sunday, for example, and Johnson nonetheless sells alcohol on Sunday, he
has violated the law.

A common law system, by contrast, does not issue such advance directives
or preordain legal and illegal behavior. What jurists rely on, instead, are the
rulings and reasoning that courts have employed to resolve earlier cases. By
studying these, courts infer the salient principles. Rather than having courts
deduce from a general rule the appropriate application to a particular case,
the common law method relies on inducing lessons by analogy with other
cases. The law is articulated incrementally – literally, case by case – through

---

[10] For elaboration, see W.J. Waluchow, *A Common Law Theory of Judicial Review*,
New York: Cambridge University Press, 2007, p. 48. Still other of the British documents include
the Provisions of Oxford (1258), Provisions of Westminster (1259), Statute of Marlborough
(1267), Statute of Rhuddlan (1284), Instrument of Government (1653), Humble Petition and
Advice (1657), and Union with Scotland Act (1706).

[11] See Melvin Aron Eisenberg, *The Nature of the Common Law*, Cambridge, MA: Harvard
University Press, 1988, p. 1.

[12] Roscoe Pound characterized common law as "a mode of judicial and juristic thinking, a mode
of treating legal problems rather than a fixed body of definite rules," quoted in Edlin, p. 22.

an extended trail of discrete disputes, rather than through more sweeping, top-down, preemptive pronouncements.[13]

Finally, "common law" is also often used to refer not to a historical period or practice nor to a characteristic method, but to a substantive legacy: that body of legal conventions that emerge from the use of the common law method. That is, specific rationales that are repeatedly affirmed by courts to justify their rulings come to enjoy the status of law on this view. Insofar as these are regarded as proper guidance for future decisions that will apply the law, it is these that actually govern. The principle that a man should be permitted to plead his case in court, for example, or the idea that freedom of speech does not protect speech that poses a clear and present danger to others, or the idea that a man should not be punished for using force in self-defense, are offspring of common law. In this third sense, then, "common law" refers to the substantive legal doctrine that the historical reliance on common law has bequeathed to us.

These three senses are often mingled in discussions of common law. Since our purpose is to investigate the ultimate authority of law, it is the second and third senses that are most salient. For many people view the common law method as the proper means of determining what the law ultimately is. The reasoning and results of particular cases, on this view, are to be respected as legally sovereign. Thus, we are also interested in the doctrine that results from common law reasoning, since that is accorded the status of authoritative law.[14]

B. The Case for Common Law Authority

Why might one think that the common law – that the results of its distinctive judicial method – should enjoy final legal authority? While many legal thinkers would draw lessons from the common law without according it the throne of full sovereignty, it is important to recognize that many others do. In the view

---

[13] As Benjamin Cardozo characterized it, "The common law does not work from pre-established truths of universal and inflexible validity to conclusions derived from them deductively. Its method is inductive." Benjamin Cardozo, *The Nature of the Judicial Process*, 1921, New Haven, CT: Yale University Press, p. 22.

[14] It is accorded that status in practice, that is, when it is treated as an equal or superior to other law, if not always in explicit profession. David Strauss, however, makes this authoritative parity plain, as we will see presently.

While the ensuing discussion will use the term in ways that sometimes highlight one or more of these closely entwined senses, readers should have no problem in following the reasoning.

of "traditionalists," precedents can come to acquire authority at least equal to that of a formal constitution. As Strauss describes this view,

> If practices have grown up alongside the text, or as a matter of interpreting the text, or *even in contradiction of the text*, those practices too are entitled to deference if they have worked well for an extended time. An old precedent that has been accepted by subsequent generations is, under the traditionalist component of the common law approach, on a par with the text.[15]

This is a strong thesis. According to this view, "provisions of the text are no more entitled to obedience than any other longstanding practice." The "text of the Constitution is analogous to the holding of an earlier case."[16]

Strauss characterizes his own view as "rational" or "tempered" traditionalism: He would give precedent the benefit of the doubt, but not ironclad authority.[17] Yet the relative strength of his devotion to constitutional text and to common law is not fully clear. For in his more recent work, Strauss evinces great reverence for the common law. Law is a set of customs, he maintains, that acquire authority without any identifiable point of origin. The authority of the common law "comes from the law's evolutionary origins and its general acceptability to successive generations."[18] While Strauss would not discard the Constitution, he writes that "other things being equal, the text should be interpreted in the way best calculated to provide a point on which people can agree."[19] Thus, the authority of the text is attenuated by social attitudes. And he approvingly claims that our constitutional system has in fact become a common law system in which precedent and past practices are as important as the Constitution itself.[20]

Beyond the particulars of Strauss, what is important is that many people see real strengths in common law practices that warrant our according it legal authority. Let me briefly recount several of the specific considerations frequently employed to argue for its command.

First, because of its emphasis on deference to precedent, common law allegedly lends great stability to a legal system. Rather than having courts "fly solo" and reach decisions independently of other courts, the common law

---

[15] Strauss, "Common Law Constitutional Interpretation," *University of Chicago Law Review*, volume 63, no. 3, Summer 1996, p. 897, emphasis added.
[16] Strauss, "Common Law Constitutional Interpretation," pp. 898 and 899.
[17] See Strauss, "Common Law Constitutional Interpretation," pp. 895 and 879.
[18] Strauss, *The Living Constitution*, pp. 37–38.
[19] Strauss, *The Living Constitution*, p. 106.
[20] Strauss, *The Living Constitution*, p. 3. Waluchow also defends common law constitutionalism on the grounds of its attunement with democratic values. See *A Common Law Theory of Judicial Review*, Note 10 in this chapter.

practice of reaffirming past decisions serves to entrench the kind of constancy and predictability that are important elements of the Rule of Law. In this way, it seems also to serve justice.[21] Constancy can certainly foster people's perception of justice, which itself can strengthen a legal system's ability to do its job. That is, law that was less steady in its application – that fluctuated more erratically – would encourage the belief that we are in fact ruled by the subjective preferences of individual officeholders rather than by the steadfast application of abiding legal principles. This would naturally diminish people's inclination to respect the law. People are more likely to obey a legal system that they regard as basically just. And more important than the perception of the legal system's justice is the fact that through its adherence to prior rulings, the common law method more consistently delivers like treatment of like cases. This, its advocates argue, is essential to actual justice.

It is important to appreciate that advocates of common law do not necessarily endorse courts' passive acquiescence to absolutely any rulings that previous courts happened to serve up. Some of them view the common law, both in historical practice and as properly practiced today, as representing a deliberate effort to make a legal system ever more rational and more just. One of the common law's signature principles through the ages has been that "law ceases where reason ceases."[22] According to Edward Coke, a luminary in common law's historical practice, the common law may overrule acts of parliament on grounds of "common right and reason."[23] And an "integral feature" of all common law systems, according to Douglas Edlin, is the judiciary's obligation to resolve legal disputes in an effort to achieve justice.[24] In other words, many see the common law as a justice-furthering means of building the law.[25] While deference to common law could take on a more submissive character, at least some of its champions seek to preserve a commitment to proper principles.

A second line of support for common law is epistemological. Common law allegedly employs a realistic model of how human beings acquire knowledge. People learn in stages, through experience from particulars. Common law reflects the gradual and inductive character of learning and develops a legal system accordingly. Through its deliberate, case-by-case method, our body of law builds incrementally, as different voices add, subtract, and revise previous

---

[21] See Edlin, pp. 38–39, on the manner in which respect for *stare decisis* seemingly promotes a cluster of values, including predictability, reliability, equality, expediency, stability, impartiality, objectivity, and adjudicative integrity.

[22] Edlin gives the Latin formulation on p. 172.

[23] Coke, opinion in *Dr. Bonham's Case*, quoted in Edlin, p. 54.

[24] Edlin, p. 124.

[25] Edlin, pp. 112–113 and 114–115. Also see James Stoner, *Common Law Liberty*, Lawrence, KS: University Press of Kansas, 2003, pp. 10–16.

conclusions. It is, in short, a sensible procedure in light of how man actually gains knowledge.

Third and closely related, the common law approach evinces humility concerning the limits of anyone's ability to identify ideal law. Rather than assuming that great wisdom can be concentrated in a central rule-making body or document, it respects the wisdom that can be gained by drawing on many minds.[26] Somewhat in the style of crowdsourcing, advocacy of the common law method is premised on the belief that we are most likely to reach good rulings by drawing on the reasoning of a number of thinkers.[27] As Strauss casts it, common law is guided by attitudes of humility and cautious empiricism rather than by algorithm.[28]

Yet another flank of support claims that common law aptly reflects the actual character of our legal system. The common law method respects the design of the U.S. system, for instance, as a mutlicomponent network in which numerous parts perform discrete functions. Like a symphony played by an orchestra, the product results from the contributions of many. By refusing to plant final command in any single, disproportionately powerful voice, the common law best allows each to offer its distinctive value.

Common law methods are also realistic, allegedly, in another way. The law, as it is actually applied to govern individual cases, does not simply flow

---

[26] Cass Sunstein celebrates this feature in some of his work. See *A Constitution of Many Minds: Why the Founding Document Doesn't Mean What it Meant Before*, Princeton: Princeton University Press, 2009, and *One Case at a Time*, Cambridge, MA: Harvard University Press, 1999. Bruno Leoni also emphasizes this in *Freedom and the Law*, Indianapolis: Liberty Fund, 1991.

[27] The idea has ancient roots. Cicero reports that according to Cato the Elder (also known as Cato the Censor, 234–149 BC):

> The reason why our political system was superior to those of all other countries was this: the political systems of other countries had been created by introducing laws and institutions according to the personal advice of particular individuals like Minos in Crete and Lycurgus in Sparta, while at Athens, where the political system had been changed several times, there were many such persons, like Theseus, Draco, Solon, Cleisthenes, and several others.... Our state, on the contrary, is not due to the personal creation of one man, but of very many; it has not been founded during the lifetime of any particular individual, but through a series of centuries and generations. For he said that there never was in the world a man so clever as to foresee everything and that even if we could concentrate all brains into the head of one man, it would be impossible for him to provide for everything at one time without having the experience that comes from practice through a long period of history.
>
> Quoted in Leoni, *Freedom and the Law*, p. 88.

For use of this idea far beyond the legal realm, see James Surowiecki, *The Wisdom of Crowds – Why the Many are Smarter than the Few and How Collective Wisdom Shapes Business, Economics, Societies and Nations*, New York: Doubleday, 2004.

[28] Strauss, *Living Constitution*, p. 40.

from a unitary, authoritative text. Law does not directly speak its answers to specific questions. Rather, its meaning and its applications rest in ideas about the law that have evolved over time. Disputes are settled by the doctrine that has emerged from judicial reasoning in earlier cases. Much of contemporary tort law, for example, emerged from the resolution of unusual cases that had not been anticipated by rules set in advance. Legal standards of responsibility, accordingly, developed through the reasoning employed in those cases. The point is, common law allegedly provides the best way to understand our legal system's actual practices; descriptively, it paints a more accurate portrait than the alternatives. Even today, under a much revered constitution in the United States, when courts rule, the legal text is often secondary, playing only a marginal role in most Supreme Court opinions.[29]

Finally, a somewhat bolder claim is sometimes made. The merit of the common law allegedly lies not merely in its descriptive accuracy (assuming that it *is* descriptively accurate). It lies in the quality of its work. Common law can boast a strong track record. Its governance has delivered major contributions to estimable legal principles, as we have already noted, spanning such areas as contracts, tort liability, and free speech.[30] In the eyes of Strauss, most of the great revolutions in American constitutionalism have taken place not by formal amendment, but by the courts' sometimes bold analysis and use of previous court rulings to strike out for reforms.[31] Important advances in civil rights and gender equality are among the most conspicuous instances.[32] It is not the language of the Constitution, in other words, but ripeness of societal attitudes that most effectively brings about change. So this, too, is apparent reason to embrace common law authority.

3. THE INADEQUACY OF COMMON LAW AUTHORITY

Historically, the common law has undeniably made valuable contributions to objective law. These do not justify its occupying the position of ultimate legal authority, however. As I explain why not, bear in mind that my aim is not to debunk common law per se, but to guard against our overestimating its value and according it a role that it does not warrant. My concern is exclusively with

---

[29] Strauss, *Living Constitution*, pp. 33ff.

[30] Strauss attributes several entrenched conventions in free speech law (concerning obscenity, fighting words, and libel, for instance) to common law provenance. See chapter 3 of *A Living Constitution*. In a similar vein, see Stoner, chapter 2.

[31] Strauss, *Living Constitution*, pp. 33ff, and "Common Law Constitutional Interpretation," p. 884.

[32] Strauss, *Living Constitution*, pp. 125–132. Today, one might add gay marriage to his examples. More generally on this, see his chapters 4 and 6.

the authority that it should wield, as we investigate the locus of *ultimate* legal authority in a proper legal system. And were common law to hold final legal authority, either in whole or in part, the objectivity of a legal system would be undermined.[33]

A. Law's Stability

The first problems with common law's authority concern its purported stability. The stability actually provided by common law is much more modest than is often supposed. In limited circumstances, where wide agreement on the proper resolution of legal questions is the norm, common law rulings are most likely to enjoy a cordial reception and bring correlative stability. The more large and heterogeneous a society, however, the more frequent and more fierce people's differences about legal rulings are likely to be, defying the image of legal tranquility that common law apologists promise. Indeed, international law that attempts to govern a diverse "international community" is increasingly codified, for this very reason. The problem is not unique to societies that govern people of diverse belief systems, however. Even among those who share basic outlooks, disagreement is natural when the law confronts the genuinely difficult questions posed by new realms of human experience (property rights in cyberspace, for instance, or legal responsibility for certain uses of genetic technologies). In short, even if common law has at certain times engendered relative consensus and stability, it could not realistically claim to offer that benefit in most societies today. Intense criticisms of court rulings in the United States on a range of issues (medical care, affirmative action, etc.) amply testify to this.

Quite apart from the actual degree of stability found under any regime, however, a more serious problem lurks: The common law method overvalues stability. Its plodding pace of reform is complacent about rights infringements. This alone renders it ill-suited to command sovereign authority. Even if common law methodology does, in the famous phrase of Lord Mansfield, gradually "work the law pure,"[34] we cannot assume that the mistakes eventually corrected are petty inconveniences to those who are governed by them. The

---

[33] One could critique the arguments that we have just surveyed in much greater depth than I will here. Were our task an assessment of common law in its own right, I would challenge several of the assumptions in the very formulations that I have just presented. For our purposes, however, to deny that common law authority should reign supreme and to show the need for a written constitution, my critique will be more abbreviated – adequate to clear the path for my own account of legal authority, I hope, but not nearly as muscular as I believe as one could deliver.

[34] Mansfield, cited in Edlin, p. 8.

ponderous, piecemeal development of the law under a common law regime carries the cost of entrenching error and perpetuating injustice. While the common law may self-correct eventually, in the meantime, real people suffer the impact of the misuse of government power. Obviously, this possibility is not unique to the common law method; any type of legal regime might make mistakes and there will always be a "meantime" during which invalid exercises of legal power injure innocent people. The common law method, however, by leaving law's boundaries murky, the pace of reform slow, and the path of reform halting, tentative, and comparatively accidental, exacerbates this danger and inflicts avoidable damage to individuals' rights. Top-down directives – thoughtful, principled rules – would better serve the mission of government.

Strauss's contention that even under his tempered common law constitutionalism, "[o]ther things being equal, the [constitution's] text should be interpreted in the way best calculated to provide a point on which people can agree,"[35] is hardly reassuring. For it prizes consensus about a reading more than the validity of that reading agreed upon. And the obvious danger is that a society's consensus will be unjust – that people will agree about the acceptability of a law that violates individual rights, resulting in respect for a presumed legal authority that defies its reason for being. (It is possible that Strauss intends the "other things being equal" condition to block that possibility, but exactly what that clause excludes, and why, is unclear, and that very unclarity only compounds the problem. It is difficult to assess common law's claim to authority when the bounds of that authority remain obscure.)[36]

Common law methodology is, quite simply, too passive in correcting misuses of legal power to serve as the final repository of legal authority. It permits ongoing deviation from a legal system's moral authority. Despite the individually good ideas that it has sometimes offered, as a method, common law lacks a sufficiently deliberate, systematic means of trying to weed out error. The

---

[35] Strauss, *Living Constitution*, p. 106.

[36] Also consider Strauss's explanation of why the text of the Constitution is binding: due to "the practical judgment that following the text, despite its shortcomings, is on balance a good thing to do *because it resolves issues* that have to be resolved *one way or the other.*" (*Living Constitution*, p. 105, emphasis added) Here again, he treats the fact that an interpretation of text will resolve a dispute, rather than *how* it resolves it, as paramount. The propriety of the resolution in applying the existing law to specific individuals is secondary to the fact of the resolution, as such. This shows disdain for the proper function of government.

I discuss kindred problems concerning the pace of legal change and social consensus as secondary considerations in objective judicial review in "Reckless Caution: The Perils of Judicial Minimalism," NYU *Journal of Law and Liberty* volume 5, no. 2, 2010, pp. 347–393. Our discussion of Minimalism in Chapter 6 will also bear on this.

proper exercise of legal authority – the use of force – is not something we can patiently wait to "back into," whenever we happen to get around to it.

B. Law's Identity Is Not Fixed

A still deeper weakness explains why common law could not serve the ends of either stability or justice: under its rule, the law is not fixed. Law's identity is pliable, in ceaseless flow, evolving in ways that widen, narrow, reverse, leap ahead, or veer off along extraneous, tangential paths. Because common law's boundaries are neither firm nor explicit, judges are actually less constrained by it than they would be under certain alternative types of authority. Indeed, the "it" itself is nebulous, since common law is continually being made and remade.[37]

The point is not that human beings can only be bound by rules that are written. A person can be objectively obligated by unwritten moral principles, for instance, and might conscientiously abide by those obligations. The point, rather, is that under a method by which any law's scope and borders are avowedly fluid, that law can have no definite identity, whether written or unwritten.

One might suspect that this criticism is overstated. The common law does contain certain identifiable rules and doctrines, after all. Further, we all have a basic understanding of the instruction to abide by precedent. And surely, one would think, that instruction implies that certain judicial rulings would be out of bounds. So common law methodology does seem to offer meaningful guidance.

This response does not rescue common law from the problem, however. For legal professionals who seek the trail of precedent that govern in a particular case frequently differ over exactly what the salient precedent *is*. It is standard practice for attorneys to search for precedents that support competing sides of a case – and often, to find such conflicting precedents. Add to this the fact that different judges will be most impressed by different aspects of arguments in their search to find the governing precedents and it becomes plain that the common law method permits considerable variation in identifying the law and, correspondingly, in applying it. However much agreement on precedent may sometimes emerge, disputes about precedent are all too familiar. Common law's method is simply not as bound by "the past" – anonymous,

---

[37] Scholars have long noted the tension between common law governance and the Rule of Law ideal. Jeremy Bentham considered common law utterly untenable for this reason. See Frederick Schauer, "Is the Common Law Law?" *California Law Review*, volume 77, 1989, pp. 455–456, and Waluchow, pp. 197–199.

impersonal, uninflected by human judgment, and constraining – as its champions profess.

Note that nothing in this argument accuses either lawyers or judges of bad faith. For the problem stems from the nature of common law: The fact that its "law" is not conceived as definite rules of specified scope makes such variations in interpretation inevitable, even by those who most earnestly strive to be objective. The anchor of objectivity, the object that *is* the law and to which jurists are asked to be faithful, is, by the standards of common law jurisprudence, amorphous. As a result, differing understandings of law's proper application are inescapable.

And this feeds into a deeper problem that we have already glimpsed. When the common law commands final legal authority, individual rights become precarious.

Recall Strauss's contention that it has often been legislative acts and judicial rulings that have propelled important progress in the United States, rather than constitutional amendment.[38] This is true. It does not follow, however, that that mode of effecting such changes is *in principle* and in the role of a society's fundamental mode of governance equally as effective as formal rules deliberately adopted to issue clear direction and to accurately reflect the boundaries of the law's legitimate powers. In fact, thanks to the uncertain status and tentative grip of even the best of common law's insights, its rule is decidedly inferior. Under common law, the most enlightened advances are vulnerable to reversal precisely because their authority is never affirmed more decisively. When truths are stumbled upon in the comparatively hit-or-miss way of common law, their staying power can hardly be relied upon. (As one aspect of this, notice that a common law ruling cannot be asserted with any real muscle. However strong the language that justices might use to defend their ruling and articulate its intended sweep, *how* significant a given decision is is determined not by that court on the basis of its interpretation of the governing law. It is left, rather, to the choices of people who come later and who happen to consider somewhat similar cases. Consequently, while a given person living under common law might hope that certain court rulings will influence others down the line, his rights enjoy no more security than such hope provides.)[39]

---

[38] His major example is racial desegregation. See *Living Constitution*, chapter 4.

[39] A version of this problem might be thought to attach to other modes of governance, as well. For courts' rulings' actual practical effects are always dependent on the cooperation of other government officials, both at the time they are issued and in the future. Common law's weakness in this regard is distinctly acute, however, because common law renounces the kind of "check" that is provided by an enduring objective standard, such as a written constitution.

All of this reveals that, in more basic terms, the common law method fails
to acquit its responsibility to *the law*. It defers the determination of what constitutes law to a shifting cast of characters and to whatever continuities those
people might maintain – which has the effect of bestowing legal authority
on those people. De facto, they are empowered to establish the law. In this
way, common law governance offers a thoroughly social, subjectivist model
of legal authority. Its subjectivism is obscured by the large numbers of people
who might affirm many of its conventions. But the foundation of an objective legal system – the function for which a legal system holds the unique
coercive power that it does – is replaced by consensus. We are ultimately
governed by the agreement of enough people ("enough," loosely, to keep the
operation going).

A related observation exposes a different facet of this problem. Respect for
common law as definitive of what the law *is* expands "the law" to include
ancillary opinions, assumptions, and practices, all of which may sometimes
make valuable contributions to our understanding of the law, but which are
nonetheless not the very same thing as the law. Let me explain.

Respect for previous court rulings is often defended as means of respecting
the work of courts, which are presumably rendering the law in good faith.
Given that some body in a legal system must make a final determination of
what the law decrees and that the judiciary is the designated body, deference
to its rulings seems sensible. What is crucial to keep in mind, however, is that
courts' reasoning and rulings are attempts to clarify and apply the law; they are
not the law itself. Some of their attempts succeed, others fail. Yet even at their
best, their reasoning and rulings must not be mistaken for the very thing that
they seek to understand.

In a related vein, we must not mistake the power of courts for the authority
of courts. Frequently, a court rules in a particular manner and the people who
live in its jurisdiction respect its ruling as legally definitive, subsequently conducting themselves accordingly. In this way, the court's ruling governs how
legal power is actually used. This does not erase the difference between power
and authority, however. The fact that people comply does not show that they
should comply (should, on the basis of legitimate authority rather than practical expediency). We sometimes erroneously accord respect to people who do
not warrant it (in a family, in business, or on intellectual issues, for instance),
just as we sometimes grant people a power that they do not legitimately possess.

While no check is foolproof, a definitive standard provides far greater protection than does law
whose identity is avowedly fluid. Keeping the limits of government power "off the books" is
hardly the best way to secure individual rights or to provide objective law.

And people who hold power sometimes exercise it in ways that exceed their authority. The point is that these same possibilities arise in a legal system. The fact that a court characteristically does get its way does not entail that its way *is* the law. To believe that it is would revert to the view that might makes right and thus reject the entire question of authority as a sham.[40]

In short: While court rulings are necessary to resolve specific cases and while earlier rulings can sometimes illuminate how a present case should be decided, those rulings are not the equivalent of the law. Longstanding deference to certain rulings sometimes explains *how* a given law is typically understood and applied, but no interpretation of law is necessarily correct and no entrenched tradition of interpretation can dissolve the difference between interpretation and object of interpretation. The rulings of common law should not be confused with the law itself.

C. Selective Examples Obscure Governing Principles

A very different concern about common law concerns its touted track record. Advocates of common law authority are sometimes selective in the specific doctrines they cite to defend it. By cherry-picking the examples, we can burnish common law's image to a more alluring finish than is warranted. An objective assessment demands that we confront its missteps as well as its contributions.

In terms of Strauss's contention that legal progress is often achieved thanks to common law practices, it is important to appreciate that his argument is colored by the comparison class he has chosen. When contrasted with a system that fails to recognize equal rights for blacks, for instance, a judicial ruling that boldly changes this puts the common law method on the side of justice. When contrasted with a system in which the equal rights of blacks are already forthrightly proclaimed and explicitly incorporated into a constitution as a principle of enduring validity, however, the common law's episodic epiphanies lose their luster. Alongside common law's episodic embarrassments (such as the *Korematsu* ruling), they no longer support the idea that common law is the better *system*. *Korematsu v. United States*, 323 U.S. 214 (1944).

[40] A related point may be helpful to correct another possible confusion. There are good reasons to hold that the commission of one mistake by a court does not invalidate the authority of that court. A court that errs in good faith by misapplying the law in a particular case may properly retain its overall authority. It is important, however, to understand the reason for this. The explanation is not that a court's authority simply is whatever it says it is (that is, that authority flows from the exertion of power). A misuse of legal power, whether deliberate or inadvertent, remains a misuse, and it is important to name it as such. The reasons for an erring court's retaining authority stem, rather, from the difficulty of its task (objective evaluation within the highly complex enterprise of a legal system) as well as reasonable expectations of a fallible body. The immediate point is simply that one need not assume that legal authority is determined by legal power in order to accept this view of a court's authority.

The record of common law regimes is hardly uncheckered. They have not offered a steady stream of moral progress, the uninterrupted ascent of justice. It is misleading to focus, as discussions of common law typically do, so overwhelmingly on Great Britain, which represents the model's finest accomplishments. Not all common law societies have been as enlightened. The traditions nourished in some result in repugnant, rights-trampling practices (in regard to women or foreigners or methods of punishment, for instance). And the problems are not confined to savage societies. Within Anglo-American law, institutionalized discrimination that violated individual rights based on race and sex were long-standing common law conventions. Courts repeatedly upheld miscegenation and antisodomy laws, for instance. In an array of areas – from eminent domain to blue laws – dubious conventions have been sheltered by common law. Even in the areas of law often claimed to have most benefitted from common law, such as free speech, the merit of some of its contributions is, at the least, arguable. A long-standing convention under British common law, for instance, was the licensing of speech: A person required a government censor's permission before he could publish.[41]

It is no doubt true, as common law advocates emphasize, that individual cases can be a valuable source of knowledge from which we should stand ready to learn. Cases are not a source exclusively of knowledge, however, and moral enlightenment is not the necessary result of the common law's methods. Once we recognize the varying merit of particular common law doctrines, it is instructive to consider: In those regions in which common law methodology has offered positive advances, what drove the value that it provided? What was responsible for its contributions?

The answer, essentially, is rational philosophy – rational beliefs concerning the pivotal moral and political principles. In the case of Great Britain, the evolution of common law was guided by the people's commitment to critical moral ideas. It

---

[41] While this practice was initiated by the Crown, generations of courts reinforced it. In the United States, the courts have introduced differing levels of protection for speech of differing types. Political speech, for example, is typically seen as especially worthy of protection (more so than artistic or commercial speech, for example) because of its relationship with government policy. Strauss implies his condemnation of the prior restraint practice, while he applauds the now conventional distinctions between strengths of legal protection afforded to different types of speech (*Living Constitution*, pp. 75–76). I, by contrast, have never heard a convincing basis for providing an individual greater legal protection, or less, depending on his particular exercise of his rights. As long as a person's speech *is* an exercise of his rights (and as such, does not interfere with any other person's rights), whether he speaks profoundly, tritely, or numbingly boringly about politics, theater, business, or the weather is not the concern of the law. The immediate point is obviously not this aspect of speech law. It is the broader, inconvenient truth that what constitutes a laudable convention of common law is itself quite contentious.

is no accident that those who have studied British common law repeatedly cite its devotion to reason and to justice, to principles of equity and the "natural rights of Englishmen."[42] Appeals to such principles testify to the need for a moral basis to ensure the propriety of the legal system. Common law traditions detached from a moral compass are nothing to celebrate. For well-intentioned judges and salutary traditions are not sufficient to safeguard individual rights.[43]

The larger point is that the value that has been generated in any common law system arises not from those features that distinguish it as common law – from the fact that legal doctrines emerge incrementally, bubbling up from scattered cases rather than issuing from principled design. Rather, the value in common law has resulted from the extent to which courts and conventions have embraced appropriate principles, whether self-consciously or not. All that is admirable and worth emulating in common law stems from its devotion to reason and to rights, from its devotion to individuals' equal freedom and correlatively, to individuals' equal standing before the law. The common law has been good, in short, insofar as it has served the proper purpose of an objective legal system.

D. The "Wisdom" of the Common Law

All of this justifies our rejecting the notion that common law should enjoy final legal authority. Nonetheless, the fact that the value of common law stems from its reliance on certain principles also suggests serious shortcomings in its

---

[42] Recall our earlier discussion of these in section 2 and Notes 21–24 in this chapter. In the words of Coke, "Reason is the life of the law" (quoted in Edlin, p. 64). Also see Edlin, pp. 54, 67–68, 74, 84, 122–123.

[43] For this reason, I view Strauss's contention that the most impressive achievements of American constitutional law are actually the product of the common law (p. 46) as exactly the reverse of the truth. Courts have delivered some brave, farsighted rulings that broke from long-standing, egregiously unjust conventions, but the propriety of these rulings stemmed not from *their* having issued them, but from their substantive merits. And when a court does "get it right" in regard to a specific meaning of law, that must be affirmed through the prism of the relevant principles. It is only when it is that a legal system's mission – the security of individuals' rights – is truly served. Unless the full basis for a good decision is directly recognized and affirmed, it may prove merely a passing fancy of transient value.

None of this is to minimize the courage of certain courts or the enormously beneficial results of some such rulings. And it was, of course, the power that courts hold that enabled them to bring about these results. My point, though, is that the *propriety* of the great legal advances is not a product of the peculiarly common law character of certain rulings. It is, rather, a function of the underlying principles of the relevant laws being more properly understood than they previously had been. And if courts' occasionally truly insightful, convention-breaking rulings are to be embraced as real achievements of a legal system, they should not be left in the murky, fluctuating tides of common law. Their propriety must be solidified in the terms of a constitution, as I shall discuss in section 4.

portrait of knowledge. So let me make a few observations about those before concluding this critique.

First, defenders of common law tend to exaggerate the "wisdom of crowds" and its role in forging a proper legal system. (In this context, that phrase refers to the ideas generated by both contemporary crowds and historical ones – that is, the people whose beliefs were represented by the centuries of tradition, conventions, and precedents which common law champions.)[44] Large numbers of individuals certainly can usefully contribute to our understanding of the proper application of law, and historically they clearly have contributed. The value to a legal system of crowd knowledge, however, stems not from its crowdy-ness – from the number of minds supporting an idea – but from the validity of its underlying logic: *Is* this the objective way of respecting the principles inherent in our legal system, or not? Collaborative products are not *necessarily* more worthwhile than solo efforts. And it is individuals who must logically assess the verdicts of crowds – by reason, rather than by number.[45]

A second epistemological issue is more basic. Contrary to the claims of some, common law does not reflect an accurate portrait of the way in which human beings acquire knowledge – at least, not of the process by which it can ultimately be held *as knowledge*. While the inductive learning prized by common law methodology generates one type of knowledge, it does not exhaust the field. And it is not sufficient to pilot an objective legal system. Although much knowledge begins through the sort of individual observations that are featured in common law reasoning, this is, literally, where it begins. Observations of particular concretes are at best preliminary, an embryonic stage on the path to knowledge which further requires the deliberate, objective integration of such observations with preexisting knowledge, in order to form valid general principles.[46]

Under the common law methodology, judges rely heavily on reasoning by analogy, comparing one case with others in order to determine the proper resolution of the case before them. How is a judge to draw lessons from those cases that he considers, however? And which cases should he consider? What makes *these* cases similar and all those that he does not consider dissimilar? As we all know, distinct incidents tend to be alike in certain respects and unalike in others.

---

[44] The term comes from the book by Surowiecki, cited in Note 27 in this chapter.

[45] Strictly, there can be no knowledge held by a group that is not the same in its basic character *as knowledge* as the knowledge attainable by an individual. The same essential standards govern all genuine knowledge, regardless of who or how many people might hold it.

[46] For a good discussion of the crucial role of integration in forming inductive knowledge, see David Harriman, *The Logical Leap: Induction in Physics*, New York: Penguin, 2010.

Without going into detail, the point should be plain (and I am hardly the first to notice it).[47] Two or more cases can only be compared *by some yardstick*, in terms of specific characteristics. Any conclusion drawn by analogy on the basis of distinct cases necessarily employs a standard (at least implicitly) by reference to which similarities are detected and conclusions are drawn. If a given legal conclusion is to be valid, then use of that standard must be valid. But we can only establish that by appeal to deeper, wider premises.[48]

Moreover, when the lesson drawn by a court in a particular case is valid and truly should inform analysis of future legal questions, we must understand the underlying principle responsible for this. A court must distinguish decisions whose legitimacy is local to the case at hand from those of wider validity. Our observation earlier that precedent can be a source of error as much as of knowledge simply underscores the fact that experience *by itself* does not teach anything. Awareness of a long trail of judicial rulings does not imprint knowledge on a person, ensuring his grasp of all the right lessons from those cases. Whether or not the particular conclusion that a jurist draws from such history is valid depends on the premises that he accepts and the inferences that he draws. In short, the common law method does not, in the end, accurately depict how knowledge is acquired. It is too partial and too superficial to model how a belief attains the status of knowledge.

My final observation returns us to a more fundamental issue. Even if the wisdom of the common law is exaggerated by some of its advocates and is, strictly speaking, a misnomer, the contributions to legal knowledge that have arisen through the use of common law reasoning cannot be gainsaid. What is crucial to our inquiry, however, is the fact that wisdom, however vast, does not bestow authority. Knowledge does not alter law. Knowledge even of better ways of shaping a given nation's law does not license the substitution of that knowledge for the law. Such knowledge should naturally be used to reform the law, through legally authorized means. But it is a mistake to treat superior knowledge as sufficient to alter what the law is and where a legal system's final authority rests.

Obviously, a legal system that is best equipped to fulfill its function will draw knowledge from whatever resources provide it and will remain open to

---

[47] See, for instance, Ronald Dworkin, "In Praise of Theory," in *Justice in Robes*, Cambridge, MA: Harvard University Press, 2006, pp. 65–72. Dworkin observes that "analogy without theory is blind," p. 69.

[48] As a simple example: The observations that Green's use of force against Singh was taken in self-defense and that Morales's use of force against Johnson was taken in self-defense and that this similarity between the two cases is pertinent depends on the wider belief that force used in self-defense occupies a different legal status than does force used for predatory purposes.

revision, should it discover its own deficiencies. My critique does not deny that we can learn from the practice of common law. It does reject the elevation of common law to the throne of sovereign legal authority, however, for the reasons we have explained and because of the distinct benefits made possible by a written constitution. So let me now turn to those.

4. A WRITTEN CONSTITUTION AS ULTIMATE LEGAL AUTHORITY

The moral authority of a proper, objective legal system, we saw in Chapter 4, rests in its serving the purpose of government – specifically, the protection of individual rights. Legal authority is derivative from a government's moral authority and the legal authority of a given regime must respect its moral boundaries.[49] A written constitution that serves as the single, overt, definitive repository of a system's ultimate law is the best means available for doing that – for fulfilling the function of government while constraining the needed legal power from exceeding its mandate.

It is easy for those of us in the United States, because we live under a constitution that has been emulated the world over, to underestimate the accomplishment that an essentially sound constitution represents. A proper constitution is a tremendous intellectual achievement. It is not merely a compendium of previous rules and rulings that have proven popular, but the product of discriminating thought concerning the fundamental purpose of government, the specific powers that a government should possess in order to fulfill that purpose, and the best means of implementing those powers in the actual mechanisms of an operating legal system. Constitution writers must have both the expansive vision to identify the range of activities

---

[49] In the founding period, these convictions concerning the purpose of government and a government's moral authority determining the legitimate extent of its legal authority were ubiquitous, manifesting themselves in numerous forms. James Madison held that a majority in a society "may do anything that could be *rightfully* done, by the unanimous consent of the members," but "the reserved rights of individuals ... are beyond the legitimate reach of sovereignty" (quoted in Timothy Sandefur, *The Conscience of the Constitution: The Declaration of Independence and the Right to Liberty*, Washington, DC: Cato, 2013, pp. 6–7, emphasis in original). Thomas Jefferson observed that "no man has a natural right to commit aggression on the equal rights of another ... and this is all from which the laws ought to restrain him" (quoted in C. Bradley Thompson, "On Declaring the Laws and Rights of Nature," *Social Philosophy and Policy* volume 29, no. 2, Summer 2012, pp. 124). One also finds express affirmation of the purpose of government as the protection of individual rights in many state constitutions of the day. See Scott Gerber, *To Secure These Rights: The Declaration of Independence and Constitutional Interpretation*, New York: New York University Press, 1996, pp. 90–92. New York State, Gerber reports, adopted the Declaration of Independence as its preamble, p. 92.

that an objective legal system needs to perform as well as the penetration to recognize the practical ramifications of its powers being assigned in one particular way rather than another. They must consider the different character of a bicameral or unicameral legislature, for instance, or the effects of placing war powers with an executive or spending powers with a legislature or the different reasons why it might be advisable to require a simple majority for the enactment of certain types of laws and a higher threshold for other types. Numerous such questions confront them. In answering, framers must at once maintain a mountain-top perspective on the essential, proper work of a legal system, keen to all of its major responsibilities, while also, in determining how these can best be accomplished, keeping each of the specific powers that it creates riveted to the system's fundamental reason for being. They must be guided throughout by the legal system's mission of protecting individual rights.

The basic challenge is to create a legal system that holds enough power to be effective, but not so much as to exceed its moral authority. The more intricate challenge is to identify the specific instruments through which this can be done. Among other things, constitution makers must anticipate unclarities and possible tensions between different organs of the legal system and clearly delineate respective tiers and domains of authority. While a common law judge must, to resolve a given dispute, determine which other cases are relevantly comparable and which precedents to honor, the construction of a constitution brings such reasoning to a dramatically higher conceptual plane. It requires sophisticated reasoning about the best arrangements *in principle*, in all similar cases. Those crafting a constitution must consider every possible power of government and action of its agencies as *of a kind*, identifying the appropriate kinds of powers for a government to possess based on a full, clear-sighted grasp of the implications of affirming a given principle not only for a case at hand, but for countless unique circumstances.[50]

The ambition of a constitution, in other words, is far greater than that of a given common law ruling, and the demands of writing a proper constitution are correspondingly much greater. The result, however, is inordinately more valuable.

---

[50] As Ayn Rand observed in an interview, "It is not enough to agree on principles. Holding the right political principles does not tell you automatically how to put them into practice. It does not tell you what institutions must be established to preserve freedom.... The job of keeping a country free is very complicated, and a constitution is indispensable." Rand, quoted in *Objectively Speaking: Ayn Rand Interviewed*, eds. Marlene Podritske and Peter Schwartz, New York: Lexington Books, 2009, p. 44.

Notice that, when compared with the governance of a written constitution, common law methodology is quite primitive.[51] And its reasoning by analogy without full identification of the justifying principles is simply not the timber from which to build a durable, objectively constrained legal authority. The common law's diffuse and provisional character and the forever-uncertain status of the law that emerges from it keeps it from reliably serving the legal system's function. Any genuine contributions that individual common law rulings might offer, as we have seen, remain vulnerable as long as their legal propriety is so tentative. In light of this, it makes much more sense to integrate our knowledge of proper legal principles and solidify our commitment to their authority by adopting the framework of a written constitution to serve as sovereign law.[52]

Historically, it stands to reason that as the concept of individual rights gradually came to be more clearly understood over the centuries, our understanding of the proper relationship between the government and the individual and correlative beliefs about adequate forms of legal authority would be affected. While Britain's common law and unwritten constitution had provided admirable protections in the progressive strengthening of individuals' legal status, the sharper identification of rights as grounded in the individual rather than as privileges granted by the crown made it more logical to embrace a formal, definitive statement of this, to protect these rights more robustly. Indeed, the

---

[51] I stress: its *method* is relatively primitive; some of its deliverances have been sophisticated. John David Lewis observes the more advanced conceptual work demanded of those who write a constitution than is demanded of those who write legislation in "Constitution and Fundamental Law: The Lessons of Classical Athens," *Social Philosophy and Policy* volume 28 no. 1 (2011), pp. 25–49. Yet even legislation drafting is more demanding, in certain respects, than the case-by-case rulings of common law.

[52] Rand took a dim view of the common law's suitability for contemporary governance. In an extemporaneous answer during a post-lecture question period in 1972, she observed,

Common law is good in the way witchdoctors were once good: *some* of their discoveries were a primitive form of medicine, and to that extent achieved something. But once a science of medicine is established, you don't return to witchdoctors. Similarly, common law established – by tradition or inertia – some proper principles (and some dreadful ones). But once a civilization grasps the concept of law, and particularly of a constitution, common law becomes unnecessary and should not be regarded as law.

(A response given at the Ford Hall Forum, 1972, quoted in *Ayn Rand Answers: The Best of Her Q&A*, ed. Robert Mayhew, New York: New American Library, 2005, p. 44, emphasis in original.)

  Notice that those who write a constitution face some of the same questions that confront a common law judge, but they must address them on much deeper terms. Constitution writers must, in effect, consider the question of what *should* be treated as binding precedent, answer on the basis of law's fundamental function, and shape the powers and interactions of government bodies accordingly.

American revolutionaries' break from Great Britain was animated, in part, by the parties' differing conceptions of what a proper constitution is and should provide.[53] In defending the superiority of a formal constitution, John Dickinson captured the basic idea in a 1768 pamphlet. A free people, he wrote, are "not those over whom government is reasonably and equitably exercised, but those who live under a government so constitutionally checked and controlled that proper provision is made against its being otherwise exercised."[54]

Firm rights require firm protections. A written constitution most effectively secures them.

Even apart from any thought of common law, the basic fact is that the question of proper legal authority must be guided by the purpose of the legal system and the freedom of action that is at stake. As long as we steer our thinking by these, the virtues of a written constitution become evident. For a written constitution honors these values on a number of fronts: It makes the identity of law *firm* and *fixed*. It correspondingly makes the law more *knowable* and thus better able to *guide*. It is less susceptible to conflicting interpretations and thus more likely to be *applied consistently*. Even more importantly, it is best suited to *govern properly*, in accordance with the moral authority of a legal system and the reason for which it exists. Let me elaborate.

To claim that under a written constitution, law's identity is firm and fixed is not to say that constitutional law is immune either to differing interpretations or future change; it is to say that at any given time, the law has a definite character. People might understand it or misunderstand it, but there is an *it* to be understood and honored. And the knowledge that there is a definite law is likely to engender more strenuous efforts to identify what that law is so as to follow it. In this way, constitutional fixedness bolsters the integrity of the legal system by fostering law's more consistent application.

A written constitution also makes the law more knowable. It is more clearly communicated to the governed and governing alike, thereby reducing the incidence of conflicting understandings. Some disagreements will still arise, of course, but the clarity of a single voice explicitly stating the law minimizes the ground for reasonable disagreement. This is beneficial not only for purposes of planning (enabling people to know what legal treatment to expect). It also means that, to the extent that a constitution is a sound one that establishes the sorts of powers and safeguards that it should, that legal system will

---

[53] For an illuminating discussion, see C. Bradley Thompson, "Revolutionary Origins of American Constitutionalism," in *History, On Proper Principles: Essays in Honor of Forrest McDonald*, eds. Stephen M. Klugewicz and Leonore Ealy, Wilmington, DE: ISIS Books, 2010, pp. 1–27.

[54] Dickinson, "Letters from a Farmer in Pennsylvania," quoted in Thompson, p. 23; I modernized punctuation and spelling.

better perform its work. The stated law will more efficiently guide people to
the proper kind of behavior – that is, to the sort of actions that the protection
of rights demands. Less friction in understanding the law means that a legal
system is both better able to guide people and better able to guide them *to* the
appropriate course of rights-respecting action.

A further advantage of a written constitution: The more that a government's
laws and their proper application are thought about in advance, contemplated
at a distance from the pressures of particular cases (the locus of common
law), the more likely the conclusions are to be uninfected by peculiarities of
isolated disputes. Addressing the question of good law from the more comprehensive perspective of a constitution better positions us to make law in a
manner that adheres to the foundational principles of the legal system as a
whole. In adopting a written constitution to serve as bedrock legal authority,
a legal system accepts the responsibility of abiding by the reason for which it
enjoys power. Under a constitutional framework, we more directly engage the
proper governing principles and certify our commitment to those principles
as reigning not just for the day, but for all seasons – for all cases of the same
basic kinds. As Benjamin Cardozo put it, a constitution states "not rules for
the passing hour, but principles for an expanding future."[55]

In all these ways, a constitution significantly promotes the integrity of a
legal system. Without a constitution, deviations and inconsistencies in the
application of law are inevitably much more likely, since the law's identity
is so much more difficult to pin down. Even when common law judges seek
to ground their rulings in broader legal principles, because their focus is naturally on narrower bands of cases, they are less likely to identify those principles as carefully or as deeply as they would be led to, had they been directly
contemplating the principles that should cover *all* cases of the same type as
well as which types, themselves, are properly subject to legal control. The
construction of a constitution simply demands more basic and more principled thought concerning the mission and correlative mechanics of proper
law. Thus the point is not simply that a constitution better serves a legal system's internal integrity. More fundamentally, a written constitution is a better
means of fulfilling a legal system's proper role.

In Chapter 2, I explained the objectivity of a legal system as turning on
three basic issues: what a legal system does, how it does it, and the authority by

---

[55] Cardozo, *Nature of the Judicial Process*, p. 83. A constitution is built to last as well as to
have broad scope. The U.S. Constitution's imposition of formidable conditions required
for its amendment reflects the conviction that this most fundamental form of law should be
made and altered by an especially thoughtful process. The power of the law, and the stakes,
demand this.

which it does what it does. While this chapter's concern fastens on the third, it is clearly closely entwined with the *how*: In what form should ultimate authority be constituted? In what mechanism should it be situated? The standard for answering remains the same as it is for every dimension of law: the purpose of government – the specific function that a legal system is properly created to fill.

We have also seen (in Chapter 3) that the Rule of Law ideal demands that a society's law be given a determinate identity that is communicated to all. This is necessary, at least, if *it* is truly to govern. This condition is certainly not sufficient to provide an objective legal system, but it is a prerequisite. Reliance on legal conventions, sound as some of them may be, is not the best means of fulfilling the law's function. Individual rights are far more secure when the powers by which they are to be protected are conceived in terms of fundamental principles, thought through in terms of their practical implementation, and then carefully articulated. For the purpose of safeguarding rights, such systematic deliberation is critical. By imposing firm, philosophically considered limits on government power, a written constitution best disciplines a legal system to adhere to its mission, best guards against its exceeding its moral authority, and best enables it to accomplish its mission.[56]

While I have stressed the significant advantages of locating ultimate legal authority in a written constitution, it is important to recognize the limitations of such governance. A constitution is neither omniscient nor infallible and does not provide a comprehensive set of answers to all possible questions concerning its application. Even under an essentially good constitution, thought will always be needed in order to properly apply it. (We will say much more on this when discussing judicial review.) Fresh insights may sometimes advise altering the constitution or traditional understandings of its proper application. Nonetheless, my point remains that when we *have* identified the foundational principles of an objective legal system, responsible government demands that we affirm our abiding commitment to these in the clearest available terms, with the formal institutionalization that a written constitution alone can provide.

The proper exercise of a government's moral authority – a legal system's allegiance to its reason for being and its fulfillment of its mission – demands clear statements of legal power's purpose and parameters. To restrict legal power to its rightful exercise, we must articulate (in broad but practicable terms) the legitimate means of exercising that power. No device can assure

---

[56] Todd Zywicki discusses aspects of this in "The Rule of Law, Freedom, and Prosperity," foreword to *Supreme Court Economic Review*, volume 10, University of Chicago, 2003, pp. 1–26.

that the people holding the legal reins will use them as they should. Rulers might defy the limits set by a constitution as much as they might defy the boundaries of common law, of the will of God, or of any other presumed authority. A document that crystallizes the proper guiding principles of an objective legal system and that translates those principles into specific rules for administering the law's power are the best safeguards available to us, however. A written constitution is the best means of administering objective law.[57]

5. A RECONCILIATION?

Given that common law has offered considerable wisdom over its course, one might naturally wonder about a hybrid system of shared authority. Perhaps legal sovereignty need not rest entirely with either common law or a written constitution. As we noted earlier, few today would suggest that we abandon a written constitution and simply respect common law, instead. In fact, the current U.S. legal system seems to be an amalgam: the rule of a canonical constitution substantially supplemented by practices delivered by common law. Don't we view both as authoritative? And doesn't that offer the best of both possible worlds?

The fatal problem with any such attempt to combine the two rests in a legal system's need for resolution – and more fundamentally, in objective law's need for resolution on the proper grounds. By its nature, *final* authority cannot be divided. Subordinate tiers and interlocking spheres within a legal system are unproblematic, as long as their exact jurisdictions and relationships are clear. Ultimate authority itself, however, cannot be equivocal. For a legal system's ultimate arbiter to be less than decisive would defeat its point, leaving open the very questions that it is charged to answer. It would prevent that system from accomplishing its work. When long-standing common law holds that mixed race couples should not be legally permitted to marry and a constitution reflecting objective legal principles holds that they should, what is to be done? Notice that the problem here is twofold. The hybrid ruler would not be able to resolve cases without the aid of some further considerations and it would not be able to resolve cases in a manner that reliably respects the proper principles of governance.

While it is true that, in the unfolding of history, we have acquired many sound beliefs about proper law from both common law and constitutional

---

[57] I discuss various aspects of constitutional government in the lecture "Constitutionalism: The Backbone of Objective Law," presented before members of the Norwegian Progress Party, Oslo, May 14, 2014. Lecture on file with author.

practices, it does not follow that joint, shared authority is the best means of serving a legal system's function. Indeed, it is hard to know how this seemingly modest proposal would actually work. *How* would authority be shared? In cases of conflicting directives from the two types of authority, which would hold sway? We can easily imagine variations on the interracial marriage example. Common law and constitutional provisions could (and often do) point to conflicting resolutions concerning suffrage, modes of punishment, treatment of the mentally ill, uses of executive power, and in a host of other disputes. Would proper resolution depend on the nature of the conflict, or on the nature of the issue in question? Why would a constitution reign in one case and common law in others? On what basis would their domains and rank be determined? And if these were not predetermined, would such a coalition authority be able to actually rule? Worse, any compromise of the proper principles in deference to common law traditions would be a betrayal of the legal system's moral authority. For a legal system's mission is not the protection of individual rights *as tempered* by traditional beliefs about those rights.

One could obviously attempt answers to the questions I have posed, but none could escape the basic problem. The character of common law governance is fundamentally antithetical to that of a written constitution. The common law's comparatively accidental, patchwork, forever-tentative refusal to commit to the law's definite identity and the fluid "law" that results cannot be reconciled with the governance of a written constitution, which reflects the clear identification of an objective legal system's most basic purpose and principles and expresses these by means of firm, stated rules (which, among other things, set boundaries around the uses of legal power).

The fact that respect for a judicial precedent has, at times, helped move us toward a superior legal practice sometimes misleads people, I think, into supposing that the common law is equally valid, in principle, and thus ought to be accorded final authority. This does not follow, however. While a sound judicial precedent might signify the moral superiority of a specific insight over the constitution that is in force at a certain time or over the theretofore dominant understanding of that constitution, it does not demonstrate that the common law as such warrants legal authority. To the extent that the substance of common law (in some of its particular judicial rulings or doctrines) rests on reasoning that should, in fact, be applied to other cases, it should be adopted not because those rulings are the *originators* of legal authority; not because they are the most fundamental source or determinant of that authority. Rather, good common law reasoning warrants respect when and insofar as it adheres to the objective principles of a proper legal system – principles that are better respected when systematically sought, identified, and subsequently incorporated into a formal, written constitution. Common law "authority" is derivative from the antecedent authority of objective law. Properly, common law does not speak in its own voice, but simply articulates the voice of preexisting truths that independently warrant respect.[58]

Finally, it is important to recognize that however innocently intended the suggestion of hybrid legal authority might be, hyphenated constitutionalism can be as corrosive to objective law as open opposition to constitutional governance. A number of modifications of constitutionalism have been suggested in recent years (including "common law constitutionalism," "living constitutionalism," "justice-seeking constitutionalism," "popular constitutionalism," and "democratic constitutionalism").[59] While not every type of hyphenated constitutionalism would sabotage a constitution's authority,[60] any support for a constitution that is coupled with an *equally weighty* obligation to serve some other ends (such as the democratic will of popular constitutionalism) can only work against a proper constitution's ability to perform its function. Commitments that are equal on paper are unequal in practice, where one or the other must rule in order to resolve any particular case. For as long as common law and constitutional instruction coincide, of course, no problem arises, but the possibility of their diverging creates the need to establish the supremacy of one or the other. And the deeper, moral authority of law – a legal system's reason for being – demands that the proper principles, as incorporated into a written constitution, reign supreme.

The upshot is, while the common law can be a useful auxiliary in clarifying the demands of a legal system, it should hold no authority of its own. At most, it is more like a junior partner than a coequal. For no amalgam of common law authority and constitutional authority can successfully serve the law's proper purpose.

6. CONCLUSION

In this chapter, I have argued that the ultimate authority within a proper legal system should reside in a written constitution. By setting it against governance by common law (a system that has fostered numerous valuable practices over the years), we have seen that a written constitution offers unmatched

---

[58] Edlin discusses the relationship between common law and constitutional authority, pp. 84ff and 87–88.

[59] In addition to Strauss and Edlin, see, for instance, recent work of Akhil Amar, Larry Kramer, and Jack Balkin.

[60] The exact threat to objective law depends on the exact meaning and content of each, as well as on how they are defended by their different advocates.

protections. There is no substitute for the sophisticated intellectual integration of principles that a constitution represents and, correspondingly, no substitute for the objective, firm identity that a written constitution gives to the law, with all of the attendant benefits of clarity, surety, consistent application, and so on, that enable it to protect individual rights most muscularly.

My aim has not been to condemn common law as such, but to deny the proposal (which we encounter implicitly more often than expressly, particularly in widespread calls for deference to precedent) that it should enjoy shared final authority with a written constitution. This notion must be wholly rejected. Indeed, it is this sort of mistaken use of the common law rather than the common law itself that creates most of the problems I have pointed to.

A written constitution is not legal nirvana, promising the omniscience of its makers or transparent answers that will dissolve all further legal disputes. It is, however, the most effective means by far of maintaining a legal system that governs as it should. A written constitution is optimally conducive to maintaining the genuine rule of the *law* and to serving the function for which a legal system enjoys the power that it does. And it confines legal power (as securely as any such device can) to that system's specific, delimited moral authority.

Just as the moral authority of the law informs the best placement of authority within a legal system, so the identification of ultimate legal authority should inform the meaning and application of specific laws in specific cases, which is the issue at the heart of judicial review. So we can now turn to the implications of all of this for that. In light of my account of an objective legal system and its proper moral and legal authority, what does objective judicial review consist of?

PART II

IMPLICATIONS FOR JUDICIAL REVIEW

6

Judicial Review – The Reigning Accounts' Failure

1. INTRODUCTION

Having established the principal features of an objective legal system, we can now turn to judicial review. What are the implications of my account for guiding an appellate court to carry out its work in a manner that is itself objective and that supports the objectivity of the legal system as a whole?

Domestic debate about the proper modes of judicial review has been intense over the past few decades. While the discussions are sometimes animated by differences over a specific judicial nominee or passions concerning a particular issue (health care, guns, or gay marriage, for instance), the stakes clearly transcend any such single controversy. For judicial review determines the manner in which courts understand the law and, correspondingly, the way in which legal power is actually used. Courts are our last resort in "guarding the guardians" – in keeping those who govern within the bounds of the law.

In this chapter, I will examine five competing accounts of proper methodology in judicial review: Textualism, Public Understanding Originalism, Democratic Deference or Popular Constitutionalism, Perfectionism or Living Constitutionalism, and Minimalism. Classification in this area is fraught, as the array of accounts that scholars have defended do not fall into conveniently creased compartments; they can be sorted and labeled by a number of cross-cutting measures. Several figures and theories may qualify for membership in a few of the competing camps.[1] These five, however, under whatever labels, dominate both the scholarly and popular debate and they do so for good reason: each carries a definite appeal. While I shall argue that that appeal ultimately proves misguided (often, offering partial truths that neglect critical

---

[1] Other helpful divisions of various positions are given in Sotirios Barber and James Fleming, *Constitutional Interpretation*; and Philip Bobbitt, *Constitutional Fate*, New York: Oxford University Press, 1982, among others.

aspects of the full context), these accounts present many of the considerations that need to be reckoned with in order to chart an ultimately sound judicial method. Identifying their respective shortcomings will thus help us to home in on those features most vital for the objective exercise of judicial review. (Although I will discuss certain figures who advocate these different theories, my aim is not to refute any particular thinker so much as to convey the core of each position and the core of its inadequacy.)

It is important to recognize at the outset that the proper methodology for judicial review *is* a difficult question. As is often remarked, it is the vexing cases that reach the high courts and that occasion the greatest attention from scholars. The issues posed are typically intricate, demanding highly abstract thought concerning the application of legal principles to circumstances that may be thick with at least apparently conflicting features (conflicting, that is, as indicators of an action's lawfulness). It can be extremely challenging to determine the objective resolution in a given case, let alone to articulate the proper method for resolving all similar cases. The difficulty is compounded when one labors without a firm grasp of the fundamental values that ground objective law.[2]

Fortunately, our discussions of objectivity and its basic requirements in a legal system give us the framework for answers to this question. As I have stressed throughout, form follows function: The proper way to do anything depends on what it is that you are trying to do. Accordingly, we must first identify the function of judicial review – which is to accurately render the meaning of existing law. A court's role is interpretive. A court is not to add to the law or to alter the law, but to ascertain its meaning so as to illuminate its proper application in practical use. This will sometimes involve a court's adding to that which had been previously expressly *articulated* concerning the meaning of the law, but it does not permit its adding to that meaning itself. More precisely, a court may not add to the law whose meaning is being interpreted. The law predates any interpretation of it and a law has the character that it does independently of any interpretation of it. Judicial review plays the role of a midwife, you might say, helping to bring a law's meaning to life in a particular case, but it is not a parent. A court is to deliver a law's meaning by clarifying its legitimate application in a particular context, but it is not to bring something new into existence.[3]

---

[2] Justice Scalia nonetheless maintains that many allegedly hard cases are "easy." Speech at the American Enterprise Institute, quoted in John Voorhees, "Justice Scalia Explains Why He Finds His Job So Easy Sometimes," *Slate*, October 5, 2012, accessed online.

[3] Based on its interpretation of the relevant law, a court determines what action should be taken to give practical effect to its ruling. Some theorists make a great deal of the difference between this latter activity (often called adjudication) and interpretation and some distinguish among

In a very direct way, therefore, the role of judicial review is to safeguard the Rule of Law. Obvious as that may seem, it can be an important reminder of courts' obligation to adhere to the actual law rather than to some near relation that lurks in the vicinity. And the Rule of Law that truly warrants preservation, as we saw in Chapter 3, is that of an objective legal system. Thus, a court's work must be conducted in a way that honors the parameters of such a system. This means that it must understand the law in terms of its three major dimensions: what the legal system does (in the substance of its rules and actions), the manner in which it does it (its administration, including the making and enforcing of law), and the authority by which it acts (the license that distinguishes a legal system from a powerful but wrongful intimidator). Objective validity sets definite boundaries around each of these; objective judicial review must interpret the law in a way that respects these boundaries.

Given the tremendous power of courts, their obligation to respect a legal system's authority bears special emphasis. Because courts police the law while no other body polices the courts, the courts bear an acute responsibility to police themselves – in particular, by ensuring that they remain within the bounds of *their* authority. Since a legal system's legal authority is valid only insofar as it remains within its moral authority, a court must continually ask both whether it is overstepping its specific authority within the legal system (as set by the written constitution) and whether it is reading the law in a way that would overstep the legal system's moral authority, allowing it to exercise more power than is justified. Because the court commands such tremendous power, it must be especially vigilant to guard against its own assumption of a moral authority that the legal system does not possess. For no mechanism within a legal system (including the judiciary) could hold greater moral authority than does the system itself.

In what follows, I will consider each of the five schools of judicial methodology in turn, first offering a brief presentation of its core claims and reasoning and then a critique. Both presentation and critique will be compressed, since my goal here is simply to convey the heart of these positions and their inadequacy by the standard of objective law.[4] While the analysis of each school will

theories of judicial review that attend more to one or the other. My point is not to deny this distinction, but simply to observe that the question of the proper implementation of a ruling by the legal system must be subordinate to the court's primary responsibility of finding the meaning of the relevant law (i.e., interpreting). For a vigorous defense of the importance of the distinction vis-à-vis Originalism, see Gary Lawson, "Originalism Without Obligation," *Boston University Law Review* volume 93, no. 4, July 2013, pp. 1309–1318.

4 I have offered in-depth critiques of the Public Understanding view in "Originalism's Misplaced Fidelity: 'Original' Meaning is Not Objective," *Constitutional Commentary* volume 26, no. 1 (2009), pp. 1–57; and of Minimalism in "Reckless Caution: The Perils of Judicial Minimalism," *New York University Journal of Law and Liberty* volume 5, no. 2, 2010, pp. 347–393. My paper

naturally follow some of its advocates' particular emphases and arguments, I am guided throughout by the basic values that we have established as critical: the function of a legal system, the conditions required for the Rule of Law, the basic requirements of any objective process, and the three pivots of an objective legal system. With these in mind, it will be much easier to recognize the failings of these accounts.

2. TEXTUALISM

Originalism is the view that the meaning of law is the meaning that its terms had at the time that the law was enacted. Law's meaning is fixed. "Originalists believe that the Constitution should be interpreted to mean exactly what it meant when it was adopted by the American people," Antonin Scalia has explained.[5] In order to follow the law, contemporary courts should seek out that historical meaning and apply the law accordingly

On reflection, it turns out that "original" meaning can itself be taken to mean somewhat different things, thus Originalism has been developed into a few distinct forms. All of them are animated largely by an aversion to the notion of a "Living Constitution," the belief that "the meaning of the Constitution must adapt to changes in values and circumstances."[6] Such a mutating constitution, in the Originalists' view, typically represents the intrusive manipulations of presumptuous judges and thwarts the will of the people. It upends legal stability and is antithetical to the Rule of Law. The "whole purpose" of a constitution, in the mind of Scalia, is to prevent change.[7] Originalism is thus well characterized as "a family of theories." As Larry Solum and Robert Bennett write, Originalists "are united by their agreement on two core ideas. First, the linguistic meaning of the Constitution was fixed when each provision was framed and ratified. Second, the original meaning of the constitutional text should be regarded as legally binding."[8]

"Why Originalism Won't Die – Common Mistakes in Competing Theories of Judicial Interpretation" addresses a few different schools, with particular attention to Textualism. *Duke Journal of Constitutional Law and Public Policy* 2, 2007, pp. 159–215. "Originalism, Vintage or Nouveau: He Said, She Said Law" indicts all forms of Originalism. *Fordham Law Review* volume 82, no. 2, Fall 2013, pp. 619–639.

5   Scalia, quoted in Steven Kreytak, "At A&M, Scalia Rails Against Judicial Reinterpretation," *Austin American-Statesman*, May 6, 2005, Section B, p. 1.

6   A characterization from Robert Bennett and Lawrence Solum, *Constitutional Originalism: A Debate*, Ithaca: Cornell University Press, 2011, p. vii. We will look at the Living Constitution view further in section 5.

7   Scalia, *A Matter of Interpretation*, ed. Amy Gutmann, Princeton: Princeton University Press, 1997, p. 40.

8   Bennett and Solum, *Constitutional Originalism*, p. 35.

The earliest wave of Originalism identified original meaning with lawmakers' intent. On this view, the role of the Supreme Court is "simply to ascertain and give effect to the intent of the framers of the Constitution and the people who ratified [it]."[9] Larry Alexander, a contemporary advocate, contends that "the meaning of a legal norm is just its authorially intended meaning."[10]

My concern here, however, is with Textualism, which builds on a critique of the Original Intent thesis. Textualism is the particular form of Originalism that holds that meaning resides in the plain words of the legal text. Its best known champions are Hugo Black and Justice Scalia, although the central idea has been articulated for centuries. Joseph Story, the nineteenth-century legal luminary whose *Commentaries on the Constitution of the United States* (1833) were widely studied for generations, argued against those who would have us reconstruct the thinking of an earlier era that "there can be no security to the people in any constitution of government if they are not to judge of it by the fair meaning of the words of the text."[11] I will concentrate on Scalia as the spokesman for Textualism, both because of his influence as a sitting Supreme Court justice and because he writes and speaks liberally to defend this view. In his most recent book, he and coauthor Bryan Garner explain that "Textualism, in its purest form, begins and ends with what the text says and fairly implies."[12] In a recent interview, Scalia maintains that "words have meaning. And their meaning doesn't change."[13]

9   "A Declaration of Constitutional Principles," 1956, drafted by Senator Sam Ervin of North Carolina, quoted in Justin Driver, "Ignoble Specificities," *The New Republic*, April 5, 2012, p. 32.

10 Larry Alexander, "Originalism, The Why and the What," *Fordham Law Review* volume 82, no. 2, Fall 2013, p. 540. Other advocates of the Intent view include William Rehnquist, Raoul Berger, former Attorney General Edwin Meese, Stanley Fish, John Manning, and Sai Prakash. Richard Ekins has recently defended intent as the proper principle of interpretation for statutory law. *The Nature of Legislative Intent*, Oxford: Oxford University Press, 2012.

11 Story, quoted in Bobbitt, p. 25. For a fuller discussion of Textualism, see Bobbitt, chapter 3, pp. 25–38; Barber and Fleming, pp. 67–70; and Suzanna Sherry and Daniel Farber, *Desperately Seeking Certainty*, Chicago: University of Chicago Press, 2002, pp. 10–28.

12 Antonin Scalia and Bryan A. Garner, *Reading Law: The Interpretation of Legal Texts*, St. Paul, MN: Thomson West, 2012, p. 16.

13 "In Conversation with Antonin Scalia," Jennifer Senior, *New York Magazine*, October 14, 2013, p. 24. Historically, some of law's most influential thinkers have expressed this view, though it is important to bear in mind that, because Originalism's distinct species had not yet been clearly delineated, speakers' sometimes refer indiscriminately to intentions, text, and meaning, thus mention of any one of these does not necessarily signify the deliberate rejection of other forms of Originalism. William Blackstone wrote that "the fairest and the most rational method to interpret the will of the legislator, is by exploring his intentions at the time when the law was made" (*Commentaries on the Laws of England*, 1765–69). Joseph Story held that "the first and fundamental rule in the interpretation of all instruments is, to construe them according to the sense of the terms, and the intent of the parties" (*Commentaries on the Constitution*,

Much of Scalia's case for Textualism consists of his reasons for rejecting the Original Intent view, which lures many others who share his opposition to Living Constitutionalism. Essentially, Scalia emphasizes the difference between that which is intended and that which is said. While these two can coincide, they do not necessarily. People misspeak, at times. (I said "catch;" I meant "batch.") People also express themselves clumsily, on occasion, garbling their intended meanings and consequently being misunderstood. The supremacy of text as the ultimate repository of meaning should thus be obvious, Scalia reasons. *That* is what lawmakers wrote, debated, and enacted; that is what is subsequently presented to the governed as the law; so that is what is law. The only thing that could justify deviations from the text would be changes to that text – changes effected by deliberate means that conform to the text's own strictures concerning its alteration. Indeed, Scalia argues that the reason we demand clarity in law is precisely the belief that it is the words that *are* the law. "Men may intend what they will; but it is only the laws that they enact that bind us."[14]

Further, any alternative to Textualism would defy the democratic character of our legal system, effectively seizing the power of making law from the people. While the people will sometimes enact foolish laws, Scalia contends, it is not the role of the courts to tell us when we do. The courts' role is to discern and announce the meaning of the law, not to second-guess whether a given law should be a law. "In an age when democratically pre-scribed texts (such as statutes, ordinances, and regulations) are the rule," he and Garner maintain, "the judge's principal function is to give those texts their fair meaning."[15]

In my account of an objective legal system in Chapter 2, I argued that part of the requisite objectivity rests in the overtness of laws: what the laws that govern us *are* must be a matter of publicly available record. The Textualists would add that our means of providing that public access is language. Indeed, whenever people are uncertain about what was meant by a person or a rule or a law, the first natural question is, "Well, what did he say?" or "What did they write?" It is words that convey our meanings, the Textualists reason. To govern

---

1833). A more infamous figure, Supreme Court Justice Roger B. Taney, wrote in his *Dred Scott v. Sanford* decision (1857) that the Constitution "speaks not only with the same words, but with the same meaning and intent with which it spoke when it came from the hands of the framers, and was voted on and adopted by the people of the United States." Further, "The duty of the court is, to interpret the instrument they [the drafters of the constitution] have framed, with the best lights we can obtain on the subject, and to administer it as we find it, according to its true intent and meaning when it was adopted."

[14] Scalia, *Matter of Interpretation*, p. 17.

[15] Scalia and Garner, *Reading Law*, p. 3.

by anything other than the relevant legal text would therefore not satisfy the condition of law's open accessibility and would not be fair.

Essentially, the Textualists urge: Go by the words. That is how we communicate. That is what we write down as the law. So that is what should govern.

Critique

As with all of the theories that we will consider in this chapter, rather than attempt an exhaustive critical audit, I concentrate on those features most salient to the core necessities of an objective legal system.[16] From this perspective, two failings stand out. Textualism suffers from a constricted understanding of abstraction – of the objective meaning of words – and correspondingly (at least by implication), it attributes the ultimate authority of law to the beliefs of people. This results in a model of proper judicial review that renders the law subjective, rather than objective.

Abstraction – The Meaning of Words

In Chapter 1, I explained the basic nature of objectivity. In any thinking or decision-making process, to be objective is to be guided, at the most fundamental level, by the nature of the objects in question. Objectivity is not a function of who believes a particular proposition or of how many believe a proposition (among other common confusions), but of that proposition's basis in reality. And recall that objectivity is used to facilitate the acquisition of knowledge. The point of being objective is to "get reality right." These basic truths carry significant implications for the viability of Textualism's portrait of language.

Given the Textualists' focus on words, it is crucial to recognize that words designate concepts. Apart from proper nouns, that is, words stand for concepts and concepts stand for *kinds* of things. A word refers to all the discrete instances of things of the same kind. The word "car," for example, refers to all cars; the word "father," to all fathers. In some cases, the number of referents is huge; in others, it may be small. The reference class of "twins" is considerably smaller than the reference class of "siblings." The point, however, is that a word designates all those existents that in fact share those characteristics that

---

[16] I offer much more detailed critique of Textualism in "Why Originalism Won't Die," and in "How Activist Should Judges Be? Objectivity in Judicial Decisions," lecture presented at OCON (Objectivist Conference), San Diego, July 2005. On file with author or available at: https://estore.aynrand.org/p/160/how-activist-should-judges-be-objectivity-in-judicial-decisions-mp3-download.

distinguish things of that kind (a car, a father, a twin) from things of other kinds. (I will refine this further, as I proceed.)[17]

The basic problem with Textualism is that text without context is empty. Words alone, in and of themselves, do not mean anything. Apart from human beings' deliberately employing words to convey specific mental content, words do not signify. Meaning is a human convention. As such, the content of people's minds is an ineliminable part of any account of language's meaning. Words are mere markings – scratchings on paper, pixels on screens, sounds in the air. What a word or string of words means (and is naturally taken to mean by a language's speakers) depends largely on the context in which it is used. Consider the difference between the same words spoken in jest and in earnest, or the same words pronounced to underscore or to mock. Or words that are commonly understood to have more than one sense. The phrase "Show me your hand," uttered by a physician in an examination room, means something different from "Show me your hand" barked by a poker player. If I place an object before you and instruct "Please cut," exactly what my statement invites you to do depends, in part, on whether that object is a deck of cards, a birthday cake, the script of a play, or a lawnmower. The objective meaning of any text is a function of the words used as well as the conventions generally govern-ing the use of those words as well as other aspects of the particular context in which they are used on a given occasion.[18]

Crucial as words are to meaning, then, they are not the whole of it. In opposing the Original Intent school, Textualists are correct that intent is not a sufficient explanation of meaning and that legal meaning is conveyed *through* words. Yet meaning is not one and the same as words and it is not contained entirely inside those words, like a nut within a shell.[19] Language is a device

---

[17] I explain this in greater depth in "Why Originalism Won't Die," and "Originalism's Misplaced Fidelity."

[18] Several other critics also target this feature of Textualism. See, for instance, Ronald Dworkin, "Comment," in *A Matter of Interpretation*, Gutmann ed.; and David Sosa, "The Unintentional Fallacy," *California Law Review* 86, 1998, pp. 919–938. Although Scalia professes to recognize the importance of context (*Matter of Interpretation*, p. 37), his treatment of certain examples reveals that he does not do so in the way that is required for objectivity. Consider, for instance, his remarks about the meaning of the Equal Protection clause in *Matter of Interpretation*, pp. 148–49: "Is it a denial of equal protection on the basis of sex to have segregated toilets in public buildings, or to exclude women from combat? I answer [these questions] on the basis of the 'time-dated' meaning of equal protection in 1868." In other words, he does not respect the contemporary context as relevant to the interpretation of meaning. We will say more about this in regard to a different example, the "cruel and unusual punishment" clause, shortly.

[19] Notice that meaning is sometimes conveyed by means other than language, such as by facial expression, body language, tone of voice, action, conspicuous inaction (e.g., in defiance of one's simultaneously spoken words, such as, "Let's all rush there immediately!"). For a legal system, language is the most objective means of expressing its powers and rules.

to facilitate human knowledge and communication, but it is not a substitute for knowledge or mental content. Consequently, statements of law do not "whisper in our ears" the answers to questions concerning their meaning and application.

As if realizing that words do not vacuum seal meaning and that strict Textualism thus could not actually be practiced, Scalia at times allows that the way to respect the text is to abide by what speakers of the time meant by the words used.[20] This proposal, so sensible on its face, is actually ambiguous. What original speakers "meant" can itself mean at least two significantly different things:

(1) the exact list of items referred to by a word that the language speakers at the time would have provided

or

(2) the precise criteria that those people employed for determining which items a word referred to (and by implication, their expected applications of the term)[21]

Option 1 does not accurately capture what words mean, however. When you and I discuss cars, for example, we are referring not only to those specific cars that you or I have directly encountered. We are referring to all existents of the kind *car* (which is why a third party may join in with valid corrections to some of the claims that either of us has made about cars).[22] The point is, a list of referents (as option 1 would have it) is too restricted a class to represent the meaning of a word.

---

[20] Scalia and Garner, *Reading Law*, p. 16. "In their full context, words mean what they conveyed to reasonable people at the time they were written – with the understanding that general terms may embrace later technological innovations." Also see *Matter of Interpretation*, pp. 140–141. On this, Scalia seems to overlap with the Original Public Understanding view, the strain of Originalism that I will consider next. Note that certain of my criticisms of Textualism will also apply to that view.

[21] Each meaning is implied in different passages in Scalia's writing. The first meaning is implied when, for instance, Scalia contends that "cruel and unusual punishment" refers to only those punishments that were considered cruel and unusual by the Constitution's authors according to the standards of their day (p. 145). At the same time, Scalia explains that he would apply the constitutional prohibition of cruel and unusual punishments to "all sorts of tortures quite unknown at the time the Eighth Amendment was adopted" – yet he further contends that what that law abstracts is "not a moral principle of cruelty" but "*the existing society's* assessment of what is cruel." Its meaning is "rooted in the moral perceptions *of the time.*" *Matter of Interpretation*, p. 145; the first emphasis is mine; the second is Scalia's. The position that emerges from Scalia's struggle with this ambiguity is, at best, contorted.

[22] It is also why people call in to National Public Radio's "Car Talk" to gain understanding of particular cars that the hosts have never seen. The hosts *know cars* – and not only those cars that they have known.

While the second meaning of "meant" – the idea that it is language users' selection criteria that are pivotal – may thus seem a stronger account than the first (after all, we do need to make sure that the *kind* that a word refers to is constant, over time, such that canaries are not smuggled into a discussion of cars, or canoeing into a discussion of laws about commerce), even this second possible meaning does not withstand scrutiny. People's understanding of the essential characteristics of a given phenomenon is fallible and may be mistaken at any given time. Insofar as a discussion of cancer concerns cancer, though (and not simply what people think about cancer at time *t*), option 2 is incorrect.

In short, neither of these construals of what the original speakers "meant" captures the objective meaning of words. The deeper problem responsible for this is that Textualism fails to appreciate the open-endedness of concepts.

"Open-endedness" is Ayn Rand's name for the fact that a word stands for all things of the relevant kind, rather than for simply the particular concrete instances of that kind with which particular speakers are acquainted *or* for simply the criteria that speakers employ in determining which things qualify as members of the relevant kind. People's understanding of the proper criteria for kind inclusion is fallible. Because words designate things,[23] however, rather than people's ideas about things, language's original users' correctable beliefs about the governing criteria are not the appropriate standard by which to measure words' objective meaning.[24]

This open-ended character of concepts does not imply that meaning may be dictated unilaterally by the fancies of a given speaker, nor that meaning is elastic, as the Textualists might naturally fear. Rather, the idea is that a word refers to all those existents of the kind in question – be they known, unknown, or at present misidentified by many or all people. When we gain a better understanding of some phenomenon (of cars, cancer, whales, toxins, schizophrenia – anything) or when we develop new techniques for engaging in a

---

[23] By "things," here, I mean existents (as discussed in Chapter 1), that is, actual phenomena of all kinds, encompassing physical objects, properties, actions, relationships, beliefs, desires, goals, emotions, etc.

[24] Open-endedness is an immensely important dimension of objectivity. For much fuller explanation, see Ayn Rand, *Introduction to Objectivist Epistemology*, pp. 17–18, 26–28, 65–69, 98–100, 147, 257–258; Leonard Peikoff, *Objectivism: The Philosophy of Ayn Rand*, pp. 78, 103–105; Allan Gotthelf, "Ayn Rand's Theory of Concepts: Rethinking Abstraction and Essence," pp. 9, 16–17, 23; James G. Lennox, "Concepts, Context, and the Advance of Science," in *Concepts and Their Role in Knowledge*, pp. 116–122, 125–126, 132; and Lennox, "Response to Burian," pp. 2–5, 211. For open-endedness's specific importance to the proper interpretation of law, see my discussion in "Originalism's Misplaced Fidelity," pp. 30–34.

particular activity and revise our definitions accordingly (think of online dating or digital photography), we are not pulling an illicit bait and switch of the
sort that Originalists warn against. We are not changing the subject. A word
names a concept, and that concept encompasses all those existents that are of
that distinct kind.[25]

What is crucial for understanding the failure of Textualism is the fact that,
because concepts are open-ended, we can correct earlier speakers' understandings of meaning without thereby betraying words' meaning or defying
the law. Indeed, if meaning is to be objective, we must correct previous errors.
If the words of a legal text are to mean certain definite things and not others
(which is exactly what the Textualists properly seek) and if they are to stand
for actual phenomena (those activities that constitute speech or the establishment of religion, etc.), then we must always proceed on the basis of the best
knowledge available at the present time.[26]

Notice that Textualism's conception of language makes meaning perversely
self-referential. In order to know a word's meaning, it directs our attention
inward to speakers' beliefs and linguistic practices rather than to the phenomena that their language attempts to identify. It would analyze the words
"speech" or "religion," for example, as representing the ways in which certain
people used the terms "speech" or "religion" at a certain time rather than by
reference to the particular characteristics that distinguish certain actions as
speech or as religious.

In truth, however, language is not about itself, nor about its speakers. The
word "cancer" does not *stand for* what we know now about cancer. Rather,
it refers to that phenomenon – the particular kind of disease that is cancer.

---

[25] To take another example, consider cyber-spying. Even if cyber-spying had not been imagined
100 years ago (when the basic concept of spying was already thoroughly familiar), insofar as
cyber-spying shares the essential distinguishing characteristics of spying, it *is* a form of spying
and our contemporary concept of "spying" must accommodate it.
    While there is no quantitative limit on the number of items that may belong to a given
kind, there is a definite qualitative limit that is determined by the set of particular characteristics that distinguish members of that class. A quick illustration: While "positive prime numbers" may include an infinite number of figures, it does not include *any* figure. Only those that
are in fact positive prime numbers qualify. For more on why open-endedness does not threaten
legal stability (at least, not stability of the type that is objectively desirable), see my discussion
in "Why Originalism Won't Die," pp. 200, 210.

[26] See Rand, *Introduction to Objectivist Epistemology*, pp. 66–69, 17–18, 147; and Peikoff,
Objectivism, pp. 103. On the contextual nature of definitions and the revising of definitions as
reflecting changes and refinements in our understanding of relevant phenomena, see Rand,
Introduction, pp. 40–54; Lennox, "Concepts, Context, and the Advance of Science," Note
24 in this chapter. In application to law, see Smith, "Why Originalism Won't Die," pp. 185,
199–201, and "Originalism's Misplaced Fidelity," pp. 46–52.

The use of a concept *reflects* what we think now, but it does not make that – our state of belief or knowledge – the subject of the discussion or the object of reference. As David Brink has observed, "The reference of our words is determined by the way the world is and not by our beliefs about the world." Accordingly, he writes, "Meaning is not to be identified with, and reference is not determined by, the descriptions that people associate with, or their beliefs about the extension of, their words."[27]

When people coin concepts or learn to use concepts that are already in circulation, properly, we remain open to new knowledge and better understanding of those things that we currently know only partially and imperfectly. Correspondingly, we remain open to revising our definitions of the words that name our concepts (be they controversial legal concepts or any others). A definition identifies the nature of the units subsumed under a concept,[28] but since that identification is necessarily limited by human beings' context of knowledge at a given time, if we come to learn more about the relevant phenomena that enables us to identify more accurately those essential features that distinguish existents of the salient kind, we should revise our definitions accordingly. The assertion of a term's objective meaning ("cancer means thus and such;" "whale means thus and such;" "marriage means thus and such") does not presume our omniscience or infallibility concerning the referents of words. When a small child first learns a particular word (such as "bear" or "banana") and we consider him now to understand it, showing sufficient adeptness at deploying the word to refer to the appropriate kinds of things, we do not imply that he now knows all that a person ever can know about things of that kind (bears, bananas). Ideally, he will gradually come to learn much more about those things that he initially grasps relatively crudely and incompletely but nonetheless adequately, for generally reliable sorting and meaningful, correct use of the term. We should all seek to graduate to more refined (and thus more useful) definitions of concepts, as the growth of our knowledge of relevant phenomena warrants. In short,

---

[27] David O. Brink, "Legal Theory, Legal Interpretation, and Judicial Review," *Philosophy and Public Affairs*, Spring 1988, volume 17, no. 2, pp. 117 and 121. Note that if this were not the case, words could not have enduring meaning and laws could not govern us tomorrow, let alone for decades. Each new instance of a kind that presented some previously unanticipated variations would have to be treated as belonging to a different kind. Online shopping would not be a type of shopping, for instance, but a wholly new phenomenon, requiring identification, classification, and legal evaluation from scratch. Even some who agree with Scalia that "a legal text's original public meaning is determinative of its meaning today" recognize that "a legal text can do more than its drafters imagined." See Steven G. Calabresi and Julia T. Rickert, "Originalism and Sex Discrimination," *Texas Law Review*, volume 90, 2011, pp. 1–101.

[28] This is essentially the definition of definitions given by Rand, *Introduction*, p. 40.

the revision of words' definitions and the open-ended character of concepts, far from threatening objectivity, reflect the fact that objective meaning is knowledge-*welcoming*.[29]

The appropriate alternative to the dreaded Living Constitution of Textualists' nightmares, then, is not law that is static, its text to be read as a petrified forest binding us to rules that tell us not about the phenomena named by those laws (about speech, religion, commerce, etc.), but only about how certain words were used in the past. Yet that is the "meaning" that Textualism instructs judges to unearth and to follow. In fact, and contrary to Scalia, the point of a constitution is not to "prevent change" of the sort that Textualism would bar, through its refusal to admit the growth of knowledge. A constitution *is* to place certain kinds of boundaries around the use of legal power, to be sure. It is precisely because we should seek to identify correctly what the legitimate boundaries are, however, that our understanding of legal language must remain open to improved understandings of terms' meanings.

It is important to recognize that a court that corrects earlier errors is performing a positive service. Suppose that a certain earlier understanding of the meaning of a term (e.g., "persons") was incorrect and was so in a way that rendered a specific legal provision that used that term (or the conventional application of that provision) unconstitutional. The law in question was not, in fact, an objective, valid law. Also suppose that that mistake was not recognized to be a mistake until many years after its enactment and use. When a court today corrects the mistake by refusing to honor it as if it were valid law, it is not being arbitrary, merely indulging its peculiar biases.[30] Rather, it is proceeding by the best evidence and judgment that it has. That is a court's responsibility. When a court first respects blacks as "persons," for example, fully entitled to all the same legal rights as whites despite a long trail of popular understanding and legal precedent that did not respect blacks as persons, that court is attempting to understand the actual referents of the law. Correcting an earlier mistake about the meaning of "person" *is* being objective. It is part of the ongoing

---

[29] To frame the idea slightly differently: When people use a word, they do not freeze for eternity their unique understanding of the essence, definition, or roster of referents of that word at that time as *the* immutable standard that properly governs all subsequent use of that word. Meaning is not chained to the prevalent understanding of the referred-to phenomenon on a particular date. Rather, we select a word to refer to a particular *kind* of thing, recognizing that we are neither all-knowing nor error-immune in our understanding of that kind. Accordingly, we remain open to recalibrating our precise understanding of the essential distinguishing characteristic of that kind. This means that we are open to the redefinition – the objective redefinition – of a concept.

[30] Such a court is not necessarily being arbitrary; obviously, any court is capable of proceeding in an arbitrary manner.

effort to "get reality right" and it is disciplined by the same logic that distinguishes all objective thinking. If the price of legal stability were the arrest of our intellectual development to that attained by a particular date, it would not be stability worth having. For it would not serve objective law.

To make use of the categories that I introduced in Chapter 1, observe that Textualism employs an intrinsicist model of language meaning and thus of law. (It is implicitly intrinsicist, not necessarily self-consciously.) Textualism conceives of meaning not as objective (representing a certain relationship between a mind and an existent), but as intrinsic: Meaning is inherent within individual words, if only we would listen. Judicial decision making, correspondingly, is seen as a relatively passive, mechanical chore. Judges are not to actively and conceptually judge, in order to determine the proper application of a law to particular circumstances, but to serve as unthinking couriers who simply deliver law's prefab answers. Any thought on the part of judges concerning what some legal text means (as opposed to what certain previous people thought it meant) is rejected by the Textualists as an unjustified intrusion on law.

In truth, however, even a written constitution, for all of the security that it helps to supply, is not a set of ready-made answers, there to be plucked off the shelf to resolve individual cases. Nor is it a failsafe guarantee that the law will be correctly applied, as long as judges honorably do their duty. Written law provides the ground for correct answers to questions of application, but that ground is abstract and must be digested by individual human reasoning in order for anyone to arrive at valid answers concerning laws' application. The failure to recognize this and, instead, to treat words themselves or original speakers' beliefs about words' referents as legally decisive is, by implication, to assign legal authority to those speakers qua speakers – that is, to some people's beliefs simply because they are those people's beliefs. Far from preserving law's objective meaning, Textualism drains objectivity from law by "socializing" its meaning in this way. It subordinates objective meaning to some set of people's beliefs about meaning. And this feeds into the second, closely related major failing of Textualism. Its untenable intrinsicism collapses into subjectivism.

Collapse into Subjectivism

Textualism's mistaken view of abstraction leads to it to misunderstand law's proper authority. However unwittingly, reliance on its theory of meaning has the effect of "authorizing" legal power that is not actually warranted. Textualism licenses exercises of legal power not on the basis of their objective propriety (their work in fulfilling the function of government), but on the grounds that they represent the beliefs and desires of particular men – the earlier speakers of the contested language – despite the fact that those beliefs and desires may be completely unjustified.

Textualism's account of language implies that legal power may be exercised, at bottom, according to the dictates of certain men. The reason for this is not that those men are thought to be correct about how legal power should be used, based on their sound grasp of the salient political and legal philosophy. Rather, we are all properly governed (on its view) according to whatever they thought words meant when they enacted those words into law. Under Textualism, words' meaning is not objective. It is not grounded on the nature of the existents referred to. (Again, recall Scalia: "Words have meaning. And their meaning doesn't change." No updates required. No corrections permitted.) Correspondingly, law's meaning is not objective and law's authority is not objective. The "objective," on its view, simply is: that which certain people would say that it is. A given conclusion or policy is objective because certain people say so (just as a given word means *x* because certain people believed that it does).

The essential problem is that this cedes inappropriate authority to people's beliefs. We are to honor those laws that our forebears enacted not because they are valid by objective standards, but because they are ... theirs and, well, they got here first, they beat us to the lawmaking punch. Consequently, the protection that is normally afforded by having written law is completely undone. By holding that lawmakers make not only the law but the very *meaning* of the law – by treating them as infallible authorities on *that*, on the meaning of words – the legal system is released from any limitations imposed by the *objective* authority of a legal system. That is, if some privileged set of language speakers and their lawmakers may declare unconditionally what language itself means and we are all subsequently beholden to it, they may define themselves (and the legal system) out of any obligation to respect the boundaries of objective law. The point is not that this is the conscious, deliberate intention of particular lawmakers or of Textualists; I do not believe that it is. The point, rather, is the damage done by the fatally flawed premise that rests at the bottom of the Textualist view of language meaning. On its view, a word's meaning is reduced to: that which some people believe about the word's meaning. And the law's authority is reduced to: those people's beliefs about authority. Their say-so trumps objective authority; truly, people's wishes are in charge. This is subjectivism through the back door.[31]

---

[31] I pursue this line of criticism of lawmakers as "meaning makers" in greater detail in "Originalism, Vintage or Nouveau: *He Said, She Said* Law," Note 4 in this chapter.

Textualism claims that the plain words provide the meaning of the law. In truth, we have seen, they could not possibly provide this. That account of language's meaning is hopeless in theory and impossible in practice. Text needs context; intelligibility needs humanity. Consequently, the way that Textualists attempt to practice their creed (in treating the law *as if* it had objective meaning) is by giving the power to assign words' meaning to whomever passes a law. But it is in this way that Textualism's untenable intrinsicism collapses into subjectivism. Because meaning is not actually lodged within words alone, words' purported meaning must come from somewhere else. In Textualism's practice, that somewhere is typically either a judge's own beliefs (projected onto the law) or a judge's beliefs about the historical language practices of the original lawmakers (*their* beliefs). The problem is that either of these is subjectivist. Instead of adherence to laws' objective meaning, this Textualist model of meaning offers us governance by some people's subjective preference.[32]

Lest one suspect that I distort Textualism's implications, Scalia has made the subjectivism plain. He does not regard individual rights as objectively valid claims, the protection of which is a legal system's proper, authorizing mission. Rather, he contends, rights themselves are products of majority wish. "Do you want a right to abortion?" he asks. "Create it in the way that most rights are created in a democratic society: persuade your fellow citizens and enact a law."[33] "You think there's a right to suicide? Do it the way the people of Oregon did it and pass a law! Don't come to the Supreme Court!"[34] The purported objectivity of law's meaning, in other words, turns out to be *intersubjectivity*: what a number of people happen to agree to.

This is not a mere quirk of Scalia, with which other Textualists might disagree. The Textualist account of language is logically committed to it. On the premise that a word means nothing but what a certain group of people think

---

[32] I discuss this collapse further in "Why Originalism Won't Die," pp. 205–208, and in "How Activist Should Judges Be? Objectivity in Judicial Decisions," lecture, Note 16 in this chapter. In a recent essay, Steve Durden somewhat similarly argues that Textualism does not truly constrain judges. "Textualisms," *British Journal of American Legal Studies* 2013, retrieved from http://papers.ssrn.com/sol3/papers.cfm?abstract_id=2256679.

[33] Quoted in Kreytak, "At A&M, Scalia Rails Against Judicial Reinterpretation," Note 5 in this chapter. Scalia has made similar claims on other occasions. See, e.g., "Captial Commentary: Lawmaking and the Supreme Court," The Center for Public Justice, March 16, 1998, retrieved from http://www.cpjustice.org/stories/storyReader$222. "You want a right to abortion, create it the way most rights are created in a democracy: pass a law. If you don't want it, pass a law the other way."

[34] Quoted in Margaret Talbot, "Supreme Confidence: The Jurisprudence of Justice Antonin Scalia," *The New Yorker*, March 28, 2005, p. 42.

it means just because they think that, objective law is a farce. Objective any-thing is impossible.

At the start of the chapter, I noted Scalia's belief that notoriously hard con-stitutional cases are actually easy.[35] Any initial surprise at this view should now be dissolved. The Textualists' constricted understanding of concepts leads to a reductivist model of judicial review in which judges interpreting a legal text are simply pursuing historical facts about language use, rather than engaging questions about language's meaning and the actual nature of the phenom-ena that laws refer to (about whether gay sex is within a person's rights, for instance, or whether abortion is within a person's rights or whether certain types of GPS surveillance constitute a search). If you suppose that language is not conceptual and does not refer to external existents, in other words, the judges' task *is* comparatively easy. Historical investigation of word use poses its own challenges, to be sure, but it is a very different kind of challenge and answers are more easily empirically verified than answers to more philosoph-ical questions.

The Textualists' aim to anchor language's meaning and thus to prevent the floating, fluctuating "meanings" that others would sometimes supply is right-minded. A word does mean *some*thing – which implies, of course, that it may not legitimately be read to mean many other things. This premise is both true and important for an objective legal system. Yet a law's meaning does not consist of text alone, nor can it be equated with speakers' expected applications of a text or term in specific cases. Textualists are right to seek the firm meaning of law, in other words, but they misidentify what it is that gives a law its meaning.

It is important to recognize that at one level, Textualists avowedly seek to avoid subjectivism. While most Textualists agree with Scalia's subjectivist determination of which rights we have (viewing individual rights as simply the product of a majority's preference), it is the text, they insist, that identifies what the *law* is. Thus, text is what judges are obligated to uphold. Their rev-erence for text, in other words, is intended to guard against a different form of subjectivism, namely, judges elevating their personal preferences over the enacted preferences of the people.

Unfortunately for Textualism, objectivity does not consist of adherence to subjective opinions. In its keenness to avoid rule by the opinion of individual

---

[35] In a 2012 speech, he observed, "The death penalty? Give me a break. It's easy. Abortion? Absolutely easy. Nobody ever thought the Constitution prevented restrictions on abortion. Homosexual sodomy? Come on. For 200 years, it was criminal in every state." Speech at American Enterprise Institute, see Note 2 in this chapter.

judges, Textualism offers an alternative that is, in principle, no better: rule by the opinion of the masses. The number of opinions may be greater than those of a few robed officials and their having written the text on an earlier date may lend the veneer of legitimacy, but the underlying subjectivism remains. Strict devotion to a subjectively reached conclusion does not a proper legal system make. While subjectivism on the part of judges undoubtedly would undermine an objective legal system, as Textualism fears, so does subjectivism at the system's very base, in the determination of which rights we possess and correlatively, what authority the government has, as necessary in order to protect them. Judicial fidelity to the legal text can accomplish no worthy purpose if what that text is is itself misguided, representing the unjustified use of force. The legitimate function of government cannot be served when what that function is is trumped by the winds of political popularity. It is a thin notion of objectivity, and one utterly incapable of preserving individual rights, that Textualists espouse.

In the end, because Textualism labors under a mistaken understanding of what language means, it labors under a mistaken idea of what law is. This corrupts its account of judicial review. Its prescribed methods would not serve the proper function of the enterprise. Instead of upholding the law – the objective meaning of objective law – Textualist review would serve the subjective beliefs about law and legal power held by a particular set of men. It would elevate original meaners over objective meaning. This does not preserve the Rule of Law. And it does not advance the mission of the legal system, the protection of individual rights.

3. PUBLIC UNDERSTANDING ORIGINALISM

Public Understanding Originalism is, according to Randy Barnett, one of its leading lights, the thesis that law's meaning is "the public or objective meaning that a reasonable listener would place on the words used in the [relevant legal] provision at the time of its enactment."[36] Rather than identifying meaning with text, what is important to the Public Understanding school is "the meaning actually communicated to the public by the words on the page."[37] And this, naturally, depends on the ordinary, everyday understanding that people have of the language that they use. In slightly more formal terms,

---

[36] Randy E. Barnett, *Restoring the Lost Constitution: The Presumption of Liberty*, Princeton: Princeton University Press, 2004, p. 92.

[37] Barnett, "The Gravitational Force of Originalism," *Fordham Law Review* volume 82, no. 2, Fall 2013, p. 413.

Larry Solum characterizes Public Understanding Originalism as "the version of originalist theory holding that the communicative content of the constitutional text is fixed at the time of origin by the conventional semantic meaning of the words and phrases in the context that was shared by the drafters, ratifiers, and citizens."[38]

The Public Understanding school shares with other forms of Originalism concern for constancy and fidelity. It rejects interpretation that "updates" the law in a way that actually alters it. Adherence to the law must be to law understood as what it meant *when* it was meant. Unlike Textualism, however, it sees meaning as resting in the understanding of a text that is natural during the era in which it was adopted. When words signify, after all, they signify *to* human beings, to a group of people. It is in people's minds that words live; it is minds that comprehend and communicate the "mental content" or specific ideas that are merely signaled by a text. The objective meaning of the law, Public Understanding advocates conclude, can only reasonably be construed to represent that content that speakers at the time would have taken it to represent.[39]

Public Understanding's principal advance over Textualism lies in its more sophisticated account of language. One of its foremost advocates, Keith Whittington, incisively exposes the inadequacy of a purely text-bound account of meaning.[40] The Public Understanding conception, he explains, recognizes

---

[38] Solum, "Originalism and Constitutional Construction," *Fordham Law Review* volume 82, no. 2, Fall 2013, p. 459. Here again, classification can grow complicated, given that some who emphasize text to elucidate meaning would agree that the historical period's understanding of a text is also vital. Michael Paulsen, for instance, identifies himself as "an original, public meaning textualist. I believe that the single correct way of constitutional interpretation is to attempt faithfully to apply the meaning that the words would have had to a reasonably well-informed speaker or reader of the English language at or about the time the text was adopted." "Debate on the Original Meaning of the Commerce, Spending, and Necessary and Proper Clauses," in *Originalism: A Quarter Century of Debate*, ed. Steven Calabresi, Washington, DC: Regnery, 2007, p. 253. And so-called New Originalists build on the Public Understanding thesis to further advocate constitutional "construction" (about which, more later). Yet while all New Originalists are Public Understanding Originalists (at least, according to some), not all Public Understanding Originalists would go as far as the New Originalists. For discussion of New Originalism, see *Fordham Law Review* volume 82, no 2; Solum, *Legal Theory Blog*, Lexicon, # 071, retrieved from http://lsolum.typepad.com/legal_theory_lexicon/, and Bennett and Solum, *Constitutional Originalism*, pp. 2–4, 18, 170–172, 175–178, 56–60.

[39] Scalia and other Textualists sometimes speak in ways suggesting that they also believe this (e.g., Scalia and Garner, *Reading Law*, pp. 16, 33), yet they do not consistently honor this view.

[40] Keith E. Whittington, *Constitutional Interpretation: Textual Meaning, Original Intent, and Judicial Review* (Lawrence: University Press of Kansas, 1999), chapter 3 and pp. 99, 170, 209–212. Jeffrey Denys Goldsworthy also offers a more sophisticated understanding of language in "The Case for Originalism," in *The Challenge of Originalism: Theories of Constitutional Interpretation*, eds. G. Huscroft and B. W. Miller, Cambridge: Cambridge University Press, 2011.

that language is a convention and argues that the only way to honor language is to respect the conventions that governed at the time when a law was adopted. The conventional way of using a term in 1787 *is* what any use of that term in 1787 means (including any laws' use of that term).[41]

This view of meaning also paves the ways for constitutional "construction," the idea embraced by many Public Understanding advocates, including Whittington and Barnett, that, because strict interpretation cannot answer all questions posed concerning the contemporary applications of laws, courts may sometimes construct an answer that is not simply derived from the meaning of the preexisting law. The basic reasoning beneath this idea is simple. Roughly: laws can be vague or incomplete; meaning is a function of men's understandings; men's understandings are typically incomplete. Therefore, the law will sometimes need to be supplemented.

Many find this judicial ability to construct attractive in part because it enables the Original Understanding view to be better adapted to contemporary circumstances. And with this emendation, Originalism has brought longtime critics such as Jack Balkin and Sandy Levinson into the fold.[42]

While the Public Understanding school charts important differences with strict, "plain words" Textualism, it insists on the supremacy of the *original* public understanding for two primary reasons: because that is what was agreed upon and because that is what was written – deliberately adopted and affirmed in writing. Thus, its basic rationale is straightforward.[43]

First, the people's sovereignty in adopting law would be fraudulent if the meaning of the words they used in so doing could be altered by later "interpreters." Adherence to the original meaning is mandatory, if we are to give effect to the will that the people expressed when making the law. If people today are dissatisfied with their predecessors' choices, the Constitution provides specific avenues for altering the law that resulted from those choices. In order truly to respect the law, however, we must abide by the original public understanding of that law unless and until we formally alter it.[44]

---

[41] Barnett, *Restoring*, pp. 89–94, and Whittington, p. 35.

[42] For more on construction, see Solum, "The Interpretation-Construction Distinction," *Constitutional Commentary*, 27, 2010, pp. 97–118; Jack M. Balkin, "The New Originalism and the Uses of History," *Fordham Law Review* 82, pp. 641–719; Balkin, *Living Originalism*, Cambridge, MA: Harvard University Press, 2011; Barnett, *Restoring*, chapter 5, pp. 118–130; and Whittington, pp. 7–15, 157–159, 171–175, 196–197, 204–208.

[43] Not all advocates of Public Understanding endorse both reasons, however. I discuss the differing arguments of Whittington and Barnett in "Originalism's Misplaced Fidelity," pp. 6–13.

[44] I elaborate on this in "Originalism's Misplaced Fidelity," pp. 6–8. Also see Whittington, chapter 4, especially pp. 95–99, 108–110, and 152–156, 159.

The second line of argument seems especially compelling in light of my own urging of a written constitution as a crucial means of ensuring objective legal authority. Barnett and Whittington reason that we put the law into words in order to objectify it and make it more readily knowable to all concerned. The point of writing law would be defeated, however, if we allowed later interpretations to depart from the originally understood meaning of the language.[45] The clarity and security that are sought by writing the law would dissolve if those words may be read in ways other than the way in which original users understood them. A constitution cannot serve its purpose (of identifying government powers, specifying spheres of authority, and correlatively limiting a legal system's power) if its language is pliable. Whittington contends that "the people can constrain their governmental agents only by fixing their will in an unchanging text" with unchanging meaning.[46]

All of this adds up to an account of law's meaning that is purportedly more true-to-experience than Textualism and more objective than any of the competing accounts. Learning from the Textualists' mistakes while still striving to be faithful to the law as enacted, the Public Understanding school claims to provide a more objective account of law's meaning – which is critical, obviously, if we are truly to be governed by *law*. Barnett trumpets Public Understanding Originalism as an advance "from subjective to objective meaning."[47] Words *are* the key to legal meaning, as the Textualists insist, but words in their originally understood sense.[48]

Critique

Unfortunately, the Public Understanding school suffers from some of the same fatal mistakes that afflict earlier forms of Originalism. Despite its somewhat more sophisticated grasp of how language works, in terms of those features that are most critical to law's objectivity, its modifications of Textualism are inconsequential. Rather than repeat all of the relevant criticisms that I explained

---

[45] See Barnett, *Restoring*, pp. 96, 98–99, 104–106, 117; Whittington, p. 58.

[46] Whittington, p. 56. This bears some affinity with the "Iron Grip" argument for Originalism, my label for the contention that genuine legal interpretation is *necessarily* Originalist. See, e.g., Gary Lawson, "Originalism Without Obligation," pp. 1311–1315; Solum, *Constitutional Originalism*, pp. 95–96; and Whittington, "The New Originalism," *Georgetown Journal of Law and Public Policy*, 2, 2004, p. 612. I critique this bold argument in "Originalism, Vintage or Nouveau," pp. 623 and 629ff.

[47] Barnett, *Restoring*, p. 94. He also equates the public meaning with the objective meaning when presenting the core meaning of the Public Understanding view, p. 92.

[48] Again, for a slightly fuller presentation of the Public Understanding position, see my "Originalism's Misplaced Fidelity," pp. 8–13.

in assessing Textualism, I will focus on Public Understanding's more distinctive and apparently stronger features to show how even these succumb to the same basic failings. While some overlap in the critiques is unavoidable, I will develop certain more targeted criticisms here that should actually fortify the case against all forms of Originalism.

To begin: the Public Understanding Originalists' insistence that interpretation not replace the concept originally expressed in a law with a different concept is perfectly sound. In this sense, what the original speakers thought does demand our fidelity: we must abide by that same concept. We must also recognize the error in their view of what such fidelity consists of, however, namely, the belief that we must adhere to the precise definition and criteria that original speakers held when using a term to the exclusion of all correction of these that results from our further learning about the phenomena in question (that is, about the relevant class of referents). As I discussed briefly in regard to Textualism, to revise the definition of a concept or to alter the exact criteria by which a concept is applied is not, in fact, to break faith with that concept or to abandon it. Obviously, it could be in a given case, as some purported corrections may be either logically invalid or, worse, deliberate attempts to swap reference to one kind of thing for another. Yet genuine refinement of our understanding of a phenomenon (in law, in natural science, in any realm, be it our understanding of persons or searches or tomatoes or AIDS) is perfectly possible with no change of subject and no breach of fidelity. Indeed, such improvements in the depth or width or precision of our knowledge are desirable. Anyone who cares about objectivity should welcome them. For these reflect our better understanding *the object*.

Public Understanding advocates insist that constitutional fealty requires that the law today be taken to mean what it meant *when* it was meant, as I put it earlier. Their reasoning, however, relies on an equivocation over the meaning of "what it meant" in that assertion. Yes, contemporary interpreters must honor the same concept insofar as we may not substitute a different one (for example, by reading a law's reference to "banks" to designate land bordering a body of water when the context makes clear that it was used to designate certain financial institutions, or reading a law's reference to "gay behavior" to designate a lighthearted manner of action when the context clearly indicates its reference to homosexual activity). But no, we are not bound (not properly or objectively) by the state of most people's understanding of that concept's governing criteria at a particular historical time (e.g., their precise understanding of "banks" in either of those two senses). In other words, "what it meant" cannot be taken to mean simply "those particular referents and/or the precise criteria for identifying a word's referents that some set of men once believed that a word stood for." A word's meaning and people's beliefs about a word's meaning are two different things. Related, to be sure, but distinct.

While it is understandable for Originalists to seek to secure the legal system from free-roaming judges who would take unjustified liberties with the law under the guise of interpretation, Textualists and Public Understanding Originalists alike labor under a misguided notion of the type of security that language can provide. Written language is an important basis for the objective operation of a legal system, as I argued in Chapter 5, but it cannot provide some sort of error-repellent, foolproof, thought-precluding assurance of law's proper application. Pointing either to written text or to a text's original understanding is not enough to guarantee the law's objective governance today.

Remember that language is *about*: words point to existents, to the specific instances that a particular word identifies as units of specific kinds (be those existents physical objects, properties, actions, emotions, relationships, etc.).[49] The language that people use to express certain ideas represents reality. Inescapably, it reflects a certain understanding of reality at a given time, but what words *refer to* is existents, and not simply beliefs about existents. Since earlier language-users were as fallible as the rest of us, contemporary judges (like all interpreters of law) must continue to think, if they are to see that laws are properly, objectively applied. That is, if they are to see to it that it is the laws that govern, rather than some earlier people's subjective and potentially erroneous beliefs about the meaning of the laws. Even written laws do not make their proper application self-evident. Putting things in writing does not put them beyond thought; it does not obviate people's need to reason, in order to understand and objectively respect the law that is written. The words used to state a law reflect man's thoughts about existents but they do not replace the existents as the fundamental referents of their words or, as such, as the fundamental determinants of meaning.[50]

A different angle might help make this clearer. While the Public Understanding Originalists rightly recognize that the language of the law is important to the meaning of the law, they stumble over the fact that while language is the means of expressing the law, a given understanding of that

---

[49] More strictly, it is not words but human beings who "identify" kinds and members of kinds; words are simply the labels that we employ to refer to those things. That is significant, however: words refer – and words refer to things.

[50] It may be helpful to note three distinct elements that are all involved in what people routinely think of as "meaning:" the *ideas* in language users' minds when they use language; the particular *words* they use to name and express those ideas; the *referents* of those words – that is, the mind-independent existents that their ideas seek to understand and that their words intend to designate (such as cars, cameras, cases of cancer, cases of commerce, and so on). The different species of Originalism tend to confuse these in a variety of ways.

language is not just the same thing as the law. To express is not to constitute; it is not to be or to become *one and the same thing as*. A means of expressing something is just that: a means – of expressing something that is distinct from the expression of it (i.e., a means of conveying content whose existence and whose character is distinct from the expression of that content). To express my affection for a friend is to express something that predates my telling him about it; to express, at a meeting, my opinion that a petitioner's appeal should be denied is to share with others a conclusion that I have reached. I could just as easily hold that conclusion without expressing it.[51]

In the course of expressing a claim, we are not creating that claim or constituting its content. When it comes to erecting a legal system, what is potentially confusing is the fact that a statement of law *is* vital to its very creation as law. That is, it is only by taking certain actions (filing a bill by a certain deadline, allowing a particular period for public comment, securing certain votes, signatures, etc.) that we constitute a proposed rule as bona fide law. And the required steps typically include the formal statement of that law. It is not the case, however, that we are, through that very action (making the statement), making the law's *meaning* – the meaning of the words in which the law is expressed. This is what is crucial.

Contrary to the implications of the Public Understanding view, lawmakers are not meaning makers. This is why subsequent language users may, perfectly fairly and objectively, correct earlier misunderstandings of the exact definitions and referents of the concepts that were written and made law. The meaning of a word depends, at the most fundamental level, on the nature of the things it refers to and not on what a group of people thinks it refers to.[52] The Public Understanding advocates, however, confuse these two: if people at time *t* thought that a particular word meant thus and such, then that is what it means, they insist. Case closed. In this way, however, Public

---

[51]   Sometimes, the two are reached in such close proximity to one another that it can be hard to disentangle them, as when I only form a definite judgment about an issue in the course of a conversation about the subject. I might not have previously "put together" the material in my own mind. Nonetheless, my conclusion is one thing and my expression of it to anyone else is another – as is evidenced by our recognizing the phenomena of sometimes choosing not to express one's opinion.

[52]   Recall Brink's observation that the meaning and reference of words is given by the way the world is rather than by our beliefs about things, see Note 27 in this chapter. Also see Brink's discussion in "Legal Interpretation, Objectivity, and Morality," Brian Leiter, ed., *Objectivity in Law and Morals*, pp. 12–65. In a similar vein, Michael Moore contends that meaning depends on how the world is constituted. Michael S. Moore, "Semantics, Metaphysics, and Objectivity in the Law," paper presented at Conference on Objectivity in the Law, University of Texas at Austin, April 4–5, 2008, and "A Natural Law Theory of Interpretation," 58 *Southern California Law Review*, 277–398 (1985) at p. 337.

Understanding fails to capture the objective meaning of law. For it is only by attending to the nature of words' referents that we actually respect laws' objectivity. Remember: the aim of objectivity is to get reality right. And thus, in judicial review, to answer such questions as: *Is* that a search? *Is* that religious exercise? *Is* that a taking? A tax? Probable cause? While other people's beliefs about words' meaning can sometimes help us to answer these questions correctly, those beliefs are not the reality that we are after. When Joe Citizen is trying to understand what the law demands of him, he needs to know what the *law* is referring to.[53]

All of this allows us to see a still deeper problem. In an important sense, Public Understanding Originalism does not actually offer an account of what law means; on that issue, it passes the buck. Instead of directly trying to figure out what meaning *is* and then articulating and defending its answer, the Original Understanding school instructs us to obey some previous people's beliefs about meaning, regardless of whether those beliefs are justified. Our engagement with the Public Understanding position might be characterized roughly as follows:

QUESTION: *What is the meaning of the law?*
PUBLIC UNDERSTANDING SCHOOL: *That which those people thought was the meaning of the law.* ("Those people" here refers to speakers of the language at the time that a law was enacted.)
QUESTION: *Why should we respect their opinions as valid?*
PUBLIC UNDERSTANDING SCHOOL: *Because that's what the words mean. That's what they thought they mean, so that is what they mean.*

This answer is not responsive. It makes a claim about *whose* thought should be considered the meaning, but does not supply good reason why, or even a genuine account of what that meaning consists of. It is hollow. At best, it returns us to the initial question: What is the meaning of the law?[54]

Like other forms of Originalism, Public Understanding centers its attention on original-ness, the date of a word's use. Yet when we are seeking the meaning of language, past-ness is beside the point. For the date of a belief about a word's meaning does not determine what that meaning is. It does not dictate the nature of those existents that are members of the kind designated by the term.

---

[53] I discuss this confusion much further in "Originalism, Vintage or Nouveau: *He Said, She Said Law*" and discuss related issues in "Originalism's Misplaced Fidelity," and "Why Originalism Won't Die."

[54] Recall Barnett's statement of Public Understanding's core thesis: Law's meaning is "the public or objective meaning that a reasonable listener would place on the words used in the [relevant legal] provision at the time of its enactment" (Note 36 in this chapter). In other words, meaning is equated with someone's (or some group's) belief about meaning.

It tells us nothing about those actions that are, in fact, searches, takings, or taxes, for instance.

Meaning is not settled by the calendar. (And those who condemn Originalism for constricting society by the "dead hand of the past" often fall into this same error.) The contemporary currency of a belief about words' meaning no more certifies that belief as valid than does the old age of other beliefs about meaning damn those beliefs as invalid (as bemoaners of "dead hands" contend). Time is not the question. The calendar obviously can help us to ascertain *word usage* prevalent in a given time (for instance, to learn whether a certain population used the phrase "domestic violence" to refer to strife on the streets or to strife between family members in the home). And that can be a valuable aid in determining which concept it is that a word in a particular legal provision designated. Once that has been learned, however (e.g., that "banks" in this law referred to financial institutions), it is crucial to recognize that the way a word is understood and the meaning of the word – the nature of its referents (in any of its distinct usages) – are two different things.[55]

To put the problem in yet a different way: Originalists' critical error is to confuse objective meaning with original meaning. More exactly, it confuses objective meaning with earlier *beliefs* about a word's meaning. Yet it is objective meaning that a legal system requires, if it is to possess genuine moral authority. The point of establishing law – of writing it, enacting it, and subsequently abiding by it – is to serve the proper work of government, the protection of individual rights. Lawmaking is one means of fulfilling that solemn function. To adhere to a past understanding of a law that itself is not objective, however (in that it contains materially significant mistakes about a concept's referents) on the ground that it *was* the past understanding is to surrender objective law to subjective opinion.

Beneath its professions of objectivity, what all of this reveals is that the Public Understanding view is every bit as subjective as Textualism and the Living Constitutionalism that Originalists disdain. Why are we to honor the original understandings? In essence, we are told: because they reflect the beliefs of those people who enacted the law. This is explicit in some of the reasoning given on Public Understanding Originalism's behalf, such as in Whittington's arguments appealing to popular sovereignty.[56] Yet even

---

[55] Note that in the background of complaints about being restricted by lawmakers of the past often lurks the assumption that legal authority is a product of people's agreement. The reason why "those old dead guys can't bind us today," it is presumed, is that *we make our own agreements, thank you very much*. As I explained in Chapter 4, however, this is an invalid notion of the legal system's authority. Some related discussion arises in Part 4 of this chapter.

[56] Whittington, *Constitutional Interpretation*, pp. 132, 152–156, 159.

Barnett, who seeks to shed populism and to ground law in individual rights that are steadfast in the face of challenges from mass opinion, cannot escape it. For the central proposition of the Public Understanding school weaves this subjectivism in, committing it to a form of popular sovereignty, whether or not it wishes this. It does this not by giving majorities the direct power to vote on individual rights (as the Textualist Scalia would). By effectively giving the people the power to vote *on the meaning of language*, however, the result is the same. Because the Public Understanding view grants a particular set of people (original speakers) the complete and unimpeachable power to determine what the enacted law means, they hold that same power to dictate rights and to veto rights. Even if we were to discover that earlier people made mistakes about the referents of certain laws or about the true or full meaning of pivotal legal concepts, the Public Understanding theory prevents us from correcting them. By its method, original lawmakers enjoy license to rule as they do not because they are thought correct in their grasp of relevant phenomena nor on the premise that they have an accurate grip on the actual moral authority of the legal system, but simply because they thought certain things. That is treated as legally binding: their having thought so. That is the "authority" behind a legal system's use of its coercive power, which courts and the rest of us are bound to obey. Obviously, the original lawmakers had to satisfy further procedural conditions concerning filing deadlines, quorums, votes, and so on, to enact the rules that they chose. But those formal safeguards are treated not as a means of facilitating our enjoying a legal system that rules in a way that is consonant with its actual, objective authority, but simply to ensure that *some* body gets to rule and that everyone knows clearly who that is. The ideal of having a legal system that holds the moral authority to act as it does is subordinated to clarity and constancy for their own sake. That which matters most for an objective legal system – a legal system that possesses valid authority – matters little, under Public Understanding.

This critique may seem harsh. Here again, I do not mean that Public Understanding advocates are all consciously committed to these things. My point, rather, is that these are the implications that their principles of word meaning inescapably entail.

To see Public Understanding's subjectivism more starkly, consider some of Barnett's own explanations of the meaning of "original meaning." "If the public at the time of ratification understood the term 'commerce' in the Constitution to include trade, exchange, and navigation," he writes, "then that is its original meaning."[57] Notice what is absent in this account: any concern

[57] Barnett, *Restoring*, p. 293.

for the actual nature of commerce.[58] Even on the subject of rights – the very
thing that Barnett is keen to assert as the impermeable moral bulwark that limits the reach of majority opinion – he reveals that his notion of rights' meaning
is not truly objective, at all. Barnett blithely asserts that "Originalists no more
need to discern the content of actual or real rights than they need to discern
activity that is 'really' commerce. Instead, they can seek either the original
intent of the framers or the original meaning of the text."[59]

Scalia and Barnett are closer than Barnett might like to think. In Barnett's
understanding of original meaning, reality ("actual or real rights," as he puts
it, or actual commerce or actual speech) is one thing and language's meaning something else. If these happen to coincide on a given occasion such that
the popular understanding of a word depicts reality, so be it; if they fail to
coincide, no worries. Either way, Barnett joins other Public Understanding
Originalists in urging that courts should uphold earlier beliefs, and reality be
damned. (Which in this context implies: rights be damned.)

As is the case with much Originalist reasoning, Public Understanding gains
traction because it emphasizes a partial truth: Human beings do play a vital
role in initially establishing particular words' meaning. That is, we establish
the specific auditory-visual code of symbols by which the words of a language
will designate distinct concepts. We choose the letter sequence "c-a-r" to designate cars, "c-o-m-m-e-r-c-e" to designate commerce, and "c-o-o-k-i-n-g" to
designate cooking. We must not be misled by this limited role, however, into
concluding that words' meaning consists of *nothing but* earlier language users'
choices of symbols or that meaning is wholly determined by those choices.
Because the Originalists (appropriately) seek to honor the original *concept*
enacted into law but because they do not understand the nature of concepts,
they date-stamp meaning to match minds' contents on a certain date rather
than to represent the nature of the thing that language was used to refer to (the
actual nature of cars, of commerce, of cooking). This does not provide the
objective meaning of language (nor of the law). The mistake is well-intended,

---

[58] Nor does such a concern surface in Barnett's surrounding discussion. He pays careful attention
to other evidence of how the people of the time used "commerce" and related terms and to
what they thought these terms referred to. For accounts of historical word usage and historical
thought, we are all in Barnett's debt for the extensive research he has done. Yet none of this
gets at the actual meaning of the phenomena in question – the objective meaning of "commerce" or "navigation" or "shipping," and so forth, as grounded in the actual nature of these
activities. See my discussion of Barnett on "commerce" in "Originalism's Misplaced Fidelity,"
pp. 36–38, and of a similar mistake in Whittington, concerning veneration of so-called original
meaning at the expense of objective, reality-anchored meaning, pp. 39–40.

[59] Barnett, *Restoring*, p. 255.

insofar as it seeks to avoid concept swapping, but it is nonetheless a mistake. And a damaging one.

The bottom line is that Public Understanding Originalism is not an attempt to "get reality right." At best, we might say that it fastens on the wrong "reality:" word usage. For it does seek to ascertain earlier people's beliefs about the words they used in laws. (In asking, for example, "How did *they* use 'commerce'?") But it is not concerned with the actual character of the phenomena that the concepts designated by laws' words refer to. On its model, to ascertain the original Public Understanding that contemporary law must follow, we are not to concern ourselves with whether segregated public schools deliver equal protection of law, for instance, but with whether earlier majorities thought that they did (as reflected in their use of words). We are not to think about whether a black is a person or a woman is a person, but about whether earlier people thought that they were (as reflected in their use of words). In fact, however, because the exercise of legal power is not about the use of words but about the use of coercion (handcuffs, fines, prison walls), the authority behind legal power cannot be settled by findings about the use of words. Law's authority must be objective. We must strive to get reality right – to understand the phenomena that laws' words refer to.[60]

The advocacy of constitutional "construction" to supplement interpretation by some Public Understanding Originalists, I think, does nothing to bolster their cause. The term itself is equivocal and has been used to describe somewhat different things.[61] Larry Solum describes construction as "the translation of the semantic content into rules of constitutional law" and "the determination of legal effect,"[62] while Barnett characterizes construction as the determination of "whether an object falls within or outside the ambit of a vague term."[63] If construction is not to license departures from law's original meaning, it is important to specify its legitimate boundaries, yet here, too, advocates disagree over its proper employment. Whittington endorses construction as "essentially creative" and "essentially political," while Barnett resists, contending that the

---

[60] And here, we glimpse what is valid in the "dead hands" objection: If or when meaning is treated as the Originalists treat it, regarded as a cryogenically preserved historical artifact that is intrinsically obligatory, then such fealty to the past strangles objectivity and defeats the point of objective law. Properly understood, fidelity is valuable not for its own sake but insofar as it is a means of maintaining the legal system's objectivity and thereby serving its larger purpose.

[61] Barber and Fleming complain, "We've never seen anyone use the distinction between construction and interpretation consistently," *Constitutional Interpretation*, p. 97.

[62] Solum, Legal Theory Blog, April 29, 2008, retrieved from http://lsolum.typepad.com/legaltheory/2008/04/reply-to-griffi.html, and "Originalism and Constitutional Construction," Abstract, *Fordham Law Review* 82, 2013, p. 453.

[63] Barnett, *Restoring*, p. 120.

legal text constrains permissible construction.[64] Solum identifies three distinct modes of construction – by politics, by principle, by original methods – each of which would carry different practical implications.[65]

Even if its advocates were to arrive at a single, coherent, and consistently used notion of constitutional construction, however, it would not help the case for Public Understanding Originalism. For the alleged need for construction rests on an emaciated image of interpretation. The interpretation of conceptual expression is not the stenographer's task of passively recording dictation; it is not robotic compliance with paint-by-number-style instructions. In the process of applying a concept to a particular situation (asking, for instance, "Is *this* an exercise of speech?" or "Is *this* an impediment to religious practice?"), the fact that a person must think in order to find the answer does not mean that he must add something to the law. Determining whether a concept encompasses a particular concrete is not an exercise of building or creation. While those who assert a need for construction are correct that application of the Constitution requires more than mindlessly taking dictation, it does not require something more than interpretation. For the rational application of an abstract rule to previously unidentified cases *is* rational interpretation.

The root of the confusion lies in the fact that, like Textualism, Public Understanding Originalism fails to appreciate the open-endedness of concepts – the fact that a concept's meaning encompasses more than just those items previously explicitly identified as members of the kind in question and more than just those aspects of the conceptualized units than have been previously recognized. If one assumes that the meaning of a concept straitjackets us to the particular understanding of that concept that was widely held at a certain date, then the application of the concept to novel circumstances *would* demand a new activity, different from interpretation; something like construction would be called for. Given that concepts are open-ended in the way that I explained in section 2, however, the rational interpretation of concepts can do far more work than the construction lobby supposes. Their notion of interpretation, in other words, is constricted by their unduly narrow conception of concepts' meaning.

In the end, by all the critical yardsticks, judicial review conducted according to Public Understanding Originalism fails. It would not foster the Rule of Law; it would not help to fulfill the function of a legal system; and it would not serve the objective substance, administration, or authority of law. By locating the fundamental authority of a legal system in certain men's beliefs, Public

---

[64] Whittington, *Constitutional Interpretation*, p. 5; and Barnett, *Restoring*, p. 122.
[65] Solum, "Originalism and Constitutional Construction," Note 38 in this chapter.

Understanding Originalism "authorizes" uses of coercive power that may be completely unjustified. Far from the objectivity that it wishes to provide, its method is thoroughly subjectivist. The Public Understanding notion of meaning surrenders us to the rule of those particular men who installed the laws and their beliefs about laws' meaning, rather than to laws – and to laws' actual meaning. Correspondingly, it fails to protect individual rights. Legal power is unleashed to do whatever those original lawmakers and meaning fixers thought it may do. The Constitution offers no sanctuary, since its meaning, too, is treated as merely that which the people of a certain time thought that it was (based on their beliefs about its words). We may correct nothing by appeal to objective analysis of rights or persons or of any concept, for we have arrived too late on the scene.

4. DEMOCRATIC DEFERENCE/POPULAR CONSTITUTIONALISM

Our next school of thought about the proper method of judicial decision making is what I will call the Democratic Deference view. Its various iterations have acquired numerous labels – Popular Constitutionalism, Democratic Constitutionalism, Democracy-Reinforcing Judicial Review, Political Process Theory, and Consensualism, among others – and advocates offer slightly different accounts of its primary aims, bases, and requirements. The bond that transcends their differences is the belief that the people should have a greater role in shaping law.[66] The essence of the view is the conviction that courts should defer to the will of the people. (I will use "Popular Constitutionalism" and "Democratic Deference" interchangeably.)

Advocates of Democratic Deference are legion in the academy, in the White House, on the bench, and on the political hustings and occupy positions across the political spectrum.[67] Bruce Ackerman, Larry Kramer, Mark Tushnet, Newt Gingrich, and the Tea Party have all been associated with one or another version of this outlook.[68] Theodore Roosevelt repeatedly claimed

---

[66] Erwin Chemerinsky, "In Defense of Judicial Review: The Perils of Popular Constitutionalism," *University of Illinois Law Review*, 2004, p. 675.

[67] Jeffrey Rosen has noted "an explosion of writing by liberals who subscribe" to Popular Constitutionalism over the past several years. "Judge Mental," *The New Republic*, March 15, 2012. Writing in 2012, Tom Donnelly reports that Popular Constitutionalism has been discussed in more than 800 law review articles since 2000. Donnelly, "Making Popular Constitutionalism Work," *Wisconsin Law Review*, 2012, p. 163, Note 11 in this chapter.

[68] Other right-wing political organizations also embrace Democratic Deference, such as the Judeo Christian Council for Constitutional Restoration, which sponsored a 2005 conference on "Remedies to Judicial Tyranny." See Mark C. Miller, *A View of the Courts from the Hill: Interactions Between Congress and the Federal Judiciary*, Charlottesville: University of Virginia

that the court should not interfere with the people's will and that voters should enjoy greater latitude to override Supreme Court decisions.[69] Woodrow Wilson famously opposed "mechanical" governance and maintained that we are "accountable to Darwin, not to Newton."[70] Wilson lamented the Constitution's "overemphasis on individual rights" and reasoned that a properly constitutional government should "adapt to the will of the whole people based on the historical realities of the era."[71]

From the bench, such figures as Harvie Wilkinson, Richard Posner, William Douglas, and Oliver Wendell Holmes all sing from this missal. Wilkinson's recent book worries about judicial "disablement of democratic majorities" and warns against courts' "constitutionalizing" contested political questions.[72] Posner frequently criticizes court rulings for insufficient deference to local preferences and cultural diversity.[73] Holmes once remarked that he had no basis for evaluating a law other than by reference to "what the crowd wants."[74]

The Democratic Deference thesis is encountered by implication perhaps as often as by its explicit, theoretical articulation. When particular court

Press, 2009, p. 181. Gingrich has warned of the danger of "a court which imposes elite values in variance with the country," quoted in Miller, p. 10; also see p. 181. For some of Gingrich's more recent professions in the same vein, see Rosen, "Judge Mental," p. 8; and more generally, see Christopher W. Schmidt, "Popular Constitutionalism on the Right: Lessons from the Tea Party," *Denver University Law Review* volume 88, no. 3, pp. 523–557.

[69] See Barry Friedman, *The Will of the People: How Public Opinion Has Influenced the Supreme Court and Shaped the Meaning of the Constitution*, New York: Farrar, Straus & Giroux, 2009, p. 382; and Rosen, "Judge Mental," p. 8.

[70] Discussed in Howard Gillman, "Political Development and the Origins of the 'Living Constitution,'" p. 3. http://digitalcommons.law.umaryland.edu/cgi/viewcontent.cgi?article =1052&context=schmooze_papers, a paper adapted from Gillman, "The Collapse of Constitutional Originalism and the Rise of the Notion of the 'Living Constitution' in the Course of American State-Building," *Studies in American Political Development*, 11, Fall 1997, pp. 191–247.

[71] Don Wolfensberger, "Is Woodrow Wilson's 'Living Constitution' Mortal?" p. 4, paper available in conjunction with Congress Project Seminar on "Is Our Constitutional System Broken?" held at the Woodrow Wilson International Center for Scholars, Sept. 17, 2010. Retrieved from http://www.wilsoncenter.org/event/our-constitutional-system-broken. On Wilson's views, also see Paul Rahe, "Montesquieu's Natural Rights Constitutionalism," *Social Philosophy and Policy*, Summer 2012, pp. 51–53.

Over the course of his intellectual life, Wilson wrote several pieces concerning the nature and proper rule of constitutional government. See especially his *Congressional Government: A Study in American Politics*, Baltimore: Johns Hopkins University Press, originally published 1885, Johns Hopkins paperback edition 1981; later updated as a series of lectures given at Columbia University in 1907.

[72] J. Harvie Wilkinson III, *Cosmic Constitutional Theory: Why Americans Are Losing Their Inalienable Right to Self-Governance*, New York: Oxford University Press, 2012, pp. 106, 108.

[73] Richard Posner, "In Defense of Looseness," *The New Republic*, August 27, 2008, pp. 32–35.

[74] Quoted in Jeffrey Rosen, "Why Brandeis Matters," *The New Republic*, July 22, 2010, p. 25.

decisions are criticized (as they frequently are) for veering "too far from main-stream opinion" on an issue, the clear implication is that the court should adhere to the majority's sentiments. During the debate over the gay marriage cases before the Supreme Court in March of 2013, for example, many people argued that it would be a mistake for the court to "shortcircuit democratic debate" with an overly bold ruling, thereby inviting a replay of the decades of divisiveness that followed its *Roe v. Wade* decision.[75] Courts are frequently advised to allow "experimentation in the states" or to "permit the political process to play out, finding its own resolution" of a controversial issue. Dialogue is a frequent motif in the Democratic Deference school, favored as a means of fostering consensus around legal rulings. Jack Balkin and Reva Siegel have written that the court should engage in dialogue with the American people, responding to "popular visions of the Constitution's values and ... [translating] these values into law."[76] "On questions of constitutional interpretation," the Democracy Deferrers agree, "judges should view themselves in a dialogue with the people and their elected representatives."[77]

Notice that at least some of the Originalist arguments that many people find persuasive rely on a kindred premise that deference is due to the democratic will. We should defer to the original meaning of words, Originalists often argue, because that best expresses the people's wishes. And the people are sovereign. Democratic Deference theory eliminates concern with *original* meaning, but agrees with Originalists that the people's will should rule. It simply champions the will of people today, since that is who is governed by today's laws.[78]

While the thrust of Popular Constitutionalism's concern is clearly to give the people what they choose, it is important to recognize that advocates do not see themselves as abandoning questions of laws' meaning. Larry Kramer, for

[75] Justice Ruth Bader Ginsberg is on record as believing that *Roe* was poorly decided for these reasons. See Jeffrey Toobin, "Heavyweight," *The New Yorker*, March 11, 2013, p. 43.

[76] Quoted in Jeffrey Rosen, "What's a Liberal Justice Now?" *New York Times Magazine*, May 31, 2009, p. 52.

[77] Schmidt, "Popular Constitutionalism on the Right," p. 528. Miller discusses the dialogue "movement" on pp. 5–12. Justice Ginsberg is known to favor the court's opening "a dialogue with the political branches," Toobin, p. 43.

[78] Some champions of Democratic Deference would deny the legitimacy of judicial review all together, rejecting the final sovereignty of the Supreme Court. See, for instance, Mark Tushnet, *Taking the Constitution Away from the Courts* (1999); Tushnet, "Our Rights, Not the Court's," *Wall Street Journal*, June 29, 2013; Jeremy Waldron, *Law and Disagreement*, New York: Oxford University Press, 1999; and Waldron, "The Core of the Case Against Judicial Review," 115 *Yale Law Journal* 1346, 1348 (2006). Many others, including Gingrich and Lino Graglia, periodically at least intimate this view. See, for instance, Rosen quoting Gingrich in "Judge Mental," p. 8.

instance, claims that it is final *interpretive* authority that rests with the people.[79] In Barry Friedman's account, it is through "judicial responsiveness to public opinion that the *meaning* of the Constitution takes shape."[80] "Consensualists" such as Michael Perry believe we should honor "the current social consensus on what the words of the document mean."[81]

The school's core idea, again, is that courts should defer to the will of the people. Perhaps because of its several variations, scholars frequently observe that the theory "defies easy definition."[82] Yet the unifying contention is that "the American people (and their elected representatives) should play an ongoing role in shaping contemporary constitutional meaning."[83] The law should be determined through inclusive dialogue. The result is the people's enjoyment of "interpretive autonomy from the judiciary."[84]

What, then, is the argument for this position? Its case is relatively simple. Judicial deference to the popular will allows full play to the democratic character of our Constitution. The most direct line of reasoning appeals to the legal system's authority. Where does that authority come from?, the Deference school asks. What is its source? *Why* is the Constitution our law?

Its answer: Because the people accepted it as such. In our system, the people are sovereign. So much so, in the view of Ackerman, that majority sentiment can sometimes alter the Constitution by means other than those specified in Article 5.[85] As a self-styled "Constitutional dualist," Ackerman distinguishes "normal lawmaking" from periods of "constitutional politics" marked by "higher lawmaking," occasions on which the people are intensely engaged, mobilized, and express their will in ways that override the formalities of Article 5. Just as the people are empowered to alter our constitution, so we

---

[79] Larry D. Kramer, *The People Themselves: Popular Constitutionalism and Judicial Review*, New York: Oxford University Press, 2004, p. 8.

[80] Friedman, p. 383, emphasis added. The public's reaction to a court ruling is a crucial part of how the meaning of the Constitution is determined, he maintains, p. 382. Note that Friedman's book presents a historical study rather than direct advocacy of Popular Constitutionalism.

[81] Discussed in Barber and Fleming, p. 67.

[82] Donnelly, p. 160. Chemerinsky writes that "there is no precise definition of the concept" of Popular Constitutionalism, p. 675; Schmidt contends that it is best conceived as a "spectrum" of views, p. 530.

[83] Donnelly, p. 161.

[84] Schmidt, p. 528.

[85] Bruce Ackerman, *We the People: Foundations* (volume 1, 1991); and *We the People: Transformations* (volume 2, 1998). See especially *Foundations*, pp. 15–16 and 50–56. This process, he believes, responds to the complexities of modern American politics. *Transformations*, p. 6. For a slightly fuller presentation of Ackerman's exact position, see my lecture "How Activist Should Judges Be? Objectivity in Judicial Decisions," Note 16 in this chapter.

are empowered to alter how it can be altered. Ackerman rejects constitutional objections to this as hypertextualist.[86] Justice Stephen Breyer likewise supports the idea that "courts should take greater account of the Constitution's democratic nature when they interpret constitutional and statutory texts" by emphasizing that governments "derive their just powers from the consent of the governed."[87] Breyer favors judicial restraint so as to expand the arena for democratic decision making.[88]

Another influential advocate of Democratic Deference is John Hart Ely, who proposed that the U.S. Constitution is distinguished not by its commitment to certain substantive principles (such as individual rights) so much as by its structures for ensuring procedural fairness. And those procedures that it requires are deliberately democratic in character, designed to facilitate rule by the people's wishes, he contends. Constitutional requirements concerning warrants and juries and equal protection, for example, are intended to ensure that everyone receive a fair hearing, but what a "fair hearing" means (and thus, what should govern, in the end) is that which most of the people would accept as a fair hearing. It is only in this way that a people can truly be self-governing. The responsibility of the courts, correspondingly, is to interpret laws in a way that mirrors the people's wishes. While the mechanics of governing are left to the decisions of the people's elected representatives, it is crucial for courts to ensure that those decisions are truly representative. If the people's will is to be sovereign, judges must attune themselves to that will in their readings of the law.[89]

While Popular Constitutionalism's array of advocates might emphasize somewhat different arguments for the propriety of judicial deference and different means of best providing that deference, the basic, shared thesis is that all branches should serve the will of the people. Government "by the people" requires that judicial review listen to the people.[90]

Critique

When we appraise the Democratic Deference model of judicial review by the standards of an objective legal system, its failings are more readily visible, I think, than are those of Textualist or Public Understanding Originalism.

---

[86] See discussion in Farber and Sherry, *Desperately Seeking Certainty*, p. 98.
[87] Stephen Breyer, *Active Liberty*, New York: Knopf, 2005, pp. 5, 132.
[88] Breyer, *Active Liberty*, p. 37.
[89] John Hart Ely, *Democracy and Distrust: A Theory of Judicial Review*, Cambridge, MA: Harvard University Press, 1980, see especially pp. 6–7, 73–104, 135–179.
[90] I discuss the basics of the Democratic Deference view a bit further in "Why Originalism Won't Die," pp. 171–173.

Democratic Deference fails on all three measures that are most vital to objective law – those concerning a legal system's substantive laws and policies, its manner of administration, and its authority for governing. Correspondingly, rather than fostering the Rule of Law, courts' deference to democratic will would deliver us to the Rule of Men. And by so doing, it would utterly fail to perform the function of law. Let me elaborate.[91]

First, consider this model's position on the three cornerstones of legal objectivity. *What* may a legal system do, under this account of proper judicial decision making? What will be the substance of its laws? Whatever the majority chooses. *How* will the legal system be operated? In what manner will its coercive power be administered? However the majority thinks best. What is the *warrant* for the legal system's exercising its power in the ways that it does? The fact that most people support its being used in that way. "Because we want to" is the license for government action.[92]

Popular Constitutionalism's most critical error is this last, its position on law's authority. Its prescription for judicial review rests on the consent theory of authority's source. When courts are advised to hew close to public opinion (on gay marriage or abortion or privacy, for instance), the implication is that that should have the final say – that popular will is the ultimate arbiter of legality.[93] Champions of different versions of Democratic Deference might protest that my analysis fails to capture their distinct nuances or fortifications, yet no subordinate subtleties can escape the essence of the view. The instruction to courts to accommodate the public's thinking on an issue indisputably implies that the agreement of the governed supplies the authority of government. (Indeed, this premise is overt in some of the reasoning on behalf of Popular Constitutionalism; recall Ackerman and Breyer, among others.) On this view, the law has no authority other than that which the people decree. Courts, correspondingly, may not deliver any interpretations that are at odds with that.

---

[91] To the extent that certain defenses of Originalism also allege the sovereignty of democratic will, they are subject to some of the same criticisms that I make here.

[92] Strictly, the popular will cannot be simply equated with the majority will, as Democratic Deference advocates would not all advocate direct referenda on contested questions followed by judicial deference to whichever views carry a majority's support, in each case. The exact meaning or referent of "the popular will" and its cognate terms is ill-defined and fluid, in most defenses of Democratic Deference. For our purposes, it will suffice to continue to use "majority will" as a convenient shorthand for this sometimes elusive idea of "the people's will."

[93] Observe that the reverse is not true: While the Democratic Deference account presupposes the consent theory of legal authority, consent theory does not commit one to Democratic Deference as the single appropriate method for judicial review. Many Originalists, for instance, accept consent as the basis of law's authority without endorsing the Democratic Deference judicial posture.

The problem, however (as demonstrated in my explanation of law's moral authority in Chapter 4) is that popular will is not the source of law's authority – not of the authority of an objectively valid legal system. To suppose that it is would slide into the belief that might makes right. *Because we want it* is no more valid a moral justification when pressed by a large number of well-meaning people than when it animates a small gang of malevolent, thuggish dictators. We must not let the principle at stake be obscured by who the "we" is, on a given occasion, or by what it is that "we" want.[94]

Part of the appeal of Popular Constitutionalism stems, I think, from a confusion over the nature of objectivity. Some of its partisans are motivated by the desire to minimize the bitter contentiousness that so often surrounds questions of law's meaning. The way to do that, they assume, is to satisfy the greatest number of people – in other words, through deference to majority will. Controversy, from this perspective, is evidence of the absence of objectivity, thus the way to achieve objectivity is to tame controversy. What could be fairer than a vote? Not necessarily a formal vote, but its effective equivalent: having the court confine its rulings to align with the weight of public opinion.

Unfortunately, this approach completely bypasses objective law. Instead of instructing courts to assert the answer to questions of legal meaning (e.g., of whether a college's affirmative action policy is or is not compatible with equal protection) and instead of positing a general means of determining what the objective meaning is, Popular Constitutionalism withdraws, preferring to cater to social peace. That is its paramount good. And in this way, Democratic Deference equates the "objective" with the "most widely agreed upon," elevating a social condition (people's relative harmony about a law's meaning) over the ascertaining of actual meaning. In other words, its methodology "socializes" objectivity, converting a question about existents (What does the law's language refer to and *does* this particular policy violate equal protection?) into a question about people (What are people's beliefs about this policy?). Under this view, being objective is not an effort to "get reality right." It is a compromise. It is whatever opinion about the relevant reality will most mollify the most people.

---

[94] It is important not to confuse the plausibly stronger case for a closely related position with the reasoning for the Democratic Deference view itself. On the question of what the judiciary should demand in order to *implement* a particular ruling most effectively, people often contend that bold measures far afield from mainstream opinion will trigger destructive backlash. That may be an argument for going slowly. I am not here endorsing it, but it is certainly a plausible argument. Regardless, my point is that such implementation is a different question from a court's best means of ascertaining what the law *is*. I will say more about this issue in Chapter 8.

"Socialized" objectivity, unfortunately, is subjectivism – a fact obscured by the number of subjects whose opinions are indulged.[95]

By treating the law as "that which most people support," in practice, Democratic Deference replaces the Rule of Law with the Rule of Men. Correspondingly, it surrenders the stable framework that a law-governed society demands. Law can hardly be clear or knowable if it is in continual flux, transformed by the winds of political opinion. When strong gusts sweep *many* people's minds, on its view, so is our law changed.

One of the purely practical problems with this concerns the determination of when the requisite change has taken place. How are courts to discern when enough minds have changed – and changed in sufficiently deep ways – to warrant a reading of a law that differs from the reading of that law in the past, given that the law has not been altered in any more formal or overt way? (At least, "the law" as we ordinarily think of it.) Ackerman's positing of periodic episodes of "higher lawmaking" is notoriously open to dispute concerning when such episodes actually occur.

The emergence of the Tea Party movement in recent years nicely illustrates the fragility of law under a Democratic Deference regime. While it is political Progressives who have historically been more associated with Popular Constitutionalism, many of the conservative and libertarian voices in the Tea Party have also advocated applications of the Constitution that reclaim the power of the people.[96] One conclusion from this is obvious: "The people's will" is itself splintered. Progressive advocates of Democratic Deference and conservative advocates of Democratic Deference typically seek different, if not diametrically opposed, government policies – *and* contend that their demands reflect the popular will. Obviously, they cannot both be right. Further, consider the electoral fortunes of these conflicting camps and the implications for the law, under the Democratic Deference view. If we are to understand the law as essentially that which the greatest number of people would like it to be, the question arises: When a large number of Tea Party candidates are elected to Congress and displace Progressive incumbents, does the law change? Such that the Tea Party version of constitutional meaning should prevail? (Equal Protection does not condone affirmative action programs, for instance, and federal health care mandates are not a tax.) Do our laws change at least until an election cycle later, when the Tea Party may lose seats and a Progressive

---

[95] See related discussion in my "'Social' Objectivity and the Objectivity of Value," *Science, Values, and Objectivity*, eds. Peter Machamer and Gereon Walters, Pittsburgh: University of Pittsburgh Press, 2004, pp. 143–171.

[96] See Schmidt, Note 68 in this chapter.

reading again becomes sovereign? How many candidates must win or lose? What about the moderates who gain office, those who do not conveniently fall into either camp? What *is* "the mandate" of a given election? (We leave aside the additional reality that the Tea Party and Progressive movements themselves encompass members of sometimes significantly differing views on particular laws.)

These tangled practical questions are simply the most superficial indicators of the much more basic problem. Under the Democratic Deference view of law's meaning, the political trumps the legal. Indeed, the difference between the legal and the political is dissolved. The judiciary's object is to understand not what the law means, but what public opinion (fragmented, inconsistent, informed or confused as that may be) would like.[97]

A grain of truth in the Democratic Deference view no doubt helps to explain people's confusion about this. The majority's preference *may* play a limited role in a proper legal system. For certain confined purposes (such as the selection of legislative representatives), it is unobjectionable for a majority's will to be decisive. We must not mistake the circumscribed role for majority will *within* the bounds of valid legal authority for that which supplies the authority of that system, however. In simpler terms: Public opinion is not what justifies the use of force.[98]

Note that while individuals' consent is required to authorize particular types of government action that would, without that consent, infringe on their rightful freedom of action, individuals' consent is not *sufficient* to render something a proper, objectively valid law. For it is not sufficient to authorize the use of coercive power or to justify the infringement of anyone's rights. As we explained in Chapter 4, the powers legitimately bestowed on a government may not exceed the powers within the bestowers' own authority; I may not confer on anyone the authority to use force in ways that I myself do not possess. No law that is adopted solely on the basis of the people's wanting it, therefore, could qualify as valid.

Finally, consider the implications of the Democratic Deference account of law's meaning for the *function* of a legal system. Contrary to its implications,

---

[97] And courts are to be tea-leaf readers in more senses than one. Louis Michael Seidman has openly called for the dissolution of the legal-political distinction. He argues that we should treat the Constitution merely as a symbol whose "meaning" depends on one's political premises. Seidman, *On Constitutional Disobedience*, New York: Oxford University Press, 2013.

[98] Slightly more fully: There are procedurally proper and improper ways of administering an objective legal system. Decision by the preference of a majority is one legitimate means of making certain decisions (not all, by any stretch), but those decisions must remain within the boundaries of the legal system's authority. Majority preference may decide who will fill certain government offices, for example, but may not determine the scope of powers of those offices.

the function of the law is not: to give people whatever most of them would like. That aim does not warrant the use of force. "Most of us really want those people to ... pay these wages/stop praying at those mosques/have *this* kind of marriage/enjoy their guns/not have those guns" does not justify a government's forcing "them" to do as "us wants." Yet that – pleasing the largest bloc of people – is Popular Constitutionalism's mandate for judicial review. That is what courts are to uphold. And in this way, judicial review by Democratic Deference detaches the exercise of legal power from it proper mission. When what the law *is* is politicized to suit social preferences by the premises of Democratic Deference, courts are directed not to uphold the law and its expressed limitations of government power, but, instead: people power.

Historically, appeals to the democratic will have sometimes leant the sheen of legitimacy to horrendous injustices. While laws prohibiting interracial marriage, for instance, long reflected the majority's will in many jurisdictions, they did not represent valid exercises of legal power. Before its 1967 ruling in *Loving v. Va* (which struck down legal prohibitions on interracial marriage), the Supreme Court effectively deferred to majority will when it refused to hear a similar challenge to Virginia's law twelve years earlier.[99] The result was twofold: a contented majority of Virginians; the ongoing abuse of all those individuals denied the freedom to marry whom they pleased for every day of their lifetimes in the intervening years.[100]

In short, judicial review conducted on the policy of Democratic Deference valorizes the people's will and misunderstands the authority of law. For the number of people who may wish to do something does not self-confer the authority to do it. Objectivity does not consist in consensus. Legal authority does not stem from consensus.

It is important to appreciate that in practice, Popular Constitutionalism fundamentally alters what a constitution is. It treats a constitution not as a framework placing firm boundaries around the permissible powers of government, but as the assortment of actions taken by government bodies,

---

[99] *Loving v. Virginia*, 388 U.S. 1 (1967). The earlier case was *Naim v. Naim* 197 Va 80; 87 S.E.2d 749 (1955). The court had directly upheld the prohibition on interracial marriage in 1883 in *Pace v. Alabama*. 106 US 583, cited in Clark M. Neily III, *Terms of Engagement: How Our Courts Should Enforce the Constitution's Promise of Limited Government*, New York: Encounter Books, 2013, p. 27.

[100] For more on the basic history, see Richard Delgado, "Naim v. Naim," *Nevada Law Journal* volume 12, 2012, pp. 525–531. Notice that the democrats' plaint "but the people aren't ready for this" shares with Originalism a misplaced concern with time. Originalists ask: "Is this what *they* thought, back then?" while Popular Constitutionalists ask "Is this what *we* want, now?" Both bypass the appropriate question: Does the government possess the authority to do this, or not?

somewhat reminiscent of the historical British view of a constitution. As Bradley Thompson characterizes that view, the British conceived a constitution as "an inheritance, a compound of political and legal institutions."[101] Essentially, it is that collection of actions that a nation's legal officials have taken. Thomas Paine, by contrast, defended the American conception of a constitution as "a thing antecedent to a government.... [It] is not the act of its government, ... [rather] the government is ... governed by the constitution."[102]

The similarity of historical British Constitutionalism with Popular Constitutionalism is not perfect. The set of actions taken by government agencies is not just the same thing as the set of legal "interpretations" that enjoy the greatest current popularity. Yet what the two notions share is the important belief that at bottom, people's opinions should rule (whether those opinions be ascertained more directly by reading the pulse of the popular will [Democratic Deference] or less directly, by inferring it from the actions taken by the people's representatives in various offices of government [the British conception]). Either way, opinion should determine how the government's power is employed. The understanding of a constitution as fixing boundaries within which a government must confine itself is cast aside, replaced by a constitution that is pliable, ever in the making. Democratic Deference in judicial review would treat the written document as more a suggestion box than a stated commitment to specific, definite restrictions.

Consider: What does it mean for a law or government action to be "constitutional," under Democratic Deference? What is the critical requirement? It is not conformity with the rules laid down in a written constitution. Nor is it adherence to the principles that underwrite those rules. Rather, to be constitutional is to be in tune with the polls. The way to make something legal is, essentially, to make it popular.

As the name "Popular Constitutionalism" suggests and as with any hybrid ideal, the relative strengths of its primary components need to be clarified. Which of these two values holds ultimate command: that which is popular or that which complies with the Constitution? When the written constitution is subject to override by democratic will, the answer is clear – and the

---

[101] For discussion of the contrast between the British and American Founders' views of a constitution, see C. Bradley Thompson, "Revolutionary Origins of American Constitutionalism," in *History, On Proper Principles: Essays in Honor of Forrest McDonald*, eds. Stephen M. Klugewicz and Leonore Ealy, Wilmington, DE: ISIS Books, 2010, pp. 1–27. Lord Bolingbroke crystallized the British view in 1735: "By Constitution we mean, whenever we speak with propriety and exactness, that assemblage of laws, institutions, and customs, derived from certain fixed principles of reason ... that compose the general system, according to which the community hath agree to be governed." Quoted in Thompson, p. 5.

[102] Paine, *Rights of Man*, 1790, quoted in Thompson, pp. 6–7.

document's safeguards are a mirage. Such an invertebrate constitution cannot protect individual rights.

Courts are, as they are often accused of being, a counter-majoritarian institution. This is because the U.S. Constitution is a counter-majoritarian institution. Individual rights are a counter-majoritarian phenomenon. And that is what objective law is empowered to uphold.

5. PERFECTIONISM/LIVING CONSTITUTIONALISM

The next school holds that judicial review should revolve around neither words' original meanings nor contemporary popular will. It advocates a more openly philosophical approach to the determination of laws' meaning. Perfectionism is the belief that courts should be continuously engaged in the betterment of our legal system. Our predecessors were fallible, after all, and their legal policies were sometimes blinded by the norms of their era (consider race, gender, or punishment, for instance). Moreover, it reasons, earlier law that may have been perfectly valid in its context can be rendered obsolete by changing social conditions. The law, accordingly, should be seen as a living organism. If it is to govern over an extended period, law must evolve to suit current conditions and maturing moral convictions. Indeed, one might argue, it is only with this kind of a commitment to shape the law to be its best that we can truly serve the proper aims of a legal system.

I am using the term "Perfectionism" to encompass figures and ideas that are often referred to under the rubric "Living Constitutionalism," or sometimes (a little more selectively applied) a "philosophic reading" or "moral reading" of law. (I will use "Perfectionism" and "Living Constitutionalism" interchangeably.) Certain of Perfectionism's concerns also arise in Democratic Deference theory and in the Minimalist school that we will consider in the next section. While no bullet-point platform enumerates necessary and sufficient commitments that allow easy classification of particular thinkers, the core idea has been clearly articulated by a number of figures.[103]

Thurgood Marshall denied "that the meaning of the Constitution was forever fixed at the Philadelphia Convention."[104] During his Senate confirmation hearings for appointment to the Supreme Court, he agreed that the role of the

---

[103] In some contexts, it would be appropriate to distinguish Perfectionism from Living Constitutionalism on the grounds that what animates "living" law in the latter need not be the effort to perfect the law, as in the former. For our purposes, however, because the two are alike in those features that are most salient to their objectivity, we need not distinguish.

[104] Quoted in Jill Lepore, "The Commandments," *The New Yorker*, January 17, 2011, p. 74. This was in an address celebrating the bicentennial of the Constitution.

court was "to ascertain and give effect to the intent of the framers" only with a caveat: "Yes, with the understanding that the Constitution was meant to be a living document."[105] In later years, Marshall characterized the judge's role as to "do what you think is right and let the law catch up."[106]

William Brennan is widely regarded as the paradigm of Living Constitutionalism. To ascertain the law's meaning, he explained in a 1980's speech, "The ultimate question must be: what do the text of the words mean *in our time?* For the genius of the Constitution rests not in any static meaning it might have had in a world that is dead and gone, but in the adaptability of its great principles to cope with current problems and current needs."[107]

Correspondingly, Brennan believed that judges should emphasize "the transformative purpose" of the constitutional text, which embodies an "aspiration to social justice, brotherhood, and human dignity."[108] Earlier in his career, Brennan had sounded the same theme, claiming that "courts have a creative job to do when they find that a rule has lost its touch with reality and should be abandoned or reformulated to meet new conditions and new moral values."[109] In a similar vein, Benjamin Cardozo held that "the great generalities of the Constitution have a content and a significance that vary from age to age."[110]

---

[105] Quoted in Justin Driver, "Ignoble Specificities," *The New Republic*, April 5, 2012, p. 32.

[106] Quoted in Deborah L. Rhode, "Letting the Law Catch Up," *Stanford Law Review* 44, A *Tribute to Justice Thurgood Marshall* (Summer 1992), pp. 1259–1265. (Rhode had served as a clerk for Justice Marshall.) Retrieved from http://www.jstor.org/discover/10.2307/1229058?uid =3739920&uid=2129&uid=2&uid=70&uid=4&uid=3739256&sid=21102060146441.

[107] Quoted in Justin Driver, "Robust and Wide Open," *The New Republic*, Feb. 17, 2011, p. 39, emphasis added.

[108] Brennan, quoted in Calabresi, *Quarter Century*, pp. 6–7.

[109] Brennan, 1957 speech at Georgetown, quoted in Driver, "Robust and Wide Open" p. 39; as well as in Calabresi, *Quarter Century*, p. 7.

[110] Benjamin Cardozo, *The Nature of the Judicial Process*, Yale University Press, 1921, p. 17. Cardozo also writes that "the content of constitutional immunities is not constant, but varies from age to age," pp. 82–83. Recall from section 4 Woodrow Wilson's contention that we must understand law's meaning as continually evolving: "Living political constitutions must be Darwinian in structure and in practice," quoted in Rahe, p. 52. Also see James W. Caesar, "Progressivism and the Doctrine of Natural Rights," *Social Philosophy and Policy* volume 29, no. 2, Summer 2012, p.177; and Lepore, "The Commandments," p. 74. The early twentieth-century political progressive and journalist Herbert Croly advised that we should not be "hypnotized and scared into accepting the traditional constitutionalism, as the final word in politics," quoted in Eldon J. Eisenach, "Some Second Thoughts on Progressivism and Rights," *Social Philosophy and Policy* volume 29, no. 2, Summer 2012, p. 196. Note, too, that in extolling the common law (as we saw in Chapter 5), David Strauss held that the Constitution can be changed without formal amendment – which also reflects the idea of Living Constitutionalism. While the common law's cautious, slow-paced image seems at odds with Living Constitutionalism's air of radical reform, Strauss's book's title – *The Living Constitution* – is indicative of the basic harmony of these views.

The phrase "Living Constitutionalism" is hurled as an epithet at least as often as it has been translated into a practical program of judicial methodology. The figure who has developed the most systematic, sophisticated articulation of both the theory and its prescribed practice is Ronald Dworkin. His work has been extensively studied, intensely debated, and enormously influential. I will thus use his theory to represent the Perfectionist belief that law must change and grow in order to be alive to present realities. The role of judges in applying the law, correspondingly, is to help it to have the best life that it can. Whatever a law's original meaning might have been, a legal system's vitality demands that it be interpreted in ways that advance our ideals in contemporary conditions.

For Dworkin, the law of a nation cannot be reduced to a set of rules.[111] Law also encompasses principles whose authority does not depend on prior enactment or formal recognition. Indeed, it is these principles that breathe life into law. They are the constant, the enduring guideposts, with stated rules serving simply as the means by which to achieve these ideals. Correspondingly, Dworkin advocates a principled understanding of law. In contrast with the theories that we have considered thus far, neither words, intentions, nor popular understandings, either historical or contemporary, can tell us all we need to know to apply law.

In his now well-known metaphor, Dworkin presents judicial review as akin to the composition of a chain novel, a cooperative enterprise undertaken by a series of authors over an extended period of time.[112] In writing a chain novel, one person starts a tale, another fills in chapter 2, another chapter 3, and so on. Each installment should develop the tale further, consonant with what has gone before in plot, characterization, and the like. (Today, many television series are written in this manner.) Dworkin contends that, in like fashion, a judge must see decisions as part of an ongoing story. His role is to interpret what has been said so far as well as to move the narrative forward – to advance and perfect the legal system. The proposal is not that judges should attempt

---

[111] Dworkin has elaborated his view in a wealth of writing across decades, including responses to various critics. The basics of his theory are most systematically elaborated in *Law's Empire*, Cambridge, MA: Harvard University Press, 1986, especially pp. 176–275, but valuable amplifications and clarifications are found in *A Matter of Principle*, Cambridge MA: Harvard University Press, 1985, especially pp. 119–177; *Justice in Robes*, Cambridge, MA: Harvard University Press, 2006; *Freedom's Law: The Moral Reading of the American Constitution*, Cambridge, MA: Harvard University Press, 1996; *Taking Rights Seriously*, Cambridge, MA: Harvard University Press, 1978; and "Comment," *A Matter of Interpretation*, ed. Gutmann, Note 7 in this chapter, among other places.

[112] Dworkin, *Law's Empire*, see especially pp. 225–238. Also see Dworkin, "'Natural' Law Revisited," *University of Florida Law Review* 34 (1982).

to perfect the system in a single stroke, but in those ways that the relevant case suggests, while sensitive both to legal precedent and contemporary moral attitudes.

To reach his decisions, Dworkin's ideal judge stands under two basic demands. First, his contribution must "fit" in the sense that it adequately conforms to the story as it has unfolded so far – to previous laws and applications of those laws. As such, it must be something that other judges might have written, had they been assigned this particular case. Second, the judge's contribution must aim to make the legal system the best it can be. (Think of this as the "bestness" or optimizing condition.) Judges should rule in ways that contribute to a cohesive story and to a *good* story, resolving new disputes by advancing the law while remaining faithful to those principles that have governed before and should govern the whole. The check against inappropriate activism rests in the obligation to be faithful to the character of the system that has emerged thus far; a judge is not a solo short story writer, free to devise independently a self-contained tale however he likes.[113]

In contrast to the Textualists, Dworkin believes that the legal text alone is of limited value. On his view, the meaning of law can be understood only in light of the larger purposes behind it. "Lawyers are always philosophers," Dworkin writes, meaning that they must always engage in philosophical reasoning to determine what a law means and demands.[114] Consequently, a judge should regard the provisions of a specific law, of a constitution, and precedent as expressions of an underlying philosophy of government and he should rest his decisions on the relevant principles of that philosophy. Dworkin calls his theory "law as integrity" to reflect the belief that a legal system should be an integrated whole whose individual parts and provisions reflect a unifying core of commitments and that form a tightly woven fabric. A judge must weave his rulings in particular cases into this broader fabric. When the language of a law does not readily tell a judge how to apply it, the question to pose is not about words or about speakers' intentions or public understandings. Rather, the question for judges to be guided by is: Which decision is required by our system's political philosophy and will most advance its goals?

---

[113] See *Law's Empire*, pp. 398–399. In different essays in his Legal Theory Blog over the years, Larry Solum has offered several helpful explanations of different aspects of Dworkin's view. See, for instance, Legal Theory Lexicon 65 on The Nature of Law, retrieved from http://lsolum .typepad.com/legal_theory_lexicon/2008/05/legal-theory-le.html and Legal Theory Lexicon 59 on Law as a Seamless Web http://lsolum.typepad.com/legal_theory_lexicon/2006/10/ the_law_is_a_se.html.

[114] *Law's Empire*, p. 380.

What legitimates this, in Dworkin's view, is the Constitution itself. It is not simply a series of words. Whereas Scalia would have judges heed only the text, Dworkin contends that the Constitution expresses ideas and that judges must read between the lines to grasp those ideas that give meaning to the text on the page. Abstract principles are as much "the law" as any other provisions enunciated in the Constitution.[115] Consequently, judges must seek out those principles and interpret in a way that maintains the legal system's philosophical integrity and strives to perfect it.

In sum, Dworkin's method seeks to provide the best of both worlds: the stability offered by respect for the past as well as progress in the perpetual betterment of law. By viewing the law as organic, all Living Constitutionalists would agree, we should recognize judges' important role in fostering its healthy growth.[116]

Critique

While I shall focus my critique of Perfectionism primarily on Dworkin's specific rendition of it, my purpose is not to indict *him* so much as to examine those features that most centrally affect the objectivity of judicial review and of the larger legal system it is meant to serve. If Dworkin or any other figure is able to escape one or another of my particular criticisms, so much the better for his account. *Better* only superficially, however. For the principles of my critique will stand, I believe, to indict the essence of the Living Constitutionalist view in any incarnation. And seeing this should advance our appreciation of what judicial review should and should not consist of, if it is to serve objective law.[117]

---

[115] See "Constitutional Cases," in *Taking Rights Seriously*, pp. 147–149, and *Law's Empire*, pp. 225, 243.

[116] Again, I am focusing on Dworkin's as a particularly sharply developed version of the perfectionist perspective. Barber and Fleming describe their own theory, despite its drawing on elements of Textualism, intentionalism, consensualism and pragmatism, as basically a kind of Dworkinianism which endorses Dworkin's belief that "fidelity in interpreting the Constitution as written calls for a fusion of constitutional law and moral philosophy." *Constitutional Interpretation*, pp. 189–192. Fleming also offers an insightful discussion of the affinity between Jack Balkin's "Living Originalism" and Dworkin's Perfectionism in both theories' aspirational characteristics and both endorsing a moral reading of the Constitution. See Fleming, "The Balkinazation of Originalism," *University of Illinois Law Review* 3, 2012, pp. 669–682.

[117] The critical literature on Dworkin is voluminous. Among many worthwhile critical essays of Dworkin's view, see Christopher L. Eisgruber, "Should Constitutional Judges be Philosophers?" in *Exploring Law's Empire*, ed. Scott Hershovitz, Oxford: Oxford University Press, 2006, pp. 5–22; James E. Fleming, "The Place of History and Philosophy in the Moral Reading of the American Constitution," pp. 23–39; and Jeremy Waldron, "Did Dworkin Ever Answer the Crits?" pp. 156–181, both, also in Hershovitz. Dworkin responds to his critics in Hershovitz, pp. 291–311, as well as in many of the essays in *Justice in Robes*, among other places.

On first acquaintance, Perfectionism offers a lot to like. It pulses with vibrancy. On its account, judges are not weighed down by the errors of history. Perfectionists recognize the indispensable role of philosophy in shaping a legal system and in subsequently understanding and applying its provisions. Dworkin emphasizes the integrity of a proper legal system, which *is* essential to its objectivity, if it is to serve its authorizing mission.

Further, at least some versions of Perfectionism reflect a more sophisticated understanding of language and word meaning than do many Originalists. I must underscore the qualifications in this claim, for some Living Constitutionalists rely on woefully subjectivist conceptions of meaning while some Originalists have a much more nuanced grasp of language than others. Dworkin, however, is particularly strong on the role of context in establishing the objective meaning of abstractions and his work has greatly contributed to legal philosophers' understanding of the difference between the intended meaning of a term and the expected applications of that term. One might interpret "cruel and unusual punishments," for example, either as a shorthand for a specific, finite list of punishments that constitute that class of punishments in the minds of certain people at a certain time (the term's "expected applications" sense) or, alternatively, one might interpret "cruel and unusual punishments" as a concept, open-ended in the ways that I have explained and – significantly – as requiring present users' additional thought, in order to determine valid applications of that concept in concrete cases. We can infer from the constitutional framers' open embrace of the death penalty in legal practice, for instance, that the death penalty was not on their mental lists of cruel punishments, yet arguably, it *is* cruel. That is, one might plausibly argue that the death penalty qualifies as among those actions that the concept of cruelty encompasses (the concept, as distinguished from the expected application of the word "cruelty").[118]

In developing this distinction, Dworkin refined our understanding of both what is right-minded in many versions of Originalism and what is wrong-footed, thereby motivating his own theory's attempt to marry allegiance to existing law (the "fit" condition on judicial review) with philosophically guided discretion to make the law better (the optimizing or perfecting condition). His theory

---

[118] To put the point from a slightly different angle: Insofar as courts should be faithful to the meaning of existing law, Dworkin illuminated the distinct kinds of speaker intention that one might believe are salient to that meaning, namely, what lawmakers intended to say and what lawmakers intended to be the consequence of their saying the things that they did. See Dworkin, "Comment," in *A Matter of Interpretation*, ed. Gutmann, pp. 116–122, and related discussion of the distinction between concepts and conceptions in *Law's Empire*, pp. 170–176. (I do not mean to imply my own view of capital punishment with this example, but simply to illustrate the different ways of interpreting the clause's meaning.)

liberates courts from the clock-bound confines of earlier people's thinking that reigns on the altars of Originalists.

Finally, the Perfectionist school is appealing insofar as it is unafraid to assert judges' role as an active one – intellectually active. Judges must be fully engaged as thinkers, it contends, in order to acquit their responsibility to understand the law's abstract concepts in the relevant context and as components of a larger, philosophically conceived legal system.

(It is also worth noting that, due to the open-ended nature of concepts, the law *is* "living" in one undeniable respect. Language "lives" in that what people later understand a word to mean can objectively extend beyond what was understood about a word in an earlier era. As our knowledge of a phenomenon expands, our understanding of both a word's exact roster of referents and, more basically, of the exact characteristics that distinguish those referents as a unique class, are open to correction [correction that does not betray the original concept]. This fact implies that we can and should expand and contract the "list" of itemized referents that those who originally used a concept might have provided. It also implies that we may revise the definition that they might have provided [refining the definition of "whale," for instance]. Indeed, the need to revise initial misapprehension and crudeness is natural, given that knowledge about any subject typically grows on the basis of further experience and further reflection. Certain concepts obviously represent phenomena that are much simpler or much more familiar from direct experience than others, such that revisions of these would be much less natural or less frequent. The point is simply that as knowledge grows, understanding of concepts' meaning grows. Objective law – a legal system that seeks to "get reality right" by correctly identifying the relevant facts concerning the function of government, individual rights, infringements of rights, and so forth – must be sensitive to this.)[119]

Its several elements of appeal notwithstanding, Perfectionist judicial review is fundamentally inimical to objective law. While Perfectionists are right that meaning is not reducible either to script on a page or to the associations in earlier men's minds and that courts must attend to the philosophy inherent in a legal system, its conception of exactly how courts should do this is seriously misguided. And the confusion stems, I think, from a misshapen understanding of what the law itself is.[120]

---

[119] As noted earlier in the chapter, much more on the open-ended nature of concepts and how it is important to proper interpretation of law can be found in my essays "Originalism's Misplaced Fidelity" and "Why Originalism Won't Die."

[120] For greater elaboration on some of the arguments to follow, see my critique of Dworkin's theory in "Why Originalism Won't Die," pp. 173–179.

Perfectionism's Image of Law

Perfectionism operates on an invalid image of law. On just a little reflection, the chain-novel metaphor makes this plain. For according to it, the law is ever in-progress; it has no fixed identity. Novelists are *authors*, after all, and fiction is *creative* writing. Judges, on this model, play the analogous role of making the law – a role that is actually assigned by our Constitution to the legislative and executive branches rather than the judiciary. The inherited law that courts work from (such as written Constitutional provisions, statutes, agency-issued regulations) is merely a draft, on this view, not to govern until edited and extended by a contemporary court which strives to make the law better. But this means, as Douglas Edlin explains, that for Dworkin, "the substantive content of the law is not identified prior to adjudication (and possibly changed as a result of the adjudicative process); the content of the law is *determined through* the interpretive process of adjudication."[121]

Consider the actual practice of this method. When courts follow Dworkin's prescription, what is treated as the ultimate root of legal authority? As its bedrock foundation? It is not the Constitution or written law, nor even the principles reflected in that law. Rather, it is judges' ideals *coupled with* those received legal materials; these, together, are sovereign.

In fact, however, the law has an identity that people are to follow regardless of whether courts are ever involved. People's *understanding* of the law and of its objective application certainly tend to evolve, over time; *that* may be an ongoing work in progress. And we can and sometimes do deliberately change the law through formal, constitutionally stipulated procedures. What is crucial to recognize, however, is that at any given time, "the law" refers to something with a definite, discernible identity. A specific law says some things and not others. People might argue more or less frequently or more or less reasonably about the proper application of different laws. We debate provisions of the First Amendment and of the Fourth Amendment far more often than Article II's age or birthplace conditions of eligibility for the presidency, for instance. Yet regardless of how difficult it can be to answer some

---

[121] Douglas E. Edlin, *Judges and Unjust Laws: Common Law Constitutionalism and the Foundations of Judicial Review*, Ann Arbor: University of Michigan Press, 2008, p. 30, emphasis added. One might object that, to be exact, it is only law that is challenged in court that is treated as a draft, not necessarily all law. Yet insofar as Dworkin instructs courts to fit their resolution of particular cases with a broader view of the seamless web that a legal system is, even laws that are not directly challenged are subject to being changed (and in effect, being treated as merely a draft) by courts' decisions in cases that center on other elements of the law. That is, insofar as the resolution of Case X involves a courts' reconceiving the broader image of the various parts and dimensions of the legal system as a whole and of how these work together, *all* law stands to be altered.

of the questions that arise concerning laws' proper application in particular cases, each provision of law possesses a distinct identity and expresses a distinct legal condition. It is precisely this that judges are called upon to elucidate. We could hardly live under the Rule of Law if the law were made in the very process of being "applied." The notion is incoherent; that which has no identity does not exist and that which does not exist cannot be applied, either properly or improperly.

I suspect that the attraction to Dworkin's view stems, in part, from a failure to distinguish between two familiar senses of "meaning" that people often use when referring to a law. Sometimes, we have in mind the meaning of the words, that is, the semantic meaning, the *overt, readily accessible to anyone who can read the language* meaning that has a definite identity prior to anyone's interpretation of it in a given case. Call this Sense A. (In this sense of meaning, the meaning of "search" is different from the meaning of "speech," insofar as the different words simply refer to different types of activities.)

Other times when we discuss a law's "meaning," however, we have in mind something different, namely, *the practical effect* that will result from the judiciary's ruling about a law's semantic meaning. Call this Sense B. Because the court declares the legally mandatory understanding and application of a disputed law, the resulting requirements for people's actions can seem to be the "real" meaning, given that that is what will actually control how governors may govern and how individuals are treated by the legal system. It is thus quite natural for people to say that "the court's ruling means that the university will have to halt its admissions policy" or that "the ruling means that the company will have to rehire those workers" or that "the city will have to allow that protest in the park."

What is crucial is to recognize that Sense B is a different and merely figurative sense of "meaning." Indeed, to treat Senses A and B as interchangeable would imply that courts could never be mistaken in their interpretations of law. For whatever ruling a court issues will, in fact, carry practical effects for the people living under that legal system. However unjustified a particular ruling might be by the standards of law's semantic meaning and fully objective meaning, the law does "mean" whatever a court says it means *in that second sense* of carrying practical effects. But this exposes the folly of conflating the two. And this conflation, in turn, props up the supposition that the law has no meaning antecedent to a court's "interpretation" of it (the supposition that is implicit in Dworkin's account). Since the courts do determine laws' practical effects (at least for a certain period, until they may be felled by later courts' rulings or other changes in the law), if the meaning of the law just *is* its practical effect (as in Sense B), then law has no meaning until supplied by the court.[122] Rather than Living Constitutionalism, this might be better dubbed Legal Creationism.

Indeterminacy

Another widespread confusion also lends Dworkin's account undue credibility. This concerns the law's much-lamented indeterminacy. Examining this notion more closely further exposes the errors in Dworkin's portrait of law and of courts' proper relationship to law.

Many legal philosophers assume laws' indeterminacy in misleading ways that rest on ill-founded expectations of what "determined" law is and provides. While claims of legal indeterminacy come in varying forms and strengths, the basic claim is that "the laws ... do not determine legal outcomes." A modest version holds that "in most (or almost all) of the cases that are actually litigated, the outcome is underdetermined by the law."[123]

What is misleading is this: While it is true that the particular, concrete applications of law are not determined in the sense of being specifically and expressly preordered (e.g., "appellant Jacobsen should be given a new trial;" "appellant Lopez should not be granted the religious exemption to permit his company's hiring policy"), the law does "determine" the ways in which legal power may and may not be exercised. The fact that a law does not issue, in advance, a set of uniquely acceptable actions for legal officials to take in applying that law to a particular situation does not entail that its identity or its implications for governance are indefinite. (Here again, people's understanding of its identity and implications might be unsettled, but that is distinct from the object about which their understanding is unsettled itself having no identity.)

A meaningful abstraction (such as "no warrants shall issue, but upon probable cause" or "no religious test shall ever be required as qualification to any office")[124] means something definite – and not various other things. Because any law is an abstraction (including relatively narrow provisions, such as the

---

[122] This would apply, at least, to law whose application is challenged and ruled on by the courts. Much law is applied without prompting anyone's protest and thus carries practical effects without courts weighing in. Insofar as any law might be challenged, however, the fact remains that under Dworkin's theory of judicial review, a law's identity at any given time is at best presumptive.

[123] Larry Solum, *Legal Theory Blog*, Lexicon # 36 "Indeterminacy," retrieved from http://lsolum .typepad.com/legal_theory_lexicon/2004/05/legal_theory_le_2.html.

Solum provides a good discussion of the basics of the question, including its relationship with Legal Realism and Critical Legal Studies. Note that I use "laws" here to encompass cases, regulations, statutes, constitutional provisions, and other legal materials.

[124] U.S. Constitution, 4th Amendment and Article VI.

stipulation that "no person except a natural born citizen … shall be eligible to the office of President"),[125] it will permit a certain range of applications and disallow many others. That some abstractions' applications are less commonly contested than others does not alter their being abstractions and as such, their requiring judgment on the part of those persons responsible for applying them to concrete cases. Even when judges may exercise discretion within a certain range, what is important is that the law sets the boundaries of that range.

While a given law might be indeterminate in the sense of its being very vaguely and ambiguously drafted, my point here is that there is nothing in the nature of law that necessitates that. "Abstract" does not mean indefinite.[126]

What is true in legal philosophers' references to law's indeterminacy is the fact that the proper application of abstract rules requires thought on the part of those applying them. We cannot simply press a button and have an abstraction's legitimate applications unspool before us. (There *isn't* an app for thinking.) Abstract rules are not accompanied by exhaustive inventories cataloging all the conceivable actions that would and would not violate those rules. Yet it is a mistake to confuse judges' explicit articulation of that which is implicit in a rule or of that which can be logically derived from a rule (which occurs whenever a law is applied to a particular case) with ex nihilo creation. To draw a logical inference from law L is not to spawn a brother to L. And it is a costly mistake, because the conflation of the two encourages the belief that law must be supplemented by the courts. That is, if the law itself is viewed as always, necessarily indeterminate – incomplete in its instruction and thus unable to govern outcomes – then judges must "complete" law by making it something other than it was beforehand. Judicial lawmaking is not merely permitted, on this view, but positively required.[127]

Beyond the intricacies of determinacy, the more basic problem is hard to escape. Because the Living Constitutionalists view the law as less complete

---

[125] U.S. Constitution, Article II.

[126] And "open-ended" in its proper, objective sense does not mean amorphous in essential character (just as the fact that "multiples of 3" is an infinite number does not entail that non-multiples may be included among its referents). We must also recognize the difference between a law and the statement that expresses that law. Some ambiguities might arise from poor expression; others, from incoherence in the very concept of the law in question which precede the issue of its clear and accurate expression. For related helpful discussion, see Brink on distinct senses of "judicial discretion," Brink, "Legal Theory, Legal Interpretation, and Judicial Review," p. 112.

[127] As an example of this confusion, consider Cardozo's claim that, because judges must fill in law's "gaps," the work of the appellate judge is essentially similar to that of a legislator. Speaking of judges and legislators, he writes: "The choice of methods, the appraisement of values, must in the end be guided by like considerations for the one as for the other. Each indeed is legislating within the limits of his competence." Cardozo, *Nature of the Judicial Process*, pp. 112–113.

and less definite than it actually is, they compensate by expanding the role of the judiciary. This is fairly plain in Dworkin's theory.

The heart of Dworkin's judicial guidance rests in its twin guideposts of fit with the past and "bestness," optimizing, as judges pursue a progressive trajectory of improvement, steadily making the law the best it can be. The critical literature on Dworkin has examined each of these in depth, with the most natural questions concerning the exact meaning of each guideline and the relationship between them, especially in regard to their comparative weight. For our purposes in assessing the objectivity of his theory, I will concentrate on the second. For the requirement of fit between present rulings and previous law is certainly valid, at least in principle, even while much hinges on the exact kinds and degrees of fit that are required. Dworkin's second, perfectionist plank, however, is fundamentally at odds with a proper requirement of fit and it is here that his theory's objectivity comes undone.

If courts are to make the law the best it can be, a crucial question is: "best" by what standard? On what basis are judges to determine? Dworkin's response is fatally flawed, for he allows judges' personal beliefs about ideal law to shape their "development" of the legal narrative. In truth, however, for an accurate understanding of existing law, such personal beliefs are utterly beside the point.

As his defenders would no doubt rush to observe, Dworkin does, at times, stress that the judge's role is interpretive, confined by the obligation to fit a ruling with previous law. And it is only among "eligible" readings that judges should strive to improve the law.[128] Yet Dworkin also endorses "creative" interpretation and "constructive" interpretation.[129] Law as integrity "begins in the present and pursues the past only so far as and in the ways its contemporary focus dictates," he writes.[130] It aims "to justify what [the laws' authors enacted] ... in an overall story worth telling now."[131] In doing this work, a judge's "own moral and political convictions are ... directly engaged."[132] He is to "draw on his own convictions about justice and fairness and the right relation between them" and reject "the rigid idea that judges must defer to elected officials."[133]

Such a judge should not be taken for an activist, Dworkin assures us, since "he will refuse to substitute his judgment for that of the legislature when he

---

[128] Dworkin, *Law's Empire*, p. 231. Also see pp. 255 and 397–399.
[129] *Law's Empire*, pp. 228, 255.
[130] *Law's Empire*, p. 227.
[131] *Law's Empire*, p. 227.
[132] *Law's Empire*, p. 256.
[133] *Law's Empire*, p. 398.

believes the issue in play is primarily one of policy rather than principle."[134] Notice the implication, however (which nothing in Dworkin's ensuing passage counters): When a judge believes that a principle *is* involved, the judge many override the law. In Dworkin's ideal, judges should aim to "impose purpose over the text or data or tradition being interpreted."[135] Note "impose." Dworkin uses the same term later, when he writes that properly, the judge "tries to impose order over doctrine, not to discover order in the forces that created it" as he "struggles toward ... a scheme for *transforming* the varied links in the chain of law into a vision of government now speaking with one voice, *even if* this is very different from the voices of leaders past."[136] And Dworkin heartily acknowledges that on his account, judges are "authors as well as critics," called upon to make judgments that are "subjective" and "aesthetic."[137]

This is not reassuring to those concerned for the Rule of Law.

What is potentially confusing is the fact that judges should, indeed, seek out the best understanding of the language that expresses law, using objective standards to attend to the full context. I agree with him on that. In the case of a legal system, this will typically involve teasing out implicit premises and principles. Judges are not to employ any standard other than that, however. For doing so would displace the existing law. Judges should draw on the philosophy that is *in* the law, in other words, but not impose their own. The law is not a puppet and judges should not be ventriloquists, speaking their own views while pretending to be the voice of the puppet.

While Dworkin's appreciation of the philosophical character of the law and of its proper interpretation is a welcome advance over the reductivist reading of text espoused by certain other schools of judicial review, in the end, Dworkin's judge is overly philosophical. More exactly: he is invited to engage in philosophical judgment of an inappropriate type. Part of the problem is Dworkin's inclusion of judges' personal philosophies, as we have just seen. But the defect is even deeper. By urging judges to make use of a nation's underlying political principles *in the particular ways* that he does, Dworkin elevates those principles over the actual law that has been enacted. Yet the philosophy behind a legal system and the laws of a legal system are not the same thing. Even when Dworkin's judge is proceeding not by his personal political values but by those of the legal system, it is critical to respect this difference between laws and philosophy. Let me explain.

---

[134] *Law's Empire*, p. 398.
[135] *Law's Empire*, p. 228.
[136] *Law's Empire*, p. 273, emphasis added.
[137] *Law's Empire*, pp. 229, 231.

A law that is inconsistent with a nation's underlying political philosophy may still be consistent with its bedrock law. For a constitution itself might, in some of its provisions, depart from the basic philosophy that inspires it and that informs most of its individual provisions. (The original U.S. Constitution includes such instances, most notably in its treatment of slaves.)[138] That our Constitution may not consistently uphold its own guiding philosophy, however, does not give judges the license to correct the law and subject the nation to a different constitution, as revised by them (Constitution-*plus*, a more perfect model). Rational interpretation of law requires that judges engage in philosophical thought; it does not require that they assume the role of philosopher kings. Judges' role is not to devise the philosophy that will inform the law, nor to choose the laws by which to implement that philosophy. The Rule of Law – even in a legal system that is grounded on sound moral and political philosophy – must be respected by judges as the rule of *law*.

Dworkin may be right, then, that judges should read the Constitution as reflecting an underlying philosophy and that they should make use of that philosophy, when interpreting its provisions. It would nonetheless exceed their interpretive function for judges to apply that philosophy when it is contradicted by specific provisions of the Constitution. As a quick illustration, suppose that our Constitution included a provision authorizing complete government control over citizens' travel, domestic and foreign. The fact that this betrays the principle informing the Constitution's recognition of individuals' freedom of speech and of religion and of property and of assembly (among others) would not license judges to treat travel as equally free, ignoring the explicit restriction on travel. Philosophy is fair game for judges to employ, as long as it *is* the philosophy that is reflected in the Constitution. When that philosophy is expressly contradicted by a particular provision, however, a court must yield to the written law. To do otherwise would enthrone judges as sovereign over the law, rather than sovereign in the application of existing law. It would sanction a usurpation of law*making* authority (Constitution-making, in this case) that the judiciary does not rightfully hold.

Simply put, interpreting law in its best possible light and philosophical context is a different activity from making the law better by altering the law itself. Dworkin's prescription for judicial review would do the latter. It would subject us to the rule of philosophy rather than the Rule of Law. While it is true that proper law must itself be philosophically justified, this does not erase the difference between philosophical justification and legal justification.

---

[138] Many would argue for other features falling into this category, pointing to the Constitution's treatment of women, eminent domain, commerce, or taxation, for instance.

To address a possible concern: It is true that the objective Rule of Law must itself be premised on proper philosophical foundations. As I sought to establish earlier and have maintained throughout, a system's fundamental legal authority can be valid only if it rests on legitimate moral authority. In order for a society to be governed objectively, however – in a way that can properly serve its function of protecting individual rights – we do need to have a legal system rather than merely: police, armies, and philosophers. We need an intermediary body of *laws* and we need to respect them as laws, rather than as cosmetic veils between philosophical conclusions and coercive muscle which judges are free to dismiss when they have a better idea of what the properly governing philosophy would say.

Some might object that we stand to gain better protection from the legal system when judges may correct philosophical errors, given that unjustified laws can violate individual rights. That last is certainly true: Philosophically unjustified laws can inflict serious damage and should be changed. The issue here, however, is how that should be done and by whom. To grant judges the prerogative to correct a legal system's philosophy or its sometimes flawed implementation of its philosophy in its formal law would replace the Rule of Law with the rule of those men. They would be men who are legally trained, in this case, yet they remain men whose legal authority properly arises under the Constitution, and does not supersede it.

Dworkin is correct that certain conclusions of political philosophy inform a legal system and affect the objective meaning of that system's laws. He is correct, further, in maintaining that judges should make use of these values in finding the proper application of laws. Those political values that judges may legitimately rely on are legitimate, however, only insofar as they are embedded in law. Political values as such, independent of the adopted law, have no purchase on courts' reasoning, given that courts' function is to apply the law.

↬

"Law as integrity" is a promising label, but the integrity that Dworkin's judges are to uphold floats unmoored from those anchors that could make it objective. For Dworkin, what is most important is that a judge's rulings cohere – but not with the relevant reality (a legal system's actual laws and its implicit stands on underlying philosophical principles concerning individuals' freedom or rights or government authority, for instance). On his view, judges' rulings should cohere, rather, with the opinions of others: their predecessors and contemporaries as legal authors and interpreters. Perfectionist judicial review affords a louder voice to today's beliefs than would the Originalists and a louder voice to past beliefs than would the Democratic Deference advocates.

It also reserves the definitive voice for the beliefs of judges themselves. At its roots, however, it is a subjectivist prescription for judicial review. What validates judicial decisions on this view is consensus, some degree of agreement among other opinions and current judges. The *authority* of law – indeed, the identity of law – is an ongoing negotiation.

The result is that the conduct of judicial review by this method would not fulfill its proper function. Nor would it advance the larger function of the legal system. If judges are to uphold a "Living Constitution" at the expense, at times, of the U.S. Constitution, the law is less knowable and the law is less stable. Indeed, what "it" is is completely unsettled. Individual rights, which are to be protected by law, are correspondingly less secure. This method makes the law *not* the law, in practice, given that what it treats as binding is, instead, that which judges deem best (a Constitution-*plus*, as I put it earlier). This is not the Rule of Law. And this is not an objective legal system.

6. MINIMALISM

Our last school to consider is Minimalism, the view that courts should resolve cases by issuing narrow rulings that deliberately steer clear of broad principles and far-reaching implications. Judges rule properly to the extent that they meticulously assess "one case at a time," as Cass Sunstein puts it, in the most case-specific ways possible.[139] Sunstein provides a clear exposition of the view, explaining that Minimalist judges strive to rule on "narrow" and "shallow" grounds while eschewing ambitious theories. Whatever changes in legal practices might be effected through judicial rulings should be small and incremental, as judges resolve as little as necessary in order to decide the dispute at hand. As Sunstein elaborates, Minimalists "favor decisions that are narrow, in the sense that they do not want to resolve issues not before the Court," and decisions that are "shallow, in the sense that they avoid the largest theoretical controversies and can attract support from those with diverse perspectives on the most contentious questions."[140] Ideally, judges leave "as much as possible undecided."[141] Accordingly, a Minimalist court avoids "clear rules," "abstract theories," and "final resolutions."[142] By so doing, the judicial footprint is minimized.[143]

---

[139] Cass Sunstein, *One Case at a Time*, Cambridge, MA: Harvard University Press, 1999.

[140] Sunstein, "Of Snakes and Butterflies: A Reply," *Columbia Law Review* 106, 2006, p. 2242.

[141] Sunstein, *One Case*, pp. 3–4.

[142] Sunstein, *One Case*, pp. ix–x.

[143] In this vein, Justice Samuel Alito has described his judicial philosophy as centered around "not trying to decide questions that are too broad, not trying to decide questions that don't have to be decided, and not going to broader grounds for a decision when a narrower ground is available." Confirmation Hearing on the Nomination of Samuel A. Alito, Jr. to be an Associate

The bold moves of Living Constitutionalists are anathema to the Minimalist, who "distrusts visionaries,"[144] is wary of theoretical "ambition," and "prizes stability."[145] "Justice is not to be taken by storm," Justice Cardozo once observed, but "is to be wooed by slow advances."[146] Arguments concerning the legal status of gay marriage and abortion that warn against the court's going "too far, too fast" or "gratuitously inflaming our political divisions" thus reflect the dispositions of the Minimalist. Rather than seeking to resolve cases definitively, he believes that courts should leave issues open to further conversation.[147]

On the substantive political principles that inform a legal system, Minimalism is neutral.[148] By adhering to a course of moderation, patience, and compromise, judges avoid "taking stands on the deepest questions in social life"[149] and the "most contested questions of constitutional law."[150] Minimalism is not aligned with any particular ideology. As Sunstein explains, there may be "liberal minimalists and conservative minimalists; majoritarian minimalists and Originalist minimalists; 'active liberty' minimalists and 'negative liberty' minimalists."[151] It is an ecumenical mode of review.

In the same spirit, judges are advised to be flexible about Minimalism itself. "[T]here are times and places in which minimalism is rightly abandoned,"

Justice of the Supreme Court of the United States: Hearing Before the S. Comm. on the Judiciary, 109th Congress 318–19, 492 (2006), at 343.

[144] Sunstein, *A Constitution of Many Minds: Why the Founding Document Doesn't Mean What it Meant Before*, Princeton: Princeton University Press, 2009, pp. 36, 38, 39.

[145] Sunstein, *A Constitution of Many Minds*, p. 38. Also See Barber and Fleming, *Constitutional Interpretation*, pp. 140ff.

[146] Benjamin Cardozo, Lecture at Yale University Law School (1923), quoted in *The American Journal of International Law* 29, 1935, p. 32. Also see Cardozo, *The Growth of the Law*, New Haven: Yale University Press, 1924, 133.

[147] Ruth Bader Ginsburg is among those who spurn the idea that "large-scale social change should come from the courts," Jamal Greene describing her jurisprudence, quoted in Jeffrey Toobin, "Heavyweight," *The New Yorker*, March 11, 2013, p. 43. In the same spirit, Sandra Day O'Connor has maintained that "when we are concerned with extremely sensitive issues ... 'the appropriate forum for their resolution in a democracy is the legislature.'" Quoted in Jeffrey Toobin, *The Nine: Inside the Secret World of the Supreme Court*, New York: Doubleday, 2007, p. 51. O'Connor, in turn, was quoting Oliver Wendell Holmes. Also see Alexander M. Bickel, *The Least Dangerous Branch*, New York: Bobbs-Merrill, 1962, p. 70; and Sunstein, "Debate on *Radicals in Robes*," in *Originalism: A Quarter Century of Debate*, ed. Calabresi, p. 313. For more on the basic character of Minimalism, see Neil S. Siegel, "A Theory in Search of a Court, and Itself: Judicial Minimalism at the Supreme Court Bar," *Michigan Law Review* 103, 2005, pp. 1951–1958.

[148] See David Strauss's emphasis on neutrality in "Panel on Originalism and Precedent," in *Originalism: A Quarter Century*, ed. Calabresi, pp. 217ff.

[149] Sunstein, *A Constitution of Many Minds*, p. 42.

[150] Sunstein, *Radicals in Robes: Why Extreme Right-Wing Courts are Wrong for America*, New York: Basic Books, 2006, p. 27.

[151] Sunstein, "Snakes," p. 2241. Sunstein does not capitalize "Minimalism."

Sunstein cautions.[152] Stephen Breyer describes Minimalism not as a "general theory" to be applied in a uniform way, but as akin to a musical score that permits players to emphasize one theme rather than another in different performances.[153]

At its core, Minimalism is a jurisprudence of deference – deference to existing law, to previous courts, to the will of the people.[154] It "makes a large space for democratic self-government."[155] And its value neutrality helps to explain its appeal across familiar political divisions. Minimalism is evidenced in the writings of Edmund Burke and Oliver Wendell Holmes; in the reasoning of Sandra O'Connor, John Roberts, and Samuel Alito no less than in Ruth Ginsberg, Stephen Breyer, and Cass Sunstein.[156]

The appeal of Minimalism is not difficult to see. Several considerations, partially overlapping, all seem to recommend it. (Some of them echo arguments we have already encountered on behalf of Popular Constitutionalism and Living Constitutionalism, and some chime with rationales beneath the common law.)[157]

One line of argument holds that the Minimalist course of small, unobtrusive steps fosters stability and predictability, which are essential elements of the Rule of Law. By avoiding radical breaks with reigning legal practice, a nation's law will be most constant and most knowable. The Minimalist drive to find common ground, moreover, shows respect for people of "diverse perspectives,"[158] which itself will engender people's respect for the legal system.[159] Minimalist restraint can thus serve, albeit indirectly, as an effective means of keeping the social peace.[160]

---

[152] Sunstein, "Snakes," p. 2243. Sunstein also discusses this in *One Case*, pp. 54–60.

[153] Breyer, *Active Liberty*, p. 7.

[154] As a central means of respecting existing law, Minimalism pays significant attention to legal doctrine, that is, the reasoning and rules of earlier courts. For discussion of "Doctrinalism" in its own right (rather than as a strand within Minimalism), see Bobbitt, pp. 41–51; and Barber and Fleming, pp. 135–140.

[155] Sunstein, *Radicals*, p. xv.

[156] Among political conservatives, the preferred label for Minimalist review is "judicial restraint" and it is often advocated in response to perceived judicial activism. Not all arguments for restraint, however, are Minimalist.

[157] I elaborate on the core commitments and arguments for Minimalism at greater length in "Reckless Caution: The Perils of Judicial Minimalism," *New York University Journal of Law and Liberty* 5, 2010, pp. 347–393.

[158] Sunstein's phrase, quoted earlier, "Snakes," p. 2242.

[159] See Strauss, "Common Law Constitutional Interpretation," p. 908. While Strauss self-identifies more as an advocate of common law jurisprudence than as a Minimalist per se, he defends common law largely by reasoning that is Minimalist (as do many advocates of common law).

[160] See Strauss, "Common Law Constitutional Interpretation," p. 907; Sunstein, *Radicals*, pp. 27–29.

Another apparent strength is Minimalism's ideological neutrality. Judicial review *should* be value free, its advocates contend, thus judges should refrain from asserting their views about a just society or good government and should serve, instead, simply as impartial umpires of others' disputes.[161] Rather than taking sides in fractious debates, Minimalist review would deliberately bypass "the deepest questions about ... the meaning of the free speech guarantee," for example, or "the extent of the Constitution's protection of 'liberty.'"[162] A Minimalist bench thereby allows for "reasonable pluralism."[163]

Yet another professed virtue rests in Minimalists' intellectual humility. Since even the most enlightened jurist's knowledge is naturally limited and since yesterday's sure bet often seems a foolish error, in hindsight, it would be hubris for a court to suppose that it knows better than all the generations of voters, legislators, judges, and framers whose reflections have crafted the law that they inherit. Because "no one, and no court, has a monopoly on wisdom," Sunstein reasons, it is best to "give many minds an opportunity to contribute."[164] This is what the modest, moderate path of Minimalism allows. It best positions the court to draw on others' wisdom to reach sound solutions – eventually – and to limit the damage that results from its inevitable errors. Small steps risk less.[165]

In this way, Minimalism also maximizes flexibility. By attending exclusively and closely to the particulars of the case before it, a court resists the temptation to tie the hands of others in the legal system. To borrow a phrase from Felix Frankfurter, it avoids "putting fetters upon the future."[166] A Minimalist court stands ever-ready "to accommodate new judgments about facts and values," Sunstein boasts.[167]

Finally, the single most important argument for Minimalists of all ideological stripes is the contention that its approach optimizes the democratic character of our government. On the belief that courts tend to remove too many issues from the control of the people, the Minimalist course of restraint would

---

[161] A view prominently championed by Justice Roberts, cited in Toobin, *The Nine*, p. 281. Sunstein cites Adrian Vermeule as another vigorous contemporary advocate of this sort of neutrality, "Debate on *Radicals in Robes*," in Calabresi, p. 289.

[162] Sunstein, *Radicals*, p. 28.

[163] Sunstein, *One Case*, p. 50.

[164] Sunstein, *A Constitution of Many Minds*, p. 45. Justice Roberts has agreed that "we need a more modest" Supreme Court. Quoted in Neily, *Terms of Engagement*, p. 121.

[165] Justice Brandeis once observed of the court, "The most important thing we do, is not doing," quoted in Bickel, p. 71.

[166] Frankfurter, *Youngstown Sheet and Tube Company vs. Sawyer*, 343 US 579 (1951) at 596, concurring opinion, quoted in Sunstein, *A Constitution of Many Minds*, p. 44.

[167] Sunstein, *One Case*, p. x. Also see p. 44.

allow the largest possible space for the people to rule.[168] The less that the courts decide, the more that the people decide. Thus, Minimalism maintains that in all but the most egregious cases of a constitutional violation, judges should defer to the democratic will.[169] As Breyer reasons, narrow judicial decisions enhance democracy by allowing ongoing "conversations" to mold future law.[170]

Critique

On analysis, Minimalism proves no more objective a method by which courts should exercise judicial review than do the other schools. Minimalism does offer a somewhat different style of guidance in that it is not so much a direct account of what the law means as it is a prescription for how judges should proceed, in cases when the law's meaning is most disputed. This is not a strength, however. It only pulls courts further from objective law.

Having developed an extended, in-depth critique of Minimalism in a separate paper, I will not recount all of its major failings here.[171] As with the other schools surveyed in this chapter, I will concentrate on those weaknesses that are most critical from the standpoint of a legal system's objectivity. At bottom, we will see that the very concept of Minimalism is incoherent. It does not, in fact, isolate a distinctive, logically unified method of judicial reasoning. Consequently, it does not genuinely guide the judges who are to follow it. In practice, its instruction licenses rule by the subjective opinions of individual judges.[172] And the reason that Minimalism urges such timid judicial review is an erroneous view of a legal system's proper ends.[173] By prizing, above all,

---

[168] On this view, more ambitious judicial methods (such as Dworkin's) "rob popular majorities of the opportunity to deliberate about, and through deliberation to reach consensus about, divisive moral issues," Barber and Fleming, p. 140. And whatever advantages might arise from having judges make decisions "are outweighed by the superior democratic legitimacy of political decision-making," Christopher J. Peters, "Assessing the New Judicial Minimalism," *Columbia Law Review* volume 100, no. 6, October 2000, p. 1476. Also see Peters, pp. 1458, 1459, 1469; and Sunstein, *A Constitution of Many Minds*, p. 111.

[169] See Sunstein, "Debate on *Radicals in Robes*," in Calabresi, p. 313, and *Radicals*, pp. 45–46.

[170] Breyer, *Active Liberty*, p. 72; also see pp. 5, 37. Justice Elena Kagan testified at her Supreme Court nomination hearings that the justices' role "must also be a modest one, properly deferential to the decisions of the American people and their elected representatives." Quoted in Neily, p. 122.

[171] Smith, "Reckless Caution," Note 157 in this chapter.

[172] Strictly, "it" cannot be practiced, if I am right that it has no firm identity, thus even to speak of its instruction "in practice" is a misnomer. This can only be its purported practice, as we shall see.

[173] "Timid" in aura, if not in fact, in its commending modest steps of limited ambition.

social peace and the will of the people, Minimalism mislocates the ultimate seat of legal authority and thereby diverts courts from attending to those features of a legal system's substance and administration that are vital for it to provide the objective Rule of Law. Let me elaborate on these charges.

Minimalism treats size as the pivot of proper judicial decision making, championing rulings' narrowness over breadth. What this actually instructs a judge to do is muddied by the fact that narrowness (like breadth) is a relative concept; it can be measured along different dimensions, such as the legal precedents for a ruling or the expected impact of a ruling. Impact itself divides into different types, such as impact on popular support for the court or impact on entrenched societal conventions (concerning the availability of abortion, for instance). These can sometimes point in conflicting directions, making two significantly different court rulings both seem Minimalist, by different measures of the "minimal." A very narrow legal *basis* for a ruling might undo the prevailing application of a law in a way that carries extensive practical repercussions, for instance (such as by uprooting entrenched police practices concerning the right to remain silent). Or a merely slightly different reading of just a few words of a legal provision, depending on the words, could bring a broad impact. (Consider the contested commas and phrasing of the Second Amendment and the implications drawn for gun control.) Which type of breadth matters?

In defending modest, small-scale rulings, it certainly sounds reasonable for the Minimalist to claim that a court should not decide issues not before it (as Justice Alito did in his confirmation hearings).[174] Yet much of what is in question is how much *is* before the court in a given case.[175] To apply the law to a particular controversy requires a judgment on what the law is, which naturally includes a judgment about its scope. (E.g., ruling that the Equal Protection clause prohibits a disputed hiring policy, or that the exercise of religion permits a firm's noncompliance with a federal health insurance mandate.) We have no reason to suppose that the scope of laws will always be narrow, however. The reach of some laws is broad. ("All firearms" as opposed to "22-caliber pistols," or "all abortions" as opposed to "abortions that occur during the third trimester.") When confronting a broad law, what does Minimalism counsel? Should a judge misrepresent the law, so as to adhere to the small-bore course of Minimalism? Or should he abandon Minimalism in such a case? By making size the test of judicial virtue and ignoring the fact that laws come in different "sizes," Minimalism's

---

[174] See Note 143 in this chapter.
[175] Alito's references to avoiding decisions that are "too" broad and to questions that "don't have to be decided" completely sidestep the standards employed to determine what does need to be decided and what constitutes too much breadth.

instruction is not actually a means of illuminating the law. It elevates judgments of size over judgments of law.

Notice a related problem: If certain kinds of narrowness are to be fostered but other types are to be avoided (so as not to reach *too* contentious a ruling, for instance), what is the basis for the difference? And won't that basis necessarily smuggle in some substantive commitments? A judge must, at least implicitly, rely on certain qualitative grounds for favoring one type of judgment rather than another. He must value narrowness of basis more than narrowness of impact, for instance, or close adherence to precedent more than close adherence to contemporary opinion. While Minimalism purports to be neutral on matters of substance, in other words, its noncommittal perch is untenable. To the extent that a judge sought to follow it, he would necessarily be relying on values other than those provided by the law. (This would also undermine the stability that Minimalism purports to provide.) The point is, Minimalism's core instruction – "do little!" – is useless unless supplemented by judgments about values.

To see this more vividly, focus on Minimalism's basic instruction to courts: *Minimize.* Minimize what? The lines of reasoning defending Minimalism suggest a number of things:

- the size of the steps taken by a court
- the pace of change in legal practices
- the impact of rulings on law
- the impact of rulings on society
- the textual, or the doctrinal, or the philosophical bases for rulings
- the ambition of rulings

Yet this is not all. Minimalists advise that other factors should also be taken into account, including:

- the desirability of gaining support from people of "diverse perspectives" and the means of gaining that support
- the desirability of gaining consensus on the court and the means of gaining that consensus[176]
- the weight of precedent
- the place of values in a legal system
- the stringency of Minimalism itself

[176] This is an aspect of Minimalism emphasized by Chief Justice Roberts. When nominated to be Chief Justice, Roberts expressed the desire that the court reach a greater number of unanimous decisions, which he thought would be an indication that justices were taking an appropriately narrow, case-bound approach. "The broader the agreement among the justices, the more likely it is a decision on the narrowest possible grounds," he explained. Quoted in Toobin, *The Nine*, p. 308. I discuss Roberts's view a bit further in "Reckless Caution."

What does all of this add up to? What is the practical takeaway for a judge? It is hard to tell.

What this assortment of considerations actually reveals, on reflection, is that Minimalism's signature directive is hollow. "Do little" or "do the least" has no content. By itself, such instruction offers no guidance. Its ultimate vacuity is embarrassingly exposed when Sunstein claims that certain landmark court decisions widely understood as engendering extensive change to legal practices – *Brown v. Board of Education* and *Lawrence v. Texas* – are, in fact, Minimalist – Minimalist, at least, in certain respects.[177] Moreover, he believes that Minimalists should be Minimalist about Minimalism itself. Recall that while "minimalism is generally the proper approach," in Sunstein's view, "there are times and places" in which it "is rightly abandoned."[178] "No sensible person could embrace minimalism in all times and places," he explains.[179]

Being "sensible," in other words, trumps Minimalism. Yet what *is* "sensible"? What standard governs whether a judge should or should not follow Minimalism in a given case? That is up to the judge; Minimalism does not tell him. A judge should faithfully practice Minimalism, in other words – except when he shouldn't.

This is judicial improv.[180]

Minimalism reflects a misguided attempt to forge into a single method a potpourri of goals, values, actions, and attitudes that are fundamentally different in kind. The legal basis for a ruling, for example (such as the narrowness of its doctrinal footing), is an essentially different kind of consideration than the controversy that one expects to be provoked by a ruling. Similarly, the accommodation of "*new* judgments about facts and values" (another of its desiderata) is an essentially different kind of aim than the aims of judicial humility or of legal stability.

Minimalism's disparate desiderata are simply incommensurable. They do not reflect a shared purpose or common justification. And they are not anchored in the objective authority of law; Minimalists do not endorse them on the ground of their purported necessity for the mission of protecting individual rights. Consider: Why should a court be concerned with the Minimalists' various ends? And how concerned should a court be? What is the relative

---

[177] Sunstein, *A Constitution of Many Minds*, pp. 40, 55, Note 49 in this chapter. *Brown v. Board of Education*, 347 US 483 (1954) and *Lawrence v. Texas* 539 US 558 (2003).

[178] Sunstein, "Snakes," p. 2234.

[179] Sunstein, "Snakes," p. 2242.

[180] Truly, this is a do-it-yourself policy – not in the innocent sense of "use your judgment to follow this policy," but rather, in instructing judges "use your judgment to make the policy."

weight of each of those ends that its various arguments defend? Individual Minimalists are left to answer for themselves.[181]

The upshot is that Minimalism does not cohere into a singular, definite form. The word does not name a valid concept. Correspondingly, it cannot issue distinctive guidance. Its incoherence in conception, in other words, necessitates its erratic governance, in practice. Minimalism's cornucopia of instruction collapses into none. Because it offers no systematic explanation of why *these* particular factors are critical or of their unifying mission and authority and because the weights and ranks of its disjointed directives are not provided, would-be practitioners are free to prioritize those desiderata in mutually conflicting ways. Even the same judge may emphasize one aspect of Minimalism in one decision and another in another decision (as Breyer's analogy with a musician playing passages differently on different occasions brings out). Minimalism's touted flexibility deprives it of the ability truly to constrain a judge who would practice it.

(And this is why it is difficult to determine whether or not particular jurists are Minimalists. Many judges tend to be Minimalist by certain yardsticks and not by others, or Minimalist by some measures in some cases and not in others. Passages from Justice Kennedy's opinion in *Kelo v. New London*[182] read as quite Minimalist, for instance, yet Kennedy galls many as the antithesis of Minimalist in *Lawrence* and *Windsor*. Justice O'Connor sounds Minimalist themes in some of her affirmative action opinions,[183] and strikingly un-Minimalist principles in her *Kelo* dissent. Yet even this assertion, characterizing a jurist's Minimalism in a specific opinion, would probably not hold up under the ever-shifting light of the Minimalist lava lamp. Obviously, a judge who subscribes to any judicial method could practice that method inconsistently; that is not a problem unique to Minimalism. The acute problem here is that, by Minimalism's promiscuous standards, it cannot identify what an inconsistency *is*.)

The larger point is that what it is for a judge to practice Minimalism is so elastic as to be meaningless. The protean character of its counsel can sanction nearly any judicial action. It is difficult to conceive of a ruling that would not find Minimalist footing under at least one of its multifarious aims.

---

[181] It is no accident that many Minimalists are positivists. They deny that rights are anything other than products of the democratic will (or of some combination of democratic will and other factors) and thus do not regard rights as a principle that should – or can – discipline the exercise of legal power. Having rejected the moral and conceptual framework that *should* govern the exercise of legal power (namely, the legal system's function of protecting individual rights), it is much more natural to urge that judicial review be guided by a bouquet of different flowers.

[182] *Kelo v. New London*, CT 545 U.S. 469 (2005).

[183] See *Richmond v. Croson* 488 US 469 and *Grutter v. Bollinger* 539 US 306.

(Remember that even *Brown* and *Lawrence* can qualify as Minimalist.)[184] And for the ordinary citizen who simply seeks to understand the implications of a Minimalist ruling for his own future conduct, Minimalism's guidance is inscrutable. Consider Justice Kennedy's hedge in his concurring opinion in *Kelo*, the Minimalist-reasoned eminent domain decision that precipitated a decidedly un-Minimalist backlash. Kennedy wrote that by allowing the particular taking of property in that case, the court did not "foreclose the possibility that a more stringent standard of review … might be appropriate" for other takings. Addressing the logical question of the basis for determining which standard would apply for different cases, his answer was not very helpful: "This is not the occasion for conjecture as to what sort of cases might justify a more demanding standard."[185]

This is the Minimalist mode. By deliberately shunning the principles that would explain the similarities that unite different cases, Minimalism leaves us guessing.[186]

To sum up, at the base of Minimalism's failings stands its misguided consecration of size or scope as the standard for judicial review. This is a thoroughly red herring. The scope of a law's provisions (or of a court decision's impact or of a decision's divisiveness, etc.) does not alter a law's status qua law. And it is the law, properly, that courts are to uphold. The only scope that a court should be concerned with is whether the power exercised by the government in a particular action falls within its scope of authority. If it does not, then the "size" of the ruling – its modesty in various other respects – is irrelevant. By

---

[184] As I put it in "Reckless Caution," "If minimizing the number and range of considerations brought to bear in reaching a decision is Minimalist, and minimizing disagreement with one's judicial brethren is Minimalist, and minimizing changes in a ruling's effects on current understandings of the law is Minimalist, and reducing social discord is Minimalist, and limiting the distance from legal judgments of the past is Minimalist – and so on – and if what "minimizing" in each of these cases *is* is continually shifting – we are hard pressed to know what Minimalism is not. However radical or consequential a decision might be in certain respects, the panoply of aims and techniques claimed by Minimalism means that by other of its elements, that decision is bound to also qualify as Minimalist." "Reckless," p. 374.

[185] Kennedy, concurring opinion in *Kelo*.

[186] This significant failure has not been lost on other commentators. See, for instance, Dahlia Lithwick's criticism of the court's ruling in the high-profile privacy case concerning police use of GPS devices, "*US v. Jones*: Supreme Court Justices Alito and Scalia Brawl over Technology and Privacy," *Slate*, January 23, 2012. Lithwick complains that the ruling "gives no sense whatsoever of when and how a warrant would be required for government surveillance … or how long such surveillance could endure before privacy concerns are raised." More generally, Jeffrey Rosen has observed that Minimalist rulings that fail to make clear their underlying principles compound confusion and necessitate clairvoyance. "The Age of Mixed Results," *The New Republic*, June 28, 1999, p. 46. I explain the inconsistencies among Minimalism's array of desiderata and the ultimate incoherence and vacuity of the concept more thoroughly in "Reckless," pp. 367–372.

the same token, if that power *is* within the government's legitimate authority, a ruling's "size" is irrelevant. The judiciary's function is to safeguard the law – whatever the law is and whatever its scope. Minimalism, however, directs courts' attention to a grab bag of considerations that are fundamentally extraneous to the identity and the meaning of the law. In so doing, it diverts judicial review from its proper mission. And the reason most frequently given for minimizing the judicial footprint is to maximize the people's footprint: to afford the greatest possible space for democratic self-governance. This means that Minimalism attributes ultimate authority not to the written constitution, but to that which a majority would like the law to be.[187]

When judged by the framework of objective law, then, Minimalism's failings are clear. Minimalist review would alter radically the role of the court. A Minimalist court is to determine how legal power may be used not on the basis of what the law is at a given time, but by cobbling together some blend of peripheral considerations that it expects people of diverse perspectives to accept. The law is subordinated to courts' projections of social harmony. Minimalism treats the legal system's authority as residing not in constitutionally enacted law, but in a court-crafted cocktail of historical precedent, contemporary consensus, the flexible, the sensible, the *not too bold*, and whatever else a court might wish to consider in a given week.

Under Minimalism's premises, the very identity of law is indefinite. For Minimalism treats law as an ongoing construction project, with courts themselves part of the construction crew. The judicial lawmaking that it licenses may not be as obvious as it is under Living Constitutionalism, thanks to Minimalism's avowals of a modest, incrementalist pace. Yet to make something by small, quiet steps is no less to make it. And in doing so, a Minimalist court betrays its proper function. The practice of Minimalism (in whatever way "it" can be practiced) thwarts the Rule of Law and forfeits any claim to objectivity.

---

[187] Clark Neily likens calls for judicial restraint or minimal judicial "interference" to some sports fans' demands that referees call certain penalties infrequently (particularly in the most consequential games, such as championships, as we often hear). I agree with Neily that this counsel is ill-founded in sports as well as in law. Referees should penalize a rules violation as often or as little as they observe its occurrence. If the rules of American football ban certain actions as constituting holding or pass interference, for instance, then the frequency with which those infractions occur does not alter a particular incident's being an infraction. The sixth time that one of a team's players holds is no less a hold than the first. Naturally, a sport that wished to take frequency of occurrence into account for an action's permissibility or corresponding severity of penalty could adjust its rules accordingly, as some sports do. Neily's analogy holds, however, insofar as he is addressing calls for lax enforcement of a sport's existing and governing rules. His legal point is that neither the impact nor the popularity of a court's ruling of what the law is alters what the law is.

7. CONCLUSION

None of the five theories that we have surveyed offers appropriate guidance for the conduct of judicial review – not if it is to maintain the objectivity of a legal system and honor a proper system's function and authority. Their errors, at base, revolve around the nature of objectivity and the authority of legal power.

Wittingly or not, all five embrace methods of judicial decision making that are subjective. This is most obvious in the Democratic Deference/Popular Constitutionalism view, which treats the convergence of a number of people's beliefs or desires about a law as if that were the law. It thus enshrines a socialized form of subjectivism: The law is what we wish it to be, in virtue of that wishing. Minimalism also offers social subjectivism, albeit while mixing in assorted other considerations (smallness of change, flexibility, etc.). In the end, Minimalism holds, whatever such mixture is most socially acceptable dictates the proper judicial ruling. Living Constitutionalism and Dworkinian Perfectionism also lift the judge's gaze from the law by instructing judges to consider, instead, how a given ruling would resonate with people's beliefs about good law (our predecessors, our contemporaries, the judges themselves). Do "what you think is right," Thurgood Marshall had counseled.[188] Opinions are the tuning fork.

Whatever their other shortcomings, the two Originalist schools initially seem to avoid the subjectivist trap. Indeed, it is the firmness of historical fact that anchors their opposition to the alternatives. Yet on analysis, we have seen that they, too, collapse into variants of subjectivism. According to the Original Understanding advocates, why should the original publicly understood meaning be canonized for all time as *the* meaning of a word? Not because those original speakers "got it right." Not due to the objective validity of those people's understanding of "speech" or equality or any of the relevant phenomena. Rather, its answer is: because those people thought that. And Textualism, the notion that meaning is fully contained within the written words, is simply subjectivism in intrinsicist masquerade. Because no such vacuum-sealed meaning (detached from the specific context of human purposes and premises) actually exists that judges *could* "find," in practice, Textualism encourages judges to insert their own purposes and premises in order to "find" that which cannot be found.

The second fatal failing shared by these theories lies in the fact that each misidentifies the authority of a legal system. Since it is authority that

---

[188] Marshall's statement that I quoted earlier, "Do what you think is right and let the law catch up," clearly implies a permitted divergence between judicial review and law.

determines the legitimate substance and administration of law (its *what* and its *how*), they correspondingly direct judges who would employ their methods to sanction uses of legal power that are not objectively justified.

How does each school misunderstand authority? An essentialized refresher: Textualism assigns ultimate sovereignty to words – words in and of themselves, divorced from the context that supplies their meaning. The Original Understanding school's measure of laws' meaning as "whatever was understood by original speakers" sanctifies the content of those people's consciousnesses – whether it is valid or invalid. *That* is our ruler: their thoughts. Democratic Deference elevates the pulse of the people over the commitments of their constitution. Perfectionism treats a nation's written constitution as partial and provisional – an early, incomplete draft to be revised and extended by judges who edit and author new installments. And Minimalism, by downsizing the work of the courts whose responsibility is to preserve the governance of the Constitution, correlatively downsize the power of that Constitution, replacing it with a congeries of pragmatic devices serving disparate political ends (social harmony, modesty of impact, diversity, etc.).

The exact mistakes about legal authority are different, in each case. Yet the effects are the same: they devastate objective law. By incorrectly understanding the true authority of a legal system, legal power is unleashed to serve things other than its legitimate end: the protection of individual rights. And because legal power is coercive, in so doing, this unleashing actually sanctions the violation of those rights. When a law is taken to mean that which will satisfy people of "diverse perspectives" or that which will affect conventional legal practices only slightly (as it is, under Minimalism) – or when a law is taken to mean what a court thinks would make a better narrative (as under Living Constitutionalism) – or when a law is taken to mean what the latest polls indicate the greatest number of people would like it to mean (as under Democratic Deference) – or when a law is taken to mean what the ordinary man at the time it was enacted would have thought it meant, however limited or erroneous his understanding of the phenomena in question (Original Understanding) – or when a law is taken to mean what it says and what "it says" is construed in the "words as oracles" sense which presumes that words contain meanings apart from all speakers or context (as under Textualism) – individual rights are roadkill. The legal system is not protecting them. Even well-made laws that are objectively justified cannot constrain the legal system's uses of its power, if the meaning of those laws is distorted by such non-objective methods of "interpretation."

I do not doubt that most defenders of these schools are well intended; nor, that some of their narrower claims in arguing for their views are valid in very

different contexts, for very different purposes. On certain carefully circumscribed questions, for instance, a government *may* accede to the majority's
will and in most circumstances, Marshall's injunction to do "what you think
is right" is entirely appropriate. The problem is that these are not means of
articulating or of applying *the law*. Courts' use of such methods would thus
undermine the objectivity of a legal system. These models do not confine
courts to their proper role and, as a result, they would only obstruct a legal
system's ability to fulfill its legitimate function.

So what *would* objective judicial review look like?

7

Objective Judicial Review – Understanding
the Law in Context

1. INTRODUCTION

What, then, is proper judicial review? What method of exercising review is most conducive to maintaining the integrity of an objective legal system?

The role of judicial review is to ensure that the law of the land be respected as the law of the land – that it actually govern. Government actions that deviate from their legal authority, whether accidentally or deliberately, may not be permitted. Our aim here, then, is to identify the basic principles that should guide courts in doing this work. What are the key components of a method of judicial decision making that best positions the court to fulfill its function and genuinely uphold the law?

My account is not especially intricate. For objective review is not, in its essence, different in kind from objectivity in any other sphere. It is, rather, a direct implication of the basic character of an objective legal system that we have already explained. In order to perform their work properly, judges need a thorough understanding of the essentials of an objective legal system and facility in objectively applying general rules to particular circumstances. This is not to say that judges' task is easy, however. A number of factors complicate the work of objectively resolving contested cases.

First and most obviously, as noted in Chapter 6, appellate courts address the hard cases. It is in the nature of judicial review that it is called upon to resolve the most tangled questions concerning law's proper application. Cases typically reach high courts precisely because we have at least prima facie reason to understand their elements' legal status in two or more conflicting lights. Is the NYPD's "stop and frisk" policy a responsible form of crime prevention, for instance, or an unreasonable intrusion in breach of the Fourth Amendment? Is the policy's typical way of being applied a denial of equal protection? Are the Michigan high school's different employment policies for lay and religious faculty a violation of antidiscrimination law or simply an exercise of religious freedom?[1] Such cases call for fine-grained discernment, as judges must identify the most essential similarities and differences among multiple considerations that point in countervailing directions.

Further burdening judicial review is the fact that other agents of the legal system cannot be relied on to perform their roles faultlessly, without error. Particular laws themselves may be non-objective. Consequently, courts need to be alert to improper uses of legal power even when those uses have not been specifically challenged. In a case immediately before it, of course, someone is bringing a specific challenge that the court is called upon to address. The point here is wider, however, namely: The materials that judges are asked to work with – including the law itself – may harbor previously unsuspected transgressions of objective validity. The relevant statutes or regulations, for instance, may lack objective foundation. While courts are not free to initiate judicial review unilaterally, neither does objective reasoning permit them, in the course of considering a particular case, to ignore relevant government practices that are unconstitutional. My immediate point is not to assert how they should do that,[2] but simply to observe that because courts' rulings do not occur in isolation, such failures elsewhere in the system only make courts' identification of the correct resolution more difficult. Insofar as courts are charged to uphold the law and that law itself may be marred by non-objective features, it will be harder for them to find the valid answer.

Moreover, the legal system is, indeed, a *system* – an extensive, complex network of distinct branches that are further partitioned into numerous departments, agencies, boards, commissions, and so on. State governments, county bureaus, the armed forces, the intelligence services, a tiered judiciary – all play a role within what, as a package, is to deliver objective law. Responsibilities and authority sometimes overlap, sometimes diverge; some units are subordinate to higher agencies while others are independent; chains of accountability can be serpentine. The court is tasked with deciphering the respective domains of each component as well as their relationships to the bedrock authority of the system itself. Simply reminding ourselves of this integrated latticework, I think, indicates how difficult that can be.

---

[1]   A question raised in *Hosanna-Tabor Evangelical Lutheran Church and School v. Equal Employment Opportunity Commission*, 565 U.S. (2012), in which the U.S. Supreme Court unanimously ruled that federal discrimination laws do not apply to religious organizations' selection of religious leaders.

[2]   I will address that further in Chapter 8, which centers on the proper conduct of judicial review in less than ideally objective conditions.

Finally, the cases that courts review frequently carry profound repercussions in both the number of people who stand to be affected and the magnitude of the impact on their lives. Correspondingly, these cases are emotionally charged, often intensely. However professionally detached judges may be in the fulfillment of their responsibilities as finders of the law, to maintain objectivity on issues about which large swaths of the public are emotionally invested can be difficult. "Difficult" does not mean impossible. Yet it would hardly be an objective inventory of the major challenges to objective review to ignore this commonplace feature of human psychology. Judges are as susceptible as the rest of us to having the sobriety of their judgment tugged by empathy, resentment, guilt, compassion, or other emotions. Thus, to safeguard the law, they must exert special vigilance to guard against such potential distortion. The emotional stakes of many cases are, simply, yet another reason why objective review is difficult work.

I raise all these to underscore the challenges that courts face in fulfilling their role. While the core of objectivity is the same in judicial review as in any other sphere, the specific conditions in which justices review government practices make it especially easy for judges to stray from the law. Thus, we need to be as clear as possible on the essentials of proper guidance.

In what follows, I will present the cornerstones of objective review. The account builds on the understanding of an objective legal system that I have laid out in the earlier chapters. To set the context, I will begin by highlighting two features of that framework: the basics of objective thinking and the function of judicial review. Then, in the core of the chapter, I will explain the two guideposts that are most critical if judges are to conduct review objectively: unswerving focus on the law; appreciation of the contextual character of the law. In elaborating, I will emphasize the philosophical nature of law and the way in which faulty legal presumptions can distort the relevant context.

Given my portrait of objective review, it will be important for those of us in the wider public who evaluate the decisions of courts to adjust our expectations. We must particularly resist allowing the tenacious, intrinsicist conception of law to distort our demands for judicial *fidelity* to law. I will further indicate a few very basic features of a judge's personal character that are salient to his ability to fulfill his role.

Finally, I will consider possible objections to my account. Having critiqued the major alternative schools of thought on judicial review in depth in Chapter 6, I see no need to revisit all the particular objections that their champions might raise (since, in slightly different form, I have already addressed these). I will, however, consider a handful of misgivings that a reader might reasonably have. All of these, I think, can be comfortably resolved.

One clarification of the scope of the discussion, before we plunge in. My aim in this chapter is to describe the essentials of judicial review in ideal circumstances, when the legal system is designed to respect the proper role of government and when all other components of the legal system are, at least in essential terms, operating as they should. Given that this is not the landscape that we inhabit, I will devote Chapter 8 to addressing proper review in today's less-than-ideal conditions.

2. THE FRAMEWORK

A. *Basics of Objectivity*

A proper method of judicial review draws on knowledge from epistemology (primarily, concerning the nature and meaning of concepts) as well as from political philosophy (concerning the purpose and authority of a legal system). Legal theorists often slight the former. To avoid falling prey to the errors that beset other accounts of proper judicial methodology, it is helpful to remind ourselves of the basic nature of objectivity.

The objectivity of any procedure, recall, turns on its dedication to accurately understanding the object in question and on its means of attempting to achieve that understanding. Bear in mind that the "object" need not be a material entity or something like a causal relationship between physical entities. It could be the answer to a question concerning legal abstractions, such as whether a particular police action is a search or whether a particular regulation is a violation of equal protection. Because an objective process is object anchored, it adheres strictly to those methods that most effectively enable one to understand the object in question. For human beings, that method is logic.

As I explained in Chapter 1, objectivity is not a natural property that inheres *in* certain facts and simply awaits notice by an observant spectator. Rather, it designates a specific relationship. Objectivity is a particular manner of using one's mind in order to gain knowledge. To be objective is to be guided throughout one's thinking by logical means of ascertaining the nature of the object under investigation and the answers to one's questions about it. (*Is he the best man for the job? Is this a search? An abridgement of free speech?*)

We also observed the contextual character of objectivity: the fact that the precise criteria that are necessary to be objective may vary in certain respects in different circumstances. (The exact criteria required for objectively grading one student's exam, for example, will be different from the exact criteria that are appropriate for grading another student's exam, depending on the level of the course, the purpose of the exam, the material being tested, etc.) Similarly, it is no failing of a man's objectivity if he fails to consider a relevant fact that he was unaware of and at no fault for being unaware of.

The point is that, whatever the type of judgment in question, objectivity requires a person's disciplined use of logical inference to draw conclusions based solely on relevant evidence. Objectivity does not ensure that one's conclusions will always be correct, since it cannot make us infallible or omniscient, but it is by the use of this method that a person best positions himself to reach correct conclusions.

B. The Function of Judicial Review

We also observed in Chapter 1 that in any sphere, the specific requirements of objectivity are determined largely by the function of the enterprise in which it is sought. Thus, objectivity in judicial review must be guided by understanding the function of judicial review, which is essentially to ensure that it is the law that governs, without any of its agencies exceeding their legitimate authority. The exact boundaries of legitimate authority are hardly self-evident. Even in a well-designed legal system run by officials of good faith, people frequently disagree about whether particular exercises of government power are justified. (*That* presidential commitment of military force? *That* restriction issued by the FCC?) Consequently, it makes sense to have a body whose role is to resolve these disputes. Indeed, it is because of our commitment to government's respecting the bounds of its authority and to maintaining the Rule of *Law* that we employ judicial review as an insurance mechanism against misuses of legal power. When it comes to the power of government, we want to *make sure*. When, therefore, we have good grounds to think that a government agency may have exceeded its authority, reason demands that we double-check.

In colloquial terms, one might say that while the Police police the people, working to ensure that the people abide by the law, the courts police the law. Judicial review seeks to ensure that all exertions of power in the name of the law actually are lawful. In this way, courts are not simply policing a different set of people (namely, those who work for the government). Rather, courts are also policing the laws themselves insofar as they are assessing whether specific rules and policies that are intended to carry out our system's mission are, in fact, authorized by the system's foundational law, the Constitution.

Given, then, that the function of judicial review is to preserve the sovereignty of the law, what instruction can best help judges to do that? What are the principal considerations that should guide the exercise of judicial review? While the basic answer rests in adherence to objectivity, two aspects of objectivity are most critical in this context.

3. GUIDEPOSTS

A. *The "Object" Is the Law*

If objective thinking is distinguished by its dedication to understanding the object in question, for judicial review, the fundamental object of inquiry is the law. Courts must seek to discover and preserve the *identity* of the law: what it is and what it means. To draw more practical instruction from this, it is useful to consider both some of the qualities that equip a judge to do this as well as the principal things that the law is not (but that it is commonly confused with) and which, therefore, should not influence judicial findings.

One of the most obvious desiderata for serving on a court is knowledge of law – of statutes, regulations, Presidential decrees and, most significantly, of the Constitution itself. It is also useful for judges to be well versed in the prevailing legal conventions, such as those involving doctrine, precedent, Restatements of the Law and commonly employed canons of construction. Familiarity with the full field *as it is practiced,* along with recognition of the legal fidelity that is reflected in certain practices and the deviations embedded in others, will help a judge to discriminate more astutely between what the law, properly understood, allows and forbids in a given case. A deep, wide-ranging command of the legal system's full terrain, encompassing its animating principles and its pivotal particulars, is a prerequisite for being able to reliably discern the law.

In this, a knowledge of legal history will naturally be helpful. It is the past that gives us our law, after all,[3] and our legal predecessors often engaged in instructive reasoning. Understanding the purpose and rationale beneath earlier legal actions (legislation, judicial findings, executive decisions, etc.) as well as the grounds of previous legal challenges can be valuable for understanding the full context of the contemporary disputes that courts are asked to resolve. This does not imply that an objective jurist must possess an encyclopedic knowledge of a legal system's detailed past; it simply observes that a solid grasp of major principles, precedents, and their underlying reasoning can strengthen his ability to navigate today's disputes about existing law and its valid exercise. Appreciating the reasoning for a particular historical practice (such as different terms for patents and for copyrights) might lead a judge to consider aspects of a current controversy that he would otherwise have overlooked.

---

[3] At least, unless we deliberately and constitutionally alter it.

While history is a great resource for understanding the reasoning behind the law and behind legal decisions made by those in all branches and while history can sometimes illuminate features of the legal system that would otherwise be puzzling, history does not replace the law. This is crucial. The mere fact that certain events took place or that certain decisions were made does not create authority where none exists. When our legal predecessors erred by straying from the law, subsequent acquiescence to that error or repetition of that error does not alter its being an error – a departure from the law. The reason to know legal history is to better understand the law; it is not to enable us to substitute the progression of historical events for the law (for the law that holds valid authority).

In addition to maintaining his knowledge of the law, then, the objective jurist must be meticulous in his use of logic. He must painstakingly inspect every turn of reasoning, inferences large and small, to ensure that the reasoning behind a proposed reading of a law is sound. He may not indulge groundless doubts or arbitrary hypotheses – although he must address reasonable doubts and assess all evidence and arguments, however novel, by the relevant standard. Contrary to the famous pronouncement of Justice Holmes that "the life of the law has not been logic; it has been experience,"[4] logic *is* the life of the law because it is our lifeline *to* the law, necessary to maintaining the law's integrity. Where we do not have logic in the understanding and application of law, we no longer have law. For the law – any law, like any rule – encompasses all of its logical implications. When those are defied, it is the law that is defied.[5]

Crucial for strict adherence to the law is the obligation of judges to deflect ruthlessly all extraneous factors, however fervently some might lobby for their influence. In Chapter 6, we encountered a few of these factors in the methodologies that I critiqued. A judicial ruling's size of impact, as under Minimalism, for instance, or its popularity, as under Democratic Deference, whatever their possible salience for certain other questions, I argued, simply fail to illuminate *the law*.

---

[4] Oliver Wendell Holmes, *The Common Law* (1881), p. 1.
[5] As a simple illustration: If a duly enacted federal law declares that all U.S. citizens who have reached the age of eighteen are eligible to register to vote in national elections and the state of Texas denies a twenty-year-old citizen this right for no relevant reason and under the aegis of no exceptional circumstances that the law decrees (such as the person's criminal record), then that law is not governing how that individual is treated.

Separately, I would take issue with Holmes's implication that logic is a rival of experience rather than our means of understanding experience and drawing valid lessons from it, although that is a larger issue than we should pursue here.

In order objectively to screen out immaterial considerations, it is especially important that judges understand the authority of the legal system and the justification for a particular action's or policy's being lawful. The law's authority and the law's identity go hand in hand; strictly, these issues cannot be severed. For any power or action exerted by government that lacks proper authority is not within the bounds of valid law. Consequently, objective judicial review relies on a judge's knowledge of the legal system's authority in order to know which particular assertions of that authority may be credited as genuine, binding law.[6]

Precedent

One of the implications of all this is that courts must reject the deeply entrenched practice of deference to precedent. It is not that they should shun all attention to previous decisions, reasoning, or considerations of fairness in regard to the expectations that earlier rulings have naturally created. The exact place of precedent in an objective legal system and the proper way to remedy unjustified precedents are intricate questions worth careful attention in their own right. What stands before all such details, however, is the fact that the use of precedent as the ultimate standard of judicial review – the "justification" of a ruling on the grounds of its conformity with previous courts' rulings – is completely misguided. For it bypasses the *law*.

Customary legal practices, however entrenched and however helpful they can sometimes be in shedding light on the logic of the law, are at best an intermediary in the work of identifying what the law is. To be objective, judges must resist treating helpful means of finding the law as if those aids themselves constituted the law. Judicial rulings must square with the Constitution, for that is the benchmark in a law-governed society. As Justice Frankfurter memorably put it, "The ultimate touchstone of constitutionality is the Constitution itself, and not what we have said about it."[7]

---

[6] While this will require an understanding of the legal system's moral authority, it is important not to confuse legal authority with the moral principles on which that legal authority rests. Moral principles underwrite legal authority, yet they are not the very same thing as legal authority. Once a constitution has been adopted (assuming that it was legitimately adopted), it is the legal system that that constitution erects that properly governs. For fuller explanation, see Chapters 4 and 5.

[7] Felix Frankfurter, concurring in *Graves v. New York*, 306 US 466, 491–92 (1939).
    The exclusive sovereignty of the Constitution has been clearly reflected in the grounds that Presidents have sometimes asserted for their vetoes of Congressional legislation. President James Madison explained his vetoing a public works bill in March of 1817, for example, by reasoning: "I am constrained by the insuperable difficulty I feel in reconciling the bill with the Constitution of the United States." Madison further observed that "it does not appear that the power proposed to be exercised by the bill is among the enumerated powers."

Indeed, justices have often recognized that long-engraved understandings of even such contentious and legally consequential concepts as marriage do not outweigh the objective meaning of the Constitution. "No tradition can supersede the Constitution," Justice Scalia wrote in a dissent in *Rutan v. Republican Party of Illinois*.[8] With the majority in the same case, Justice Stevens reasoned that "the tradition that is relevant in these cases is the American commitment to examine and re-examine past and present practices against the basic principles embodied in the Constitution."[9] In *Bowers v. Hardwick*, Stevens argued that "'the fact that the governing majority in a State has traditionally viewed a particular practice as immoral is not a sufficient reason for upholding a law prohibiting the practice; neither history nor tradition could save a law prohibiting miscegenation from constitutional attack.'"[10]

The point is, objective law demands that we be governed by the objective meanings of terms, as best as we can discern them, rather than by the limited understandings of those terms or of related legal practices of any set of people, our learned judicial predecessors included.[11]

Foreign Law

Another type of pressure that threatens to distract courts from the proper object of their work is the growing chorus of calls for U.S. law to emulate the

Presidents Franklin Pierce and Grover Cleveland both vetoed popular bills that would have provided charitable relief on the same explicit grounds. Pierce declared, "I cannot find any authority in the Constitution for public charity," while Cleveland explained, "I can find no warrant for such an appropriation in the Constitution, and I do not believe that the power and duty of the General Government ought to be extended to the relief of individual suffering which is in no manner properly related to the public service or benefit." All three, cited in Walter Williams, "What Our Constitution Permits," January 12, 2012, Townhall. com, retrieved from http://townhall.com/columnists/walterewilliams/2011/01/12/what_our_constitution_permits/print.

[8] *Rutan v. Republican Party of Illinois* 497 US 62, 95 n.1 (1990) Scalia, dissenting.
[9] *Rutan*, 497 US at 92, Stevens, J., concurring.
[10] Justice Stevens, dissenting in *Bowers v. Hardwick*, 478 US 186, 216 (1986). In a similar vein, Justice Kennedy wrote for the majority in *Heller v. Doe*, 509 US 312, 326 (1993) 23, "Ancient lineage of a legal concept does not give it immunity from attack."
[11] For a similar appreciation that what should govern is the law (as distinguished from what someone thinks is the law), see David Brink, "Legal Interpretation, Objectivity, and Morality," in *Objectivity in Law and Morals*, ed. Brian Leiter, New York: Cambridge University Press, 2001, p. 5 (evidenced in his claim that laws banning toxic substances ban those substances that are actually toxic, rather than those that are believed to be toxic on the date the law was enacted). I defend this view further in "Why Originalism Won't Die: Common Mistakes in Competing Theories of Judicial Interpretation," *Duke Journal of Constitutional Law and Public Policy* 2, 2007, pp. 159–215; "Originalism's Misplaced Fidelity: 'Original' Meaning is Not Objective," *Constitutional Commentary* 26, no. 1 (2009), pp. 1–57; and "Originalism, Vintage or Nouveau: He Said, She Said Law," *Fordham Law Review* 82, Fall 2013, pp. 619–639.

practices of foreign legal systems (in regard to capital punishment, privacy, sexual autonomy or medical care, for instance). Justices themselves have sometimes invoked foreign experience to support their reasoning.[12] While this, too, is a subject for more in-depth investigation, the essential thing for us to recognize is that the legitimacy of the proposal turns entirely on the specific use of foreign law that is being advocated. What, exactly, are judges advised to learn from foreign law? And in what ways is that to affect their rulings concerning American law? We have no general reason to suppose that other nations enjoy superior enlightenment concerning objective law or judicial review. Naturally, in any case in which we have specific grounds to believe that we might learn from looking abroad, it would be foolish to spurn that. The knowledge and experience of others have always provided a rich reservoir to be tapped – for certain purposes, however, and not others.

Remember that the role of the court is not to theorize about ideal law. In fact, it is lawmakers and legal theorists whose work might benefit from studying legal policies employed around the world. It is not the purview of

---

[12] Anthony Kennedy, for example, in a speech delivered at Stanford in 1986 (before his elevation to the Supreme Court) criticized the court's upholding the criminal status of homosexual sex in *Bowers v. Hardwick*, in part, by contrasting it with a 1981 decision of the European Court of Human Rights that had struck down a similar law in Northern Ireland. Several years later, writing the majority opinion in *Lawrence v. Texas*, Kennedy cited that same European Court decision in support of his conclusion. See Adam Liptak, "Surprising Friend of Gay Rights in a High Place," *New York Times*, September 2, 2013. Justice Ginsberg has defended the use of foreign law on several occasions, remarking, "I frankly don't understand all the brouhaha from Congress and even from some of my colleagues about referring to foreign law." Adam Liptak, "Ginsburg Shares," *New York Times*, April 11, 2009. Naturally, the exact judicial use of foreign law that each would endorse warrants close scrutiny.

Among the recent cases in which justices have made reference to foreign law and/or the propriety of consulting foreign law are: *Olympic Airways v. Husain* 540 US 644 (2004), see especially Scalia's dissent; *Lawrence v. Texas* 539 US 558 (2003), see especially majority at 522–524, writing that "the right the petitioners seek in this case has been accepted as an integral part of human freedom in many other countries," and Scalia's dissent; and three death penalty cases, *Foster v. Florida* 537 US 990 (2002), in which Justice Breyer's dissent cites several foreign courts on the issue of lengthy incarceration before death; *Atkins v. Virginia* 536 US 304 (2002), in which the majority opinion cites an amicus brief from the European Union (316, footnote 21); also see Scalia's dissent; and *Patterson v. Texas* 536 US 984 (2002), in which Justice Stevens's dissent, joined by Justices Ginsburg and Breyer, invokes the "apparent consensus ... in the international community against the execution of a capital sentence imposed on a juvenile" as reason for the Court to revisit the issue at the earliest opportunity."

For discussion of the basic issue, see Richard Markovits, "Learning from Foreigners: A Response to Justice Scalia's and Professor Levinson's Professional Moral Parochialism," *Texas International Law Journal* 39 (2004), pp. 367–380; and Harold Hongju Koh, "International Law as Part of Our Law," *American Journal of International Law* volume 98 no. 43 (2004). Thanks to Sam Krauss for research on this.

the judiciary, however, to assess the wisdom of policies concerning the death penalty, surveillance cameras, or anything else. A foreign accent does not change that.

The bottom line is, foreign law as such holds no independent claim on our courts' attention. For purely informational purposes, other nations' legal practices might be worth considering, but they must be subjected to careful scrutiny to cull any lessons that can be objectively applied to the understanding of existing U.S. law. Where a foreign notion or practice is at odds with U.S. law (as that is properly understood), it is completely irrelevant to the task of judicial review. For foreign law holds no *authority*, and that is what is crucial. Given that a judge swears to uphold the U.S. Constitution, for him to invoke the ideas of others as authoritative would be a brazen repudiation of his responsibility. It would abandon the Constitution and, in the mode of a Dworkinian Living Constitutionalist, it would replace the law with the jurist's beliefs about ideal law.

B. Context

As with objective thought in any sphere, part of what logic requires for objective judicial review is respect for the relevant context and hierarchy. (I will use "context" to encompass both.) Understanding both the law's reason for being and the authority behind the legal system is crucial to understanding how the government's power may be exercised and, correspondingly, how its laws may be legitimately understood. Judges must thus understand the essentials of the entire legal system: its foundations, its function, its powers, and its limits.

Remember that a proper legal system is organized around a single mission. Its *what, how,* and *why* – its substance, manner of administration, and fundamental license for exercising its power – are united by their service to that mission. This entails that the bedrock of the system's governance, its constitution, also has the particular character that it does as a means of advancing that end. The interpretation of the Constitution and of all that takes place under it, accordingly, must respect this integrity.

And this carries a significant implication for judicial review: The purpose of a legal system constrains the rational interpretation of its laws. For all of a legal system's parts should be designed and operate solely to advance its principal, overarching purpose. The proper function of an objective legal system, I argued in Chapter 4, is the protection of individual rights. That function thus limits the range of actions that are legitimately legal. That is, it limits those actions that could constitute the rational application of its constitution.

Naturally, courts must respect the particular laws that most directly pertain to the case that it is considering, be it a dispute about patents, police tactics, or public education. Logical respect for context also demands a wider lens, however, as the correct application of laws to a particular situation cannot be determined without understanding the broader laws and principles within which these are merely a part. Indeed, opposing litigants often argue that *their* position uniquely represents the proper application of that broader law to the immediate dispute.

The objective interpretation of law must be holistic. The rules of a proper legal system are not a haphazard agglomeration of policies adopted by a government, such that any one of these can, in isolation, be taken to justify a current course's legality. A proper constitution is not a scrapbook whose cut-and-paste contents each carries a freestanding meaning and authority. The logical interpretation of any of its components or any of its derivatives must respect them as elements of a larger, systematic effort to carry out the function of government. The U.S. Constitution is a conceptually sophisticated elaboration of a coherent network of powers and organs by which a government will carry out its work. Its proper application, correspondingly, cannot be Photoshopped, with its individual elements effectively cropped in ways that remove them from their meaning-giving context and thereby distort their logical implementation. Interpretation may not emphasize one constitutional clause that is relevant to a case to the exclusion of others that are also relevant, for instance, or interpret one constitutional provision in a way that would contradict another specific provision, such as by reading the Commerce Clause in a way that undercuts the Necessary and Proper Clause or by reading the Necessary and Proper Clause in a way that would violate the Fourth Amendment.

In many arenas, people readily distinguish the "spirit" of a law from its letter. In doing so, they are essentially recognizing this basic truth: context affects meaning. My stronger contention, however, is that the letter of a law cannot be understood without understanding its spirit – that is, without understanding the animating purpose and principles of the larger system.[13]

Objective judicial review, in short, must be acutely attuned to apply the law in question in ways that preserve the integrity of the whole. The proper understanding of any discrete element of the legal system rests on an understanding of the system's overarching substantive mission. And in order to be so attuned, it is especially important that judges understand the authority of law.

---

[13] The judiciary's practice of employing somewhat different standards when interpreting contracts and when interpreting constitutions exemplifies an appreciation of the role of context, as do courts' appeals to legislative history to dispel ambiguities that cloud certain statutory language when it is detached from that historical context.

Notice that an aura of legality naturally surrounds any action that government takes. This is so, at least, when the government is regarded as basically just. Where most citizens regard their government as morally proper, they will tend to assume the legality of its actions, whatever criticisms they may have of the wisdom of those actions. Simply by virtue of being a government action, that action presents itself as legally warranted. To assure that it actually is, courts must understand both the proximate authority (such as the particular relevant provision of the U.S. Criminal Code or the Code of Federal Regulations) and the deeper, underlying authority of the action in question.

Obviously, the parameters of jurisdiction are a frequent question for judicial review (in regard to state and federal responsibility for the conduct of elections or treatment of immigrants, for instance, or the respective responsibilities of the Defense Department and the National Security Agency). Objective law demands respect for the distinct domains of various government bodies as well as the domains of private individuals. What is less commonly appreciated, however, is the fact that objectivity requires understanding the underlying *moral* authority of the legal actions in question. For that is what legitimates any of the more concrete powers that government agents exert.

Recall from Chapters 4 and 5 that a constitution translates a legal system's moral authority into legal authority. Through the specific powers of the government that it creates (along with those it deliberately does not create), through the rights that it recognizes and the structure of relationships that it establishes among a legal system's various components, a constitution reflects a set of moral convictions about the proper relationship between a government and the people it governs. It is important to keep in mind, however, that that underlying moral authority is not lost in this translation; it is not replaced by the more particular laws that the legal system adopts. Rather, it is made manifest by them; it is made practically operative through those mechanisms. An objective understanding of the Constitution's specific provisions must, correspondingly, be constrained by an understanding of the moral authority that they implement and the larger project that they are the means of carrying out.

The Importance of Presumptions

A powerful way of distorting the proper contextual framework for objective review is through the misuse of legal presumptions. Presumptions per se are not problematic. When a person must repeatedly engage in a particular type of complex decision making, it is natural (and sensible) to adopt certain default assumptions so as to free up mental energy to concentrate on a situation's more unusual and more puzzling features. Because those premises that are taken for granted offstage can exert powerful influence over the conclusions drawn and legal decisions reached, however, it is critical to objectivity that the assumptions themselves be valid. They must be rationally justified and conform to the larger context.[14] In our legal system's use of presumptions, this has not always been the case.

As an example of the failure to respect the full logical context, consider the shift from the presumption of individual liberty in cases concerning the legitimacy of government action to the presumption of government prerogative. While a series of court decisions brought about this shift, most scholars would agree that two turning points came in the 1930s, in *Nebbia v. New York* and *US v. Carolene Products Company*. In *Nebbia*, the Supreme Court ruled that

> a State is free to adopt whatever economic policy may reasonably be deemed to promote public welfare, and to enforce that policy by legislation adapted to its purpose. The courts are without authority either to declare such policy, or, when it is declared by the legislature, to override it. If the laws passed are seen to have a reasonable relation to a proper legislative purpose, and are neither arbitrary nor discriminatory, the requirements of due process are satisfied.[15]

Note: "*a* reasonable relation" to a proper government purpose, rather than "is rationally justified by" a proper government purpose. If an enacted law has *a* reason in its imagined defense and, further, if it is not "arbitrary" – that is, a-rational – that is good enough; the court should approve of the law.

A few years later, the Court went further in *Carolene Products* and launched the "rational basis" test, which reigns to the present day. Justice Stone's majority opinion held that

> the existence of facts supporting the legislative judgment is to be presumed, for regulatory legislation affecting ordinary commercial transactions is not to be pronounced unconstitutional unless, in the light of the facts made known or generally assumed, it is of such a character as to preclude the assumption that it rests upon some rational basis within the knowledge and experience of the legislators.[16]

"Some" rational basis is a rather mild condition to require, in any context. For it would be satisfied even when that presumed basis is quickly, clearly, and overwhelmingly overturned by the weight of full evidence and logical reflection. ("After all, we could imagine *some* conceivable basis for their having

---

[14] The presumption of innocence is probably the most familiar of American legal presumptions that is, by the lights of the philosophy of the larger legal system, perfectly sound.

[15] *Nebbia v. New York*, 291 US 502, at 537 (1934).

[16] *United States v. Carolene Products Company*, 304 US at 152 (1938).

enacted the law.") In the context of the U.S. Constitution, however, given the philosophy behind the Constitution as well as the numerous indicators that directly call for fidelity to the government's possession of solely those enumerated powers that the Constitution expressly bestows, it is astonishing. It is flagrantly illogical.

Such deference to someone's imagining of a *possible* reason could not possibly be compatible with a constitutional order that creates a government as the instrument designed to protect individuals' rights. To claim that the government may do whatever it imagines some conceivable basis for doing is to reverse ends and means, exalting one of the government's means of fulfilling its function (the thinking of legislators) at the expense of the end that these means are authorized to serve. And if a person who is subject to such an easily "justified" law protests that his rightful freedom is victimized by this law, his plea would be defeated in court by the advised acquiescence to an imagined rationale for thinking that the government power is constitutional, regardless of whether it is. "*Maybe* the government has this power" excuses the court from figuring out whether or not it does. And permits the government to proceed as if it does.

To put the problem slightly differently: If the ultimate reason for erecting a legal system is the protection of individual rights and if that system's constitution authorizes a government to exercise only a set of specifically enumerated powers and if, further, the Constitution expressly states that all other authority is retained by the people (as it does in the Ninth Amendment),[17] it would defy reason to ignore all of that and to declare, instead, that we should presume that the government possesses whatever powers it claims to, as long as one can conceive of some reasonable basis for them, regardless of whether those powers are within the enumerated powers, are consistent with the mission and authority of the legal system, or are, even, rational. Its label notwithstanding, rationality is actually excluded by the rational basis test. For this is a use of "reasonable" that glaringly ignores the context.

The presumption of constitutionality that is crystallized in *Carolene Products* sabotages our legal system's ability to fulfill the purpose for which it was created and that its constitution was designed to uphold. Both in philosophy and in practice, it reverses the fundamental relationship between the government and the governed. Notice, too, the manner in which this standard of review

[17] The Ninth Amendment reads: "The enumeration in the Constitution of certain rights shall not be construed to deny or disparage others retained by the people." The Tenth also serves the cause of limiting government power: "The powers not delegated to the United States by the Constitution, nor prohibited by it to the States, are reserved to the States respectively, or to the people."

subjects us to rule by the thoughts of legislators rather than by constitutional authority. For its premise is roughly: *As long as legislators mean well and aren't patently insane in their action, whatever they think appropriate must be allowed to govern. It's not lunatic; therefore, it's lawful.*

This is not a policy by which to safeguard individual rights. And it is not the policy espoused by the U.S. Constitution.[18]

In *Carolene*, Justice Stone refines his call for deference to legislators in the famous footnote number 4, which retains some role for review by courts, rather than surrendering unconditionally to the powers asserted by the other branches. Yet it does so by means that actually aggravate the seminal error. Stone proposes two distinct tiers of scrutiny that courts should employ, according to the nature of the law and activity in question: strict or heightened scrutiny and rational basis scrutiny. In other words, certain exercises of government power should be subject to more stringent inspection than others, in order to pass Constitutional muster. Economic regulations, for instance, must simply be rationally related to a state interest (the rational basis level of review), while legislation that "appears on its face to be within a specific prohibition of the Constitution, such as those of the first ten amendments," or directed at "discrete and insular minorities" (such as religious or racial minorities) must meet a higher threshold of Constitutional conformity to win the court's approval.[19]

In practice, this means that some laws are treated as more law – more binding – than others. Correlatively, this treats certain exercises of individual rights as entitled to greater government protection, depending on the court's appraisal of those exercises. When you use your freedom to engage in economic activity, for instance, you are less protected than when you use your

---

[18] As a contrasting illustration of constitutional interpretation that is objectively respectful of its wider context, consider James Madison's gloss on the "general welfare" reference in the Preamble: "With respect to the two words 'general welfare,' I have always regarded them as qualified by the detail of powers connected with them. To take them in a literal and unlimited sense would be a metamorphosis of the Constitution into a character which there is a host of proofs was not contemplated by its creators." Thomas Jefferson similarly recognized that "Congress has not unlimited powers to provide for the general welfare, but only those specifically enumerated." Both quoted in Walter Williams, "What our Constitution Permits," *Washington Post* January 12, 2011, retrieved from http://www.creators.com/opinion/walter-williams/what-our-constitution-permits.html.

In the same vein, consider Justice Harlan's 1905 majority opinion in *Jacobson v. Commonwealth of Massachusetts*, 197 US 11: "Although [the] preamble indicates the general purposes for which the people ordained and established the Constitution, it has never been regarded as the source of any substantive power conferred on the government of the United States, or on any of its departments. Such powers embrace only those expressly granted in the body of the Constitution, and such as may be implied from those so granted."

[19] *Carolene Products*, footnote 4.

freedom to pray, because the First Amendment mentions religious practice. The problem is that such discrimination among individuals' uses of their rights as worthy of greater or lesser legal protection finds no basis in the Constitution. As long as a person is acting within his rights and is not violating the rights of others, the more particular way that he chooses to exercise his rights is simply not the government's business.[20]

Carolene's two-tiered scrutiny quickly gave way to the three-tiered grada- tion that rules to the present day: either strict, intermediate, or rational basis scrutiny is routinely employed, depending on whether the government inter- est at stake is deemed compelling, important, or legitimate.[21] This expansion from two to three tiers testifies to the mercurial character of standards, once you sever the legal system from its single, proper standard. Indeed, a standard whose authority fluctuates does not truly serve as a standard, at all. Its sover- eignty is subordinated to whatever other considerations determine its clout, in ruling on a particular law. While its name might still be used to lend the aura of legitimacy to legal processes ("standard" suggests rigor, principle), it has been dethroned by those considerations that actually determine the resolution of a given case.

It is noteworthy, too, that the rationale for rational basis permissiveness, at least implicitly, is the same premise found in Democratic Deference judicial review, namely, the belief that the people's will should hold ultimate author- ity. By placing legislators' decisions (which are assumed best to reflect the people's will) above the demands of the law (which may inhibit the people's exercise of its present will), through rational basis presumptions, the court is acceding to popular desire rather than upholding constitutional authority.[22]

---

[20] Remember the instruction of the Ninth Amendment. Randy Barnett and Clark Neily both offer extended critiques of the rational basis test along broadly similar lines. See Barnett, *Restoring the Lost Constitution*, Introduction, especially pp. 1–2, and Chapter 9; and Neily, *Terms of Engagement*, chapter 3, especially pp. 50–53, 61, 79, and notes 39 and 40 on p. 180, and Neily, "No Such Thing: Litigating Under the Rational Basis Test," *New York University Journal of Law and Liberty* volume 1, no. 2, 2005, pp. 897–913.

[21] For basic explanation, see American Law Institute, http://www.law.cornell.edu/wex/rational_basis_test.

[22] It is instructive to recognize a different kind of implication of the adoption of tiered scrutiny in the message sent to lawmakers. When courts effectively announce that they will take some laws more seriously than others by treating some laws as more accountable to the Constitution, they degrade the entire institution of law. And they encourage laxness in lawmaking. When a lawmaker knows that the court will not insist on the constitutionality of every government action but cares more about some types of law than others, subconsciously, at least, he may feel released from the obligation to create laws exclusively by the single, objective standard (namely, a law's necessity as a means of the government's fulfilling its function), and may instead partake of a smorgasbord of considerations that seem to support a law, all of which may be appetizing under some circumstances yet none of which necessarily passes the proper test

In addition to *Nebbia* and *Carolene Products*, a further significant distortion of the objective framework for judicial review came in *Wickard v. Filburn*, the 1942 case in which the Supreme Court unanimously ruled that Mr. Filburn's growing wheat on his farm for his family to consume constituted interstate commerce and was thus subject to regulation under Article I, section 8 of the Constitution (which grants Congress the authority "to regulate commerce with foreign nations and among the several states"). Despite the fact that Filburn's wheat was neither transported across state lines nor sold, the court reasoned that because such activity "exerts a substantial economic effect on interstate commerce" it *was* commerce.[23]

Earlier, I observed that the proper use of presumptions in a legal system must respect the larger context of that system's purposes and government powers. The failings of the *Wickard* reasoning are actually deeper than its failure to respect this context, however. For even considered apart from that, to produce something for one's own consumption is plainly not an act of commerce. If you were teaching a young student the meaning of the concept "commerce" and he offered such an example as a case of commerce, you would correct him, recognizing that he had not yet mastered its essence. Indeed, on the reasoning that the court employed ("but it conceivably could affect the market"), what activity would not qualify as commerce? By that rationale, nearly anything could. If you cook your own dinner tonight, you are not patronizing restaurants, pizza delivery services, or various other commercial food services. If you mow your own lawn or file your nails or have sex with your wife instead of paying prostitutes, certain would-be beneficiaries of your would-be business are affected. The time you spend reading or praying or sleeping *could* have been spent shopping.[24]

(constitutionality). If, when you are drafting a law, the consequences of doing so are emphatic, definite, and entail the authorization of government coercion to enforce it, you will tend to make law much more carefully than when you can assure yourself, "Oh well, this might not be enforced, anyway. The court picks and chooses; it's more forgiving of *some* unconstitutional laws. Don't sweat it."

Judicial review with a wink offers a Constitution with escape routes.

[23] Justice Robert Jackson, writing for the majority, *Wickard v. Filburn* 317 US 111 (1942). More recent cases follow in the same vein. See, for example, *FCC v. Beach Communications*, in which the Court contends that "if there is any conceivable state of facts that could provide a rational basis" for a challenged law, "it will survive rational basis review." 508 US 307, 313 (1993) cited in Neily, "No Such Thing," and Justice Roberts in the Affordable Care Act case, describing the court's role as to go out of its way to rescue statutes from unconstitutionality. Rather than using the most natural interpretation of the relevant language in its full context, Roberts maintains that "every reasonable construction must be resorted to, in order to save the statute from unconstitutionality." *National Federation of Independent Business v. Sebelius* 567 US, 2012, quoted in Neily, *Terms of Engagement*, p. 79.

[24] For more on the absence of a limiting principle, see Neily, *Terms of Engagement*, pp. 74–76.

Because its ruling is so illogical, *Wickard* may seem too crude a case for highlighting the particular role of context in objective review. Yet it is instructive in illustrating how, if one were even tempted toward such an egregiously ill-founded line of thinking, a check of the wider context of the Constitution's purpose and principles would have immediately called for reconsideration. Once the logic of context has been discarded, however, reason's guardrails are gone. And once the Court ushered in speculative review under *Nebbia* and *Carolene*, later courts were poised for *Wickard's* flight from reason.

Beyond these particular cases and the fatal reversal of presumptions which they represent, my larger point is simple. While presumptions as such can be a valuable device in facilitating the administration of justice, it is important to recognize their impact on government activity. Presumptions are a potentially powerful form in which the substance of what a legal system does – and correlatively, the degree to which an individual's rights are protected – can be significantly altered. In order to respect the full context of legal authority, therefore, the rationale for each legal presumption resting where it does must be faithful to constitutional powers and purpose. The upshot for judicial review is that, as part of its responsibility to police the law, an objective judiciary must police the use of presumptions.

Law Is Philosophical

Presumptions are simply one form in which philosophical beliefs shape a legal system's governance. The wider and more basic fact that an appreciation of our legal context must recognize is that the law is philosophical and that judicial review, correspondingly, must be philosophically informed. Objective interpretation of the meaning of the law depends on an understanding of the legal system's overall purpose and guiding principles. The Constitution did not emerge in a vacuum.[25] It is "backlit by the Declaration,"[26] having been motivated by substantive aspirations and given the specific form that it has as a means of realizing those aspirations. The framers enumerated the specific powers that the government

---

[25] I adapt from Lord Johan Steyn, who writes that "Parliament does not legislate in a vacuum. Parliament legislates for a European liberal democracy founded on the principles and traditions of the common law and the courts may approach legislation on this initial assumption." Quoted in Douglas Edlin, *Judges and Unjust Laws*, Ann Arbor, MI: University of Michigan Press, 2008, p. 180.

[26] Scott Gerber, *To Secure These Rights: The Declaration of Independence and Constitutional Interpretation*, New York: New York University Press, 1996. Also see Richard Epstein, *The Classical Liberal Constitution: The Uncertain Quest for Limited Government*, Cambridge, MA: Harvard University Press, 2013, pp. 3–16, 17–33; and Timothy Sandefur, *The Conscience of the Constitution: The Declaration of Independence and the Right to Liberty*, Washington, DC: Cato, 2013, pp. 2–3, 7.

would hold, for example, and decreed that the powers of Congress would be limited to those that are "necessary and proper for carrying into execution the foregoing powers and all other powers vested by this constitution."[27] as deliberate means of confining the government's activities to those needed to realize a specific vision of the role of government. We cannot understand the legitimate scope and meaning of any part of the law without respecting that.[28]

Indeed, as David Brink has observed, given that the objects of legal interpretation are artifacts, it makes perfect sense to appeal to the purposes that inspired them in order to clarify their meaning.[29] Alexander Hamilton's belief that courts should strike down "all acts contrary to the manifest tenor of the Constitution" testifies to the fact that the Constitution speaks not only through its explicit clauses, but also through its animating principles.[30] The idea that these principles and overarching purpose constrain the logical application of law was squarely recognized by the Court early on. In *Calder v. Bull* (1798), Justice Chase wrote for the majority that:

> The purposes for which men enter into society will determine the nature and terms of the social compact; and as they are the foundation of the legislative power, [i.e., the purposes] will decide what are the proper objects of [government authority].... There are certain vital principles in our free Republican governments, which will determine and over-rule an apparent and flagrant abuse of legislative power; ... An act of the Legislature (for I cannot call it a law) contrary to the great first principles of the social compact; cannot be considered a rightful exercise of legislative authority.[31]

[27] U.S. Constitution, Article I, Section 8.

[28] By the same token, when its overall mission is borne in mind, we can readily understand several individual provisions, such as the Ninth, Tenth, and Fourteenth Amendments.

[29] David Brink, "Legal Interpretation, Objectivity, and Morality," in *Objectivity in Law and Morals*, ed. Brian Leiter, New York: Cambridge University Press, 2001 p. 26. Brink also characterizes legal interpretation as a "philosophical enterprise," pp. 34, 42–44.

[30] Hamilton, *Federalist* # 78. Edlin's book on common law is largely an effort to illuminate the indispensable role of principles in a legal system as a whole and in courts' reasoning about the meaning of its laws. See Edlin, especially pp. 52, 55. Joseph Raz maintains that one of the defining features of a constitution is its embodiment of an ideology ("its provisions include principles of government [democracy, federalism, basic civil and political rights, etc.] that are generally held to express the common beliefs of the population about the way their society should be governed"), Joseph Raz, "On the Authority and Interpretation of Constitutions," in *Constitutionalism*, ed. Larry Alexander, New York: Cambridge University Press, 1998, pp. 153–154. On the propriety of principled interpretation of constitutional provisions, also see Bernard Siegan, *Drafting a Constitution for a Nation or Republic Emerging into Freedom*, Fairfax, VA: George Mason University Press, 1994, p. 37.

[31] *Calder v. Bull*, 3 US 386 (1798). A similar appreciation that legal meaning presupposes a larger context is reflected in the words of Edward Coke: "Though a man can tell the law, yet if he know not the reason thereof, he shall soone forget his superficial knowledge. But when he findeth the right reason of the law, and so bringeth it to his natural reason, that

By this stage of my account of objective law, the claim that judicial review should be philosophical and informed by a legal system's paramount purpose should seem relatively straightforward. Yet if taken apart from this context, it may be unnerving to many people. Won't that entail Living Constitutionalism of the sort that I criticized in Dworkin and others? Won't it allow judges to impose their own values onto the rest of us? (Their evaluations of egalitarianism or of capitalism, for instance, or of religious creeds or moral duties.)

No. But it is important to understand why not.

As I demonstrated across Chapters 2, 3, and 4, an objective legal system is not a value neutral one. Given that a government is the institution that is uniquely entitled to impose rules of social conduct by force, the question of its moral license cannot be avoided. A legal system's validity depends on its using that coercive power exclusively in ways that are morally justified. When it comes to the proper exercise of judicial review, therefore, courts cannot be blind to values. The application of law must be informed by the same moral principles that underwrite the entire system.

Objective interpretation does not permit courts to inject extraneous values, which is what people naturally worry about. The point, though, is that courts must adhere to those values that inhere in the legal system. And in our fervor to repel the inclusion of inappropriate value judgments, we too often throw out the baby with the bathwater. To reject the use of inappropriate values in judicial review does not indict all judicial regard for values. Bear in mind that I am describing the proper method of review in an objective legal system. A system that *is* objectively valid, however, is so thanks to its actually possessing the moral authority to rule; that authority is a vital condition of its legitimate governance. No actions and no laws contrary to that authority would be valid. In order for courts to ensure that the law actually governs, therefore, they must ensure that valid law governs – that is, authoritative law, law that satisfies that specific value test. Because, under an objective legal system, a law's identity depends (in part) on its authority, anyone who seeks to discern the meaning of law must be concerned with the authority of the law; the two concerns cannot be pried apart. And the authority of law reflects a stand on certain values.

The upshot is, in an objective legal system, questions of value cannot be avoided. Conclusions about what a legal system rightfully may and may not

he comprehendeth it as his own, this will not only serve him for the understanding of that particular case, but of many others." *Institutes of the Law of England*, retrieved from http:// books.google.com/books?id=sesyAAAAIAAJ&dq=edward%20coke%20understand%20the%20 reason%20law&pg=PA285#v=onepage&q&f=false.

do are dyed into the fabric of what a proper legal system is. Because neither a legal system's substantive rules nor its manner of implementing them are value-vacant or value neutral, the proper application of that legal system cannot be value neutral. When a court interprets law that incorporates value commitments, objectivity demands that it respect those commitments.[32]

While philosophy and values do play an important role in judicial review, then, it is crucial to see that my theory does not reduce to a form of Perfectionism. Given the extensive and continuing influence of Dworkin's theory and the appeal, more generally, of Perfectionist theories that would have judicial review improve the legal system (lately, sometimes called "Aspirational" theories), let me explain the differences between Perfectionism and my own view still further.

Jim Fleming, who clearly aligns with Dworkinian Perfectionist ambitions, maintains that "moral readings" of the Constitution enable us to see "that one of the main purposes of the Constitution is to exhort us to change in order to honor our aspirational principles..... Thus, the aspiration to fidelity requires rather than forbids change."[33] On my view, that is a mistake, for change is not a *purpose* of the Constitution. The Constitution's purpose is to lay out the framework for our legal system – the foundations and meta-rules establishing the most basic powers, organs, and structure of that system. While I would agree that a proper constitution will do so on the *basis* of and *informed by* noble aspirations to protect individual rights and respect men's liberty, such wider aspirations for the kind of society we will live in are not the purpose of *this* legal document.

Similarly, I differ with Fleming's belief that judicial review should "interpret the Constitution so as to make it the best it can be"[34] and with his wish to develop a "constitution perfecting theory."[35] Because "constitution perfecting"

---

[32] Note that if a nation's constitution itself contains a mistake (such as an amendment that defies the informing principles of that constitution), a court may not correct it on philosophical grounds. For a judge to ignore or defy a provision of the Constitution would be a usurpation of power and an inversion of logical hierarchy, given that the judiciary's authority is created by the Constitution and is thus subordinate to it. Because justices' oath is to uphold the Constitution, their paramount obligation is to that Constitution; they are not free to amend it, however superior a document their improvements might make it. For elaboration, see the discussion of this in Part 5 of the previous chapter as well as my lecture "How Activist Should Judges Be? Objectivity in Judicial Decisions," given at OCON 2005, pp. 26–30, on file with author, and related discussion in "Why Originalism Won't Die," pp. 208–213.

[33] James E. Fleming, Abstract, "Fidelity, Change, and the Good Constitution," *American Journal of Comparative Law* 62, Summer 2014, pp. 515–545.

[34] Fleming, Abstract, "Fidelity, Change, and the Good Constitution," p. 515.

[35] Fleming's characterization of his book, *Securing Constitutional Democracy*, in Fleming, "The Place of History and Philosophy in the Moral Reading of the American Constitution," *Exploring Law's Empire*, ed. Scott Hershovitz, New York: Oxford University Press, 2006, p. 30.

is constitution-changing, courts have no authority to engage in it. Thus, it is anathema to my view. My contention, again, is that the objective, fully contextual interpretation of a constitution that clearly reflects certain moral judgments must be faithful to *those* moral judgments, but this does not license judicial review that incorporates any further types of moralizing. Properly, the only end that courts should "aspire" to is accurate, objective interpretation of the Constitution and the specific moral judgments it finds therein; nothing more, nothing less.

Consider again Dworkin's own view. As Solum characterizes it, Dworkin's ideal judge is

> to construct a grand theory of political morality that provides a constructive interpretation of the entire institutional history of a given society. Because this theory is a theory of that institutional history, it is constrained.... But this constraint does not require a perfect match between a literal interpretation of every legal text and the content of the law. So some precedents may be categorized as mistakes, and some statutory or constitutional provisions may be given a constructive interpretation that makes them morally more attractive but does not follow every jot and tittle of the text.[36]

While I agree that some judicial precedents constitute mistakes, I differ from Dworkin by denying that these justify courts' offering a "constructive" interpretation of *constitutional provisions* to render the law "morally more attractive." For courts to make any part of the Constitution *more* attractive is for it to deviate from the actual Constitution that it is given to interpret (rather than to alter). Constraining as it may be, the literal interpretation of "legal text" and "content" *is* imperative, if we are to live under the Rule of Law.

Bear in mind that "literal" does not mean mindless; properly practiced, literal interpretation is thoughtful, objectively attuned to the relevant context and guided by logic. Anything other than law's literal interpretation, in fact, would defeat the point of a written constitution. The Constitution is not metaphor.

It is also important, for appreciating the difference between our views, to recognize that Dworkin advocates not merely courts' correcting mistaken *interpretations* of the law given by previous courts. For courts to do that is perfectly appropriate (indeed, it is part of their responsibility). Rather, Dworkin sanctions judges' "improving" the law itself. For courts to make existing law *better* is to make the law different, however. That would be usurpation of an authority that does not rest with the judiciary.

---

[36] Larry Solum, Legal Theory Blog, Lexicon 65: The Nature of Law, retrieved from http://lsolum .typepad.com/legal_theory_lexicon/2008/05/legal-theory-le.html.

Lest one protest that it is unfair to use Solum's characterization rather than Dworkin himself, a brief reminder of just a handful of Dworkin's claims that we encountered in Chapter 6 should make plain the significant differences between us. Dworkin's central metaphor of a chain novel likens judicial review to creative writing. While assuring us that the ideal judge would not substitute his own philosophical judgment for that of the legislature on matters of policy, he may use such personal philosophy, we are told, when it comes to principle.[37] A judge's "own moral and political convictions" are to be "directly engaged" in judicial review.[38] He is to "draw on his own convictions about justice and fairness and the right relation between them" and reject "the rigid idea that judges must defer to elected officials."[39]

In short, under Perfectionism, judges are counseled to make the law as good as it can be – which is a distinct enterprise from making the most sense of the law that they find. Perfectionism's instruction merges the task of legal interpreter – understander, decipherer – with that of legal reformer. And the reformer role is primary, as "better" law, in the eye of the judge, is to defeat respect for existing law. This is a dramatically different use of philosophy than in my own prescription. On my view, in order to be objective, judges must draw on the philosophy that is *in* the law, but not inject their own. Dworkin's judge may depart from the law; mine may not.

What Can't Be Written

Even as I emphasize that objective judicial review would not allow the imposition of judges' personal values, some will no doubt still resist from a different flank, insisting that for judges to be philosophical at all would be for judges to leave the law. Originalists, in particular, might contend that we commit the law to writing precisely in order to confine the legal system to definite boundaries. (Recall some of their arguments from Chapter 6.) This is true. Yet as we saw in my critique of Textualism, words alone do not transmit meaning; the thought that a string of words represents does not inhere in those audible or visual markings. Meaning requires context. This holds for the law as for anything else. And this holds for written law. While committing the boundaries of a government's legal authority to writing does provide a valuable degree of security, it is important to recognize what such writing cannot provide. A court's task is to understand the objective meaning of the law, but the *understanding* of words' meaning is simply not the kind of thing that words themselves contain.

---

[37] *Law's Empire*, p. 398.
[38] *Law's Empire*, p. 256.
[39] *Law's Empire*, p. 398.

The proper understanding of an idea can be indicated by written words (often, in very helpful ways), but it is not reducible to those words. Understanding is a conceptual process, an activity that yields (at least in many cases) an intellectual conclusion. Intellectual phenomena cannot be fully captured by means of perceptual devices, however, such as audible or visible symbols. Meaning is thicker than words.

Think of it this way: While the requirement, in an objective legal system, to write down the law *is* an important safeguard, "Write down the law" does not mean "write down the rules and the philosophy behind the rules along with the rules of linguistic interpretation and everything else that one might ever need to know in order to properly understand the meaning and objective application of the particular law that is identified by those words – and, by doing so, one will have written the meaning of the law." Such an assignment would be hopeless. The problem is not simply that the task would be endless (although it would be).[40] The deeper problem is that it reflects a conceptual confusion (a category mistake, in the lexicon of philosophy). It fails to appreciate that a word and the meaning of that word and the understanding of that word are three fundamentally different kinds of things. Intimately connected as they often are, none of the three can be fully captured in terms of the others.

The implication for judicial review is that it is a mistake to demand that objective interpretation of law shed background suppositions. They are an ineliminable condition of the understanding of words' meaning. While a legal system's rules must all be written down, the understanding of the rules cannot be.

Contrary to the Originalists' wishful thinking, objective interpretation cannot be outsourced to physical symbols, either written or spoken. Writing cannot replace reasoning. We cannot "lock in" meaning, as Barnett had dreamed, by locking out the mind.[41] To expect that we can is fundamentally to misunderstand the kind of thing that meaning is and the kind of thing that understanding is.

In sum, when we respect the context of specific laws within an objective legal system, we recognize that that system reflects philosophical conclusions and that "the law" includes values. If the law were value free, it would carry no authority. Consequently, objective judicial review must honor those values that a legal system embeds and interpret its constituent laws in light of them.

---

[40] No abstractions (laws included) could ever be understood without resting in a framework of unarticulated background presuppositions. However far one reaches in trying to articulate those suppositions, questions about *those* could still be raised.

[41] "How can a meaning be preserved or 'locked in' and governors checked and restrained if the written words mean only what legislatures or judges want them to mean today?" Barnett asks, *Restoring the Lost Constitution*, pp. 104–105.

4. CORRECTING INTRINSICIST EXPECTATIONS

All of this also underscores the need to shed the intrinsicist conception of objectivity that mars our expectations of what proper judicial review consists of. As we discussed in Chapter 1, intrinsicism is the belief that objectivity is a property inherent in certain facts and that external reality contains objective truths ready-made, for human beings either to recognize or to deny. Intrinsicism, moreover, is widely assumed to be the only alternative to subjectivism.

Several of the methodologies that we inspected in Chapter 6 were distorted by subjectivist premises. The use of Popular Constitutionalism, Living Constitutionalism, or Minimalism to determine the meaning of law would insert extra-legal factors into the court's calculus, I argued, such as a decision's anticipated popularity, or the magnitude of its expected effects, or the desirability of those effects, or prior judges' beliefs about a law. In so doing, they would replace the Rule of Law with governance by subjects' beliefs. Whether it is the beliefs of our judicial predecessors or the preferences of the voting masses or the preferences of the deciding justices themselves that a method erects as sovereign, such methods are subjectivist insofar as they subordinate the law to a higher ruler: certain subjects' attitudes toward the law. And the threat to objective law that is posed by such subjectivist review is plain. If the meaning of the law were hostage to subjective opinions, the legal status of actions would be completely unpredictable. The fact that a court ruled that a law "meant" one thing last year would provide no reason to think that it will treat that law in the same manner when it next arises (or even that it believes that it should). Whichever the set of subjects that the court accedes to, under such a volatile regime of "meaning," the law would be useless. When law has no firm identity and enduring meaning, *it* cannot govern.

In the attempt to fend off this subjectivist sabotage of the law, however, Originalists and others tend to embrace an equally invalid alternative: intrinsicism. They treat the meaning of law as wholly contained within its words, a prepackaged "given" that needs only to be honestly reported by contemporary courts in order to properly govern. In fact, however, law's meaning is not a user-proof pellet buried in the law's language; meaning is never fully contained within written words, simply awaiting extraction. As we explained in Chapter 6, the words of a constitution are not shorthands for a fixed, predetermined list that straitjackets later interpreters to an exact set of explicitly preapproved applications.[42] One cannot look up the answer to a question of abstractions' valid application in the way that one can look up the tax he

---

[42] Neily decries the notion that the Constitution is a "tape measure." Neily, *Terms of Engagement*, p. 30; also see p. 111.

owes on an IRS chart or a dollar's Euro equivalent in a currency converter. Consequently, any particular meaning or application that a judge allegedly merely "found" by such devices could not be the law's actual meaning.

Objective meaning is neither a self-evident revelation nor a social construct; it is not fully contained within text any more than it is created by people's beliefs. As explained in Chapter 1, objectivity is relational: it is not determined exclusively by reference to the object nor, exclusively, by reference to the subject. And remember what the discipline of objectivity is for – it is to guide a process of thought. A method of engaging in judicial review is a method for guiding how a person should employ his mental faculties so as to answer questions about the relationship between the abstract concepts represented in law and the particular circumstances in which people dispute law's proper application. Insofar as objectivity in judicial review is an ideal that is meant to guide volitional beings, however, the possibility of their disagreement and error is ineliminable.[43]

The law is a body of conceptual instruction; as such, it is not reducible to a list of concrete commands that can be heard and followed with no intervening thought on the part of the person following it. Applying a law is not akin to obeying orders in a game of Simon Says. For a person's thinking process to be objective, he (the subject) must act and contribute to the conclusion in a way that is not fully scripted by the material that he attempts to understand. Contrary to the implications of many Originalists, to recognize the inescapable role of the subject in a process of thinking does not license subjectiv*ism*. The fact that the activity of judgment is *performed* by a subject does not render it subjectivist, for it does not entail that the *standard* employed must be the subject's belief or preference. A person is perfectly capable of exercising his judgment by impersonal standards. I want Michaels to win; I count the ballots and report that he lost. I want the Packers to retain ball possession; I know the rules, I see the Packers' fumble clearly, I rule it a fumble. This is no less true in the more complex cases. Indeed, if objective standards were not available, our very discussion here and debate over proper methods of judicial review would be a hopeless swamp of subjectivist say-so. Scholars who engage in the debate are committed, at least implicitly, to the premise that people are capable of being swayed by sound, impersonal standards.[44]

---

[43] The fact that jurists who endorse the same judicial method sometimes disagree about the exact resolution that that method prescribes in a particular case testifies to this.

[44] What is true is that we have no way of knowing the law except through our thinking about law. It does not follow, however, that our beliefs about the law therefore simply *are* the law, that the two are one and the same thing. Nor does it follow that our beliefs become the standard by which to identify what is and is not law. This should also help us to appreciate why judicial

Objectivity is not achieved by a person's unthinking submission or unquestioning acquiescence; it does not consist of passively awaiting orders which one will robotically execute. Being objective is an active effort to understand a phenomenon and to reach valid conclusions about it, be it a law of nature or a written law of a government. Understanding legal language requires intelligent *labor*. Far from the intrinsicist implications of most Originalists, thought is not a threat to objectivity; it is its necessary means. (Not a bug, but a feature.) And contrary to the implications of many critics of "activist" judges, objective judicial review is not a no-brainer. It is the use that a jurist makes of his brain that determines the propriety of his method.

The Originalists are correct, of course, that in order to maintain the Rule of Law, a certain form of obedience *is* critical, namely, obedience of the nation's laws. My finer point here, however, is that the courts' task is to figure out exactly what the law is. Judicial review is called on precisely when someone challenges an *understanding* of the law, arguing that a particular understanding employed in a government action would be invalid. ("Surely, *that* use of the seized property does not conform to the public use requirement" or "*That* army policy does not treat women in a way that satisfies the Equal Protection Clause.") Judicial review is the process of ascertaining what the law means, and thus, what the rules that we are to abide by truly are. That cannot be accomplished simply by confirming what its language reads and awaiting insight into the answers within. Judges are not the overdressed equivalent of spell checkers. Writing the law down does not write away all reasonable questions about what the writing means nor about how the law is properly respected in different circumstances.

To wrap up this point: Intrinsicism, regrettably, is widely seen as the only alternative to subjectivism. While that label is rarely used, its core belief that an objective truth is a given truth warps many of our images of objective law and correlative expectations of what proper judicial review should look like. Our failure to shed these intrinsicist assumptions actually contributes to the very state of affairs that those drawn to them wish to protect us from – the law's subjectivist application. Because intrinsicism's model of precooked, thought-free meaning is a fiction, judges who sincerely seek to "find" the law's intrinsic meaning cannot. It does not exist. Correspondingly, they cannot follow it. When they presume that they are following it, therefore, they must actually be guided (at least implicitly) by something other than the law. What

discretion is perfectly compatible with objectivity. What is important is that discretion be exercised within the bounds that are set by the law, as that is objectively understood. For discussion of "lawful" discretion, see Karl Llewellyn, *The Common Law Tradition*, Boston: Little Brown, 1960, p. 217.

comes most naturally will be some variant of subjectivism, as they treat their own attitudes or others' attitudes toward the law as if it *is* the law.

The judge who is objective, by contrast, appreciates that intrinsicism offers no better a means to objective meaning than does subjectivism. He banishes both from his thinking. He does not expect meaning to be transparent in the law's language and he will not supply extraneous elements of subjects' beliefs in order to "finish" the law. Rather, he reasons exclusively by the nature of the law – understood in light of the relevant context – as best as his strict use of logic allows him to understand it.

5. JUDICIAL CHARACTER

Having identified the guidelines that are most critical to the proper conduct of judicial review, it is also useful to recognize certain aspects of judicial character that are vital, if this method is to have the desired effect. Two characteristics stand out. Intellectually, a judge must be an astute conceptual, abstract thinker; morally, he must have integrity, exerting both the self-discipline not to exceed his rightful power and the courage to exercise it fully.

Intellectually, objective judicial review requires keen discrimination. In order to disentangle the lacing, knotted vines of considerations that disputes brought to the high courts typically pose, a judge must be adept at sifting essentials from peripherals and at identifying the core legal principles involved. The principal activity that occupies courts engaged in judicial review is that of classification. Through the myriad idiosyncrasies of each dispute that reaches them, the recurring question that courts are called upon to answer is: "Is this a case of that?" Does the Detroit police department's use of this GPS device constitute a search? Do Georgia's voter identification requirements respect the Equal Protection mandate? Does the developer's repurposing of the seized property constitute a "public use" of it?

Judicial review's basic function is to answer the question, "Is this legal?" And it must address this at at least two levels: Does the particular action being challenged conform to the relevant legal rules? And do those rules themselves conform to the Constitution? To the basis and bounds of legal authority? In order to answer correctly – that is, in a way that preserves the sovereignty of the law – a judge must skillfully distill those features that are essential to an abstraction from those that are incidental and those features of a contested case that are essential to an action's being a member of the relevant legal category (a search, a public use, an exercise of religion, etc.) from those that are not. It is only by the acute recognition of these similarities and differences that he can maintain fidelity to the law.

The kinds of questions brought before appellate courts are characteristically close calls. (At least, they are comparatively close calls, for the purposes of conceptual classification. If the laws being challenged clearly indicated the dispute's proper resolution, courts would not grant review.) Correspondingly, there can be substantial grounds to think that *A is* a case of *B* (e.g., this police tactic does constitute a search) when in fact, on analysis, it is not. It is for this reason that judges must be especially conceptually discerning.

The second major character requirement of objective judicial review is moral. Objectivity in review requires both self-disciplined restraint and courageous assertion.

It is commonplace to observe that judicial review demands self-discipline. Judges must refrain from imposing what are truly their own preferences about what the law should be and adhere strictly to their honest understandings of what the law is. This is, indeed, a sound observation and a significant requirement. While I believe that specific charges of judicial activism are sometimes misdirected and often hurled irresponsibly, the principle behind the complaint is valid.[45] Judges, as much as the members of other branches, must confine their reasoning and their rulings to the bounds of their authority. Because their actions are not reviewed by others in the ways that agents of other branches are subject to review by the judiciary, moreover, courts bear a special responsibility to self-police. In order to police the law, a justice must conscientiously police himself. Thus judicial self-discipline *is* particularly important.

What is not usually appreciated, though, is that courts also bear a responsibility to assert fully the power of their office. Doing so is often unpopular. Because court decisions are made by small numbers of easily identifiable individuals, because judges on the highest courts are not directly elected, and because their decisions are not subject to the same kinds of review as are those of other government officials, courts are easy scapegoats for laws that people dislike. Their work is frequently denounced as "undemocratic." The profound impact of many of their rulings only intensifies hostility and calls for restraint.

In this charged context, it is especially important to recognize that objective judicial review demands that a judge exert the moral courage not to retreat from his obligation to uphold the law. Regardless of his own or others' evaluations of that law – its reception among editorialists, the legal academy, or various segments of popular opinion – and regardless of anyone's views concerning the morality or the most likely impact of a decision upholding that law (economic impact, electoral impact, etc.), a judge must scrupulously

---

[45] On different conceptions and measures of activism, see Adam Liptak, "How Activist is the Supreme Court?" *New York Times*, October 13, 2013.

adhere to the meaning of the law, the facts of the case, and deliver the logical conclusion. He may not permit anything to come between the law, as best as he can discern it, and his ruling on a particular's legality. The objective jurist does not evade the fact that if a challenged action is constitutional, it is lawful, whatever else might be said of it, and if a challenged action is not constitutional, it is not lawful. Proper judicial review demands that *he* have the courage of the law's convictions.

In short, the objective jurist accepts the full responsibilities of his role – what he must do as well as what he may not. In light of the prevalent criticism of courts' engaging in unwarranted activity (which, of course, they sometimes do), it is important to appreciate that inactivity is not the solution. For it permits extraneous considerations to trump the law. Judicial abdication is not a virtue.[46]

Seductive Red Herrings: Balance and Deference to Competence
Because courts are frequently distracted from the objective course by sober-sounding aims, it is useful to say a few words about two of the most prevalent forms of this. One common type of deviation from objectivity rests in courts' appeals to "balance" in support of their rulings. Too often, this term is a hollow catchall, a "vaporous non-standard"[47] invoked to sanction deference to extra-legal considerations. In many cases, "balance" is simply a euphemism for the compromise of the relevant legal standards to a nebulous sense of propriety.

I do not mean to condemn every judicial use of the word "balance" as constitutional heresy. Considerations of specific types of balance may be appropriate in certain cases. When they are, however, a court must explain exactly what the balance invoked refers to and why it is constitutionally mandated. What is the content of its counsel? What does the invoked "balance" actually instruct a legal interpreter to do and what is the basis on which it does so? *What* are courts to balance, and by what standard? When is balance achieved? And why is the reputed standard the appropriate one?

---

[46] In this vein, see Neily, *Terms of Engagement*; and Suzanna Sherry, "Why We Need More Judicial Activism," in *Constitutionalism, Executive Power, and Popular Enlightenment*, eds. Giorgi Areshidze, Paul Carrese, and Suzanna Sherry, Albany, NY: SUNY Press, 2014. Note that the rational basis test, discussed earlier, encourages judges to shirk the responsibility of judgment. As an example of their doing so, Justice O'Connor wrote for the majority in *Midkiff*, an eminent domain case, that a government taking is permissible as long as it is "rationally related to a conceivable public purpose." *Hawaii Housing Auth. v. Midkiff* 467 US 229 (1984). O'Connor took a starkly different view, asserting more judgment, in *Kelo*.

[47] A phrase used by Justice William Brennan in his dissenting opinion in *Hazelwood School District v. Kuhlmeier*, 484 US 260 (1988).

What is essential for the maintenance of objective law is that the answers to all such questions be determined by the Constitution. Balance of any type can be a legitimate judicial consideration only to the extent that it is consonant with the dictates of the Constitution. Without that, "balance" undermines law's integrity. When advancing some sort of "balance" actually gives extraneous considerations as much weight or greater weight than the law, it must be evicted as an interloper on the terrain of legality.

Another of the ways that courts sometimes deviate from objective law is by deferring to others' presumed greater competence. Courts will commonly avoid direct confrontation with contentious legal questions by claiming to lack the relevant knowledge. "That is for the experts to decide" or "that is for the people to decide" are frequent rationales for Minimalist rulings or for non-rulings. (I will use "competence" here to refer to knowledge along with relevant abilities.)

Now in some cases, such deference *is* objectively called for. Yet it is important to distinguish deference on the basis of others' superior competence from deference on the basis of others' possessing the relevant legal jurisdiction. Too often, courts muddle the two and invoke others' competence as a dodge. The problem occurs when a court professes that a certain legal question is beyond its purview when in fact, by law, it is not. Judges are the experts on lawfulness and they are professionally obligated to exert the judgment of that expertise.

Obviously, in numerous situations of ordinary life, consultation with experts is eminently sensible. It is for this reason that legislatures, for instance, *should* gather reports from experienced practitioners in specialized fields (munitions manufacturers, drug researchers, etc.) before crafting certain laws and that courts, too, should seek out expert testimony on certain issues in order to reach informed and objective rulings. What increasingly occurs, however, is that legitimate restraint in delaying a legal decision until important knowledge has been acquired is invoked as a pretext for courts' avoiding decisions that they can and should make. While it would sometimes be the more popular course to leave contentious questions of government action to others (as many advise for the legality of abortion, for instance), it is seldom the legal course. And when it is not, for courts to deflect these questions under the guise of others' competence is a dereliction of their duty.

Like "balance," competence per se is a red herring. Whatever the comparative competence of different agencies of government, it is not degrees of competence that confer these agencies' authority. The Constitution does not say: "Congress shall have these enumerated powers, except when it is particularly competent, in which cases it may assume more, or particularly incompetent, in which case it will have less" or "the Executive will have this set of specified powers, except when it becomes really good at making certain kinds of judgments, in which case it may help itself to the exercise of additional powers, as well, thereby shrinking the authority of the legislature, the judiciary, the states, or the people." Ability does not determine whether a particular exercise of government power is objectively justified. Whatever the special competence that a given organ of government might in fact possess, it is the Constitution that establishes that organ's authority to act. Competence, however genuine, is not a Constitution-buster. And it is not reason for courts to skirt their duties.[48]

Over the years, many people have mocked Hamilton's claim that the judiciary is the "least dangerous" branch of government, scorning the courts as a counter-majoritarian menace.[49] Yet a court that is properly fulfilling its role could be a danger only if the law that it is upholding is itself a danger. U.S. courts are a counter-majoritarian device, as I noted in Chapter 6, but they are so based on the design of a Constitution that is itself a counter-majoritarian institution. This would be problematic only if one assumed that popular will should be sovereign – an ideal that is at odds with constitutional government and the Rule of Law. For as Jefferson observed, "An elective despotism, was not the government we fought for."[50] And judicial review is a crucial bulwark against that.[51]

In short, an objective court respects the division of labor that the Constitution imposes. It accepts the limits of its authority as well as its responsibilities and it does not second-guess the Constitution by substituting its own assessments of competence and assignments of authority. Occasional rhetoric notwithstanding, it is not for members of the judiciary to be society's peacemakers or to be our leaders. Properly, judges are the law tellers. Their role is to listen

---

[48] The issue is complicated by the fact that the term "competence" is sometimes used loosely to encompass authority, as well. A court will sometimes claim, "We are not competent to judge" when in fact, it means that a certain question is not within its legal jurisdiction. I have no objection to courts doing that; indeed, they are required to. What I am spotlighting as unjustified deference, however, is a court's refusing to exercise authority that it does actually possess, as when a court claims to lack authority (under the cover of "competence" or in any other language) when what it actually means is that it does not want its authority, perhaps because of the contentiousness of a given case and the criticisms likely to follow its exercising its authority. Anyone who cowers before the responsibilities of his role has no business taking that role. For the judge who accepts the specific role of safeguarding the law but then fails to fulfill that role subverts objective law.

[49] Hamilton, *Federalist Papers*, number 78. He characterizes the judiciary as the branch that is "least dangerous to the political rights of the Constitution," p. 522 in Cooke edition.

[50] Thomas Jefferson, *Notes on the State of Virginia*, query 13.

[51] Texas Supreme Court Justice Don Willett has framed the issue thus: "Whether the surrender of constitutional guarantees is necessary is a legislative call in terms of desirability but a judicial one in terms of constitutionality. The political branches decide if laws pass; courts decide if laws pass muster." Concurring opinion in *Robinson v. Crown Cork & Seal Co*, Case No 06-0714 (2010).

attentively to competing arguments, to evaluate them objectively, to explain the reasoning behind their conclusions, and all the while, scrupulously to *follow* the law.

6. POTENTIAL MISGIVINGS

Before concluding, let me consider a few reservations that one might have about my account of proper judicial review. Given the groundwork that I have laid in earlier chapters' discussions of objectivity, of an objective legal system, and of law's authority, I can dispose of each fairly quickly.

A. *Too Scant*

From a certain perspective, it may seem that my portrait of proper review is simply too meager. The instruction to "be objective" might seem uninformative, or at best, not distinctive. After all, aren't the methods advocated by the alternative schools of Originalism, Minimalism, Popular Constitutionalism, and so forth, accounts of what judicial objectivity consists of?

Actually, I think not. While lip service to objectivity is sometimes paid in these accounts, they exert no genuine effort to penetrate the essential character of objectivity and then, on that basis, to demonstrate what objectivity specifically requires in the context of understanding and applying law. One of my principal contentions has been that a process of abstract thought cannot be reduced to a mechanical procedure. Correspondingly, an account of objective judicial review will not issue a simple, handy formula that can be mindlessly obeyed (such as, "abide by the text"). To regard the absence of *this* type of instruction in my account as a deficiency is to retain distorted expectations of the type of guidance that is needed and that is possible from a theory of proper judicial methodology. It reflects a failure to appreciate the abstract character of language and of meaning.

My account of review provides, in essentialized terms, the standard that should govern legal interpretation and judicial decision making. Courts must proceed exclusively by the law, understood by logic and in context. What we have learned over the course of the book is that the ultimate foundation and the ultimate standard for every element of a legal system is its service to the overarching mission of that system. Every aspect of a legal system is to be created and operated in ways that advance that system's reason for being – that fulfill its central function. The authority of the law can extend no further than that. This entails that the identity of the law can extend no further than that. And this entails that the exercise of judicial review (a power that is granted under that authority) can extend no further than that. Objectivity demands that a court treat nothing other than that as carrying legal authority.

Given that the dominant alternative methods of judicial review do include extraneous considerations and thus obstruct objective law, the significance of my account's instruction to be objective – along with the elaboration of exactly what that entails – should be plain. What the complaint of insufficient guidance seems to demand, however, is a formulaic technique that will replace the need for courts to engage in rigorous, objective thought when confronting a case. No such technique could uphold objective law.

B. Too Philosophical

Others might object that my method of judicial review assigns too large a role to the philosophical principles behind the law and not enough to the enacted law. The fear is that my method encourages judges to employ political theory at the expense of the law, allowing them to treat actual legal materials (statutes, doctrine, precedents, etc.) as merely a dispensable intermediary. It invites judges to philosophize, treating the Constitution more as a symbol of certain ideals than as a firm body of rules, to which they are bound.

While this type of objection might be warranted against some accounts of judicial review, it is not, against mine.[52] I have been at pains throughout to emphasize that courts may employ only those political principles that inhere in our legal system and are not free to inject any further conclusions of philosophy seminar rooms. To recognize those principles that animate a legal system and that are implicit in its constitution, however, is not to treat the Constitution as symbolic silly putty, allowing it to be manipulated by the philosophical predilections of the interpreters. It is, rather, to recognize a constitution for what it is: a set of rules that provide conceptual guidance through both the express statement of its rules and the context of commitments that underwrite those rules and that establish their authority and objective meaning. A constitution is the expression of philosophical conviction. Courts not only may make use of that in order to find the objective meaning of its components; they must.[53]

---

[52] For a spirited rendition of the charge that Dworkin's view is guilty of this, see Brian Leiter, "The End of Empire: Dworkin and Jurisprudence in the 21st Century," *Rutgers Law Journal* 35, 2005, pp. 165–181.

[53] As we have seen earlier, in their eagerness to uphold the written law, some people are unduly suspicious of anything that is not written. Yet it is natural that the philosophy that informs a constitution will not itself be explicitly written *in* the Constitution; a constitution is not a treatise of philosophy. The subject matter of a constitution is the most basic rules that will constitute and structure a legal system; the *subject* is not the philosophy that informs those rules. Correspondingly, the belief that the Constitution's words *by themselves* could dictate their meaning and proper application is misplaced.

In short, objective jurists are not to be philosophical as authors of law, but they are to be philosophically attuned interpreters of law (as anyone must be, to understand the meaning of a philosophical document).

C. Too Open-Ended

A related concern focuses on the open-endedness of concepts that is at the heart of my portrait of objectivity. Some may fear that this leaves the law too open-ended – or more exactly, open-ended in an inappropriate and danger-ous way. For it may seem to surrender the stability of law that is crucial to an objective system.

In fact, however, objectivity requires open-endedness. As explained in my critique of Textualism in Chapter 6, to deny open-endedness – to "close" or "fix" concepts' referents – would lodge concepts' meaning in the beliefs of a particular collection of people at a particular time rather than in the nature of the phenomena in question – that is, in the nature of the *objects* that a law refers to. As such, it would not be objective. It would be a form of intrinsicism.

Remember that the type of open-endedness that I have embraced is not license for simply any extension of referents that a person might assert. To say that a term's meaning is open-ended does not mean that it is boundless, stan-dardless, answerable to nothing, or that speakers may apply that term indis-criminately. The meaning of concepts is *objectively* open-ended. Concepts are open-ended strictly in the precise sense that the discrete existents that a concept refers to are not limited ("closed") by the beliefs of word users on a particular date. A concept's meaning is limited, however, by the essential identity of things of that kind – that is, by that set of characteristics that most fundamentally dis-tinguishes them from things of all other kinds. ("Religious activity," for instance, excludes countless forms of nonreligious activity; "commerce" excludes count-less forms of noncommercial activity.) That restriction is crucial.

In respecting concepts' open-endedness, we recognize the fundamental independence of existents from people's beliefs about existents. Recognition of this independence is vital if we are to be governed by the Rule of Law rather than the Rule of Men – of that set of men whose particular ideas about words' referents are permitted to govern.[54]

---

[54] Obviously, the open-endedness of concepts might be distorted in law-abusing ways by judges who do not exercise their power in good faith. And anyone who assumes the prevalence of bad faith will be especially eager to "confine" meaning within words, out of fear that any room left for an interpreter's judgment is room for abuse that will only facilitate the law's deliberate manipulation. Yet the problem in such a scenario is not with my method; it is with the practi-tioner's bad faith. And the solution is not to misrepresent the actual, open-ended character of concepts.

D. Drastic Repercussions

Finally, some might object that the adoption of my method would carry unacceptably drastic practical repercussions. The implementation of rulings reached by this method threatens to disrupt longstanding precedents and widely accepted legal practices. Originalism is often criticized for the radical implications that its use would carry for laws governing racial segregation, sexual relationships, or certain labor, environmental, or consumer protection laws, among others.[55] Parallel charges might be lodged against my account: my theory would simply be too radical in its practice to be seriously entertained.

The first part is true – the use of objective judicial review would reverse previous departures from objective law. The conclusion that that should eject it from serious consideration, however, does not follow. If the overarching end is a law-governed society and our aim is to clarify the judicial method of review that will best support that, then observations about the probable impact of different rulings have no purchase, for they say nothing about the legality of those rulings. In an objective legal system, courts are obligated to abide by the law, not by that which is most entrenched, most familiar, or most comfortable. The wisdom of the law is a separate question, which stands beyond the judiciary's authority.

This is not to commend the abrupt imposition of radical change with no regard to individuals' rights or individuals' reasonable expectations about how the legal system will treat them (expectations which the legal system itself has fostered). If significant upheaval would result from restoring an objective interpretation in an area where non-objective practices have been permitted to take root, measures can be adopted to ease the transition. I will discuss this further in Chapter 8, which concerns proper review in less-than-ideal conditions. What is most important here, though, is this: the fact that earlier rulers may have misapplied the law does not alter the meaning of the law, just as the fact that correcting such errors can bring painful consequences does not alter the meaning of the law. However disruptive it may sometimes be to restore the governance of law in areas where we have strayed from that, that is what upholding the *law* requires.

7. CONCLUSION

My account of proper judicial review, I think, is uniquely based on a sound understanding of an objective legal system and a sound understanding of objectivity itself. It is built on an appreciation of the nature and purpose of

---

[55] See, for example, David Strauss, *The Living Constitution*, pp. 12–18.

government and the fundamental mandate of a legal system. Consequently, it is best positioned to enable a court to fulfill the function of judicial review, namely, to maintain the Rule of Law. It does this in large part by respecting the authority that the legal system does and does not possess. This last is crucial, for the authority of law is critical to the identity of law – to what it is that qualifies as bona fide law.

My account does not offer a simple litmus test of legality or an easily implemented blueprint for courts to follow. Nor does it promise to "deliver us from error" with a guarantee of correct decisions. Objective decision making demands abstract thinking and abstract thinking is a volitional, fallible activity; some of the constituent choices that a person makes in using his mind (to attach significance to a particular piece of information or to minimize the relevance of another piece of information, for instance) may be mistaken. *Objective* abstract thought concerning the meaning of law is particularly demanding, insofar as it requires logical rigor throughout intricate, often multitiered conceptual relationships. While judicial review is not rocket science, it isn't a game of checkers, either. Our expectations of courts and of their proper methods must be set accordingly.

The essence of my view is that objective review proceeds exclusively by the law, with its meaning and implications ascertained solely by means of logical, context-sensitive analysis. While many accounts of judicial review profess their fidelity to law, by failing to master the core character of objective law, they do not actually provide that. Moreover, while it may seem elementary to observe that courts must abide by the law, the extraneous factors that competing judicial methodologies would have courts include make it important to insist on this. On the account that I have defended, no other considerations *as such* – popular preferences, moral principles, scope of impact, etc. – carry weight as law. Insofar as fidelity to law is what a court properly seeks, it must unequivocally reject all such peripheral considerations.

In the end, it is useful to remind ourselves of the reason to seek "proper" judicial review. Why care whether courts engage in judicial review in one way rather than another? To ensure the Rule of Law. Even more basically: to achieve the purpose of a legal system, namely, the greatest possible security for individual rights. The question to pose of any method of judicial review, accordingly, is: Does this mode of review do that? Does it confine itself to that purpose and serve that purpose more effectively than the alternatives? Only the objective method of judicial review, as I have explained it, does this.

8

Proper Review in Contemporary Conditions

1. INTRODUCTION

Objectivity is contextual. What constitutes the objective application of any rule depends, in part, on the specific conditions in which it is being applied. The judiciary's task is complicated by the fact that it is one component of a deliberately integrated system whose distinct organs are designed to work together to carry out the government's function. The American legal system today, unfortunately, is encrusted with non-objective law. Its content, its administration, and the authority behind its uses of power have all been infected by unjustified elements. Given this, should the methodology of judicial review be modified in any way? It is one thing to theorize about how judges should proceed in a legal system that is essentially working as it should, when the other branches are properly fulfilling their roles. It is another to say how judges should proceed in a system that is seriously skewed by various non-objective influences. In what ways, if any, should the judiciary do its work differently when assorted agents of the legal system are not functioning as they should and the system has strayed from its proper bounds, as a result?

To address this, I shall identify the major considerations that should guide a court if it is properly to perform its role in this setting. Given the various forces that have tainted people's notions of what objective judicial review *is* and that exert pressure on courts to deviate further from objective law, this is an important start on the work of reform. My aim in this chapter is not to detail the precise steps by which a court should respond to each of the distortions that it encounters, thus I will not issue anything like a blueprint for exactly how courts should undo errors of the past. That is a worthy project that requires more specialized investigation. My purpose, rather, is to lay the foundation for that effort by identifying the basic principles and parameters within which more concrete corrections may properly be pursued.

To appreciate the challenge faced by today's courts, I will begin by reminding us of some of the major forces that corrupt our legal system's objectivity. I will then turn to my prescriptions for judicial method. In one sense, my answer to the question of whether courts should do things differently is: only minimally. For the essence of what judicial review requires in order for courts to uphold objective law is no different, under current conditions. Yet the change that is minimal, in terms of procedural complexity, would be significant in its substance and radical in its impact. In order to proceed objectively today, primarily, a court needs to reject three-tiered scrutiny and to restore proper presumptions concerning the legal system's authority. Doing so will particularly demand one of the personal virtues that we discussed in Chapter 7 – courage.

2. CHALLENGES FOR OBJECTIVE JUDICIAL REVIEW

In order to understand the principles by which a court should navigate under current conditions, it is useful to bear in mind the principal kinds of obstacles that it faces. In very basic terms, our legal system is distorted by bad laws and bad understandings. By "bad," here, I mean invalid according to objective standards for the substance, administration, and authority of a legal system.

A. Non-Objective Laws

As we detailed in Chapter 2, the U.S. legal system suffers from numerous failures of objectivity and the courts are frequently asked to apply laws that are not themselves valid in one or more respects (usually, in regard to their foundation, formulation, or exercise). Some laws are poorly written, worded in vague or ambiguous ways that fail to issue clear and definite instruction. The law's definitions of "anti-competitive behavior," "obscenity," "indecency," "sexual harassment," and "diversity" are just a few of the most flagrant offenders that leave a great deal to the imagination of those charged to enforce the law.[1] When a particular use of such laws is challenged in court, their ambiguity invites the court to *supply* their meaning, rather than to find it. Whatever the substantive merit of Dodd-Frank's restrictions on financial transactions, even many supporters acknowledge that its unwieldy scope and untenable complexity overwhelm people's ability to comply with the law and legal officials' ability to enforce it objectively. Some of the official "clarifications" of the law's requirements themselves run to hundreds of

---

[1]   See the discussion in Chapter 2 of this book.

pages.[2] The U.S. tax code, to take a different example, is, in the droll assessment of *The Economist*, written in Klingon.[3]

Other law offends objectivity by virtue of exceeding the legal system's authority. Certain statutory and regulatory requirements exercise "authority" that government agencies do not legitimately possess – by restricting the food you may eat or the ways you may spend your money, for instance, in cases in which your doing these things in no way imperils the rights of others. (As examples, consider laws that restrict portion sizes, the rates charged for flood insurance, or money contributed to political campaigns.)

Still other legal policies are mutually inconsistent, issuing conflicting instructions that could not possibly all be satisfied. When a provision of one law directs a person to do one thing and a provision of another law (or of that same law) directs a person to do something else that makes his doing the first impossible (e.g., pricing his product neither so low as to be "predatory" nor so high as to constitute "gouging," both of which are forbidden and neither of which is objectively defined), confusion is the result for courts as well as for the average citizen seeking to comply. "The law" here is unintelligible. In these circumstances, there *is* no singular law that can be objectively understood and applied.[4]

B. Non-Objective Interpretations

Sometimes, it is laws themselves that are in tension, but often, it is non-objective interpretations of proper laws that create the friction. Consider the First Amendment's prohibition of the "establishment of religion" and protection of the "free exercise" of religion and the Fourteenth Amendment's assurance of "equal protection of the laws." Both, I believe, are objectively justified laws; they express proper legal principles. Yet particular notions of each have taken hold that pit them on a collision course, as was vividly illustrated in the controversy precipitated by the Obama administration's decree that, under the terms of the Affordable Care Act, religious institutions' health insurance plans

[2]   "Over-Regulated America," *The Economist*, February 18, 2012, p. 9, concerning the Dodd-Frank Wall Street Reform and Consumer Protection Act, signed into federal law by President Obama in July 2010. The so-called Volcker Rule is a single provision that is explained by means of answers to 348 questions, themselves divided into 1,420 sub-questions. As *The Economist* sums up the situation, "Financial firms in America must prepare to comply with a law that is partly unintelligible and partly unknowable."

[3]   "Fixing the Republic," *The Economist*, April 20, 2013, p. 72. Klingon is the language of an alien life form in "Star Trek," the popular science fiction series of television and film.

[4]   To change metaphors, the legally permissible strike zone between the two infractions is not identified.

were required to cover contraceptive services for their employees regardless of whether those services offended the institutions' religious beliefs.

The background needed to appreciate the problem is simple. The Equal Protection clause has widely been taken to justify the legal prohibition of employers' differential treatment of individuals on the bases of their race or sex or religion, among other factors. And the First Amendment has widely been taken to justify a religious exemption that excuses people who profess religious beliefs from legal obligations to act in ways that violate those beliefs. (In practice, of course, it is only those who profess *certain* religious views, since the government determines what type of belief qualifies for this exemption.)[5] Further, Congress in 1993 enacted the Religious Freedom Restoration Act, which prohibits the federal government from imposing a "substantial burden" on any religious practice in the absence of a "compelling state interest."

For our immediate purposes, set aside the question of such laws' more basic legitimacy. Simply suppose that both interpretations of what the First and Fourteenth Amendments demand were valid. The problem is that these interpretations are at loggerheads. The understanding of religious freedom as offering favored treatment (relieving a religious person of the usual obligation to obey laws) results in the predicament that at least one of these laws cannot be respected. On these conceptions of the two Amendments' meanings, it is either the case that, in order for the legal system to enforce anti-discrimination law, it must violate a religious employer's right to offer employee benefits that conform to his religious beliefs, or it is the case that, in order for the legal system to honor employers' religious freedom, anti-discrimination law is not respected, as the religious are permitted to violate equal protection requirements.

In fact, both interpretations are invalid. The interpretation of religious freedom as a religious *exemption* is profoundly mistaken. In a legal system dedicated to the proposition that each person has a right to lead his life however he likes as long as he respects the like rights of others, it makes perfect sense to recognize religious practices as among those protected activities. It

---

[5] The Supreme Court unanimously asserted the "ministerial exception" in *Hosanna-Tabor Evangelical Lutheran Church and School v. Equal Employment Opportunity Commission*, in January 2012, holding that federal antidiscrimination laws may not obstruct religious organizations' freedom to designate ministers. Retrieved from http://www.supremecourt .gov/opinions/11pdf/10–553.pdf. Coincidentally, this ruling was announced shortly before the White House announced its policy on enforcing the contraceptive coverage provision of the Affordable Care Act. In time (and most would agree, due to its hostile reception among a significant number of people), this proved to be only one of a series of evolving positions declaring how the administration would understand the provision.

makes no sense, however, to grant religious people special permission to violate law that the government deems vital to the protection of individual rights. That is, in a proper system, the premise behind every law must be that that law is a necessary means of fulfilling the government's function. No extraneous agendas may contaminate the system or deter it from that singular task. Correspondingly, we must work on the presumption that all laws are justified by their necessity to serve to that end.[6]

Against that background, the notion that a man's religion should excuse him from the obligations imposed by law (imposed on the ground that those particular laws and citizens' correlative obligations to obey them are necessary for the protection of individual rights) is tantamount to saying that religious people should be permitted to violate others' rights. In a legal system whose sole mission is the protection of individual rights, such a permission has no rational foundation. Those who interpret the religious liberty clause to bestow such special status misunderstand the framework of the Constitution and its conception of individual rights and government powers. Indeed, this reading of religious freedom itself defies *equal* protection of laws inasmuch as it grants extra legal rights and services to the religious – and correspondingly fewer legal protections to those whom the specially exempted might victimize.

Along a parallel track, we could critique any interpretation of the Fourteenth Amendment that views the legal prohibition of private discrimination as among its requirements. "Equal protection *of the laws*" does not, rationally, dictate equal treatment by private individuals.[7] The decision of whether to extend a job, a loan, a battery charge or a recommendation or of whether to engage in all manner of other relationships with another person is well within the range of an individual's rightful freedom to lead his life as he likes. For a person's declining to extend such goods would not infringe on the rights of those affected.

Obviously, some will dispute this and a deeper argument is needed to definitively validate my claim. (I offer this argument in *Moral Rights and Political*

---

[6]   This paragraph is discussing law and presumptions in a proper system, thus nothing I have said earlier about the unwarranted presumptions that prevail today and that need to be corrected should be misconstrued as in conflict with my claims here.

[7]   Section 1 of the Fourteenth Amendment reads:

   All persons born or naturalized in the United States, and subject to the jurisdiction thereof, are citizens of the United States and of the State wherein they reside. No State shall make or enforce any law which shall abridge the privileges or immunities of citizens of the United States; nor shall any State deprive any person of life, liberty, or property, without due process of law; nor deny to any person within its jurisdiction the equal protection of the laws.

Freedom, demonstrating why there can be no such thing as rights that could be respected only at the expense of other rights and, further, why the individual's right to freedom is fundamental.)[8] For present purposes, however, we can set that further debate aside. For even if one accepted this (misguided, in my view) interpretation of the Fourteenth Amendment and thought that laws banning discrimination in private relationships were legitimate, this would be incompatible with the First Amendment. It would create untenable friction that makes objective legal governance impossible. For it requires that a subjective decision be made to determine which of the conflicting Amendments is to be respected on a given occasion.

Properly understood, the First Amendment implies that a man should be free to act on the basis of his religious beliefs and to discriminate on those religious grounds, as long as he respects others' rights. (He is not free to discriminate in ways that violate others' rights to property, for instance, or that obstruct others' rights to travel or speech.) Yet even if the First Amendment were improperly understood in the way that the "exemption" notion mistakes it, such permission to break other laws would render the Fourteenth Amendment toothless. For in that case, the question of which Amendment to uphold (and which purported right: my right to break certain laws or your right not to be discriminated against) would *necessarily* be a sheer toss-up for the Court – random, unprincipled. In other words, even if we accepted the reading of the Fourteenth Amendment that I reject, that reading would be incompatible with *both* the proper interpretation and the improper interpretation of the First Amendment. (That is, if the Fourteenth Amendment forbids private individuals' discrimination on the basis of religious beliefs, it is logically in conflict with the First Amendment when that is read as protecting the exercise of religion up to the point of others' rights *and* with the First Amendment, when read as protecting the exercise of religion that infringes on others' rights. For when the First Amendment is used to protect the latter, its doing so renders the Fourteenth Amendment impotent.)

This is obviously an example of great significance and warrants more extended examination in its own right. That is not necessary for our purposes, however. Beyond the inner workings of these particular provisions, the larger point is that an invalid interpretation of a law (or of the legal system as a whole) places conflicting demands on the courts that can only be resolved by non-objective means.

[8]   Smith, *Moral Rights and Political Freedom*, see especially chapters 2, 6, 7, and 9; as well as "Rights Conflicts: The Undoing of Rights," *Journal of Social Philosophy* volume 26 no. 2, Fall 1995, pp. 141–158.

C. *Shirking and Its Consequences*

Yet another obstacle to objective law results from members of one branch of government punting their responsibilities onto others. (Indeed, this is frequently responsible for non-objective laws and non-objective interpretations.) Article VI of the Constitution stipulates that all government officials are bound to uphold the Constitution. The relevant portion reads: "The Senators and Representatives before mentioned, and the Members of the several State Legislatures, and all executive and judicial Officers, both of the United States and of the several States, shall be bound by Oath or Affirmation, to support this Constitution." This means that the judiciary is not the sole keeper of constitutionality. While the court does have final say in those cases when a law's meaning is disputed, officials in each branch are obligated to use their judgment of what the Constitution requires and permits and to perform their particular duties accordingly.

Unfortunately, today, it has become commonplace for the Congress and President to leave concern for the Constitution to the courts. Rather than risk hostile reactions to actions based on their own judgments of a law's constitutional fidelity, they frequently advance dubious laws with the glib assurance that "the courts will sort it out."[9] The Executive Office offends, for instance, when Presidents use Signing Statements to signal their belief in the unconstitutionality of a Congressionally approved bill in the very course of elevating that act into law (in effect, treating Signing Statements as a "get out of constitutional obligations-free" card). In 2002, for example, President George W. Bush signed the McCain-Feingold Bipartisan Campaign Reform Act despite his profession that "certain provisions present serious constitutional concerns" and his "reservations about the constitutionality of the broad ban on issue advertising." Nonetheless, he reassured himself in the Signing Statement, "I expect that the courts will resolve these legitimate legal questions."[10]

In contrast, recall a James Madison veto that I referred to in Chapter 7. In 1817, Madison vetoed an Internal Improvements Bill on exactly such constitutional grounds. As he explained,

> I am constrained by the insuperable difficulty I feel in reconciling the bill with the Constitution of the United States.... I am not unaware of the great importance of roads and canals and the improved navigation of water courses,

[9] Justice Scalia has complained that Congress increasingly passes "imprecise" and "fuzzy, leave-the-details-to-be-sorted-out-by-the-courts" legislation. *Sykes v. United States*, No. 09-11311 (2011), Scalia dissenting, quoted in "As Federal Crime List Grows, Threshold of Guilt Declines," *Wall Street Journal*, September 27, 2011.

[10] Signing statement retrieved from http://georgewbush-whitehouse.archives.gov/news/releases/2002/03/20020327.html.

and that a power in the National Legislature to provide for them might be exercised with signal advantage to the general prosperity. But seeing that such a power is not expressly given by the Constitution, and believing that it can not be deduced from any part of it without an inadmissible latitude of construction and a reliance on insufficient precedents ... I have no option but to withhold my signature from it.[11]

The court itself also fails in its constitutional responsibilities whenever it permits irrelevant considerations to infect its decision making. Exhibit A is its reliance on the tiered scrutiny bequeathed by *Carolene Products*, applying more and less stringent standards of review to different types of government activity. As the argument in Chapter 7 should have made clear, objectively, we have no basis for distinguishing "legitimate," "important," and "compelling" state interests or for subjecting distinct uses of government power to different tests of legitimacy. The state's sole "interest" is in fulfilling its authorized function: the protection of its citizens' rights. And the only type of scrutiny that the court should apply is logical scrutiny of whether the government authority asserted in a given case does or does not exist.

Exhibit B is the court's frequent practice of ducking difficult judgments of constitutionality in the name of the will of the people. As we have seen in earlier chapters, the will of the people is not the ultimate authority in our legal system. For courts to proceed as if it were is to inject extra-legal elements that distort their rulings and thereby allow the unauthorized use of government power. However well-intended such deference may sometimes be, well-meaning intentions do not legalize unconstitutional practices.[12]

---

[11] James Madison, Veto Message on the Internal Improvements Bill (March 3, 1817). Retrieved from http://millercenter.org/president/speeches/detail/3630.

  Also see discussion of this issue in Neomi Rao, "The Constitution: Not Just for Courts," *Wall Street Journal*, January 10, 2011. Rao cites a similar veto by President Andrew Jackson, who reasoned that "each public officer who takes an oath to support the Constitution swears that he will support it as he understands it, and not as it is understood by others."

[12] For a powerful statement rejecting several avenues of deviation from the judiciary's responsibility to the Constitution, see Justice Sutherland's dissent in *West Coast Hotel*, a 1937 minimum wage case. US 379 *West Coast Hotel Co. v. Parrish* (No. 293). Sutherland writes, for instance, that while some urge that the question of minimum wages should "receive fresh consideration ... because of 'the economic conditions which have supervened' ... the meaning of the Constitution does not change with the ebb and flow of economic events." In the same vein: "If the Constitution, intelligently and reasonably construed in the light of [its] principles, stands in the way of desirable legislation, the blame must rest upon that instrument, and not upon the court for enforcing it according to its terms." More generally, he observes, "The judicial function is that of interpretation; it does not include the power of amendment under the guise of interpretation. To miss the point of difference between the two is to miss all that the phrase 'supreme law of the land' stands for." Sutherland's dissent is worth reading in its entirety.

Over time, ill-founded legal practices nourish mistaken beliefs about proper law and such mistaken beliefs, in turn, encourage the adoption of ill-founded laws. A mutually reinforcing cycle serves, gradually, to tilt people's expectations and the prevailing standards of what valid law and proper judicial review themselves *are*. As the context shifts in this way, it becomes harder for government officials in any branch to resist. And it creates acute pressure on the courts, in particular. Longstanding misconceptions of legal authority have distorted people's ideas about what constitutes judicial overreach. Our tremendous volume of non-objective law coupled with the judiciary's frequent past acquiescence make any court that today were to employ objective standards and thus uproot familiar precedents appear to be usurping others' authority. Indeed, to correct uses of power that do not conform to the Constitution, the court must sometimes take actions that superficially resemble law*making* (in terms of the effects of their rulings). That only intensifies suspiciousness toward the court, which may subtly further pressure the court into appeasing popular sentiment.[13]

Suppose that a particular government action (a particular search or taking, for example) is challenged and that the court reaches a mistaken conclusion, allowing a government practice that is not, in fact, objectively warranted. Mistaken though its ruling may be, the fact that the court ruled in the way that it did fosters the belief that the government does possess that challenged authority. Each time that one branch of the legal system affirms an unjustified action by another (and particularly when the judiciary does so, given its special role in ensuring that the Constitution ultimately governs), it bolsters the *apparent* legitimacy of that policy, cementing its grip on public consciousness a little more firmly. This naturally increases the pressure against any government agent who would resist this by doing his work objectively, in the way that is truly warranted.

Isolated error, if quickly corrected, does little lasting damage. But several such mistakes, left to rule, nourish the assumption that that unjustified action is legitimate. Over time, this effects a gradual shift in people's expectations of government action and in accepted standards of objective law.

The point is, bad law breeds bad law. Because legal practices are adopted on the basis of beliefs, an invalid law sends the misleading signal that that law *is* legally valid. Thus, an invalid law provides the apparent justification for further deviations, in the future. And this also fosters bad methodology,

---

[13] It may also help to explain the appeal of Minimalism for jurists who, by pursuing the Minimalist tack, can maintain that they are deliberately trying not to overreach.

encouraging those who assess an action's constitutionality to attend to factors that are, by objective standards, inappropriate.

The upshot is, the greater the incidence of non-objective actions taken by other branches of government and the more entrenched people's beliefs that such actions are legitimate, the harder it will be for a court to perform its role as it should. For in such an environment, a court's objective exercise of its role will very visibly thwart the actions of the other branches. This looks suspicious to people: "Aren't the courts supposed to be comparative bystanders? On the sidelines, rarely in the limelight, as in a well-officiated ballgame?" When a court halts actions that other legal organs have taken, many conclude that it is exceeding its authority.

As should be plain from our earlier discussions, in fact, it does not imply that. The number of times that a court blocks what others in government would do bears no necessary correlation with the propriety of its course. What matters is not the number of court reversals, but their foundation (which makes studies that define judicial activism in quantitative terms misguided). Where other agents of the legal system have overstepped *their* authority by violating the Constitution, the court must intervene. Its guide is the Constitution, not the frequency of occasions on which it is called upon to correct other legal agents' misuses of it. Where a government action cannot be reconciled with the Constitution's strictures, the court's failure to act is what would truly be a breach of its responsibilities. For a court to grant counterfeit approvals to unconstitutional practices would not fulfill its job and would not serve objective law.[14]

The problem with unjustified actions by others in a legal system is not simply that it leads to a poor public image for the judiciary, however, making the court look bad by having to frequently intervene. When other legal agents exercise their powers in ways that are not objectively warranted, they make it more difficult *in fact* for the court to accomplish its work.

A legal system that includes non-objective law effectively issues conflicting instructions. It presents the judiciary with alternatives that are justified, by one standard, at the same time that they are unjustified, by another. The Rule of Law, for instance, demands that we be governed by written, public, knowable rules. Yet when one of those written rules is itself not valid (by the relevant objective standards), the same ideal of justice that demands respect for the Rule of Law's conditions seems to demand that we not require compliance with that written rule. (Imagine an immigration law that is unjust,

---

[14] Observe that the court *will* be a relatively quiet sideliner when the other facets of a legal system are operating as they should.

for instance.) When faced with such a situation, which imperative should a judge obey? Is he to apply the specific written law – essentially, because it is written? Or is he to honor the unwritten law that is part of the justification for the authority that any particular written law can command?

Prima facie, a plausible case can be made either way. While there may be a correct resolution in the end, the very complexity posed by the case is damaging. For it suggests that reason cannot arbitrate and that subjective decisions are inevitable in any legal system, requiring a court simply to *choose* which rules to apply, rather than to discover the meaning of that rule which is the valid, governing law. Such a belief not only corrodes the popular image of the court and of the legal system. It also encourages justices themselves to believe that they cannot help but resort to subjective factors. While the court *can* still discern the fundamental parameters set by the Constitution, the more credence that non-objective considerations acquire and the more such extraneous material that a court is given to weigh *as if* it warrants attention, the greater the likelihood that the court will sometimes err, basing its decisions on considerations other than the appropriate ones and thereby reaching invalid conclusions about the proper exercise of legal power.

In short, when laws are not objective – when they were not created for the right reasons or made by the right standards – they cannot be objectively applied. Not in the full-blooded, full-context manner that maintains valid legal authority. Narrowly, a court might "objectively" apply one or two limited aspects of a law (respecting its announced deadlines or required percentages, for instance), but to neglect the underlying authority of the law is not to be truly objective and is not to serve the function of government.

3. OBJECTIVE REVIEW UNDER CURRENT CONDITIONS

Does this tangle of transgressions that defy objective law alter the proper methods of conducting judicial review? Should a court proceed differently than would be appropriate under ideal conditions?

Basically: only minimally. For these distortions do not change the law. They have certainly changed people's expectations, corrupting people's beliefs about what *is* law, about how the legal system will treat different activities, and about how the legal system should treat different activities (by corrupting their underlying beliefs about the standards that validate legal action). In order to be fair to people and to proceed objectively from this point forward, the legal system should recognize its own role in encouraging expectations that will be disappointed by the resuscitation of objective standards. Nonetheless, its compass must be set by the fundamental function of the legal system and by the particular function of judicial review. In resolving the disputes that are brought before it, the court's abiding purpose is to uphold the law, ensuring that the Constitution, our bedrock legal authority, rules as our actual, final sovereign.

A. *Uniform Standard of Scrutiny*

To do this, a contemporary court must commit itself to sole reliance – thoroughly and consistently – on objective standards in reviewing all questions brought before it. The central means of doing so rests in discarding the invalid distinctions of three-tiered scrutiny and applying strict scrutiny across the board. There is no basis for granting more protection or less protection to any of the different ways in which an individual might choose to exercise his rights. As long as he is not infringing on the rights of others, the particular ways that a person chooses to exercise his right makes no legitimate difference to the way that the government should treat him. If a man speaks or prays, for instance, and is thus engaging in activities protected by the First Amendment, he should be granted no greater legal protection thanks to the "strict scrutiny" that a court typically applies to First Amendment activities than if he engages in commercial activities or culinary activities or coin collecting, which fall beyond the First Amendment's express protections. The judiciary has no basis for treating some laws as effectively second-class citizens, more easily override-able, on the premise that they do not serve interests that are as "important" or as "compelling" as others. As we have noted before, in a truly objective legal system, all laws serve the same, single vital interest: the protection of individual rights.

Correspondingly, all of a government's actions and policies warrant equally exacting judicial inspection. Under a government whose ultimate authority resides in a constitution, the constant, ongoing question for a court to pose is: Does this comply with the Constitution? On a fully objective understanding of what that means and encompasses? Yes, or no?

How should courts do this? In essence, by abandoning the rational basis test as it is customarily employed and replacing its presumption of constitutionality with the presumption of liberty. Because ours is a government of limited powers authorized to serve a specific, circumscribed purpose, the fundamental presumption should be that individuals are entitled to act free of all government interference other than that which is directly required to enable the government to fulfill its mission. The basis for this presumption is not simply ideological; it is not simply the fact that it reflects the correct principle of political philosophy (although I believe it does). What is more salient here, this orientation is *legally* grounded: It is the only positioning of presumptions that is consistent with the design, structure, and content of the U.S. Constitution. It is the only inference concerning the respective powers and authority of the government and the governed that is compatible with a legal system that expressly enumerates its limited powers and that includes such provisions as the Ninth Amendment, the Tenth Amendment, and the Necessary and Proper Clause (to cite only the most obvious relevant features).[15] For this reason (along with reasons we have gone into more fully when discussing authority in earlier chapters), logically, any time that the government seeks to do something that is not a patent exercise of its legal authority, it bears the burden of demonstrating its legal justification for doing so.[16]

The core thought, again, is that objective judicial review requires courts to restore proper presumptions. To effect this change, the judiciary must adopt and enunciate objective standards. It must put the other branches on notice by making plain its rejection of business as usual and calling attention to its commitment to adhere diligently to proper standards as its conscious, deliberate policy. Both its words and actions must be consistently of a piece, steadily sending this message through the cases it chooses to hear, its reasoning, and its rulings. Courts must rigorously hold other government officials accountable by demanding clear demonstration of the Constitutional authority for their actions and by not yielding on the basis of factors that are, at root, irrelevant (by considerations such as "balance," "modesty," "popular will," etc.). A court must not retreat from its own responsibility, in other words, to rule exclusively by the objective rendering of the Constitution.

In essence, all scrutiny of every question, regardless of the kind of government power or individual action at issue, must meticulously employ rational, objective, fully context-sensitive standards.

B. Context-Sensitive Implementation

My proposals for proper judicial review in current circumstances may provoke a natural objection. Suppose that certain legal practices are invalid, by truly objective standards. If they are long-standing, widely accepted, and deeply entrenched, however, their uprooting would carry dramatic repercussions on ordinary life (scrambling the effects of people's previous decisions

---

[15] As Madison, widely considered the Father of the Constitution, observed in *Federalist* 45, "The powers delegated to the federal government by the proposed constitution are few and defined." *The Federalist*, ed. Jacob E. Cooke, Middletown, CT: Wesleyan University Press, 1961, p. 313.

[16] Randy Barnett offers a vigorous defense of the needed reversal of presumptions in *Restoring the Lost Constitution*.

about employment or finances or living arrangements, for instance). Since misguided presumptions have been used for decades and because the legal system now includes practices that have been infected by them, the adoption of my counsel for proper review threatens to dislodge some very basic, taken-for-granted institutions that frame many of people's activities. It is natural to wonder how Social Security or labor laws or the banking system, for instance, would be reshaped under objective scrutiny. Indeed, in the course of a court's correcting these missteps, it may appear that certain Rule of Law conditions would have to be abridged, such as those requiring laws' stability or equal application or the prohibition on retroactive laws. Bear in mind that a legal system relies on presumptions largely in order to facilitate these very values. A significant shift in presumptions, correspondingly, can seem to threaten the Rule of Law.

The kind of worry here is hardly unreasonable. It does not defeat my counsel, however. Several observations should make this plain.

Valuable as the formal requirements of the Rule of Law are, remember that they are not ends in themselves. They are not freestanding goods that vie with rights for our ultimate allegiance. Rather, the Rule of Law is valuable for a practical reason, namely, to help to protect individual rights. The ideal's conditions are necessary means of restricting legal power to only those uses that are required for the legal system to fulfill that function. When uses of legal power stray from that function, they need to be corrected – out of devotion to the same principles that animate the Rule of Law itself.

Presumptions are valuable insofar as they facilitate a legal system's ability to accomplish its work. Properly employed, presumptions are not a substitute for substantive principles, but are shaped by the system's paramount principles. If presumptions are not disciplined by the overarching mission of the legal system, however, they will sabotage objective law. For this reason, courts must insist on the rational use of presumptions to keep them from corrupting the legal system's operation.

Given all this, several entrenched legal practices *would* have to be dismantled, on my view, although the explanation of exactly which is not necessary for present purposes. Here, to appreciate the need for the courts' dramatically shifting presumptions, a few points are most salient. And we should begin by acknowledging why the worry expressed in this objection is powerful. To abruptly overturn people's reasonable, longstanding, and *government-encouraged* expectations about very basic contours of legal policy that carry profound repercussions for their activities would resemble the wrong in the legal practices now being corrected. If the government suddenly seized a person's Social Security checks, for instance, without warning and against decades of legal practice, that would seem unjust in much the same way that the previous, objectively misguided rulings may have been unjust. Such radical and total reversal at a stroke is not the only possible course of effecting change, however.

As ever, context is critical. A contextual application of objectivity here would counsel a gradual transition back to a fully objective application of the relevant law. Bear in mind the difference between finding the law (determining what the Constitution truly permits and forbids) and the restoration of its objective application. Identifying what the law is does not, by itself, dictate how to "get there from here" when a large gap has grown between objective law and law's currently dominant modes of application. Because objectivity is context-sensitive, it demands careful consideration of the principled means of implementing a ruling in the immediate circumstances. Significant overhaul should be implemented with fair warning and, in some cases, by gradually phasing in the most far-reaching changes. (How gradual is appropriate will depend on a number of factors, but the calculation must be governed by the legal system's overarching mandate.) Eager as an objective court might be to correct unwarranted legal practices, given the deviant precedents and associated expectations that have taken root, it would be unjust to do so by shock treatment, abruptly eradicating policies that people have organized their affairs around and have reasonably come to rely upon. In order to be sensitive both to Rule of Law requirements and to the more fundamental values which those are designed to serve, the court should issue objective findings of law and oversee an orderly and just restoration of rule by objective standards. The best exact means of doing this is a question for specialized examination. What is crucial, however, is that we firmly distinguish the identification of what the law is – what the Constitution permits and requires – from the subsequent action that legal bodies should take in light of that identification. We must not allow legitimate concern for the latter to distort our reasoning about what *is* Constitutional.

And all of this points to the more basic fact: The entrenchment of non-objective law does not justify that law. However familiar and whatever sort of comfort people derive from the continuation of practices that are not compatible with the Constitution, these do not become compatible through sheer repetition. Frequent incidence of the breach of a rule does not alter its being a breach.

Given the cumulative sediment of mistakes in our legal system, resistance to my proposals can be understandable. The system's individual infidelities over the decades, often reinforced by their express affirmation or permitted expansion, have skewed people's thinking about proper law. The problem is not simply that people "expect their checks." Rather, our very concepts and categories for appraising government actions (what constitutes judicial activism or properly democratic processes, for instance, or the types of equality that citizens are legally entitled to) have been distorted by the conflicting messages sent by a constitution that says one thing and legal policies that imply something else.

There is no pain-free path back to objective law from non-objective practices. The difficulty of restoring objectivity in judicial review is not reason not to do it, however. For inaction would only perpetuate the illegitimate practices. Remember that what is at stake is the government's use of its unique coercive power. To allow ourselves to be ruled by comparative accidents of our history – in particular, by accidents that misused the government's power to forcibly impose its will – would be to surrender the Rule of Law to the rule of those men who misuse that legal power.[17]

The Rule of Law is not superior to the Rule of Men *just when it's convenient*, as long as the Rule of Law would not demand too much disruption. If we are to enjoy the rule of rights that the Rule of Law uniquely makes possible and, correspondingly, if we are to have a legal system of genuine moral authority, this type of disruption is, albeit painful, imperative. Mistakes are inevitable in the course of any legal system's governance. The problem is not the sheer occurrence of a misstep (damaging though that can be). The problem lies, rather, in recognizing something as a mistake in this sphere – in the use of the government's coercive power – and nonetheless allowing it. To do that would be to brazenly defy the government's mission and authority. It would be morally criminal.

To frame my point in more colloquial terms: Sometimes, big change needs to happen ("needs to" according to the fundamental principles of the legal system's authority). It is precisely because we make mistakes that we need radically to reverse our course, at times. When the impact is significant, doing so will be especially controversial. The fact that *Loving v. Virginia* did not win universal acclaim in 1967 does not mean that it should not have been decided as it was.[18] Many people cheered and many people jeered at the Court's rulings in *Brown, Griswold, Roe, Lawrence, Citizens United,* and *Windsor.*[19] Divisive

---

[17] The nature of their motivations is beside the point.

[18] *Loving v. Virginia,* 388 US 1 (1967), rejecting laws banning interracial marriage.

[19] *Brown v. Board of Education,* 347 US 483 (1954) declared state laws establishing separate public schools for black and white students unconstitutional; *Griswold v. Connecticut,* 381 US 479 (1965) invalidated certain restrictions on the use of contraception; *Roe v. Wade,* 410 US 113 (1973) recognized a woman's limited right to abortion; *Lawrence v. Texas,* 539 US 558 (2003) invalidated antisodomy laws; *Citizens United v. Federal Elections Committee,* 558 US (2010)

and disruptive as such rulings may be, they are sometimes necessary in order to be faithful to the law. If we are not willing to make such corrections, we must surrender our pretensions of being a system of objective law.[20]

It should be clear from all I have argued in earlier chapters that I am not recommending that the judiciary adopt a substantive agenda reflecting its beliefs about what constitutes good law and then exploit cases as mere tools to realize that vision. In our system, courts are obligated to treat each case on its individual merits, objectively applying the existing law to that dispute. At the same time, however, when a court rules in a case on the proper, principled grounds, it is inescapably speaking to other potential cases. Decisions based on principles are "amplified" by their nature; they apply to multiple cases precisely because they are based on deeper and more enduring characteristics that transcend the peculiarities of the given dispute (at least, they potentially apply to multiple cases; the number will depend on the number of other cases that are similar in essential kind). The point is, conclusions of principle are always expressed through a figurative megaphone that projects its reasoning out to a wider range of like cases.

Again, the restoration of objective standards in applying the law can be accomplished through a gradual, orderly period of transition. Just as any significant rules changes made by a legal system should be implemented with consideration of the rights of those affected, so should the court adjust its schedule for required compliance with its findings in large-impact cases. This is particularly appropriate, given the legal system's responsibility for having created people's misguided expectations. Courts themselves have often sanctioned practices that will now cause people to be harmed by the changes of its interpretive practices.[21] Part of the responsibility of a legal system is the communication of its rules (as reflected in the Rule of Law's requirements of promulgation and clarity). These conditions were not satisfied by invalid interpretations of the law in the past and would not be satisfied today, if drastic change were imposed without warning. The basic point is: To honor individuals' lives as *theirs* and because the mistake was ours (the government's), the sudden imposition of radical changes in the application of law would not be objectively justified.

---

struck down certain restrictions on independent political expenditures; *US v. Windsor*, 570 US (2013), struck down critical portions of the federal Defense of Marriage Act.

[20] My point is not to take a stand on any of these rulings or their reasoning, but simply to highlight that divisiveness per se is not a valid indicator of the identity of the law.

[21] "Harmed," that is, in the short run. In the larger scheme, a person benefits from living under a government of objective law. Yet once certain non-objective legal practices have been implanted, the path of correcting these carries undeniable pains.

In order for a court to proceed responsibly through this morass, then, it must commit itself to the policy of explaining itself as forthrightly and as completely as it is able. It must be clear about the exact bases for its rulings, about whether it is taking into account a particularly unusual context (beyond the sort of peculiarities that naturally attend any case), and in precisely what way. It must be transparent about what exactly it is saying and the reasoning that justifies it, indicating how narrow and case-specific or fundamental and widely applicable the governing principles. Obviously, courts already do this to some extent, but in order to perform their work objectively in conditions that have tilted far from objective standards, courts should more fully utilize their opinions to clarify the law and the standards appropriate for understanding the law. They should explain the legal justification of their rulings more extensively – more deeply, more carefully, more patiently, more thoroughly – and directly address those factors that may make their rulings seem unjustified, due to the distortions of law's non-objective applications in the past. All of this is necessary both to demonstrate the validity of their rulings and to be clear in the guidance that they provide for future applications of the law.

While the precise series of steps by which to untangle our legal system's knotted cables of illegitimacy warrants close examination in its own right, for our purposes, it suffices to reiterate the principle to keep paramount. However "settled" the unjustified practices may have become, these do not change the law itself. The authority of the legal system does not expand or contract in tandem with misuses of its power. A constitution is what it is; that is what courts are charged to uphold. All the rest is distraction. Objective judicial review demands single-minded devotion to the law of the land. Consequently, a contemporary court must restore the Constitution to the position of governing.

C. *Courage of Constitutional Conviction*

The pressures exerted by the powerful forces that distort so many of today's legal practices make it especially imperative for justices to exert one of the personal characteristics that I discussed in Chapter 7: courage. A justice must be resolute in his commitment to objectivity. He must painstakingly do his searching best to be objective in regard to all aspects of the legal questions that he faces and he must be undeterred by the criticism that is bound to attend the responsible performance of his work. (So warped has our system become that doing a good job, by truly objective standards, is likely to provoke wider criticism today than doing a poor job.)

It is important to remind ourselves that, popular rhetoric notwithstanding, consensus is not the highest ideal for an objective legal system to aspire to.

Differences of opinion among the branches are natural; our legal system is designed to resolve such differences in a way that upholds objective law. This requires that each branch robustly execute its distinct role, however, and that it fulfill its oath of constitutional fidelity. The checks and balances famously built into our system enable one branch to prevent or correct errors of the others. What such a system relies on, however, is each component's unblushing fulfillment of its role. Each must objectively judge the Constitution's parameters and conduct its work accordingly, delivering on its distinct assignment. Concern with interbranch harmony only diverts it from this work.[22] The different branches' views of the Constitution will sometimes diverge. While an atmosphere of consensus is naturally more agreeable than one of contention and while a certain type of harmony is required for a government to fulfill its charge (namely, all must accept the hierarchy of authority for resolving such disputes), consensus is not the goal of government and disagreement is not the devil. We do not license the coercive power of a government in the first place for the greater glory of "No gridlock! Agreement!" Our system functions as it was designed to and in a way that genuinely protects individual rights only when the members of each branch do their assigned work objectively. To reap the benefits of a well-designed system, each legal agent must accept his particular responsibilities and conscientiously, sometimes courageously, acquit them.

As part of this, naturally, a judge must candidly examine his own role in the decay of objective standards. Courts do sometimes make mistakes, after all, and this is often because their individual members stray from objective reasoning.[23] Thus, objectivity demands that a judge scrupulously monitor his reasoning to ensure that he is deflecting all extraneous considerations and that he is reasoning about all that *is* relevant in strictly logical ways. He must exert the courage to assert his judgment concerning the objective reading and application of the law, regardless of the scorn that it may unleash.

4. LIMITATIONS AND PROSPECTS

Some might find my account unsatisfactory because its counsel to courts is not particularly technical or tuned uniquely to today's legal conditions. I am not proposing additional policies or emergency measures for judicial review,

---

[22] The same applies to intrabranch harmony. Neily adopts a similar position in *Terms of Engagement*, pp. 29–30.

[23] Other times, it is a result of honest errors. Recall from Chapter 1 that objectivity of method does not ensure accuracy of conclusions.

so much as urging courts' recommitment to those standards that should also reign in more desirable circumstances. In the end, one might complain, my prescription for objective judicial review in today's less-than-ideal conditions is not so different from my prescription for more ideal conditions: In the best of times, I tell courts to be objective and in the worst of times, I tell courts to be objective. Shouldn't an account of these different circumstances offer something beyond more of the same?

Such a complaint seems not adequately to appreciate that judicial review is, in its essence, an intellectual enterprise. The court's day-to-day work consists of reasoning. Examining briefs, posing questions, drafting opinions, reading others' drafts, revising drafts, and discussing cases are so many means of reasoning in order to determine the objective meaning and application of law. Bear in mind also that on my analysis, the core problem plaguing our legal system is conceptual – specifically, the decay in people's understanding of what objectivity is and of what it demands, in law. If this diagnosis is correct, however, it follows that no "technical" patch or nonintellectual devices could heal our afflictions. We can only demand that courts reason about the proper application of laws by more scrupulously objective methods. While the most suitable *remedies* for legal transgressions might vary significantly under differing conditions, the essence of what is required to find the law does not. The standard for that enterprise is constant.[24]

A different strain of skepticism about the merit of my theory might caution that the prospects of judicial restoration of objective law are inhibited by structural constraints. The court is a reactive body which can act only when petitioned by others; it may not initiate the reform of defects lurking within the legal system. Courts work on a case-by-case basis, as we noted earlier, obligated to assess each dispute on its distinct merits, applying the law to that dispute rather than using its power to advance a larger agenda.

This is certainly true. Nonetheless, the judiciary can exert major influence on the objectivity of a legal system. The more scrupulously the court does its work when it does rule, the fewer occasions for challenge will arise. The more strictly, the more clearly, and the more consistently the court enunciates the truly objective boundaries of Constitutional authority, the less encouragement other agents of government will have to exceed those boundaries. We can hardly hope to eliminate questions which will reasonably arise about

---

[24] Neily's proposal that judicial nominees be asked to explain their understandings of the meanings of a number of constitutional provisions as well as of certain Supreme Court decisions reflects a kindred appreciation that the standards of proper review cannot be reduced to more mechanical formulas. See his suggestions in *Terms of Engagement*, pp. 150–153.

the faithful application of law to unusual or unusually complicated cases, but the court's conscientious fulfillment of its law-policing function can patrol the borders between the legal and the illegal in ways that make the sovereignty of the Constitution more secure. By deciding which cases to hear, by how it rules, by how it reasons in reaching its rulings and by explaining its justifications in published opinions, the court can sharpen everyone's understanding of the parameters of Constitutionality and thereby influence the kinds of laws that will be enacted in the future and the kinds of policies that law's administrators adopt.

Obviously, a justice who sought to practice my model of objective review could not reform the law single-handedly, let alone quickly. Many people and many forces create and sustain the unjustified practices that penetrate our system. Moreover, a court is not a homogeneous body. The objective jurist will not always succeed in convincing enough of his brethren to prevail in a given case.

Nonetheless, dissents register. Every ruling, every opinion, every question, and every argument that a justice offers can inch the system in a better or worse direction, toward greater or lesser objectivity, overall. Even when a valid argument loses in a given case, dissenting opinions are read, oral arguments are studied, and the reasoning that fails to command a majority today may gain traction in the treatment of later cases. The reigning legal understanding of free speech protections, to cite one prominent example, is largely a product of "the ebb and flow of precedent," including convictions that were initially voiced in judicial dissents and that gradually came to command majority support.[25]

Objective law can only be restored brick by brick; minority arguments are sometimes the bricks that lay the foundation for rebuilding. (Justice Scalia has characterized his dissents as "advocating for the future."[26]) Whatever the

---

[25] David Strauss, *The Living Constitution*, New York: Oxford University Press, 2010, p. 67. Strauss also observes that "central features of First Amendment law were hammered out in fits and starts, in a series of judicial decisions and extra-judicial developments, over the course of the twentieth century," p. 53. The clear and present danger test is perhaps the most now-entrenched example. Strauss's fuller discussion is in Chapter 3, especially pp. 63–76, and for a still wider discussion of the history of free speech law in the United States, see David M. Rabban, *Free Speech in its Forgotten Years*, Cambridge: Cambridge University Press, 1997.

    Bear in mind that it is not only judges and lawyers who read judicial opinions. Lawmakers, executives, regulators, law enforcement officials, and students, among others, can also be influenced by minority reasoning. Sheer example is also powerful. The display of some jurists' courage in refusing to go along with the expected but non-objective course can quietly embolden others to do the same.

[26] Quoted in Jeffrey Rosen, "Strong Opinions," *The New Republic*, August 18, 2011, pp. 11–12. Also see Scalia's more recent statement of this sentiment in a 2013 interview, reported in Jennifer Senior, "In Conversation: Antonin Scalia," *New York*, October 14, 2013, pp. 23–27, 80–81.

condition of the legal system around him, a judge must reason objectively about the case before his court and explain his reasoning's principles as clearly as possible. Just as the maintenance of a legal system's objectivity requires ongoing vigilance, so the restoration of complete objectivity requires patient persistence.

Again, the corrosive influences entrenched by a long trail of unjustified practices precludes any panacea; no quick or painless cure is available. It is only by recognizing the swift currents against which an objective jurist must swim, however, that we can appreciate the particular elements of objective review that are most urgently needed: the rejection of tiered scrutiny, the consistent deployment of objectively strict scrutiny, and the resolve of unshakeable integrity in courage to abide by the law.

5. CONCLUSION

In concluding, it is useful, as ever, to ground our thoughts in the fuller context. Regardless of whether a court is acting under optimal or suboptimal conditions, remember the stakes. Objectivity is not an end in itself. For a court to fail to apply the law objectively – however difficult its doing so may be, in certain circumstances – is to release government power from the bounds of its legitimacy. When the court rules without objective justification, it permits the government to do things that it has no authority to do. The casualty is individual rights. For just as a system of objective law works to protect individual rights, so unjustified uses of a legal system's coercive power destroy them. They seize from a person the freedom of action that properly belongs to *him*.

Conclusion

People are right to argue about judicial review. For the method by which courts ascertain the meaning of law determines how a legal system's coercive power is actually exercised and, correspondingly, whether individuals enjoy their rights.

The propriety of a method of judicial review, however, cannot be assessed in isolation from the larger enterprise of which it is a part. Just as words cannot be properly understood apart from the context in which they are spoken, laws cannot be understood apart from the overarching mission of the legal system that they are to serve. What is the function of a proper legal system? Why does it enjoy the unique power that it does? What is it designed – and what is it authorized – to do? Answers to these must inform the rational interpretation of any of a legal system's individual components and particular laws. For no law can mean something more than its underlying authority permits.

The specific role of judicial review, within a proper legal system, is to ensure that it is the law that actually governs. When disputes arise concerning the legitimate application of a particular law, courts are needed to discern precisely what the law means so that we can, indeed, abide by it.

What is essential, in order for a court to do this, is objectivity: the scrupulous, unwavering effort to understand the object in question (in this realm, the law) as thoroughly and as exactly as the light of logic, in the full context, permits. This demands that the court's lodestar be *exclusively* the law – not what the law should be, according to various possible measures; not what the law has sometimes been thought to be, whether by people who originally supported its adoption or by people polled last week; not what previous courts may have mistaken the law to be. Since none of these is the law, none of the schools that champion such considerations in judicial methodology can maintain the Rule of Law.

Objective review cannot guarantee correct conclusions. To understand a law is an intellectual process and, as such, inescapably fallible; no instruction for this process, however sound, can eliminate the possibility of error. While objective review is not sufficient to reach law-faithful answers, however, it is their prerequisite. The essence of objective review, again, rests in judges' riveting their reasoning strictly by the law and by logic. If a legal system is to govern by objective law, to serve its function thereby and, correspondingly, to protect individual rights, this is indispensable. The proper exercise of judicial review demands that courts do no more than this and no less.

Select Bibliography

Ackerman, Bruce. "Liberating Abstraction." In *The Bill of Rights and the Modern State*, edited by Geoffrey R. Stone, Richard A. Epstein, and Cass R. Sunstein, 317–48. Chicago: University of Chicago Press, 1992.

"Storrs Lectures: Discovering the Constitution." *Faculty Scholarship Series*, no. 149 (1984). Accessed June 3, 2014. Retrieved from http://digitalcommons.law.yale.edu/fss_papers/149.

We the People: Foundations (volume 1, 1991). Cambridge, MA: Harvard University Press.

We the People: Transformations (volume 2, 1998). Cambridge, MA: Harvard University Press.

Ahmar, Akhil Reed. *America's Unwritten Constitution: The Precedents and Principles We Live By*. New York: Basic Books, 2012.

Alexander, Larry. "Originalism, The Why and the What." *Fordham Law Review* 82 (Fall 2013): 539–44.

Alexander, Larry, and Emily Sherwin. *Demystifying Legal Reasoning*. Cambridge: Cambridge University Press, 2008.

Balkin, Jack M. *Living Originalism*. Cambridge, MA: Belknap Press, 2011.

Barber, Sotirios A., and James E. Fleming. *Constitutional Interpretation: The Basic Questions*. New York: Oxford University Press, 2007.

Barnett, Randy E. *Restoring the Lost Constitution: The Presumption of Liberty*. Princeton: Princeton University Press, 2004.

Bellos, David. *Is That a Fish in Your Ear? Translation and the Meaning of Everything*. New York: Faber & Faber, 2011.

Bennett, Robert W., and Lawrence B. Solum. *Constitutional Originalism: A Debate*. New York: Cornell University Press, 2011.

Berman, Mitchell N. "Originalism Is Bunk." *NYU Law Review* 84 (2009): 1–96.

Bickel, Alexander M. *The Least Dangerous Branch*. New York: Bobbs-Merrill, 1962.

Bix, Brian H. "Legal Positivism." In *Blackwell Guide to the Philosophy of Law and Legal Theory*, edited by Martin P. Golding and William A. Edmundson, 29–49. Malden, MA: Blackwell, 2005.

Bobbitt, Philip. *Constitutional Fate*. New York: Oxford University Press, 1982.

Bogongiari, D. ed. *The Political Ideas of St. Thomas Aquinas*. New York: Haffner, 1969.

Bolick, Clint. *David's Hammer: The Case for an Activist Judiciary*. Washington, DC: Cato Institute, 2007.

Brest, Paul. "Interpretation and Interest." *Stanford Law Review* 34 (April 1982): 765–73.

Breyer, Stephen. *Active Liberty*. New York: Vintage Books, 2005.

Making Our Democracy Work: A Judge's View. New York: Knopf, 2010.

Brink, David O. "Legal Interpretation, Objectivity, and Morality." In *Objectivity in Law and Morals*, edited by Brian Leiter, 12–65. New York: Cambridge University Press, 2001.

"Legal Theory, Legal Interpretation, and Judicial Review." *Philosophy and Public Affairs* 17, no. 2 (Spring 1988): 105–48.

Buckley, F.H., ed. *The American Illness: Essays on the Rule of Law*. New Haven, CT: Yale University Press, 2013.

Calabresi, Steven, ed. *Originalism: A Quarter Century of Debate*. Washington, DC: Regnery, 2007.

Cardozo, Benjamin. *The Nature of the Judicial Process*. New Haven, CT: Yale University Press, 1921.

Chemerinsky, Erwin. "In Defense of Judicial Review: The Perils of Popular Constitutionalism." *University of Illinois Law Review* (2004): 673–90.

Dicey, Albert Venn. *An Introduction to the Study of the Law of the Constitution*. Indianapolis: Liberty Fund, 1982.

Dworkin, Ronald. "Comment." In *A Matter of Interpretation*, edited by Amy Gutmann, pp. 115–27. Princeton: Princeton University Press, 1997.

Freedom's Law: The Moral Reading of the American Constitution. Cambridge, MA: Harvard University Press, 1996.

Justice for Hedgehogs. Cambridge, MA: Belknap Press, 2011.

Justice in Robes. Cambridge, MA: Harvard University Press, 2006.

Law's Empire. Cambridge, MA: Harvard University Press, 1986.

A Matter of Principle. Cambridge, MA: Harvard University Press, 1985.

"'Natural' Law Revisited." *University of Florida Law Review* 34 (1982): 165–88.

Taking Rights Seriously. Cambridge, MA: Harvard University Press, 1978.

"Unenumerated Rights: Whether and How *Roe* Should be Overturned." In *The Bill of Rights and the Modern State*, edited by Geoffrey R. Stone, Richard A. Epstein, and Cass R. Sunstein, 381–432. Chicago: University of Chicago Press, 1992.

Easterbrook, Frank H. "Abstraction and Authority." In *The Bill of Rights and the Modern State*, edited by Geoffrey R. Stone, Richard A. Epstein, and Cass R. Sunstein, 349–80. Chicago: University of Chicago, 1992.

Edlin, Douglas E. *Judges and Unjust Laws: Common Law Constitutionalism and the Foundations of Judicial Review*. Ann Arbor: University of Michigan Press, 2008.

Eisenberg, Melvin Aron. *The Nature of the Common Law*. Cambridge, MA: Harvard University Press, 1988.

Eisgruber, Christopher J. *Constitutional Self Government*. Cambridge, MA: Harvard University Press, 2001.

"Should Constitutional Judges be Philosophers?" In *Exploring Law's Empire*, edited by Scott Hershovitz, 5–22. Oxford: Oxford University Press, 2006.

Ely, John Hart. *Democracy and Distrust: A Theory of Judicial Review*. Cambridge, MA: Harvard University Press, 1980.

Epstein, Richard A. *The Classical Liberal Constitution: The Uncertain Quest for Limited Government.* Cambridge, MA: Harvard University Press, 2013.

———. *Design for Liberty: Private Property, Public Administration, and the Rule of Law.* Cambridge, MA: Harvard University Press, 2011.

———. *How Progressives Rewrote the Constitution.* Washington, DC: Cato Institute, 2006.

Fallon, Richard. " 'The Rule of Law' as a Concept in Constitutional Discourse." *Columbia Law Review* 97 (January 1997): 1–56.

Finnis, John. *Natural Law and Natural Rights.* Oxford: Clarendon Press, 1980.

Fish, Stanley. "Fish v Fiss." In *Interpreting Law and Literature: A Hermeneutic Reader,* edited by Sanford Levinson and Steven Mailloux, 251–68. Evanston, IL: Northwestern University Press, 1988.

———. "Intention Is All There Is: A Critical Analysis of Aharon Barak's 'Purposive Interpretation in Law.' " *Cardozo Law Review* 29 (2008): 1109–46.

Fiss, Owen M. "Objectivity and Interpretation." In *Interpreting Law and Literature: A Hermeneutic Reader,* edited by Sanford Levinson and Steven Mailloux, 229–50. Evanston, IL: Northwestern University Press, 1988.

Fleming, James E. "The Balkinazation of Originalism." *University of Illinois Law Review* 3 (2012): 669–82.

———. "Fidelity, Change, and the Good Constitution." *American Journal of Comparative Law* 62 (Summer 2014): 515–45.

———. "The Place of History and Philosophy in the Moral Reading of the American Constitution." In *Exploring Law's Empire,* edited by Scott Hershovitz, 23–39. Oxford: Oxford University Press, 2006.

Fordham Law Review 82, no. 2, Fall 2013. Symposium: "The New Originalism in Constitutional Law."

Friedman, Barry. *The Will of the People: How Public Opinion Has Influenced the Supreme Court and Shaped the Meaning of the Constitution.* New York: Farrar, Straus and Giroux, 2009.

Fuller, Lon. *The Morality of Law.* New Haven: Yale University Press, 1964.

Gardner, John. "Can There Be a Written Constitution?" In *Law As a Leap of Faith,* edited by John Gardner, 89–124. Oxford: Oxford University Press, 2012.

Gerber, Scott D. *To Secure These Rights: The Declaration of Independence and Constitutional Interpretation.* New York: New York University Press, 1995.

Ghate, Onkar. "Comments on Michael Moore's 'Semantics, Metaphysics, and Objectivity in the Law.' " Paper presented at Conference on Objectivity in the Law, University of Texas at Austin, April 2008.

———. "Natural Kinds and Rand's Theory of Concepts: Reflections on Griffiths." In *Concepts and Their Role in Knowledge: Reflections on Objectivist Epistemology,* edited by Allan Gotthelf and James G. Lennox, 148–59. Pittsburgh: University of Pittsburgh Press, 2013.

Gotthelf, Allan. "Ayn Rand's Theory of Concepts: Rethinking Abstraction and Essence." In *Concepts and Their Role in Knowledge: Reflections on Objectivist Epistemology,* edited by Allan Gotthelf and James G. Lennox, 3–40. Pittsburgh: University of Pittsburgh Press, 2013.

Green, Christopher R. "Originalism and the Sense-Reference Distinction." *St. Louis University Law Journal* 50 (2006): 555–627.

Hamilton, Alexander, James Madison, and John Jay. *The Federalist: The Gideon Edition*, edited by George W. Carey and James McClellan. Indianapolis: Liberty Fund, 2001.

Hannan, Daniel. *Inventing Freedom: How the English-Speaking Peoples Made the Modern World*. New York: Harper Collins, 2013.

Harriman, David. *The Logical Leap: Induction in Physics*. New York: Penguin, 2010.

Hart, H.L.A. "American Jurisprudence through English Eyes: The Nightmare and the Noble Dream." In *Essays in Jurisprudence*, 123–44. Oxford: Oxford University Press, 1984.

The Concept of Law. 2nd edition. Oxford: Clarendon Press, 1994.

Hershovitz, Scott, ed. *Exploring Law's Empire: The Jurisprudence of Ronald Dworkin*. Oxford: Oxford University Press, 2006.

Hogue, Arthur R. *Origins of the Common Law*. Indianapolis: Liberty Fund, 1966.

Kelly, J.M. *A Short History of Western Legal Theory*. Oxford: Clarendon Press, 1992.

Kozinski, Alex, and Misha Tseytlin. "You're (Probably) a Federal Criminal." In *In the Name of Justice*, edited by Timothy Lynch, 43–56. Washington, DC: Cato Institute, 2009.

Kramer, Larry D. *The People Themselves: Popular Constitutionalism and Judicial Review*. New York: Oxford University Press, 2004.

Kramer, Matthew H. *Objectivity and the Rule of Law*. New York: Cambridge University Press, 2007.

"On the Moral Status of the Rule of Law." *Cambridge Law Journal* 63 (March 2004): 65–97.

Lawson, Gary. "Dead Document Walking." *Boston University Law Review* 92, no. 4 (July 2012): 1225–36.

"Originalism Without Obligation." *Boston University Law Review* 93 (July 2013): 1309–18.

Leiter, Brian. "The End of Empire: Dworkin and Jurisprudence in the 21st Century." *Rutgers Law Journal* 36 (2004–2005): 165–76.

"Introduction," *Objectivity in Law and Morals*, 1–11. Cambridge: Cambridge University Press, 2001.

"Objectivity, Morality and Adjudication." In *Objectivity in Law and Morals*, 66–98. Cambridge: Cambridge University Press, 2001.

Lennox, James G. "Concepts, Context, and the Advance of Science." In *Concepts and Their Role in Knowledge: Reflections on Objectivist Epistemology*, edited by Allan Gotthelf and James G. Lennox, 112–38. Pittsburgh: University of Pittsburgh Press, 2013.

Leoni, Bruno. *Freedom and the Law*. Indianapolis: Liberty Fund, 1991.

Levy, Robert A., and William Mellor. *The Dirty Dozen: How Twelve Supreme Court Cases Radically Expanded Government and Eroded Freedom*. Washington, DC: Cato Institute, 2009.

Lewis, John. "Constitution and Fundamental Law: The Lessons of Classical Athens." *Social Philosophy and Policy* 28 (2011): 25–49.

Liu, Goodwin, Pamela S. Karlan, and Christopher H. Schroeder, eds. *Keeping Faith with the Constitution*. Oxford: Oxford University Press, 2010.

Llewellyn, Karl. *The Common Law Tradition*. Boston: Little Brown, 1960.

Locke, John. *A Letter on Toleration*. Indianapolis: Hackett, 1983.

Second Treatise on Government, edited by C.B. MacPherson. Indianapolis: Hackett, 1980.

Marmor, Andrei. "The Rule of Law and Its Limits." *Law and Philosophy* 23 (2004): 1–43.

Mayler, Bernadette A. "Towards a Common Law Originalism." *Stanford Law Review* 59 (2006): 551–600.

Miller, Fred D. Jr., and Adam Mossoff. "Political Theory – A Radical for Capitalism," In *A Companion to Ayn Rand*, edited by Allan Gotthelf and Gregory Salmieri. Malden, MA: Wiley-Blackwell, in press.

Moore, Michael S. "A Natural Law Theory of Interpretation." *Southern California Law Review* 58 (1985): 277–398.

"Semantics, Metaphysics, and Objectivity in the Law." Paper presented at Conference on Objectivity in the Law, University of Texas at Austin, April 2008.

Murphy, Mark C. *Natural Law in Jurisprudence and Politics*. New York: Cambridge University Press, 2006.

"Natural Law Theory." In *Blackwell Guide to the Philosophy of Law and Legal Theory*, edited by Martin P. Golding and William A. Edmundson, 15–28. Malden, MA: Blackwell, 2005.

Nagel, Thomas. *The View from Nowhere*. New York: Oxford University Press, 1989.

Neily, Clark M. "No Such Thing: Litigating Under the Rational Basis Test." *NYU Journal of Law and Liberty* 1, no. 2 (2005): 897–913.

Terms of Engagement: How Our Courts Should Enforce the Constitution's Promise of Limited Government. New York: Encounter Books, 2013.

Paulsen, Michael Stokes. "The Intrinsically Corrupting Influence of Precedent." *Constitutional Commentary* 22 (2005): 289–98.

Peikoff, Leonard. *Objective Communication*. Edited by Barry Wood. New York: Penguin, 2013.

Objectivism: The Philosophy of Ayn Rand. New York: Dutton, 1991.

Understanding Objectivism. Edited by Michael Berliner. New York: Penguin, 2012.

Perry, Michael. "What is the Constitution? (and Other Fundamental Questions)." In *Constitutionalism*, edited by Larry Alexander, 99–150. New York: Cambridge University Press, 1998.

Peters, Christopher J. "Assessing the New Judicial Minimalism." *Columbia Law Review* 100 (2000): 1454–537.

Posner, Richard. *How Judges Think*. Cambridge, MA: Harvard University Press, 2008.

"Legal Reasoning from the Top Down and From the Bottom Up: The Question of Unenumerated Constitutional Rights." In *The Bill of Rights and the Modern State*, edited by Geoffrey R. Stone, Richard A. Epstein, and Cass R. Sunstein, 433–50. Chicago: University of Chicago Press, 1992.

Overcoming Law. Cambridge, MA: Harvard University Press, 1995.

Prakash, Saikrishna. "Radicals in Tweed Jackets: Why Extreme Left Wing Law Professors Are Wrong for America." (Review of Cass Sunstein, *Radicals in Robes: Why Extreme Right Wing Courts are Wrong for America*.) *Columbia Law Review* 106 (2006): 2207–33.

Rahe, Paul. "Montesquieu's Natural Rights Constitutionalism." *Social Philosophy and Policy* 29 (2012): 51–81.

Rand, Ayn. "Causality vs. Duty." In *Philosophy: Who Needs It*, 114–22. New York: Bobbs Merrill, 1982.

"Censorship: Local and Express." In *Philosophy: Who Needs It*, 211–30. New York: Bobbs-Merrill, 1982.

Introduction to Objectivist Epistemology. 2nd edition, edited by Harry Binswanger, New York: Penguin, 1990.

"Man's Rights." In *Capitalism: The Unknown Ideal*, 367–77. New York: Signet-Penguin, 1986.

"The Nature of Government."In *Capitalism: The Unknown Ideal*, 378–87. New York: Signet-Penguin, 1986.

"The Objectivist Ethics." In *The Virtue of Selfishness*, 13–39. New York: New American Library, 1964.

"The Pull Peddlers." In *Capitalism: The Unknown Ideal*, 184–90. New York: Signet-Penguin, 1986.

"Thought Control" (in 3 parts). *Ayn Rand Letter*, II, no. 26, and III, nos. 1 and 2 (1973): 243–46, 247–50, and 251–56.

"What is Capitalism?" In *Capitalism: The Unknown Ideal*, 1–29. New York: Signet-Penguin, 1986.

"Who Is the Final Authority in Ethics?" In *The Voice of Reason*, edited by Leonard Peikoff, 17–22. New York: Penguin, 1988.

Rappaport, Michael, and Michael McGinnis. *Originalism and the Good Constitution*. Cambridge, MA: Harvard University Press, 2013.

Raz, Joseph. "About Morality and the Nature of Law." *American Journal of Jurisprudence* 48 (2003): 1–15.

"Formalism and the Rule of Law." In *Natural Law Theory: Contemporary Essays*, edited by Robert George, 309–40. Oxford: Clarendon Press, 1992.

The Morality of Freedom. Oxford: Clarendon Press, 1986.

"On the Authority and Interpretation of Constitutions." In *Constitutionalism*, edited by Larry Alexander, 152–93. New York: Cambridge University Press, 1998.

"The Rule of Law and Its Virtue." In *The Authority of Law: Essays on Law and Morality*, 210–29. Oxford: Clarendon Press. 1979.

Roosevelt, Kermit. *The Myth of Judicial Activism: Making Sense of Supreme Court Decisions*. New Haven, CT: Yale University Press, 2006.

Rubenfeld, Jed. *Revolution by Judiciary*. Cambridge, MA: Harvard University Press, 2005.

Salmieri, Gregory. "Conceptualization and Justification." In *Concepts and Their Role in Knowledge: Reflections on Objectivist Epistemology*, edited by Allan Gotthelf and James G. Lennox, 41–84. Pittsburgh: University of Pittsburgh Press, 2013.

Sandefur, Timothy. *The Conscience of the Constitution: The Declaration of Independence and the Right to Liberty*. Washington, DC: Cato Institute, 2013.

"In Defense of Substantive Due Process, or the Promise of Lawful Rule." *Harvard Journal of Law and Public Policy* 35 (2012): 283–350.

"Scalia's Basic Contradiction, or, Words Mean (A Potentially Infinite Number of) Things." *Positive Liberty*. Last modified November 2005. Retrieved from http://positiveliberty.com/2005/11/scalia%e2%80%99s-basic-contradiction-or-words-mean-a-potentially-infinite-number-of-things.html.

Scalia, Antonin. *A Matter of Interpretation*, edited by Amy Gutmann. Princeton: Princeton University Press, 1997.

"On Interpreting the Constitution." Wriston Lecture, given at the Manhattan Institute, November 17, 1997.

"Review of Steven D. Smith's *Law's Quandary*." *Catholic University Law Review* 55 (2006): 687–94.

Scalia, Antonin, and Bryan A. Garner. *Reading Law: The Interpretation of Legal Texts*. St. Paul, MN: Thomson/West, 2012.

Schauer, Frederick. "Is the Common Law Law?" *California Law Review* 77, 1989: 455–71.

Schmidt, Christopher W. "Popular Constitutionalism on the Right: Lessons from the Tea Party." *Denver University Law Review* 88 (2011): 523–57.

Seidman, Michael. *On Constitutional Disobedience*. New York: Oxford University Press, 2013.

Senior, Jennifer. "In Conversation: Antonin Scalia." *New York Magazine*. October 6, 2013. Accessed June 4, 2014. http://nymag.com/news/features/antonin-scalia-2013-10/

Sherry, Suzanna. "Why We Need More Judicial Activism." In *Constitutionalism, Executive Power, and Popular Enlightenment*. Edited by Giorgi Areshidze, Paul Carrese, and Suzanna Sherry. Albany: SUNY Press, 2014.

Sherry, Suzanna, and Daniel Farber. *Desperately Seeking Certainty*. Chicago: University of Chicago Press, 2002.

Siegan, Bernard H. *Drafting a Constitution for a Nation or Republic Emerging into Freedom*. Fairfax, VA: George Mason University Press, 1994.

Silverglate, Harvey. *Three Felonies a Day*. New York: Encounter Books, 2011.

Smith, Tara. *Ayn Rand's Normative Ethics – The Virtuous Egoist*. New York: Cambridge University Press, 2006.

"Humanity's Darkest Evil: The Lethal Destructiveness of Non-Objective Law." In *Essays on Ayn Rand's*. Atlas Shrugged. Edited by Robert Mayhew, 335–61. New York: Lexington Books, 2009.

"The Importance of the Subject in Objective Morality: Distinguishing Objective from Intrinsic Value." *Social Philosophy and Policy* 25 (2008): 126–48.

Moral Rights and Political Freedom. Lanham, MD: Rowman & Littlefield, 1995.

"Neutrality Isn't Neutral: On the Value-Neutrality of the Rule of Law." *Washington University Jurisprudence Review* 4 (2011): 49–95.

"Objective Law." In *A Companion to Ayn Rand*, edited by Allan Gotthelf and Gregory Salmieri. Malden, MA: Wiley-Blackwell, in press.

"Originalism, Vintage or Nouveau: *He Said, She Said* Law." *Fordham Law Review* 82 (2013): 619–39.

"Originalism's Misplaced Fidelity: 'Original' Meaning is Not Objective." *Constitutional Commentary* 26 (2009): 1–57.

"Reckless Caution: The Perils of Judicial Minimalism," *NYU Journal of Law and Liberty* 5 (2010): 347–93.

"Rights Conflicts: The Undoing of Rights." *Journal of Social Philosophy* 26 (1995): 141–58.

"'Social' Objectivity and the Objectivity of Value." In *Science, Values, and Objectivity*, edited by Peter Machamer and Gereon Walters, 143–71. Pittsburgh: University of Pittsburgh Press, 2004.

Viable Values: A Study of Life as the Root and Reward of Morality. Lanham, MD: Rowman & Littlefield, 2000.

"Why Originalism Won't Die: Common Mistakes in Competing Theories of Judicial Interpretation." *Duke Journal of Constitutional Law and Public Policy* 2 (2007): 159–215.

Social Philosophy and Policy 28, no 1. Winter 2011. Theme: "What Should Constitutions Do?"

Solum, Lawrence B. *Legal Theory Lexicon*. Retrieved from http://lsolum.typepad.com /legal_theory_lexicon/.

"Originalism and Constitutional Construction." *Fordham Law Review* 82 (2013): 453–537.

Sosa, David. "The Unintentional Fallacy." *California Law Review* 86 (1998): 919–38.

Stoner, James. *Common-Law Liberty: Rethinking American Constitutionalism*. Lawrence: University Press of Kansas, 2003.

Strauss, David A. "Common Law Constitutional Interpretation." *University of Chicago Law Review* 63 (1996): 877–935.

The Living Constitution. New York: Oxford University Press, 2010.

Sunstein, Cass R. *A Constitution of Many Minds: Why the Founding Document Doesn't Mean What It Meant Before*. Princeton: Princeton University Press, 2009.

"Of Snakes and Butterflies: A Reply." *Columbia Law Review* 106 (2006): 2234–43.

One Case at a Time. Cambridge, MA: Harvard University Press, 1999.

Radicals in Robes: Why Extreme Right-Wing Courts are Wrong for America. New York: Basic Books, 2006.

Surowiecki, James. *The Wisdom of Crowds: Why the Many are Smarter than the Few and How Collective Wisdom Shapes Business, Economics, Societies and Nations*. New York: Doubleday, 2004.

Tamanaha, Brian Z. *On the Rule of Law: History, Politics, Theory*. New York: Cambridge University Press, 2004.

Thompson, Bradley C. "The Revolutionary Origins of American Constitutionalism." In *History, on Proper Principles: Essays in Honor of Forrest McDonald*, edited by Stephen M. Klugewicz and Lenore T. Ealy, 1–27. Wilmington, DE: ISI Books, 2010.

Toobin, Jeffrey. *The Nine: Inside the Secret World of the Supreme Court*. New York: Doubleday, 2007.

Tribe, Laurence H., and Michael C. Dorf. *On Reading the Constitution*. Cambridge, MA: Harvard University Press, 1993.

Tushnet, Mark. *Taking the Constitution Away from the Courts*. Princeton: Princeton University Press, 2000.

Waldron, Jeremy. "The Concept and the Rule of Law." *Georgia Law Review* 43 (2008): 1–20.

"The Core of the Case Against Judicial Review." 115 *Yale Law Journal* (2006): 1346–1406.

Law and Disagreement. New York: Oxford University Press, 1999.

"The Rule of Law and the Importance of Procedure." In *Getting to the Rule of Law*, edited by James E. Fleming, 3–31. New York: New York University Press, 2011.

"Thoughtfulness and the Rule of Law." *British Academy Review* 18 (2011): 1–11. Retrieved from http://www.britac.ac.uk/review/18/index.cfm.

"Vagueness and the Guidance of Action." In *Philosophical Foundations of Language in the Law*, edited by Andrei Marmor and Scott Soames, 58–82. New York: Oxford University Press, 2011.

Waluchow, W.J. *A Common Law Theory of Judicial Review*. New York: Cambridge University Press, 2007.

"Constitutionalism." In *The Stanford Encyclopedia of Philosophy*, edited by Edward N. Zalta. Retrieved from http://plato.stanford.edu/archives/spr2014/entries/constitutionalism.

Whittington, Keith E. *Constitutional Interpretation: Textual Meaning, Original Intent, and Judicial Review*. Lawrence: University Press of Kansas, 1999.

"The New Originalism." *Georgetown Journal of Law and Public Policy* 2 (2004): 519–613.

Wilkinson, J. Harvie. *Cosmic Constitutional Theory: Why Americans Are Losing Their Inalienable Right to Self-Governance*. New York: Oxford University Press, 2012.

Wright, Darryl. "Reason and Freedom in Ayn Rand's Politics." In *The Philosophy of Capitalism: Objectivism and Alternative Approaches – Ayn Rand Society Philosophical Studies*, volume 3, edited by Gregory Salmieri and Robert Mayhew. Pittsburgh: University of Pittsburgh Press, forthcoming 2016.

Zywicki, Todd. "The Rule of Law, Freedom, and Prosperity." Foreword to *Supreme Court Economic Review* 10 (2003): 11–14.

Index

Printed in February 2023
by Rotomail Italia S.p.A., Vignate (MI) - Italy